The Guernica Generation

BOOKS IN THE BASQUE SERIES

A Book of the Basques
by Rodney Gallop

In a Hundred Graves: A Basque Portrait
by Robert Laxalt

Basque Nationalism
by Stanley G. Payne

Amerikanuak: Basques in the New World
by William A. Douglass and Jon Bilbao

Beltran: Basque Sheepman of the American West
by Beltran Paris, as told to William Douglass

The Basques: The Franco Years and Beyond
by Robert P. Clark

The Witches' Advocate: Basque Witchcraft
and the Spanish Inquisition (1609–1614)
by Gustav Henningsen

Navarra: The Durable Kingdom
by Rachel Bard

The Guernica Generation: Basque Refugee
Children of the Spanish Civil War
by Dorothy Legarreta

THE BASQUE SERIES

Basque children arriving in Belgium, being greeted by Belgian nuns, 1937. (Photo courtesy of Javier Goitia)

The Guernica Generation

Basque Refugee Children of the Spanish Civil War

Dorothy Legarreta

UNIVERSITY OF NEVADA PRESS
RENO, NEVADA 1984

Basque Series Editor: William A. Douglass
University of Nevada Press, Reno, Nevada 89557 USA

Designed by Dave Comstock
Printed in the United States of America

Library of Congress Cataloging in Publication Data
Legarreta, Dorothy
The Guernica generation

(Basque series)
Bibliography: p.
Includes index.
1. Spain—Civil War, 1936–1939—Children—Spain—País Vasco. 2. Spain—History—Civil War, 1936–1939—Evacuation of civilians—Spain—País Vasco. 3. País Vasco (Spain)—History. 4. Children—Spain—País Vasco—History—20th century. I. Title. II. Series.
DP269.8.C4L44 1984 946.081 84–13136
ISBN 0–87417–088–5

CONTENTS

Prologue ix

Preface xi

Introduction 1

1. War and Evacuation in Euzkadi 8
2. Finding Refuge in France 51
3. The Basque Refugee Children in Britain 99
4. Belgium: Flemish and Walloon Hospitality 135
5. Basque Children in the Soviet Union: The Sovieticos 156
6. Switzerland, Denmark, the United States, and Mexico 174
7. The Repatriation to Euzkadi 201
8. Aftermaths 241
9. The Summing Up 297

Appendixes 334

Notes 351

Bibliography 381

Index 389

PROLOGUE

In the year 1937, nearly twenty thousand Basque children left their parents and homeland for unknown fates in France, Britain, Belgium, the Soviet Union, Mexico, Switzerland, and Denmark. They were refugees of the Spanish Civil War, nominated for evacuation by desperate parents after the terrible bombing of Durango and Guernica. In a modern era, to those numbed by countless scenes of the plight of refugees flashed instantly around the globe by the media, this one small cohort of war's victims may seem insignificant. Surely, in terms of sheer horror, atrocity, and numbers, the world was to witness much worse. Jews, Biafrans, Cambodians, and Vietnamese were all to provide hideous examples of human desperation on a massive scale. Nor did the Basque children ever provide the now-classic image of the refugee waif in rags, whose spindly arms, distended stomach, and sunken eyes all bespeak hopelessness and resignation. Yet there is a special importance, indeed a uniqueness, in this modest evacuation of Basque children: they were the first to be displaced by the bombs of modern warfare, the first to capture the world's attention. Warfare has never respected the able; henceforth, it would scarcely respect the young. This is a crucial distinction, since it projects that day's disputes into the future, by implicitly or explicitly condoning genocide.

PREFACE

This book was written as testimony to the Guernica generation of the Spanish Civil War. Beginning in the Basque province of Vizcaya in 1937, the use of massive aerial bombardment, incendiary shells, and strafing against an unprotected population ushered in a new era of civilian suffering in battle. The subsequent evacuation of thousands of young children to refuge far from their parents and their homeland, detailed in the following pages, was the first such event in a tragic series continuing to the present day.

Contemporary interest in the history of modern refugee peoples is increasing. This is reflected in growing scholarly concern to document the impact of what has been termed the "Century of the Refugee" upon those affected by such forced migration.* We need only contemplate the two major world wars, the several revolutions within various world powers, and the decolonization of the Third World to sense the profound effects such upheavals have had on the populations involved. This is particularly true of the children, the most vulnerable victims of war. The Basque child refugees of 1937 were the earliest manifestation of this current phenomenon, possibly excepting the Armenian children and untold thousands of Russian orphans during the first quarter of this century. These two groups, however, were quickly gathered up into orphanages, if unaccompanied, or resettled with their

*A representative list of publications on the refugee problem in the twentieth century may be found in "Works Consulted or Cited."

families in the countries offering safety.[1] The special significance of the Basque child refugees lies in the fact that they served as a harbinger of the coming world conflagration. Unlike the Armenian or Russian children, they became a political embarrassment to the European nations who hosted them. During the late thirties, much of Europe was jockeying for position in the impending global conflict. The children from the north of Spain who were welcomed into France, Britain, Belgium, Denmark, Switzerland, the Soviet Union, and Mexico gave a human face to the bitterly opposed ideologies of that era. Representing the full spectrum of political doctrines of the period, from Anarchism to Fascism, these children symbolized, in microcosm, the forces in the Civil War in Spain, which were soon to ignite the Second World War. In some cases, giving them sanctuary was in opposition to the official stance of the host country; in others, it gave substance to the orthodox rhetoric of the government. Wherever they were sent, the "Basque Babies" acted as a political catalyst, innocently serving to confront the appeasement of some, test the professed neutrality of many, and provide an illustration of benevolence essential to others.

Much of the text of this volume is in the words of over one hundred of the Basque refugee children, interviewed as adults in middle age in 1979–80. Retrospective oral histories were gathered from among those evacuated to the five major host countries—France, Britain, Belgium, the Soviet Union, and Mexico. Because most of the children were ultimately repatriated, the majority were interviewed in their own homes in the Basque provinces of Spain. Substantial groups in each country, however, never returned from exile. These Basques, excepting those in the Soviet Union, were questioned in their adopted country. Testimony was also obtained from a handful of parents still living, and from Basque, British, and Mexican auxiliary personnel, including several Basque priests who lived with the children as expatriates. Because of the general dislocation of the period covered in the book, and the concomitant destruction of many records, those located for interviews comprise a purposive (non-random) sample. Each was chosen, however to reflect the range of experiences found in the settings provided in the host countries. The study plan, based upon an open-ended questionnaire, included traumatic effects on young children due to separation from their parents, and those factors influencing the maintenance of ethnic identity. (See Appendix I for a summary account of the Basques interviewed, and Appendix II for the interview questionnaire.)

Archival research was also carried out in public and private collections in each host country, excepting only the Soviet Union.* Extended participant observation in all but this one country, as well as correspondence over a four-year period with many of those involved in the evacuation, yielded other data. Throughout the book, the refugee interviews appear without footnote reference as indented excerpts, one paragraph to each respondent. Since many requested anonymity, particularly those from the Soviet Union, only public figures are identified. Archival material and other published work is also indented, and is referenced in a footnote.

This work does not purport to be a history of the Spanish Civil War in the Basque provinces. For scholarly accounts of this conflict, the references in the Bibliography (end of volume) are suggested. It is, rather, the Civil War in the north of Spain and its aftermath as seen from the perspective of the children who experienced these events, and recounted by them from memory in their own words. Although these anecdotal accounts contain a historic validity of their own, a series of factual insertions in the text will serve as guides.

This study was made possible by a fellowship from the Council for the International Exchange of Scholars, through the United States-Spain Treaty Grant. However, it could not have been written without the cooperation and generous assistance of the scores of Basques who consented to be interviewed and who shared with me precious memorabilia,

*Travel to the Soviet Union was discouraged by American consular officials during the period of my research in Europe (1979–80) as a result of the Afghanistan incursion. However, the Hoover Institute Collection at Stanford University provided useful published material for the period.

journals, letters, and photographs. Without the encouragement of many family members in Vizcaya, particularly Jesús Legarreta Bilbao, valuable contacts with leaders of the Basque Nationalist Party, Basque clergy, and with many of those who fled Spain in 1936–39 would have been impossible. A network already begun in Morelia, Mexico, was extended with such help back to the several countries in Europe which gave refuge to the children of the Guernica generation. I wish to thank those who assisted in the translation of Basque, Flemish, French, Danish, and Russian materials: Jesús Legarreta, Frank Callier, Margaret Harvey, Lars Neldested, and Eric Pittman, respectively. William A. Douglass, of the Basque Studies Program of the University of Nevada, Reno, has given me invaluable editing assistance as the book developed.

This volume is dedicated to the memory of my father, Raimundo Legarreta Marcaída, who in 1917 brought with him to America a few oak leaves from the sacred tree at Guernica, as a reminder to himself and his family of his Basque heritage.

Dorothy Legarreta
Berkeley, 1984

INTRODUCTION

The Basques who live in the north of Spain today are the descendants of a venerable people; they are considered by some to be the modern remnants of a paleolithic stock. Many are still rooted to their small green landholdings, from which they wrest a hard living. For hundreds of years, these subsistence farms (*baserriak*) have been the basic economic unit of the countryside, passing undivided to the chosen son or daughter, usually upon the occasion of this child's marriage.[1] The impartibility of the land imbues it with a marked significance, particularly to the several sons and daughters in each generation who must seek a livelihood elsewhere. Many emigrate; others live and work in the growing urban centers. Ideally, each landholding supports three generations of the family living together upon it, and thus serves as the foundation of the Basque social structure. Even in the case of actual physical departure of the children, the family on the land continues to draw the scattered members "home" on weekends to help in the fields, and even attracts those who emigrate to make frequent voyages back to the *baserria*. Basque family structure, with its base in the soil, continues to be stable, firmly adhering to the values of the Catholic church. Marriages are for life, and the children are beloved and carefully reared. Because of a set of specific blood factors unique to Basques,[2] marriages have traditionally been endogamous and, frequently, within the kinship network. This has been the practice even among the communities of Basques who have become established over the past four centuries in the New World.

The sea, which forms one border of the Basque country, has complemented the soil as an economic base. Prowess as merchant sailors, whalers, and fishermen has been the result of the respectful partnership the Basques have formed with the oceans. Whether from a farm or fishing background, however, certain consistent cultural traditions, such as early admission to adulthood, and a propensity, for obvious economic reasons, to emigrate, are important as a frame of reference for the account of the evacuation of young Basque children which follows.

The homeland of the Basques, *Euzkadi*, contains four Spanish and three French provinces* in a land mass totaling under 100 miles square. In the Spanish provinces, particularly in Vizcaya and Guipúzcoa, autonomy from the reigning kings of Castilla had been won by the twelfth century. From the Middle Ages, governance was based on a system of foral rights (*fueros*) which spelled out the legal and political rights inherent in a society of free men.[3] Through the *fueros*, Basques were exempted from conscription into the Spanish army and from taxes to the crown. In addition, their elected leaders enjoyed a veto power over royal edicts. The manner of choosing those who would speak for them in political and legal matters was best exemplified in Vizcaya. Here, in the ancient market town of Guernica (*Gernika*), stands the descendant of a particular oak tree, where, for centuries, the heads of each family clan from every town or rural parish met periodically to cast the vote for their representatives to a primitive parliament.[4]

In the beginning of the last century, profound political changes were generated in the Basque provinces by the war against Napoleon's France, coupled with internal conflicts between secular liberal reformers and traditionalists. These culminated in the Carlist civil wars,[5] which pitted the modern urban coastal provinces (Vizcaya and Guipúzcoa) against the more traditional rural citizens of landbound Alava and Nava-

* In Spain: Vizcaya, Guipúzcoa, Navarra, and Alava. In France: Soule, Labourd, and Basse Navarre.

rra. Foral privileges, already eroded, came to an end. This split between the persistently pro-Carlist rural conservatives of Navarra and Alava and the industrialized coastal provinces was to reappear a century later during the Spanish Civil War. Then, General Mola's Insurgent army easily subdued Republican forces to bring these areas into partnership with Spanish Nationalists.

In Euzkadi, throughout the reigns of both Alphonse XII and XIII and the dictatorship of Primo de Rivera (1923–30) the birth and growth of modern Basque nationalism roughly paralleled the burgeoning of industrialization. Particularly in Vizcaya and Guipúzcoa, the major cities of Bilbao and Pasajes grew into ports of international importance. Iron mining, steel fabrication, manufacturing, and the shipbuilding industry all flourished. It was during this period, or about the turn of the last century, that Basque nationalism also emerged, drawing the sons of many of the new Basque industrial giants into its folds. At first, nationalism made only small local ripples as its founder, Sabino de Arana, developed his ideology and potent symbolism. Arana, the son of a major Bilbaoan shipbuilder, set out to revitalize a flagging Basque consciousness. One of his major concerns was the restoration of the Basque language, Euskera, which had fallen to the status of a local patois, restricted to the rural areas. He renewed such cultural symbols as the songs and dances of Basque folklore, collected the rich oral tradition of Basque folktales, and even designed a new Basque flag, the red, green, and white *ikurriña*. Finally, and more pragmatically, he founded a new political party, committed to autonomy, the Partido Nacionalista Vasco (PNV).

The ideology of the PNV closely reflected the major tenets of Arana's personal philosophy. Translated into a political platform, the PNV was to be strongly Catholic; it would seek to unify the four Spanish Basque provinces (Euzkadi Sur) with the three just over the border in France (Euzkadi Norte); it espoused racial purity, seeing the Basques as a unique racial stock to be insulated from miscegenation. Arana also stressed the centrality of Euskera as a living language; he sought to achieve autonomy from Spain by non-violent means; and his platform embraced strong elements of social justice, including the redistribution of land, through a democratic form of government.[6] During the first decades of the twentieth century, and especially after the imprisonment and untimely death of Arana, the party, with its companion labor union, the Solidaridad de Trabajadores Vascos (STV), enjoyed phenomenal growth. Under Primo de Rivera, however, the PNV was suppressed. Only Basque cultural activities such as folklore and language were permitted to continue from 1923 until 1931.

In part, the anti-Spanish stance of the PNV was a reaction to the massive in-migration of non-Basques to Euzkadi as industrialization proceeded. Thousands of families were drawn from marginal rural lives outside Euzkadi by the promise of factory jobs in Bilbao, Eibar, or San Sebastián. An industrial proletariat was thus grafted onto the ethnically Basque farmers, fishermen, and new industrialists. These Spaniards are even today referred to by Basques as the "*Maketos*" or even "*Koreanos*" for their darker skin and shorter stature.

In Euzkadi, many of the immigrants joined the national Spanish parties of the Left, especially the Socialists with their sister union, the Unión General de Trabajadores (UGT), the Communist party, or the Anarchists, with their Confederación Nacional de Trabajo (CNT). These ethnically Spanish workers tended to be much less strongly Catholic, much less interested in regional autonomy, and much less conservative in their political orientation than were the Basque Nationalists in the PNV. The major strength of the PNV came from those living in the rural areas and small towns of Vizcaya and Guipúzcoa and belonging to the lower middle class. Neither the factory workers nor the upper middle-class Basques, who supported the Spanish Left and Right respectively, saw utility in its ideas. Similarly, the rural and urban conservatives of Alava and Navarra continued to support Carlist traditionalists. These differences were to manifest themselves again and again during the Spanish Civil War, as fought in Euzkadi, and as we shall see, in the evacuation of the child refugees from the battlegrounds.

In 1931, Spain emerged from six decades of monarchy and

dictatorship with the proclamation of the Second Republic. Elections were held throughout the country which resulted in victory for the strongly anticlerical Republican Left, essentially representing the lower middle class. The government, led by Manuel Azaña, was committed to social reform, some regional autonomy, the secularization of education, and the inauguration of a constitutional democracy. In the Basque provinces, the PNV, after nearly a decade of clandestine operation, adopted a pro-Republican position. It called, as well, for immediate autonomy consistent with the new federalism espoused by Azaña and his government. Throughout Euzkadi, the PNV worked to draft and then ratify a statute granting the Basques a measure of self-government.

However, the course of the short-lived Second Republic was never to be smooth. The Catholic church, the aristocracy, and the newly rich coalesced into a strong Rightist force which opposed the land reforms and secularization of Azaña's government. A worldwide economic depression added to the instability of the new republic's financial status. The parties of the Left, particularly the Anarchists, called a number of general strikes, which disrupted communication and transportation. A bitter and violent rivalry developed among the Left parties and their respective unions. The drafting of a national constitution, particularly those articles dealing with the separation of church and state, also fueled old Spanish passions.

In the Basque provinces, this issue, coupled with the conservative ideology of the PNV when compared to that of the Socialists, Communists, and Left Republicans in Azaña's government, led to profound disaffection. This was exacerbated as the plans for Basque autonomy foundered in the Spanish Parliament on the issue of religious freedom. Even within Euzkadi, there was internal dissension since the largest province, Navarra, withdrew from the campaign for Basque autonomy, and Alava, also predominately rural, showed diminishing interest in participating in a separate government within Spain. The PNV's base continued to be in industrialized Vizcaya and Guipúzcoa.

During the election held late in 1933, a further barrier to the

Basque nation emerged when the moderate Right, strongly opposed to regional autonomy, gained victory in Spain. At the national level, the republic moved to the Right, and Leftist forces retaliated with planned insurrections in newly autonomous Catalonia and in Asturias in 1934. In Euzkadi, there was sharp cleavage, as the PNV remained neutral, while the Socialist and Communist parties and their sister unions supported these strikes. Polarization increased, making Basque autonomy an even more problematic issue.

During the following year, the PNV began taking a more radical stance. Its union, the STV, supported the workers imprisoned as a result of the violent Civil Guard repression which followed sympathy strikes held in Euzkadi to demonstrate solidarity with the striking Asturian miners.

By 1936, national elections in Spain revealed the unbridgeable chasm between the Left and the Right. The Left had joined in a Popular Front coalition, which included the Left Republicans, the Socialists, Communists, a Revolutionary Communist Party, the Partido Obrero de Unificación Marxista (POUM), and the Anarchists. Arrayed against this were the Catholic church, the Carlist monarchists, and the Right. The PNV was, of course, still strongly pro-Catholic, but was also committed to autonomy and social justice. In Euzkadi, this election dramatized the three-way split in the region's politics. The Leftist Popular Front won seven seats, the PNV won nine, and the Carlist Rightists won eight (most of these being from Navarra). The PNV was the strongest single party in Euzkadi, but had actually polled a smaller popular vote than in 1933, due to extreme polarization of the Right and the Left. In Spain as a whole, the Popular Front won a rather narrow plurality but it was one that secured it a large majority in the composition of the new parliament.[7]

Azaña, once again head of state after the defeat of Alcalá-Zamorra's Right-Center government, tried to maintain the Republic. However, the cleavages within the Popular Front were deep, and the nation fell into mass strikes, agrarian revolt, political assassinations, and anti-clerical violence. On the other hand, the deposed Rightists were not idle. Seeing the Popular Front victory and the ensuing chaos as inexorably leading to a Bolshevik Spain, the army and the Right began to conspire to overthrow the elected government with a military coup.

One of the Basques interviewed reflected on those first months of the Popular Front government:

> All that last summer before the Civil War was marked by a strange ambience, full of rumors, endless proclamations from every political tendency, a continuous campaign to discredit every other point of view. Perhaps ours was the first generation to experience psychological warfare; to learn the power of propaganda to enliven or to demoralize; to live through official lies. We knew how guinea pigs must feel, in our foretaste of the world war to come, the first to be waged for the minds of people.

CHAPTER ONE

War and Evacuation in Euzkadi

Europe outside the Iberian Peninsula in 1936 was arranging its political alliances in a desperate rivalry made ominous by the activities of the Fascist dictators, Mussolini and Hitler. Italy's quest for extra-territorial hegemony saw black-shirted troops march into Abyssinia in 1935. By its lack of meaningful actions in this invasion, the League of Nations made evident its impotence to the world. The profound attachment of the Great Powers to neutrality was clearly demonstrated to the dictators, thus whetting their common appetite for additional conquests. The Papal State in Rome openly supported the Fascist invasion, a clear portent of the position of the Holy See in the coming Civil War in Spain.

With the twilight of the League unmistakably apparent, a struggle among the greater and lesser international powers for world domination commenced. In this paroxysmic effort, Spain was to become the augury:

> If the Western powers [France, Britain] commanded it [Spain], they might hope to succeed in establishing contact via the Mediterranean with the Soviet Union and any other potential allies on the eastern flank of the "Rome-Berlin Axis." On the other hand, if the Central Powers commanded the Iberian Peninsula, they might not only liberate themselves from the nightmare of war

on two fronts, but might put their Western opponents in this quandary.[1]

Following the military coup in Spain, international opinion immediately moved to characterize the major Spanish political forces as a projection of the then-dominant European ideologies: "democracy" meant a parliamentary system stripped of clerical influence; "communism," a range of proletarian forces, from Bakunin anarchism to Marxism; while to "fascism" was ascribed military, royalist, and clerical elements. Throughout the Western Hemisphere, public opinion was inflamed over the moral issues involved in the struggle in Spain, and bitterly divided over how to influence the conflict. All the major countries were united, however, in a common fear that this war might kindle a full-fledged confrontation between the Axis and the Western Powers.

The Spanish Civil War had erupted on July 17, 1936, outside peninsular Spain with the revolt of garrison troops in Spanish Morocco. Led by a young career officer, General Francisco Franco, this insurrection was joined immediately by a planned series of uprisings arranged by General Emilio Mola within Spain. Army and Civil Guard units quartered in Spain's major cities were confronted with a forced choice. Though a good number became part of the Rightist coup, most retained loyalty to the Republican government which had taken power in 1931. Thus, Madrid, Barcelona, and Alicante were loyal to the elected government, while Málaga and Burgos joined the Insurgents.[2]

In the north, in the Basque provinces, both Navarra and Alava were rapidly subdued by troops quartered in Pamplona and led by the top Insurgent leader, Mola. Particularly in Navarra, residual Carlist and Rightist sentiment was already manifest in eight thousand seasoned paramilitary troops who eagerly augmented the Insurgent garrisons. Members of the Basque Nationalist party, committed to autonomy, fled to Bilbao from both provinces, as their offices and clubs were destroyed and their activities prohibited. Some, under intense pressure, joined the Insurgents.

In highly industrialized Guipúzcoa and Vizcaya, calmness

reigned. There, municipal governments, newly empowered after the Popular Front victory the previous February, continued loyal to the Republic.[3] An exception was San Sebastián, where a short-lived coup attempt was soon quelled by the local militia, though the casino, yacht club, and major hotel were briefly occupied by revolting troops.[4]

The outbreak of civil war is clearly recalled by those in Guipúzcoa who experienced it:

> I remember perfectly that we were on school vacation. Quite naturally, we devoted ourselves to playing. Soon, however, rumors began of an impending military uprising, perhaps in Africa. We hung around the few radios people in our barrio had, until news of the coup began. Truthfully, my idea of the revolt and its causes was not that clear, but, at thirteen, I knew it would be in opposition to the Republic, and by undemocratic means.

> Our tragic Civil War was begun by one faction in the army, with the complementary help of the church, the industrialists, and the estate owners, all naturally against the existing popular democratic Republic. Without the assistance of Italy and Germany, and their massive shipments of war planes, tanks, artillery, and well-trained troops, the military coup would not have lasted very long. Here in San Sebastián, just a day later, the shelling began, by the Insurgents from rooftops, using arms from the barracks. They took the center of town, but the local militia, with their few rifles, fought back and liberated it.

Throughout Guipúzcoa and Vizcaya, regional councils of defense were hastily organized, based on union and political affiliation. The PNV joined with the Leftist political parties, ranging from Left Republicans to Anarchosyndicalists. Basque Nationalist leadership saw clearly that the Civil War was "a struggle between civil rights and Fascism; Republic or monarchy,"[5] and that the history of the Basques as a democratic and free people precluded any choice but that of remaining loyal to the elected government.

The Civil War in the Basque provinces within the larger frame of the Spanish nation's conflict reverberated throughout the Basque kinship network. Families unsympathetic to the Insurgent cause hurriedly moved north to provinces more hospitable to their political views. Children who had blithely gone to church or union summer camps outside Euzkadi, in the Rioja, Alicante, and Logroño, could not be reunited with their families in Republican territory.[6] The divided loyalties between many family branches were to be played out in the organized battles which began in eastern Guipúzcoa by mid-August. By then, General Mola had marched south from Navarra toward Madrid, leaving Carlist Colonel Beorlegui in charge at Pamplona. Beorlegui led his red-bereted troops from Pamplona across the Navarrese border to positions in the mountains of northeastern Guipúzcoa. His objectives were to seal the French border completely at Irún, and to conquer the two Basque provinces remaining loyal to the Republic.[7]

It was strategically important to capture the Basque gateway to France over the Bidasoa River. The Popular Front government of France, led by Léon Blum, had manifested strong pro-Republican sympathies privately. Its official policy, however, became quite different: the implementation of the "Non-Intervention Policy." The American ambassador to Spain at that time wrote:

> History is still curious about the genesis of the Non-Intervention plan, through which the European democracies aligned themselves stubbornly, if ignorantly, on the side of the Fascists against the Spanish democracy. It is now fairly established that this plan was hatched in London, and that Blum was practically blackmailed into acceptance. Otherwise, England would withdraw her guarantee to maintain the frontier of France and support France in a possible war with Germany, unless France abandoned her right, under international law, to sell arms and ammunition to the democratic republic that both France and England recognized as the legitimate, legal government. This amounted to an ultimatum, and the Blum government yielded to the threat.[8]

This plan, ostensibly intended to localize the Civil War, was to apply to all nations, including, of course, Italy and Germany. What actually happened was that only the democracies signed the pact, stopping all arms shipment to Republican Spain during the battle for San Sebastián and Irún. The Axis powers and Portugal never signed. During the next two and one-half years, troops and arms from the Fascists came in freely for the Insurgents. Only Russia and Mexico, seeing the bankruptcy of the Non-Intervention policy, sent military advisors and small quantities of armaments into Republican Spain.

Children who witnessed this first campaign in Euzkadi recall the dawning of war very vividly even forty-five years later:

> When the rebellion of the "Glorious one" [Franco] began, we at first found it an amusement. We watched our older friends from the barrio go to the front, with a few rifles left over from the Carlist battles, and we pretended to be revolutionaries, too, filling sandbags for the militia's defenses. It was just playing a new game to us.
>
> For a while, it seemed a prolonged summer holiday. Schools in Guipúzcoa never reopened after that August, and we had all day to roam the streets. I collected dud shells from the Rebel cruiser *Cervera* that landed near our barrio. I even put one in front of the *ayuntamiento* [city hall].

However, from the moment Beorlegui ordered the Insurgent attack from mountain positions overlooking Irún and San Sebastián, the Basque militia was doomed. Untrained, armed with shotguns ordinarily used for shooting birds, without naval or aerial support, the multiparty Basque junta, joined by Civil Guard loyalists, fought bravely but without hope.[9] Beorlegui's troops were presently joined by the army of General Mola, primed by stunning victories in Andalucía. Fascist assistance also arrived. Italian planes bombed the two cities, and an airlift using German Junkers brought seven hundred crack Moroccan Foreign Legionnaires to join Mola and Beorlegui.[10] The Insurgent navy steamed up to the harbor nearby and shelled the cities at will.

Throughout eastern Guipúzcoa, Basque families began to

suffer the impact of total civil war. The battles all through August became more and more intense.

> I'll never forget the first bombardments from the Rebel destroyer *Velasco* anchored outside San Sebastián. All my friends would run to the beach each morning. We would watch for the puff of smoke from its big guns as our signal, then shout out in unison the seconds elapsing until we heard the detonation. Then we would listen for the whistle of the ball's flight until it landed, nearly always short, in the bay in front of us. Once in a while they had the range right, and the shots exploded right behind us, in our own barrio.
>
> All above us were the Italian planes helping Franco: we had not a one. At first, they just dropped propaganda leaflets, telling us to surrender or be killed. Then, the bombs started.
>
> We all listened every night to the Rebel news broadcasts: Quiepo de Llano and others. They warned us about the Moors from the legions in Spanish Morocco, who killed the little ones and had no respect for women. We knew they were on their way to fight us.

The psychological warfare had at least some effect, because, already, Basques had heard reports of the savagery of Moroccan troops in Andalucía. News of bloody Insurgent reprisals in Badajoz against captured Republican militia, including the killing and burning of even the wounded, had also reached the Basque country. The Moors were known to carry long knives to use for silent, nocturnal forays, to strip corpses of jewelry, and gold teeth, and to be totally devoid of "Christian principles."[11] And it was becoming well known that Franco took few, if any, prisoners of war. On the other hand, families in Guipúzcoa also saw a number of French and Belgian volunteers who fought side by side with the Basque militia:

> Even a Jew from Frankfort came to fight in San Sebastián. There was much enthusiasm, but too little training and organization: an idealistic, romantic defense against highly trained militarists.

The Exodus

Women, children, and men too old or infirm to fight began to leave the two besieged cities. Evacuation became wholesale by the end of August, when five thousand women, children, and old men crossed the International Bridge to France in three days.[12] The refugees took with them only a few clothes and household goods. Because the volunteer militia defending the northeastern cities and towns of Guipúzcoa depended upon their families for food and shelter, their base for daily maintenance disappeared. No alternative could be arranged, and morale dropped sharply. On September 4, Irún was abandoned and set afire by the Anarchists. Basque militia moved into San Sebastián. Also foredoomed, it escaped incendiarism, but fell to General Mola on September 12.[13]

According to figures compiled by the Basque government, some forty thousand Basques crossed into France during this period (or until October 7, 1936) "uncontrolled and under personal initiative," on foot, or in vehicles or boats. Of this number, some thirty-two thousand (those of military age) were sent on to Catalonia to fight again in later campaigns. This left about eight thousand Guipúzcoans in France in the fall of 1936.[14] Most families, however, had chosen to head west toward Basque cities, such as Eibar, which still remained in Republican hands, or to go on to Vizcaya.

This Basque exodus can best be reconstructed by picturing the countryside before the outbreak of the Civil War. Guipúzcoa is small in size, and the existing system of roads traversed a very hilly terrain. The narrow highways soon became clogged with fleeing families, their household goods, and sometimes their livestock.

> Guipúzcoa was like a market, full of people moving in every direction, looking for ways to reach Bilbao. Everyone was crushed by the rapid defeat. They loaded burros, they loaded wooden carts drawn by oxen. The few trucks and cars that were available were requisitioned, very few in those days. Some had to flee on foot.[15]

Many of the children who walked or rode to Eibar, then on to Durango, Bermeo, or Bilbao in September of 1936 were among those to be evacuated from Euzkadi the following spring and summer. They were urged along the medieval pilgrimage route to Compostela by reports of the tragic executions of the militia who had remained in San Sebastián, the excesses of the Moorish Legionnaires in the Insurgent army, and the hope that safety could be found in Vizcaya.

Of the eighty thousand inhabitants of San Sebastián, fewer than twelve thousand were left when General Mola arrived.[16] The experiences of one family who stayed behind are typical. The daughter, then eight years of age, recalls:

> I can never forget those terrible days. My father was well known, being an official of the Bank of Guipúzcoa. He left early in August, taking bank funds to safety in Bilbao. My older brother went with him, to enlist in the Basque militia. My mother and two sisters and I were in our house near the plaza when the Insurgents entered. She, they put in jail immediately, as they couldn't find my father. My older sister, the prettiest girl in town, they shaved her head and put her to cleaning the urinals of the troops. Our good neighbors helped us out with food. We three were made to dance with the Insurgent troops in the plaza, along with all the other young girls in town, whenever they played their music. The Moroccan soldiers were barbarians, and there were incidents. This went on for nine months, we three under "house arrest," and my mother in prison. When the Red Cross got us permission to join my father, we didn't want to leave my mother, and my sister was ashamed to go with her bald head. There were no wigs in those days. Finally, the Falange released my mother to a convent, where she was put to sewing military shirts. Later, they permitted us to go to Pamplona, but we still lacked a Safe Conduct,* and had to go clandestinely. We arrived at night, carrying the name of a friend our neighbor had recommended. My mother asked directions of a policeman, speaking, of

*A document necessary for travel within Insurgent-held territory.

> course, in Euskera. He rebuked her, saying "Madame, you should use a Christian tongue here." He took us a long way to the house, a couple without children, pleasant, but very pro-Franco, really addicted to his cause. Clearly, we couldn't stay there, so we all went to a furnished room, where we shared the kitchen with five families. The police watched us closely. My mother got work sewing. There we stayed until my father sent us word to go to France. He sent us to a smuggler, who took us over the border in a taxi. The smuggler's son drove, a Carlist *requete*, red beret and all, but the money for this "cargo" was good, and they put politics aside. In France, the people were very cold, insulting us as the "Scum of Spain" and "Red Spaniards." My mother found work, and we three were later sent to adoptive homes, good ones, in Belgium.

The tens of thousands of civilians who fled eastern Guipúzcoa found little organized help. The PNV was able to requisition some public buildings en route to offer shelter. The advancing Insurgent armies did not yet strafe the refugees or attempt to cut the roads to Vizcaya. Local militia, later to be incorporated into the "*Gudari*" ("Warrior") units of the Basque army, maintained guard in the towns, using arms from the Civil Guard armories. The limited available assistance was given freely to all, regardless of political affiliation. There was a great deal of mutual help and solidarity. As the refugees reached the major towns in Vizcaya, an aid organization was hastily improvised through the sponsorship of the major political parties and trade unions.[17]

Basque Autonomy and Formation of the New Basque Government

At this same time, the Spanish Republican government, headed by Largo Caballero, was trying to unify the many groups comprising the Popular Front in order to create a viable army throughout the regions of Spain under its control. Caballero made overtures to the newly formed Basque leadership, the All-Basque Junta, promising them that the long-awaited Autonomy Statute would be ratified. In return, the Junta was to appoint a representative to serve in Caballero's cabinet. All the formalities were completed by October, and an Autonomy Act, nearly identical to that drafted by the PNV in 1931, was accepted by the Republican parliament.[18] As Madrid was now under Insurgent assault, the statute was signed in the new wartime capital, Valencia. Manuel Irujo of the PNV entered the Popular Front cabinet, first as Minister without Portfolio, but later, as Minister of Justice, serving to humanize the war through prisoner exchanges. The All-Basque Junta, elected by municipal councils in the Republican zone of Euzkadi, chose as its leader an ardent, charismatic nationalist, José Antonio Aguirre.

Throughout the Spanish Civil War, the strongly Catholic Basque leadership was to be a rather curious anomaly in the anti-clerical stance of the Popular Front. An anecdote from autumn, 1936, captures this:

> Aguirre, the President of the Basques, was at that time in Madrid, waiting for a copy of the Act granting Home Rule, in order to proclaim it officially in Euzkadi. A poor Basque woman came to his lodgings, disclosing to him that a monk was hidden in her house who had the Holy Eucharist with him. Aguirre called two soldiers of his Basque Guard, and went to the slum, where the monk was found hiding in a cupboard. Next day, when the aeroplane landed in Bilbao and the official delegation advanced to welcome the statute, they were met by these words, "Stand, we bring the Lord." Amidst a deep religious silence, the Host was carried to Our Lady of Begoña (church) and given in communion the following morning to the Basque Nationalist authorities and members of the new autonomous government.[19]

To underscore the statute, military help was promised by Caballero and one shipment of arms was actually delivered late in September by the now decimated Republican fleet.

During these weeks, General Mola marched rapidly west through Guipúzcoa, meeting very little defensive action. Resistance was organized near the Vizcayan border by mid-October. The Insurgents were repulsed at Eibar, and Mola withdrew his forces back to Navarra. The eastern as well as the southern border of Vizcaya remained quiet during a welcome hiatus lasting almost exactly six months.[20] The new Basque government could turn its attention to building a military defense. At the same time, Aguirre began to organize assistance for the hordes of war refugees from Guipúzcoa and the political refugees from Navarra and Alava.

Within the newly formed government, a very extensive bureaucracy developed with surprising speed. PNV leader Aguirre, elected as president in a historic ceremony in the foral center of Basque liberty, Guernica, immediately named himself Minister of Defense. He appointed a cabinet heavily weighted to the PNV. Three key cabinet posts, Interior, Justice, and the Treasury, went to members of his party; the Socialists were given Industry, Labor, and Social Assistance; the Left Republicans, Trade and Supply; Basque Nationalist Action (ANV) was given Agriculture; and the Communists were awarded Public Works. Neither the Anarchists nor the Left-oriented trade unions were represented in cabinet posts.[21]

Asistencia Social (Social Assistance)

This cabinet post, headed by Juan Gracia, a prominent Socialist, was charged with developing a complete system of social services for the citizens of Euzkadi, particularly for those who were refugees. The range of assistance soon available exemplified the particular care and importance certain observers have noted as being characteristic of Basque humanitarian efforts.[22] Public dining rooms in requisitioned schools throughout Vizcaya fed forty thousand refugees each day.[23] Clothing, shoes, and other necessities were distributed gratis and in an equitable manner. A model orphanage for children of Basque soldiers killed in combat was opened in Bilbao. Hospital services for the civilian and military victims of war were augmented. More than 100,000 refugees were relocated in requisitioned apartments or homes, many in the poorer sections along the river in Bilbao.

After we fled San Sebastián, we made our way to Durango, to live with cousins of my mother. By the next March, we fled again for our lives, this time to Bilbao, on the river, in the top flat of an old house, where an aunt of my father lived.

Those without relatives fared less well:

> We refugees from Guipúzcoa were parceled out among Basque families in Bilbao. We were given space in a trucker's home, right next to the railway station. We all slept on the floor. But it was hard to get enough food, because, being from elsewhere, we didn't know the area or the people.

The municipal administrations from Basque towns in Guipúzcoa and other areas now under Insurgent rule were reconstituted in Vizcaya. These city officials assisted in relocation, in the distribution of food and clothing, and served as a trusted information network among the refugees. Through their efforts, scattered family members could be reunited, news of casualties among relatives reported, and information about family members taking refuge in France or Catalonia relayed.[24] Those who fled from Navarra, Alava, and Guipúzcoa thus learned of the execution of women. Scores of Basque priests were also imprisoned, and over a dozen were executed by the Insurgents.[25]

Throughout the Basque government's few months of life in Euzkadi, assistance to the refugee and civilian population was a priority, second only to defense. Refugee workers from abroad who came to offer help found the work of this ministry impressive:

> In Vizcaya and Santander we went to see a great number of places where the Asistencia Social, the official social welfare organization, was housing and caring for all those who would be destitute. There are no waifs and strays; no old people begging. The Asistencia Social has collected them all, as well as the hundreds of thousands of refugees, and not only are they given the best food available (we know because we saw it and had opportunities to compare), but the people appointed to look after them are a combination of experienced people, such

as matrons and doctors, and young people with vision who help the children with their lessons and think out amusements for them. In Bilbao is one children's home being quickly prepared (with accommodation for two hundred). Well-known Basque painters were painting large mural studies—one was a magnificent fishing smack, one a study of mother and child, one a country scene with a hiker. . . . Of course, though the scarcity of food outweighs all else, there are other needs. . . . I remember a babies' home where for 200 babies, bottles were being prepared with water and a little flour.[26]

Ministry of Justice and Culture

This ministry, headed by PNV spokesman Jesús Leizaola, coordinated the court system and jails throughout Euzkadi. Leizaola, a brilliant lawyer, insisted that extra-legal reprisals and terrorism against citizens presumed to be disloyal to the Republic would not be tolerated.

Women prisoners were freed and sent to safety in France. Torture in prisons was prohibited, and the new "People's Tribunals" dispensed a justice considered moderate for the times.[27] The practice of Catholicism was encouraged under the new Basque government. Many militia units had chaplains attached to them, and public worship was as fervent as ever. The *ikastolas*, the Basque language schools of Euzkadi begun in the Second Republic by the PNV, were also encouraged by Leizaola in every possible way.

Ministry of Commerce and Supply

Left Republican Ramón Aldasoro accepted the responsibility of provisioning the intricate system of free dining rooms in operation throughout Vizcaya for refugees, in addition to organizing the commissary for the Gudaris, who soon numbered over forty thousand men.

He faced an impossible labor, for the province had never produced enough food to be self-sufficient even when its population was at a normal 600,000. Now swollen by nearly 200,000 refugees, the people of Euzkadi also confronted ominous rumors of a blockade by the Insurgent navy, the destruction of traditional sources of provisions, and disruption of local agriculture and fishing due to the war. Even rural areas formerly boasting a small surplus to sell on regional market days found that their stocks of milk, pork, fresh fruit, and vegetables were needed within the family kinship network. Staples such as olive oil, rice, sugar, potatoes, and kerosene or charcoal for cooking had always come from other provinces or abroad. Aldasoro did have large stocks of lentils in storage, and Mexico had shipped in over fifty million pounds of garbanzos.[28] These two beans soon were synonymous in the popular mind with wartime life, as they provided the major source of nutrition in Euzkadi during its nine months of life. These memories are still salient:

> To this day, I cannot eat lentils without recalling those months when that was all we had to eat, day after day, with a bit of rice. Whenever my wife cooks them, they seem to give me indigestion.

A strict rationing system was implemented early in October of 1936, and all food prices were frozen at the levels in effect at the time of the war's outbreak. A typical ten-day ration for each person with a food coupon late in 1936 included a few ounces of garbanzos, half that amount of rice, a bottle of tomato sauce, and a little sugar.[29] Whenever bread was available, the ration was 100 grams. Throughout the winter and spring, however, flour was unavailable for weeks at a time. When it arrived, the loaves themselves, all produced in government-controlled bakeries, were a distant cousin of the white, crusty, fresh loaf purchased twice daily in better times by Basque housewives. The wartime loaf was heavy and gray and seemed to resist chewing. People claimed only God really knew what natural and artificial ingredients went into it, and many ailments, including impotence, were blamed on eating it.[30]

> Besides the terrible bombardments, we had to withstand the scarcity of food, for there was hardly enough to subsist on. There was only black bread, made from ingredients at hand. That bread, when you chewed it, was totally tasteless, and gave the sensation of turning to rubber in your mouth. Worse than that was the daily ration: only enough for breakfast.

> Looking back on that time, I think the hunger was worse than the bombs. It was always with you. At least, in the refuges, you felt safe from the bombardments. All we talked about was food there, too.

The cardinal sin was to waste food: one woman interviewed recalled dropping and breaking the family's ten-day ration of oil—a half-liter bottle—on the cobblestones of the "Old City" in Bilbao early in 1937. She was eight then; forty-three years later, this event was one of her most vivid memories of the war.

At the war's beginning, the old and those with written orders from their doctor were given a soup bone, and sometimes a bit of meat, for their daily broth. This, plus a liter of milk, was dispensed by Social Assistance in the first two months of its work. This had to be discontinued near the end of 1936 for lack of supplies. Refugees were assured one meal of garbanzos or lentils, some rice, and salt codfish each day in the public dining rooms. In the blocks-long great public market in Bilbao's Arenal, nothing was for sale except a few locally caught fish. Only once did the mothers complain: in late January 1937, a petition requesting milk signed by 200 women was presented to Aguirre. He could do nothing: no milk was available.[31] Only those with relatives in outlying farms saw milk, eggs, or meat. Rations were cut again in early 1937 as the food situation became critical.

Those interviewed recalled how their lives as children in wartime revolved around obtaining food to bring to their mothers:

> Our days were spent in the streets, trying to obtain food. I remember running behind the truck of "Chocolate de Bilbao" to see in what store food would be delivered, and being among the first to line up for rice or garbanzos. Sometimes we would linger near the schools, now turned into armories for the Gudaris, to get their leftovers. Their food always came first.

> From the early hours of the morning, we stood in lines to buy whatever was available. We walked to the port to bargain for a few fresh anchovies or sardines when they

were to be had. These last, cooked with orange peel as the only seasoning, were a glorious treat to us.

My mother was desperate: I became thinner and thinner. Finally, she enrolled me in a school for deaf-mutes, to ensure that I received one meal a day. They kept me for three months before they found out I could hear and talk.

Franco's Blockade

Early in 1937, Franco announced a blockade of the Basque coast. Although the Insurgent fleet was occupied elsewhere, this attempt to discourage ships carrying vital food to Euzkadi had immense propaganda value. Shippers from England, France, Mexico, and other countries became more cautious, in spite of the tremendous profits that could be made. The Basque government strengthened coastal fortifications, and improvised mine sweepers and convoy vessels from trawlers formerly used for codfishing. Fishermen from coastal towns who had followed the sea for centuries quickly learned to use the new guns mounted on their vessels. They escorted and protected food ships entering their territorial waters, and swept the seas clear of mines laid by Insurgent vessels.[32] Outside the three-mile limit, the British navy offered protection, and the announced blockade was viewed as largely fictional.

During March, the situation changed. As one preparation for the coming Northern Campaign, Franco proclaimed a total blockade of Euzkadi. This time, however, there was substance to his declaration. The battleship *España*, its batteries manned by German sailors, as well as two cruisers and two German submarines, set up a cordon in the bay near San Sebastián. This flotilla, intended to control access to the Bay of Biscay, was later joined by a German battleship, the *Graf Spee*. The Generalissimo then announced that any ship flying the flag of the countries in the Non-Intervention Committee would be stopped.[33] The announcement generated much indignation, particularly in Britain, the primary shipper to Euzkadi. A letter to the (London) *Times* of February 16, 1937, commented:

> It is intolerable that General Franco, who is a mere rebel and has no right to interfere with international shipping, should be stopping, carrying off to rebel ports, and searching peaceful ships of all nations.

On April 6, a British merchant ship carrying food to Bilbao and flying the British flag was signaled to stop by the *España*. In London, an emergency cabinet meeting was held, but came to no conclusion. The Royal Navy, acting on its own, ordered that there be no further escort of British food ships to Bilbao. Admiralty and diplomatic reports that Franco was maintaining an effective blockade over 200 miles of coastline and that the harbor of Bilbao was mined were both inaccurate. The reports perhaps reflected the pro-Franco sentiments of the British ambassador to Spain at Hendaye, Sir Henry Chilton. In reality, the Insurgents had only one battleship and the cruisers. The Basques controlled their own territorial waters: their coastal guns had an effective range of well over three miles, quite adequate to police the sea-lanes through the Bay of Biscay.[34]

Public opinion over the food blockade became aroused in England. There was absolutely no precedent for stopping food ships to either side in a civil war. Letters to the editor deplored the "Hunger Blockade" and protested the attitude of the British government in

> concurring on the idea of blockade of food ships as normal in the waging of war. The effect is not only of pain and horror and death of the civilian population, but in the distorted limbs and swollen bodies of starved children.[35]

On April 13, President Aguirre informed the British Prime Minister that

> 26 ships entered and 32 ships left Bilbao safely the previous month and not one ship had been detained or fired upon in Basque waters.[36]

In spite of this, British ships continued to be ordered to drop anchor across the border, in France, at St.-Jean-de-Luz. There were half a dozen ships, "including 3 Welsh sea captains known to the British press according to their cargoes as 'Potato Jones,' 'Ham and Egg Jones' and 'Corncob Jones.' "[37] Their cargoes were rotting, and they were losing thousands of pounds sterling, while ships were well known to be safely entering and leaving Bilbao. "Potato Jones" tried to leave, but bad weather forced him back. Finally, the *Seven Seas Spray* with Captain Roberts and his daughter Fifi made it to Bilbao—safely—on April 20. Its cargo consisted of 3,600 tons of food including oil, salt, flour and potatoes.[38] Other ships followed suit and the fictitious blockade was at an end. When the merchant ships met Insurgent ships on patrol, the latter backed off.

The breaking of the blockade, after the citizens of Euzkadi had subsisted on about forty centavos worth of food a day for months, did provide a welcome, but tragically short, respite from hunger.[39] The day following the blockade's end, the Bilbao press announced:

> There will be potatoes, rice, codfish, sugar, beans, tomato paste, and possibly wine and dried peas, and there will even be MEAT, *hombre*.[40]

Spring was beginning in Euzkadi, there was more food to be had. But Mola and Franco had already begun their campaign to crush the autonomous Basque Republic.

The War in Vizcaya

Ever since the previous September, German planes and pilots had flown reconnaissance flights over Bilbao and other Vizcayan cities. At irregular intervals, bombs fell, and the populace fled to improvised shelters in churches, or the interurban train tunnels. There were some casualties, and one twelve-year-old boy, later evacuated to England, remembers:

> I volunteered to help clear away rubble from a few houses in my barrio which had been hit. Till I die, I'll never forget the horror of finding pieces of the children who lived there among the bricks and debris.

As in the early battles in San Sebastián and Irún, these raids provided a bit of diversion to the children:

As soon as the bombardment was over, we would run to pick up the "dud" bombs, bringing them home to add to our collections.

Since we had no classes, because of the bombing, my father sent me to the country, to my uncle's farm near Munguía. There, too, the bombing began. The planes passed so low, we could clearly see the German pilots. One day, I was minding the cows, and a plane came toward me, coming lower and lower. The cows bolted, and I, who had never been fearful before, fell into a ditch. The pilot threw a pineapple grenade at me, but it didn't explode. In my ignorance, I took it to my uncle, but he was frightened, and threw it in the river.

After the loss of Guipúzcoa to the Insurgents, the battles of the Civil War shifted south to the campaign in the Madrid area. In the ensuing six-month lull in the north, Aguirre energetically organized the defense of Vizcaya. Based on an infantry (Gudaris) to man the fortified mountain outposts ringing Vizcaya, and a classic ring of ground fortifications intended to protect Bilbao, his plan did not take into account the reality of modern aerial warfare. The Basque "Iron Ring" proved no more valuable in protecting Bilbao than did the Maginot Line, a few years later, in preserving France. In addition, the construction of the heavy fortifications around Bilbao was slow and inefficient, and the engineer defected to the Insurgents with the complete plans.[41]

In the organization of his infantry, Aguirre used the multiparty model of the Republican force, with similar results. The Gudaris were organized strictly according to political affiliation, with battalions raised by six major parties, Leftist or Nationalist, in Euzkadi. Each took a name from a hero or event in earlier struggles for liberty, or current Basque martyrs. Of the seventy-nine battalions, each with 750 men, the PNV raised twenty-five, including the Arana Goiri, Simón Bolívar, and Ariztimuño, named for a politically active priest executed by the Insurgents. Eleven Socialist units chose names such as Indalecio Prieto (after the Bilbao-born Socialist leader), Pablo Iglesias, and Meabe; in the eight Communist cadres, Rosa Luxemburg, Lenin, and Karl Liebknecht were memorialized. President Azaña denoted a Left Republican unit, and Malatesta, an Anarchist one.[42]

As could have been predicted, the coordination of such a disparate force with such differing ideologies into a crack fighting army never materialized. Furthermore, the Gudaris were never to be adequately armed, though the Basque government did arrange arms purchases from neutral powers and even Germany. The Soviet Union sent a shipload of weapons, including a dozen aircraft and trained pilots and two dozen armored cars. Both were to be invaluable in the coming months.[43] But enough machine guns, ammunition, or personal arms for each Gudari never arrived. There were no anti-aircraft defenses, no suitable fields for aerodromes, and only a handful of planes.

The Gudaris as individual units distinguished themselves for bravery and tenacity under superior firepower. They also exemplified the spirit of the newly autonomous Basque nation. Every family in Vizcaya had a son, brother, father, or uncle fighting to rid their land of a foreign invader.

> My first recollection of the war was of my father, dressed in the uniform of a Gudari, when he arrived home on a day of leave. Our happiness was so great. But, the next day, he had to march away, and our sadness was even greater. Everyone in the house cried, while I was allowed to walk with him to the corner of the street (I was six), and stay a few moments at his side. That was to be the last time I saw him.

Their casual heroism made a lasting impression on the children of Euzkadi:

> I can never forget the trucks filled with young Gudaris, including my uncle, leaving the Ayuntamiento of Basauri. They were dressed with great diversity, some still wearing civilan clothes. Many had only their hunting rifles; others had only their bare arms and good will. But, a few days later, this battalion brought in a captured Insurgent flag, the first one we'd ever seen.

On March 31, General Mola launched the Northern Campaign. He wanted to gain the munitions factories of Eibar and, within Vizcaya, the iron ore deposits in the province, and the world-famous heavy industry centered in the Bilbao area. There were political and propaganda purposes to his assault as well. Taking Vizcaya would crush the Catholic Basque Republic, a thorn in the side of the proclaimed "Defender of the Faith" which the Insurgent cause epitomized to much of the world. Furthermore, since the campaign to take Madrid had floundered badly the previous month—the Italians proved very diffident fighters—a quick victory was essential for morale and propaganda reasons. Mola predicted Bilbao would be his in twenty-one days.

An all-out attack was planned. Thousands of Italian and Moorish troops were brought up to Vitoria, in Alava. An airbase was constructed there for a force of 140 Heinkel, Junkers, Savoy, and Dornier planes, including the aircraft of the famous German Condor Legion. Trained German pilots and crews, and a full range of the most modern aerial weaponry and bombs came from Hitler. Italian tanks were massed at the Vizcayan border, and quantities of heavy artillery were rushed in to headquarters in Vitoria.[44]

The offensive began with "the most terrible bombardment of a civil population in the history of the world at Durango and its adjacent villages."[45] Churches, hospitals, schools and homes were destroyed. Over 250 people were killed instantly in Durango and nearly half that number died later in Bilbao hospitals.[46] A man, then fifteen years old, remembers that day:

> It was a morning without cloud, a splendid spring day. On the horizon appeared the formation of German Junkers, protected by their fighter planes. They came so fast, there wasn't time to run the eighty meters to the refuge. We already heard the penetrating whistle of the bombs dropping on a defenseless people, and the horrible sound of exploding bombs. Our alarm siren was sounding, and the church bells were ringing to warn of the imminent danger, that we should run to the refuges. The planes ranged like buzzards upon prisoners incapable of defending themselves, having not even one anti-aircraft gun. It was a terrible massacre. Those in the churches at Mass were entombed there. Who would

> have thought the "Defenders of Catholicism" could commit such a crime?

A woman, then eleven, recalls:

> One bombardment occurred in the morning; in the afternoon came a new attack. This time, the townspeople were alerted, and went into the shelters. This sent the Franquistas on a spree, dedicating themselves to machine gun every living thing, including the cemetery, loaded with cadavers not yet buried. The wounded had been taken in every kind of vehicle to places like Bilbao, where there was medical help.

The next day, the bombing attack was repeated and the day following, a delegation from England, which included the Archbishop of Canterbury and John McMurray of the Popular Front, viewed that day's attack.[47] A boy of Ochandiano, then eight years old, recalls that twenty-six of his neighbors were killed there. He watched the corpses arrive on a truck to be buried in a mass grave nearby.

> The people had thought the planes would drop more propaganda leaflets from Mola, but instead, they dropped bombs.

The bombardment, as seen by a nine-year-old of Durango, was

> furious—it was a clear day, full of sun, which made the bombs shine brilliantly as they fell—a spectacle. We watched from the top of our house—the bombs were bright, silvery white. The church right there was destroyed as Don Carlos said Mass. Many were killed, including my aunt, and we watched them be buried the next day.

In spite of daily poundings by aerial bombardment—in Markina some three thousand bombs fell in seven months—much of the population of the Basque Republic had stayed in their villages and towns along the southern and eastern battle lines. Many homes were almost in ruins from bomb hits, with broken windows that could not be reglazed. But still Basques lived on throughout the winter, often less than a mile from Mola's troops. "This phenomenon can only be explained by the Basque love of his home and land."[48] Some families moved en masse to the Bilbao area, to the presumed safety of the Iron Ring, and doubled up with relatives there. As the fighting intensified, even the rural farms were evacuated, with one family member elected to care for the precious livestock. Within the Bilbao area, air raids became more and more frequent. Women and children became accustomed to spending most of the day in the cold, damp shelters improvised throughout greater Bilbao. There were a total of 159 Insurgent air raids in one month that spring, with over 100 planes participating. In April and May, in fact, there were only five days when the sirens did not sound. One frightening day, there were twelve separate air raids.[49] Families now remained in the refuges night and day.

> I was only nine then. Our days were lived around the air raid sirens, the race to the shelters. Our first shelter, a big warehouse, burned after a direct hit. We took to the train tunnels. But they weren't safe either, as we soon learned. The hours and days we spent in the refuges were endless, and we never knew what we would find when the raid was over and we could come out.

> Those bombardments are etched in my memory. We lived near a small air field, and were bombed daily, so we took refuge in the granary of a *caserio* nearby. One direct hit destroyed our house, and the sky was often red from the squadrons of Junkers coming over in waves. They were trying to destroy our will to fight with the Moors, Italians and Germans attacking us, burning our homes, a continuous trial.

Refuges were located in churches, basements of municipal buildings, and railroad tunnels. This last site became unpopular when the interurban train from an adjoining town ran into a tunnel full of women and children taking shelter, and killed several of them.[50] The refugee population, housed in large part near the industrial strips on either side of the river Nervión along the miles of Bilbao's harbor, bore the brunt of the bombings.

Civilian morale seemed high, in spite of continued advances by General Mola's troops, now circling close to Bilbao. Posters with the exhortation *No Pasarán* were everywhere in Bilbao. The press urged everyone to continue to resist; all able-bodied women were volunteering to build the fortifications.

The spirit of the Basques in this uneven struggle was well publicized. A representative of the National Joint Committee for Spanish Relief in England wrote:

> To the Editor of the *Manchester Guardian*
> Sir,—We have just returned from a visit to the north of Spain, where we represented the Society of Friends and the Save the Children Fund. Vizcaya, the object of so much controversy today, is sadly changed in these days of civil war. Bilbao, the capital, that gay, noisy town of former times, is haunted by an atmosphere of tragedy. Shops are open, but there is nothing to buy, no food, no fruit, no vegetables, while the cafés are full of occupants who sit reading before bare tables, the only drinks obtainable being a camomile-tea infusion or a little bad whisky. Milk is scarce, and not till the last day of our stay did we see bread, which had not been baked for three weeks. The hungry people received it like manna from heaven. . . . The sirens sound constantly, giving warning of air raids, and the streets become suddenly a seething mass of men, women, and children running to the refuges. There is no panic, no disorder, and in spite of the general terror—for the fate of Durango is fresh in their minds—everyone laughs and jokes with apparent unconcern, till the whir of the aeroplanes directly overhead causes a sudden hush, followed by a sigh of relief if they pass without dropping any bombs. Everyone is thin and haggard, but there is no talk of surrender. "Better to die fighting, for if the enemy get in we die anyway," is the feeling.
>
> Such is the spirit of the people that when we left not one showed envy of our returning to safety, not one expressed a wish to come with us—but there was one plea: "Can you arrange for our children to get away? We would not have asked this a month ago; we could not have let them go; but now . . ."

> And when we arrived at St.-Jean-de-Luz there were three English ships carrying food to Bilbao and Santander prevented from doing so because of Franco's threats. Behind us we had left starving people waiting for the food which should bring them life and hope, food which is now rotting in the holds of the ships still in France.—Yours,
>
> Bronwen Lloyd-Williams
> Lydia Mary Gee
>
> London, April 16, 1937

In the three weeks after Durango, southern Vizcaya was taken by Mola's troops, Eibar to the east fell, and the last remnant of Guipúzcoa was now in Insurgent hands. Many more refugees came to Bilbao, three thousand from Eibar alone.[51]

Guernica

A more stunning blow came on April 26 when the historic center of Vizcayan liberty, Guernica, was bombed for over two hours by the Condor Legion. For the first time, small new incendiary bombs were used experimentally in tandem with conventional aerial bombs, so that uncontrolled fires added to the bombs' destruction. It was a Monday afternoon, the traditional weekly market day, and farmers and residents from nearby villages had come in to buy or sell extra produce and stock. Guernica, a town of seven thousand, was not a military target, nor were troops stationed there, nor was it situated on a strategic road. Yet hundreds were killed instantly—estimates range from 250 to perhaps as many as 1,600, and nearly 900 were wounded.[52] The fire, which burned until late the next day, consumed most of the town.[53] Thousands were forced to flee toward Bilbao, within the supposed safety of its fortifications.

This devastating assault on their holy city stunned the Basques and sent waves of shock through the Western world. Eyewitness accounts taken by war correspondents for the London *Times, Daily Express,* Reuters, and *Çe Soir* of Paris had an immediate effect on public opinion. In England, popular feeling for the Basques rose, so that funds for the humanitarian National Joint Committee for Spanish Relief were collected in quantity. Franco first denied the bombing, trying to shift the destruction to the Basques themselves. A young Basque priest, Don Alberto de Onaindia, was in Guernica during the bombardment. His vivid testimony to Catholic groups in France and England during May undercut the official Insurgent position.[54] Children from Guernica remember that Monday well:

> There were more than the usual number of reconnaissance flights and the day somehow seemed different, more tense. When the church bells rang, many people went to the shelters, so inadequate they would now be a joke, but life was simpler then. Many bombs fell, and soon everything was burning, to the ends of the streets. Even the shelter near us, behind three houses, caught fire, by luck, after the bombardment, so that we had just left it before the houses in front caved in. We walked to the farm of our grandparents in Rigoitia. There, we were between the Rebels and the hooligans from the Asturias, a bad situation. Soon we went on to Bilbao and then we were sent to England.

The military situation in Vizcaya became more desperate:

> More than anything, I remember those last days: the anguish of continual bombardments, every hour of every day. And the food, so bad, very bad, only a little rice and garbanzos. I can never forget the bombing of Guernica, when the farm families came with their oxcarts into Bilbao, just like those from Guipúzcoa the September before.

There was no anti-aircraft protection, and the lack of suitable flat airfields and absence of spare parts kept the small air force inefficient. In spite of this, the feats of this tiny force, led by nineteen-year-old Felipe Del Rio, have become legendary. Del Rio bagged nine Heinkels before being shot down himself in mid-April.[55] The young boys who watched his exploits against Fascist planes can still describe each dogfight over forty years later:

> To all of us, he symbolized the war in the north: the few against the Fascists. We watched every clash between Felipe and the German planes. Once, we saw three German aviators parachute out of a burning fighter he bagged. We ran there, and got airplane parts for souvenirs. I found a pilot's boot, and took it to the house requisitioned for us, but my aunt threw it out.
>
> We had one old plane everyone called *El Abuelo* as it was so old and slow. But our best was one famous aviator, very well known, our idol, Del Rio. I once saw some fourteen or fifteen black bombers, German Heinkels, as I was coming home. We had about five fighter planes, but they didn't come out at first, only their bombers, dropping their bombs, "Boom, boom, boom." Then all of a sudden, our fighters, led by our adored Felipe, were on the top of the bombers, shooting them down. It was tremendous. What a brave young man.
>
> We had only eight planes, really only mosquitoes against the scores of Junkers and fighter planes they had. The most fantastic spectacle I ever saw was when our pilots bagged three Junkers, and forced the other seventeen to flee, jettisoning their bombs in the sea.

By late May, Mola's troops had advanced to the Iron Ring around Bilbao. A week later, the last plane of the Basque air force was shot down. The help promised from Valencia did not arrive. The military situation was hopeless. But at least the children should be saved.

The Evacuation's Prelude

Throughout Republican Spain, by the spring of 1937, the possibility of the evacuation of children and other noncombatants had been considered by such governmental ministries as that of Instruction and Social Assistance. As Spain's closest neighbor, France became the logical country to host the civilians who might be evacuated. Within France, such assistance was forthcoming very shortly after the start of the Civil War. The Committee to Aid the Children of Spain (*Comité d'Accueil aux Enfants d'Espagne,* CAEE) was organized by the French Popular Front in November of 1936. Its sponsorship consisted of the Leftist Confédération Générale du Travail (CGT), which included all the major trade unions in France. The consumers' cooperative movement, the teachers' unions, and other production workers' associations were also represented, as was the French League for the Defense of the Rights of Man.

The purpose of this committee was to bring into France as many refugee and orphaned Spanish children as possible. There, good care, a home, and an education would be provided for them. Working closely with the Spanish Republican government, a set of procedures was developed for each child to be evacuated. These included the issuance of an identity card, a medical inspection, vaccination, and the establishment of reception centers (*centres de triage*) to enable children to adjust to their new life for a month while in quarantine. The children would subsequently be dispersed to children's colonies, or to adoptive families, who were to be screened for good moral and health backgrounds. School instruction was to be provided in the state French schools along with French children. A system of follow-up inspections was organized.[56]

Immediately, the many member unions and other allied organizations of the Popular Front in every province of France mobilized to screen and select the thousands of working-class families needed as adoptive parents. In all, over five thousand private families were enrolled as being willing to house, feed, and clothe a refugee child. Buildings were acquired and renovated for the colonies needed for the thousands of children who could not be accommodated by families.[57] Press coverage of this unprecedented assistance was international: a clipping of the weekly *Frente Popular* of Santiago, Chile, for December 26, 1936, noted that

> The Ministry of Public Health in France and the Minister of Social Assistance in Spain had announced earlier in December in Madrid that they would cooperate to care for any children, aged five to fourteen, who would be evacuated to France "under the best conditions of peace, tranquility and affection, which are traditional in the friendly country of France."[58]

In addition, the CGT set up a fund drive throughout the French nation and, beginning in December, used the collections to send six large caravans of food to Spain. By April 1937, over three thousand tons of food had been sent to the Spanish Republic, one-third being potatoes, but including a welcome eight tons of chocolate. Cold-weather clothing and shoes for women and children were included.[59] On the Day of Solidarity, celebrated in April 1937, it was announced that twenty small colonies were already being established throughout France for refugee children.[60]

Among the first child refugees from Spain to be housed in these colonies were parties of Basque children who had fled the battles of Irún and San Sebastián in the fall of 1936. By January, very small groups of Spanish children also began to be sent across the border to these colonies. In each community, the trade unions and various political organizations took responsibility for maintaining the refugee children coming there. This wholehearted response on the part of the French Popular Front came in spite of the official French policy of Non-Intervention, announced by Socialist Premier Léon Blum only three weeks after the war began. Very probably, the political expediency of France's participation in this pact, so counter to the aspirations of the Popular Front, spurred its members to greater efforts to help the Civil War's most helpless victims.

Mutual Help in Spain

While Leftist organizations in France were preparing to receive refugee children, and sending in shiploads of food and clothing, groups within Spain itself were also mobilizing to offer help to the civilian population living in the zones held by the Republicans.

The *Socorro Rojo* (Red Help) of the Spanish Communist Party organized food and clothing distribution in Andalucía and Madrid late in 1936 and early in 1937. It set up a number of refugee colonies in Catalonia for women and children who fled from Insurgent-held territory in the south and north. These soon evolved into colonies, where food, clothing, some medical attention, and schooling for Basque and Spanish children were offered.[61]

The Spanish people distinguished themselves by the mutual assistance they practiced spontaneously throughout Republican-held territory. One observer, sent in by the British Quakers, and who was later to play an important role in the repatriation of the Basque children from England, wrote:

> One of the most heartening experiences I have ever known in my life was the observation this last December 1936 and January 1937, of what the Spaniards themselves were doing for the people who had been driven out of their homes. Since last August, hundreds of thousands have been moving eastwards and northwards. In the provinces of Catalonia, Valencia and Alicante (I speak of what I saw), they had been received with wonderful generosity. People had given them of their best—in mattresses, food, accommodation. And it was not a matter of a few days. Some we saw had been housed, fed and cared for three months or more—e.g., two hundred in la Granja Flor de Mayo. . . .[62]

The situation outside Catalonia soon became even more grave, prompting over 220,000 refugees to flee there by February.[63] Several international organizations began to send observers and help. Among these were the International Brigade, which set up hostels for refugee children in eastern Spain, as well as dining rooms in Barcelona. Here, hundreds of children were fed from left-over Brigade food, augmented by parcels of food from abroad.[64] The British Quakers set up milk canteens, as well as a dining room where thousands of children got one meal daily.[65]

The Evacuation

In Euzkadi, as in the rest of Republican Spain, the evacuation of unaccompanied children to France was an idea that took root slowly, seeming unthinkable or unnecessary to most Basque parents in Vizcaya during the first few months of the Civil War. Early in January, however, the Spanish Republican embassy in Paris sent a delegate to Bilbao to report to Sr. Gracia regarding the progress of facilities for refugee children from Euzkadi. He said that a number of colonies were ready to receive thousands of Basque children between five and ten years of age.[66] Within a few days the Basque government devised a detailed plan for the evacuation of its children. This plan exemplified the uneasy coalition of political parties, both regional and national, which comprised both the Basque Autonomous Government and the army that was to defend it during the coming Northern Campaign.

Throughout Bilbao, special desks were set up by each trade union and its parent political party. Special registration was also arranged at the Hotel Carlton in downtown Bilbao. The quota of children each of these entities could send abroad was fixed by Asistencia Social to be roughly proportional to the electoral strength each had shown in the most recent provincial and city elections, those of February 1936.[67] In this election, the Leftist national parties showed greater strength in the cities, in both Vizcaya and Guipúzcoa, than in the countryside, while the PNV made its strongest showing in the rural areas. Evacuation places in the children's expedition were awarded as follows: The PNV and its associated union, the Solidaridad de Trabajadores Vascos, received half the allocation; the Socialists, with their Unión General de Trabajadores, would have a quarter of the spaces; the Left Republicans were entitled to an eighth, and the Communists received about 10 percent. The Anarchists, and their unions, the Federación Anarquista Ibérica and the Confederación Nacional de Trabajo, garnered the balance, a few percent.[68] A publicity campaign was mounted by radio, press and the posting of handbills, urging parents to ensure their children's safety by signing them up for evacuation. The age limits were extended to twelve years after negotiation with the Spanish embassy in Paris. In Bilbao, within a few days, over 1,800 children had been registered for evacuation.[69]

In all cases, a medical screening was necessary; height and weight were recorded, and children were checked for absence of infectious diseases. Four photos of the child, some proof of age, and a vaccination certificate were required. Four copies of the file on each child were made: one to be sent to the Basque delegation in the host country; one to the Republican government, then in Valencia; one to the sponsoring agency, to follow the child to the colony or private family that became the destination; and one to remain in Bilbao with the Department of Social Assistance. As expeditions were mounted, each child was issued an octagonal heavy cardboard tag with a number, which was tied to his outer clothing upon departure. The number corresponded to the number stamped on the four files of the child's personal identity papers. This number became his identification abroad as well, particularly in England, Belgium, and the Soviet Union. Clearly, it was far more convenient for the administrators of the evacuation in the receiving country to use a number rather than the complex double, or in some cases, triple Basque names the children had been given at baptism. Many of the children felt a personal sense of loss when they became numbers instead of persons:

> I was old enough to feel resentment for being stripped of my identity for the evacuation abroad. Instead of my name, quite well known here, from both my father and mother, I became a *tripito con numero* [a little stomach with a number].

In spite of the indignation some expressed, a great many still possessed their identity tags over forty years later.

After the first announcements in early January, no further notices were printed for seven weeks. Meanwhile, meticulous preparations were made of the first group of 450 Basque children to be evacuated to France. When all was arranged, full pages of photographs of the CGT summer camp on the Île d'Oléron appeared in Bilbao's newspapers. Its virtues and many features were described glowingly: roman baths, sandy beaches, new heating plant (the site was ordinarily used only as a workers' summer resort), a full library, brand-new typewriters and sewing machines, recreation facilities. The department prepared a memorial souvenir booklet, with some of the photos, which was presented to each family sending away a child.[70] Later reports in the press disclosed that two Basque doctors and eight teachers, refugees to France from the Guipúzcoan battles, would be part of the staff. The first week in March, a reception was held in a Bilbao theater, the Coliseo Alba, for all children chosen for the first expedition. Here, a movie of the summer resort was shown, group photographs of the children taken, and final instructions imparted to the parents present by the administrators of Social Assistance.[71]

Then, the sailing date, originally March 16, had to be postponed. The Republican minister of public instruction from Valencia had issued a decision that no state-employed teachers, "be they national, provincial, or municipal," could emigrate with any expedition of children.[72] The matter was adjudicated quickly, and twelve Basque teachers did accompany the 450 children to France the following week. Even before this first expedition of March 20 was safely completed, others were in the planning stages. Parents were impressed by the success of the first evacuation, and began to exert pressure on the Department of Social Assistance to include their children on the next expedition to France, one reportedly to include one thousand children.[73] Newspaper reports of a possible expedition to Russia also appeared.[74]

Aguirre's Plea to Europe

Eleven days after this first expedition of children had left Euzkadi, the Northern Offensive began. General Mola's Insurgent forces moved rapidly toward Bilbao. The Basque defensive capability was totally inadequate to protect the civilian population. On April 27, the day after Guernica was bombed, President Aguirre sent urgent requests to the countries of Europe for asylum for women, children, and the old. In response to Aguirre's appeal, the various committees already formed to aid the Spanish Republic in such countries as France, England, Belgium, Denmark, Switzerland, Sweden*, and Holland* offered care and lodging to the unaccompanied Basque children. These committees were, in each country,

*Neither of these countries subsequently cared for children on their soil due to internal political pressures. However, both sponsored Basque children in colonies in France.

spearheaded by the Left, through the Popular Front organizations and labor unions, and aided by humanitarian groups such as the Quakers. In the case of France and England, developers of the Non-Intervention Pact, some reaction by large segments of the citizenry to this fiasco certainly undergirded their assistance. Other countries, geographically distant, notably Uruguay, Egypt, Canada, and Czechoslovakia, offered to sponsor children's colonies in France, or in Republican Spain, in Catalonia. Two Socialist countries, Russia and Mexico, offered to sponsor colonies both in their respective countries and in France.[75]

At about this same time, Franco proposed establishment of a neutral refuge zone for women and children of Euzkadi at an unspecified location. This was to be supervised by the International Red Cross.[76] The Basque government rejected the plan, noting that the atrocities committed against women in Guipúzcoa and Vizcaya did not give it the necessary credibility.[77] This proposal was widely discussed in the European press, particularly in the Catholic pro-Franco segment, and was periodically re-echoed in all the host countries to which Basque children were sent. It was clearly illusory, as no suitable site existed within Spain for the thousands of refugees at that moment enduring the Northern Campaign. Even the pro-Franco British ambassador in San Sebastián, Sir Henry Chilton, later wrote that Franco's offer had been made for propaganda purposes, to deflect world opinion away from Aguirre's plan of evacuation.[78]

In early May, the Basque army had retreated to its last line of defense: the Iron Ring, at the perimeter of Bilbao. As the Gudaris abandoned villages and towns, women, children, and the old also fled into Bilbao, compressing there nearly the nation's entire citizenry. The Insurgent air and ground offensive was now concentrated against an extremely reduced area, a classic open city of exposed civilians, unprotected and vulnerable.

The Basque government rapidly developed a comprehensive plan for the mass evacuation of the total civilian population. A major feature was to organize colonies of expatriate Basque families in France. It was announced that each colony in France of up to one thousand persons, or within a five-kilometer radius, would be a designated colony; that the Commerce and Housing Ministries of the Basque government would organize services, food, clothing, and other benefits, as well as a means of identifying those eligible to receive them; and that abuses would not be tolerated.[79] Each person would be issued identification by his political party and the Basque government. Sr. Fidel Rotaeche was placed in charge of the civilian expeditions, with Sr. Gracia of Asistencia Social continuing to supervise the evacuation of unaccompanied minor children.[80] For the actual physical transfer of the citizens of Euzkadi, all possible ships were pressed into service: merchant ships, frequently coalers; Basque carriers; even yachts. Names such as *Alice Marie*, *Goizeko Izarra*, and *Habana* became familiar to all as these and many other ships dashed in and out of Bilbao from early May until mid-June, when Bilbao fell. Even fishing boats such as *Gure Ametza* and *Itxaro Izarra* had to be requisitioned for transport.[81]

It was an unprecedented undertaking, a first chapter in the long history that was to follow.

> I do not think the full story of the evacuation of Bilbao has ever been told. The Basque government was so extraordinarily efficient and I was so filled with admiration for them that I should like to set the record straight. In addition to evacuation of children, other refugees were being sent away all the time—old people, invalids—as hospitality and transport became available. The most careful records of each child were kept by Asistencia Social, and duplicates, in the form of lists and indexes, went with each party. There were health checks and vaccinations. . . . But there is a more important aspect of evacuation than the perfection of technical detail, and that is the preparation of a right psychological approach. . . . When I arrived in Bilbao (April 24), the government had decided on this policy, but the people had scarcely begun to think about it. In less than a month, an atmosphere had been created which made the civil population realize that evacuation was the single safest precaution their government could take on their behalf. The atmosphere was created in these ways: by careful publicity; by

> absolute fairness in the choice of those to be evacuated and in the order of their going; and by the creation of confidence in the people who would be responsible, especially those in care of the children. Radio and press were requisitioned for publicity purposes; the president, his ministers, well-loved priests, and public personalities all made broadcasts. . . . In a short time, everyone was talking about evacuation and regarding it as inevitable. And the people learned wealth could claim no privileges. Another decision was the allocation of refugees from the political parties in strict proportion to their electoral representation. Whenever possible, whole families—mothers, children, elderly relatives—went together. But many thousands of young children went alone. Confidence was established in the hearts of mothers when many teachers volunteered to accompany them . . . many young women volunteered to go as aides. Thanks to an ingenious numbering system, the greatest care was taken to see that each child travelled with his own teacher or a family friend as aide. Then, because many Basques were devout Catholics, many priests accompanied these expeditions.[82]

The cost of evacuation in French and English ships was borne in part by the respective governments. England, and later France, supplied protection on the high seas.[83] Since many of the children traveled in family groups to France rather than unaccompanied to colonies, arrangements were made for families to transfer money via letters of credit.

Parents who could not leave were anguished by the choices available for their children in May and early June. A highly favored expedition to England was far oversubscribed; France, Russia, and the Republican colonies in Catalonia were possibilities, as was keeping their children with them. It was a difficult decision to make. Personal circumstances usually dictated the choice. One mother, now seventy-seven testified:

> Because of my circumstances, I sent you three away, but I wouldn't ever do so again. We lived on the third floor, your father was crippled, his legs gone since a truck accident, and I had to carry him down to the shelter in

> the old train tunnel on my shoulders. We all spent days and nights there, with the dirty stones overhead dripping on us. Food was scarce and hard to come by for all of us, and it was getting worse.

Another mother, now eighty, recalled:

> After we were bombed in Durango—my sister was one of those killed—we came by wagon to Bilbao, you four, I with the baby and pregnant besides. My husband was at the front. I was so desperate, I let my brother, the school teacher, sign you up to go.

A father, now eighty-five, wrote an extended personal memoir describing his decision:

> By the spring of 1937, medicine, as well as food, was very scarce. My poor wife's tuberculosis became much worse, and I brought her to the sanitarium in Plencia, on the seacoast. Each day, I took my boys to my mother's house in La Peña where I had been born and reared. By April, they were spending all day in the air raid shelter. One day, rumor reached them that a bomb had destroyed the building where I worked, and my ten-year-old ran to me, three kilometers away, saying he wanted to die with me. They were all three getting more and more anxious. My youngest, then eight, asked me why we didn't change the Lord's Prayer from "Give us this day our daily bread" to a more truthful "Give us this day our daily bombs," since bread could be found rarely, but raids were now every day. They became afraid to be away from me, and began to rise with me at 5:00 A.M., and stay in the air raid shelter in the basement of my workplace all day. A friend who brought milk from a nearby farm to sell gave me rice cooked with milk to feed my boys each day. My superior soon worried about their lack of maternal care and food, and sent me to Social Assistance. They enrolled my boys in a model orphanage for children whose fathers had been killed in battle, in a building close to my job. They got regular food, and even saved me some. Soon, the director decided to evacuate the entire orphanage. By then, I knew it was the only salvation. Days later, my boys were given their identity tags, with their number on the expedition list. My

> youngest exclaimed happily, "Look, Papa, what they have given us," while my middle son, always very sensitive, cried, "No, they have put labels on us, the same as sacks of garbanzos." I gave my oldest a notebook, where I wrote the family addresses, some words of counsel, and put a few family photos. This upset him, and he begged me to keep a copy of these photos, so that if he came back to older, changed parents, we could be sure he would not be given to some other family.

A collection of these letters of counsel was published in London in 1937, in a book printed by the Basque Children's Committee.[84] They were reprinted in a retranslation to Spanish, in Barcelona, in 1977.[85] In these letters, Narciso Moragrega, one of seven children of a poor miner from Bilbao's barrio La Peña, reminds his eldest son to look after his younger brothers always. He continues,

> My sons, be decisive always: if they ask if you are Red, say plainly that you are proletarian, poor, human, and Christian.

He reminds the boys of their trip to say good-bye to their mother in the sanitarium in Plencia. He closes with a "few songs with which to amuse the English children," including an air about the suspension bridge across the Nervión, the chants of the famous sardine-selling women from Santurce, and the hymn to the Virgin of Begoña, the site of their favorite walk together in better times. The final letter admonishes the boys to

> hate war, love peace. All Spanish children must pray for peace in the world, so that no other children may suffer as you have done. You have a sacred mission, as emissaries for the peace of the world.

That same night, Sr. Moragrega wrote this poem:

> Pero la cruel guerra seguía
> Y no le importaba nada de estos dramas:
> Así que cada familia besó a sus hijos
> y a toda prisa arrancaron los autobuses
> Con tan preciosa carga.
> Y llorando unos y otros estos niños

Nos decían "Adiós" con sus manecitos.
Sus pañeulos blancos parecían palomas blancas
Que en trágico vuelo huyeron del tiro del cazador.
Pues, ya la aviación y los obuses
Sembraron el terror y la muerte.
En la noche de este día, me fuí
A mi humilde buhardilla
Al nido deshecho
Donde escribí a mis hijos unos pequeños consejos.[86]

The evacuation was mounted on an immense scale: nearly eleven thousand were evacuated in May from Bilbao.[87] In June, the tempo increased: during only one week, thirteen thousand people left. The harbor in Bilbao, the six miles from the "Old Quarter" to elegant Las Arenas, where the river Nervión reaches the sea, was now a mass of humanity lining up to board the hundreds of fishing trawlers—the whole Basque fishing fleet, now utilized for the evacuation. All through the night, by floodlight, the exodus by sea continued. Tracer bullets from enemy aircraft illuminated the scene. No bombs were dropped, but the bright bullets and the mere presence of reconnaissance planes brought panic to the families fleeing by sea.[88]

After the fall of Bilbao, on June 19, floods of refugees took to the road to Santander, or attempted to reach the city by sea.[89] Both avenues were dangerous. Insurgent aircraft strafed the columns of fleeing families, and Franco's blockade had been reinforced sufficiently to harass the boats making the run for safety. Still, nearly 100,000 people left in a matter of a few days. Many were children who soon would have to flee Santander to Gijón, Asturias, and from there go on to Barcelona, suffering constant bombardment, before finally reaching safety in exile abroad. By land, every conceivable vehicle repeated the flight from Guipúzcoa ten months earlier. The most precious household goods were piled up on lorries: ancient *armorios,* the hand-carved Basque chests handed down from earlier generations, and handwoven blankets. At night Insurgent aircraft fired tracer bullets along the sixty miles of winding roadway. On June 18, 1937, *Le Peuple* of Paris reported on page one:

> Fifteen Heinkels, flying very low, first bombed the families; ten minutes later, the squadron returned, scraping the hedges, machine-gunning the refugees. This went on for two and one half hours, alternate bombing and strafing, causing many deaths and wounds.

An eyewitness reports:

> The road from Castresana to Santander was an anthill of soldiers and country people, swarming around the trucks abandoned in mid-flight; many became the victims of strafing by foreign aircraft. My mother, 80 years old, my sister (a spinster), and my sister-in-law, with her nursing baby (her Gudari husband was killed at Ochandiano) I had evacuated by fishing trawler days before. We all were reunited in a room in Santander requisitioned by the Basque government. I paid the rent with my salary earned as a guard until Santander fell; then we fled by coal boat to Barcelona. When Barcelona fell, in 1939, we fled to France, where we were placed in the concentration camp at Gurs, with Senegalese guards, very tough.

Those who fled as children to Santander as Bilbao fell have no difficulty recalling both the journey and their reception there.

> Just days before Bilbao fell, my father took me to the PNV desk in the Hotel Carlton, and signed me up for France. As the Insurgent troops came in at Archanda, he put me, alone, on a train bound for Santander, over one hundred kilometers away. He wanted to pin the pass in my pocket, but I told him I would guard it myself. I was just past twelve; that day, I became an adult.
>
> Our group went by bus to safety in Santander. The road was pitted with bomb holes, but the cadavers of those who were machine-gunned were thrown in the holes, and we hurried on.

In Santander, a center of Republican anti-clericalism, the Basque government had requisitioned the Hotel Real, one of Santander's best, as well as schools and homes, to shelter refugee families. Mattresses were thrown on the floor for sleeping, and rations of bread and cheese were given out daily. The streets were full of wounded civilians and Gudaris from the Northern Campaign. A hospital ship in the bay was filled with the most critically ill. Groups of children en route to colonies in France were kept together.

> Our group from Bermeo were all going to France together. They put us up in the elegant Hotel Real, where the rich tourists used to stay. We were five boys from the same barrio, sons of fishermen. The hotel astounded us: there were telephones in every single room.

> I fled with my mother, my aunt, and a sister-in-law, who brought with her seven small children. The Basque government issued us one room for all. Since I was already thirteen, almost a man, they sent me upstairs to sleep on a cot. I went up, opened the door, and saw an old man with a huge white beard, lying still, and obviously dead. I ran down to my mother who told me to go back up to sleep with him, on the same cot. I did go up, but lay on the floor, as far away as possible from that corpse. But, in the morning, he woke up, alive.

Already, the Basque government had sent the official Evacuation Committee to Santander, with a delegation headed by Sr. Rotaeche. He arrived four days before Bilbao fell to negotiate the evacuation of citizens of Euzkadi with the portion of the governments of Santander, Palencia, and Burgos remaining in Republican hands. He found the officials there unfriendly and uncooperative, again reflecting tensions within the Popular Front government. In spite of this, he set up offices on Avenida Rusia near the harbor, and began processing refugees and dispensing boat tickets. Problems developed immediately: the first boatload of refugees, on the *Marrakesh*, left half-empty on June 20, because the official in Santander had neglected to prepare the required document of accreditation. This boat also left without sufficient food for the voyage, and without the required doctor and nurse on board. When the boat docked in France, French officials were outraged and a series of complaints ensued. Two days later, the first boat organized by Rotaeche departed, with a full load of two thousand persons. Everything was in perfect order, drawing praise from even the Santander officials.[90] But they continued to harass the Basques: the police, for example, required proof of age beyond that issued by the Basque government. Even the canes of those over sixty were unavailing. Young boys were detained in spite of birth certificates. One refugee boy of fourteen narrowly escaped being conscripted to build trenches. Only because a Basque official from his province recognized him was he allowed to join an expedition to France.

The evacuation of Santander ended on August 26, the day that city fell to Insurgent troops. The Basque delegation had endured two months of continuous problems, culminating in the killing of three Gudaris by Santander police. In addition, Santander officials insisted that the Basques evacuate many Santander citizens and officials, and pay their expenses besides. This was done.

As the Insurgent forces entered the city, the Basque Ministry of Evacuation moved westward to Gijón, in the province of Asturias. In Asturias the officials were more cooperative, but the refugees were more desperate.

> My mother was pregnant, my father at the front. She fled with the four of us, ages four to ten, first to Santander on the train, then to Gijón. We slept on floors, lived on the rations they gave us. Finally, she got us places on a ship to Russia, kissed us "Goodbye," and gave birth to a baby who died in the war.

By September the French ports had become glutted with refugees. To slow the exodus, the *Habana*, the major carrier, was impounded by French officials in late June, and a British escort was denied her. The French ports, Bordeaux, La Rochelle and St.-Jean-de-Luz, were badly congested. The guarantee that only noncombatants were being carried could not be certified, due to lack of a British agent in Santander and Asturias.[91] Only small ships were now allowed to leave, and groups as small as thirteen appeared on the passenger registers of the trawlers and coal boats pressed into service for the evacuation.

The Basque government set up a fund of ten million francs for the children's colonies in France. An additional four million francs had been spent to help pay expenses of the fleet of over thirty British, French and Basque ships employed in the evacuation.[92] The Spanish Republican government was of little concrete help in this vast undertaking. In all, nearly 120,000 persons were evacuated: 26,000 from Bilbao, 30,974 from Santander, and 62,199 from Asturias. Of this total, all but 13,631 were citizens of Euzkadi. About a quarter of all evacuated were children under fourteen years of age, some thirty thousand.[93]

In retrospect, the verdict of many historians is that the Basques were unique in the manner in which they, through their government, cared for their citizenry. One writer notes:

> After the Northern Campaign, and again, during the mass evacuation of Catalonia, the Basques were perhaps the only political group to conduct themselves with dignity and discipline, caring for their refugees efficiently, and with their own resources.[94]

CHAPTER TWO

Finding Refuge in France

Of all the nations offering sanctuary to the refugee children from Euzkadi, France was not only the first, but she was also the most generous. This assistance came in spite of her being politically the most bitterly divided of all the host countries, regarding the contending forces in the Spanish Civil War. Her long history of offering assistance to fleeing peoples, and her geographical proximity were surely factors which overcame, at least to a degree, the refusal of the Socialist Blum government to become officially involved in any way in the conflict. There was, clearly, an overwhelming popular championing of the Republican cause in France, but a powerful minority of important business interests, military leaders, politicians, the diplomatic corps, the press, and the Catholic church had strong Rightist leanings. Léon Blum's Popular Front coalition, composed of Socialists and Radical Socialists, was only a few months old, and was relatively weak. Blum saw that any overt military aid to the Republic could topple his cabinet. French mutual assistance pacts with eastern European countries, most recently with the Soviet Union, were tenuous, and not one of them had strategic interests of consequence in Spain. Great Britain, France's major ally, was pressing for an arms embargo. Blum, in hopes of limiting the war to the Iberian Peninsula, and preserving strategic interests, acceded.[1] Nonetheless, humanitarian assistance was a feasible kind of intervention for France in 1936. One of the first forms this took was the offer of hospitality to Basque child refugees from across the Pyrenees.

France accepted a larger number of unaccompanied Basque children than did any other country. Some fifteen thousand youngsters from Euzkadi spend periods of time ranging from the specified weeks in the *centres de triage*, for quarantine and transition, to the balance of their lives. France was, as well, the first country to undertake any such arrangements, beginning with Guipúzcoan youngsters in 1936, and later, in March of 1937, welcoming the first large group from Vizcaya.

In this pioneering expedition, as in all succeeding ones, the published age limits—usually five to twelve—were not observed. Among the 450 were two- and three-year-olds sent to safety with older brothers and sisters, who might themselves be as old as fifteen. As in all subsequent evacuations, only a minority of children came without siblings and cousins. In the March cohort, many Basque families sent four or five offspring; forty of the 176 families sent three youngsters each.[2]

Some of the children were not even aware that their parents had signed them up for evacuation abroad. After the announcement in January of the first expedition from Vizcaya, weeks passed with no further news. Parents made the required preparations discreetly.

> Something I can never forget is when my parents called together us three oldest and lovingly told us that an expedition was going to France, and that they had signed us up to go, as the situation here was so bad. That same afternoon, my mother said good-bye: I have never again seen her so emotional. She stayed behind, holding the babies, at the station, while my father took us to the embarkation point. His good-byes were full of manliness: "We are in a war and we are confiding you to good people. Don't worry, it will very soon be won, and we will be together again." I didn't see him again until 1957, twenty years later.

In the first three months of 1937, everyone seemed to be

sure that the war would soon be over. Madrid had held firm, the air raids in Euzkadi were still sporadic, and both the mobilization of Gudaris and the construction of the Iron Ring were progressing. This first group of parents was quite confident that their children would not be gone for long—perhaps until the end of summer. It would thus be a good spring and summer away from poor and insufficient food, the many other shortages, and the air raids. Already for the children, the war had lost its aura of novelty and excitement. Its real horror was as yet only glimpsed by Vizcayans who had not experienced the battles of the previous year in Guipúzcoa. The walls of buildings in towns were full of posters with exhortations: "Euzkadi Askatuta," "Unidos Hermanos Proletarios," or the timely "Hay que Fortificar, Fortificar."[3] Truckloads of Gudaris went through the towns singing, en route to their quiet mountain outposts. Finally, after two months of waiting, further news came of the expedition to France.

Notices in the press and on the radio admonished "the children whose names appeared below to present themselves without pretext or excuse at the City Hall of Bilbao on Saturday, March 20, by 8 o'clock."[4] Early that drizzly morning when the 239 boys and 211 girls and their parents arrived at the massive gray City Hall, they found a dozen buses already waiting. First, each child's small suitcase was put aboard, then the loudspeaker began to call out names in alphabetical order. It was a subdued and dignified leavetaking, as parents tried to calm their children and remain dry-eyed themselves. There was a band playing as the children boarded the buses in groups of forty. Each bus had a teacher aboard who remained in charge throughout the trip. The teacher explained what would occur, and tried to keep spirits up as the enormity of this first separation became clear to the children.[5] Older children, as beloved landmarks disappeared from view, tried to mask their feelings:

> So as not to be seen as cowardly by friends or those in charge, no one cried or let his fearfulness be seen.

Some of the younger ones could not control their emotions:

> I cried and cried the whole trip. The teacher told me to stop but I couldn't: I was seven, I went alone, I was frightened to death.

In Bermeo, the children boarded British ships whose names most never forgot—the HMS *Blanche* and the HMS *Campbell*. The much-admired Basque trawlers, converted to patrol boats, were there as escort.[6] Though certain later expeditions of children were menaced by Insurgent planes and ships, this sailing was uneventful. Predictably, children became seasick; in the interviews, the recollection of the odor of vomit was universal.

In this and subsequent expeditions, the oldest child had been given strict instructions to care for the younger ones, and had been made to promise to keep the family together wherever they were sent:

> My mother told me I was responsible for my two sisters: I can never forget her exact words: "My son, promise me one thing, that you now accept the responsibility of the family; stay together." After that, I only cried in private. I was myself just nine, but I carried my five-year-old sister on board ship, and came back to help my crippled older sister up the gangplank. I lined up to get food for them both, and wiped them when they vomited.

> Since I was the oldest of my three brothers, I quickly became the father, responsible for making decisions in difficult situations. This, in spite of my having always been the mischievous and rebellious one. Even today, my brothers laugh at me, calling me "Grandfather" when I dare to give them advice. But I managed then to keep up our spirits, and we were close together on shipboard and in quarantine in France.

Unfortunately, for most children the promise faithfully made to keep the family together could not be kept. Few adoptive families in any host country except Belgium took more than one child of a family, though efforts were made to keep brothers and sisters in the same vicinity. Children sent to Catholic institutions were separated by sex, and almost invariably housed in different institutions.

Upon arrival in France, the promised white bread materialized:

> I could have all the white bread I wanted. I remember eating very slowly, so as to really taste it. They gave us hot milk, too, so hot it burned my tongue. I drank four glasses anyway. What a sensation of joy and satisfaction came over me.

The children were taken to a Socialist vacation resort, to the Maison Heureuse, a huge summer hotel. It was located at Oléron, an island between Bordeaux and La Rochelle, in the upper Bay of Biscay. The young Basques had carried with them a French flag to present to their hosts in the adoptive country. The following day, the Bilbao press reported that the children had arrived in perfect health, and they were enjoying the care of personnel from the French Popular Front, the Committee of Help (Comité d'Accueil aux Enfants d'Espagne, the CAEE).[7]

French Popular Front

The French Popular Front, through its committee of Help for Spanish Children (CAEE), did heroic work in caring for Basque children, women, and the old. Even as the Condor Legion was bombing Guernica, five reception centers and nine colonies were already receiving youngsters. By mid-June, three thousand unaccompanied Basque refugee children were being cared for by the CAEE.

In addition to organizing colonies in nearly every department in France, some 581 by the end of 1937, this organization placed large numbers of Basque children in adoptive homes.[8] These homes were of working-class families who supported such extra children at some personal sacrifice. Though France experienced the worldwide depression of the period somewhat later than did Britain and Belgium, and in a less severe manner, there was substantial unemployment throughout 1937. The two major trade unions had only very recently merged, in 1936, to form the CGT, the initiator of the CAEE. Nearly two years previously, a highly successful general strike had finally brought improved wages and working conditions to production workers in France. This same general strike in 1934 also served to unite all Left groups into the Popular Front. In the national elections of 1936, the Popular Front, led by Blum, was victorious over a Rightist coalition.[9] The French Communist Party had doubled its membership in six months; the CGT grew to four million members. Thus, in the winter of 1936 both the Popular Front and the CGT were at the apex of their power, a most fortunate circumstance for the refugee children from Bilbao.

Throughout France, the major donations to the CAEE came from thousands of French citizens, through their town councils and worker organizations. Subscription lists were published in Leftist newspapers, with a running total of donations for the Basque children printed on the front page. Many of these were from individuals sending five to ten francs, all they could spare.[10]

The generosity of the French working class was remarkable in the CGT-CAEE campaign. A letter accompanying one donation read:

> I'm sending you ten francs: please give half to the Basque children. I am a tenant farmer, and my crop was destroyed by hail. Still, I want to help the Communist Party and the pitiful Basques.[11]

Some twenty thousand people attended a large rally held in Paris by the CAEE in May 1937. There, the Popular Front program for refugee care was described: "All in need would be assisted, whether Socialist, Communist, or Basque Nationalist-Catholic."[12] The committee members located and refurbished a number of sites, usually orphanages, unused worker retirement homes, or vacant worker summer resorts, to house the children. A number of large homes were also donated; others were rented; a few temporary colonies were set up in schools closed for the summer.

During the first year alone, the CAEE collected nearly three and one-half million francs, to care for the refugee children of Spain.[13]

In the evacuation from Euzkadi, over thirty thousand children arrived in France during 1937, more than half of whom were "unaccompanied" children. Of these children who had left both parents and country behind, about five thousand were later sent on to Belgium, the Soviet Union, Denmark, or Switzerland. The balance of the children who had been evacuated without their parents, over nine thousand, were placed in adoptive homes or in children's colonies.[14] Thousands of other Basque children found shelter with their families or relatives in refugee colonies, or in private arrangements.

Late in 1937, just one year after its first organizational meeting, the CAEE could report that, already, some nine thousand children, nearly all from Euzkadi, were being cared for by their organization. Of these, about 3,600 were in the children's colonies, and over five thousand were living in adoptive homes.[15] The pioneer work of the CAEE in caring for children evacuated as a result of the Northern Campaign was thoroughly reported in the Leftist press. The correspondent in Euzkadi from *L'Humanité* wrote chilling accounts of the effects of modern warfare upon children from his own observations.[16] Articles exhorting families to offer space to evacuated children were commonplace in the weeks before Guernica was bombed, and became more frequent after this catastrophe.[17] President Aguirre's appeal to the world spurred the CAEE to greater efforts, as it prepared for the flood of Basque children shortly to be evacuated. Both *Le Peuple* and *L'Humanité*, respectively Socialist and Communist, printed daily pleas for the Basque refugees.

From Oléron to Limoges: The Dispersion

The Basque children in quarantine at Oléron from the March expedition found much to delight them. In addition to real white French bread and milk in abundance, there were no sirens or bombs or days in crowded shelters; no lines to buy the scanty food as in Euzkadi. The staff from Euzkadi and France set up classes immediately; the children had access to books written in Spanish in a large library available to them. There was ample free time to bathe in the sea, to fish, and to explore the island. Since it was still spring, no French citizens came to the spot on vacation. The children were isolated from the population, and most of the adults in charge were Basque.[18]

Visitors to this tranquil island included several Basque officials from the delegations recently established in Paris and Bayonne. In Oléron, the war seemed remote. But the news from home that arrived in frequent letters soon became frightening. In early April, the children learned of the destruction of Durango. Soon rumors circulated that more children were on their way to France, and that others would be sent on to England or Russia. Twenty days after their arrival, on April 10, their peaceful idyll on the beach ended.

Of the 450 who came, some 230 were selected to stay until May, when they would be sent on to Belgium. There, the Confédération Générale du Travail Belgique (CGT) in Brussels was finding adoptive families to care for each of them.[19] Those who were to stay in France were quickly dispersed, the single ones to adoptive families already enrolled by the CGT and awaiting their child. Exactly one hundred were chosen to open a model CGT colony at Mas Éloi, Limoges. Many were brothers and sisters, since care was taken not to separate children from the same family. With them went three teachers: one Basque, one Spanish, the third a highly trained Frenchman, who was to direct the colony. Being Communist, he was always addressed as "Comrade Ranz" by the children.

The trip to Limoges was difficult, with several train changes. It was midnight on a cold and rainy night when they finally arrived. In spite of this, there was a large crowd at the station to greet the first group of such size to come from Spain to be cared for by the Popular Front. As the children boarded waiting buses, the townspeople broke forward to hug, kiss, and press toys and caramels upon them. Many citizens were crying for joy—a most impressive welcome.

Within three days, as these attentions from the populace multiplied, Comrade Ranz wrote to thank the mayor of Limoges for such overwhelming support, closing his letter with the words: "Under the banner of '*No Pasarán*,' I take my leave of you, united in the anti-Fascist cause."[20] Mas Éloi was to be very widely publicized in the Communist press, with the children making frequent appearances at fund-raising rallies in the nearby towns for Popular Front aid to Spain.

Photos from a memorial booklet of the one hundred Basque children show them invariably smiling broadly, many saluting with a *puño*.* The colony was housed in an ancient abandoned convent, recently used as a boys' reformatory, housing two hundred inmates. A large stone building, it was described as "isolated, modest, and of severe architecture." It was modified only superficially to house and educate its new guests. Two dormitories, an infirmary, and two classrooms were set up and the kitchen and dining room were furnished spartanly. The former chapel was converted into a cinema, showing films thrice weekly. Food, though abundant, was not cooked in the Basque style, and a good deal was wasted, though French bread was eaten in abundance. In addition to a great quantity of clothing donated by the community, a new summer uniform was given to each child. It consisted of white trousers or skirt, dark blue shirt, and white socks and sandals. This was invariably worn to the frequent fund-raising affairs, to festivals, and to the municipal circus, where the children sang Basque songs, and danced, and where the obligatory collection was taken.

The major source of revenue for all the CGT-CAEE colonies was the system of promoting each child's sponsorship by adoptive parents who simply paid twelve francs weekly for the child's expenses. Besides the economic help, many adoptive parents invited the child home for the long three-day weekend the school scheduled, running from Saturday morning to Monday night. Between seventy and seventy-five of the children of Mas Éloi were adopted by individuals or groups in Limoges. The shoemaker's union—shoemaking was a major industry in the city—adopted the four brothers from one Basque family.[21]

Because of the importance of the shoe industry, the children were unusually well supplied with footwear: wooden sabots for rainy days, the white sandals already noted, and a

* The clenched-fist salute of Leftist solidarity.

pair of *kakuskas*, or rubber shoes. The three professors, French, Spanish, and Basque, gave classes four days weekly, each teaching a different level of children. French was taught daily. Afternoons were passed in letter writing, naps, walks or sports, and in bad weather, cultural activities indoors were offered. The director maintained a very close relationship with the local mayor, the adoptive families, and with the Basque delegation of Bayonne. Until Bilbao fell, close contact was also kept with Juan Gracia of Asistencia Social. Correspondence was scrupulously maintained with parents, and prior to the surrender of the city, the children even collected money to send food packets to Bilbao.

One indication of the dedication of the staff of this colony to the children was a plaintive request for payment of salary. Five months after the colony opened, Comrade Ranz wrote that not a cent had been received from the Basque government. Noting that the teachers were on duty twenty-four hours a day, he said some attention to this matter would be appreciated.[22]

The last correspondence in the Archives of the Basque Government-in-Exile in Paris from Comrade Ranz was received in November of 1939. It was a request for 800 francs to purchase new shoes for the children of the colony. All were soon to be repatriated after more than two and one-half years under his care.[23]

May and June Expeditions to France

After the March 1937 expedition sailed from Euzkadi, almost two months went by before another contingent of children was organized. The Basque government's evacuation of entire families also began in early May. By then, Euzkadi was doomed. The promised help from the Popular Front did not materialize; expected diversionary attacks on the Aragón front were not mounted as the Left parties in the Popular Front wrangled for power. But families in Vizcaya were still hopeful that their children could be spared the debacle that was clearly in store.

Until Bilbao fell, the evacuation system functioned quite well for thousands of children. A second expedition, carrying

2,375 youngsters, left Bilbao on May 5. Upon arriving at La Pallice, 800 were sent on to the CGT transition center on the island of Oléron, and the balance (1,575) to Biarritz, where they were greeted by Basque personnel of the Social Assistance department and given a breakfast of fried eggs, bread, and coffee with milk.[24] A third expedition left May 9 with 800 children, also bound for France, and a fourth left May 23 with 3,000 children in three ships bound for Pauillac, France.[25]

Working closely with Sr. Juan Gracia, the shiploads of children were divided upon arrival in France by their political affiliation, sent to the appropriate reception camps, then on to colonies or homes. Scrupulous attention was paid to each child's medical needs:

> Each child is the object of a veritable troop of doctors. The Basque children arrive poorly clothed, in a deplorable state of hygiene, undernourished, many, actually ill.[26]

A number of doctors volunteered their help, so that any medical problems were treated before the child was sent on. Even the decision on where to place an individual child, whether in a private home or a colony, was based on matching both the climate and living conditions to those optimal for that child. It was reported that of the first groups, those from the Bilbao area, some 2,500, were obviously malnourished or exhibited some physical malady or dental problem.[27] Newspaper articles commented on the squalid appearance of the Basque children, due, they noted, to the shortage of soap in Euzkadi. Articles in the Leftist press also counseled those adoptive families awaiting their child to be patient, noting, "The children will come, a load of children is not like a cargo of oranges."[28]

These first expeditions of Basque children were made up in large part of the sons and daughters of working-class parents living in the industrial belt surrounding the greater Bilbao area. Their parents were generally not politically affiliated with Basque Nationalist parties; rather, they were members of Spanish parties of the Left: Socialist, Left Republican, Communist, and Anarchist. These parties naturally had their greatest strength among the more exploited urbanized laboring classes. Later groups of children evacuated were to be composed of the strongly Catholic, strongly Basque Nationalist children of conservative small farmers from the suburban and more remote *baserriak,* with their city counterparts, the predominantly lower middle-class children of Euzkadi's shopkeepers, civil servants, and professionals. Few of the upper classes sent their children into exile. Most were openly or secretly in sympathy with the Insurgent cause, whether from disdain for Basque separatism, attachment to the monarchy, or to Rightist or Catholic traditions.

By the fall of Bilbao in mid-June, there were already fifty colonies operating in the central, southeast, and southwest areas of France, caring for nearly thirty thousand Basque refugees. The Basque government expressed profound gratitude to the Popular Front and the French government for such warm support from the Left. This support included the sponsorship of families in refuges as well as care for children in colonies or in private homes with adoptive parents.[29]

Adoptive Homes Under CAEE Aegis

The French working-class families the CAEE had enrolled as custodial adoptive parents clearly took on this task with enthusiasm. Each provided food and shelter, with the CAEE issuing needed clothing and school materials. Any medical costs were borne by the town. These children were visited monthly by Spanish nurses. In addition, the CAEE organized a staff of some fifty volunteer inspectors to visit with the adoptive families regularly and report on sickness, general living conditions, school progress, and the child's adaptation.[30]

Those Basques interviewed who had been placed by the CAEE in private families found the experience to be uniformly positive.

> My adoptive family was Communist, extraordinary people, unfailingly kind to me. In Spain, coming from a Catholic, Basque Nationalist family, my idea of Communists was of dangerous, bad people, and I was afraid of them. I learned instead how generous strangers can be.

> I was happy with my family: I stayed two years and received an outstanding education. In Spain, schools had been turned into jails. Later, I returned to the family to complete my education, taking advanced work in France.
>
> They bought me beautiful clothes, and for the first time in my life, I was taken to a beauty parlor. My braids were cut, and my hair was styled. When I looked in the mirror, it was like being in a film: I saw a 12-year-old with elegant shoes, a well-cut dress, and nicely arranged hair. I felt happy for the first time in months. They treated me like their own daughter, maybe even a little better.

All the children in adoptive families attended the public French schools. They seemed to have no difficulty learning the language and published reports noted that, by year's end, many were doing better in their schoolwork than their native French-speaking classmates.

> What was to be expected happened; the youngest of us sent into France to live with families soon forgot our own language, and became fluent in the language of our new homes and schools. I, myself, learned so well that I won a prize in French in school after repatriation.
>
> My little sister completely forgot her Basque. When we came home over two years later, she couldn't even talk to our mother.

Older children were given training in various trades, and some were apprenticed during their stay.

A number of children (over 1,650 in 1937) were placed by CAEE with Spanish and Basque families, particularly in departments such as the Loire, Gironde, and Basses Pyrénées, where old settlements of Spaniards and Basques were to be found.[31]

By January of 1938, the CAEE still had nearly 1,800 Basque children under its direct care, now grouped in thirty-eight colonies throughout France. Of these, eight were supported by Popular Front groups in Sweden, five by French municipalities, three by the French government, and one each by the Red Cross, the Socorro Rojo, and a cooperative, leaving thirteen under direct CAEE patronage.[32] This assistance represented the efforts of literally thousands of French citizens.

Catholic Assistance and the PNV

The later expeditions to France, unfortunately, fared less well, particularly those organized by the PNV. Many Basque parents were members of this party, or its affiliate trade union, the STV, which together had received about half the popular vote in Euzkadi's elections the previous year. For several reasons, however, the PNV was slower in mobilizing expeditions to accommodate PNV children than were the parties from the Left. For one, being a regional party, it did not belong to an international organization, as did the Socialists and Communists. Its base was narrow, and its resources were correspondingly small. Furthermore, it was irrevocably bound, by its genesis as a confessional party, to the Catholic church. Thus, it was not until after Aguirre's plea to the world to host Euzkadi's children, coupled with a letter written by the former Basque Bishop of Vitoria, Monsignor Mateo Múgica, by then in exile in Rome, that Catholic-Basque Nationalist help began to materialize.[33] It was in Msgr. Múgica's former diocese that the autonomous government of Euzkadi was located in 1936–37. Immediately after the Rightist coup, Alava became part of Insurgent-held territory. Cardinal Gomá, primate of the Catholic church in Spain, was quite ardently pro-Franco. His natural interest in encouraging the newly autonomous and predominantly Catholic Basque government to sever connections with the Popular Front Republican cause had earlier been made evident. In September 1936, Archbishop Gomá had a pastoral letter prepared which called for Catholic unity, and implicitly rebuked the new Basque government's move toward separatism through espousal of the Republican cause. Múgica signed the letter, albeit reluctantly. Three years earlier he himself had indicated that Basque autonomy was a viable option for Basque Catholics, even if it meant alliance with an obviously anti-clerical Republican government. In spite of his obedience in signing Gomá's letter, Msgr. Múgica was still regarded as too inclined toward Basque Nationalism and the Cardinal sent him into exile to Rome in October of 1936.[34] His hand-picked replacement was Msgr. Lauzirica, who proved to be a better supporter of the Cardinal 's pro-Franco policy than Múgica had been. The exiled bishop was characterized in the Franco press as "not feeling sufficient patriotism" and as being "Catholic, a Bishop, but too Basque."[35] As Msgr. Múgica was leaving Spain, he was interviewed in Hendaye, France. There, he commented: "I prefer a persecuted church to a protected [enslaved] one."[36]

In Rome, Múgica kept himself well-informed about events in Euzkadi, and maintained an extensive correspondence with those in his confidence. As the Northern Campaign advanced, his concern for the fate of the Basque children increased. The day after Guernica was bombed, he composed a moving letter of appeal to his former colleagues in Spain, as well as to the archbishops, bishops, and cardinals of Europe. It was written on his official stationery as Bishop of Vitoria. In the letter, he wrote that the Basque children, though innocent of any responsibility for the tragic Civil War, were the victims of famine and bombardment. He begged, "As their pastor, as one who had himself personally given so many Confirmations as he visited their parishes, that Catholic homes be found for them in countries not at war."[37]

His letter was effective—offers of help came from prelates in France, England, Belgium, and Switzerland. But now time was rapidly running out. During all of May and early June, the Basque government and the PNV, through their Minister of Justice and Culture, the noted attorney and historian Jesús Leizaola, had planned a wholesale evacuation of the children enrolled in the Basque educational system. In 1936, when Leizaola accepted the post of Minister of Justice and Culture, he relied heavily on a young Basque who exemplified the religious and cultural roots of Basque Nationalism.

Vicente Amezaga, a teacher, poet, and translator, had proclaimed the Basque Republic in 1931 with his neighbor and close friend José Antonio Aguirre. As Director-General of Instruction, he had worked assiduously in the ensuing years to develop Basque teaching materials, and to encourage the classes in Basque taught by volunteer teachers and priests in the *batzokis* (PNV clubhouses). With the granting of autonomy, this improvised system became institutionalized, with over two thousand children enrolled in the *ikastolas* by 1937.

> I taught a group of more than thirty children in the *batzoki* here. They learned reading and writing in Euskera in daily classes, and the traditional songs and dances of Vizcaya. I also taught them catechism; and there was sewing for the girls, while the boys went to the *frontón* [handball court]. On Saturdays, we always had excursions to the mountains, with chocolate for each child.

> I grew up in Guipúzcoa, in a town of 4,500, all Basque-speaking, even those from away. My brother and I would go to the *batzoki*, first learning to read Basque. We learned the little dances, then the *Ezpatadantza*. But we didn't just read and dance. The life in each *batzoki* of Euzkadi was intense. We had a theatre, giving Basque plays every few weeks, with an audience full to the rafters. There was a cultural renaissance that few today realize: competitions in theatre, dance concerts in the major cities with hundreds of groups competing. And we went to political meetings too, sitting on the stairs to listen. Irujo, Monzón, we knew them all. It was a cultural resurgence, a generation of Basques as much involved with culture as with nationalist politics.

On the day Guernica was bombed, in fact, Amezaga was in a town nearby, officially opening a new *ikastola*.[38]

Within a week after Aguirre's appeal, a project to evacuate the entire *ikastola* system, complete with teachers and aides, was begun. There would be created a series of special Basque-language children's colonies in France, a continuation, in exile, of the new education. Many parents signed their children up to emigrate, feeling confidence in an evacuation under such auspices, with teachers already well known to them. One such *andereño* (teacher) comments:

> All the families in Munguía knew me since childhood. They told me, "Go, Concha, we'll feel more secure if you are with them: please go." So I went with my class, to France.

In all, five hundred children from *ikastolas* left the Bilbao area, some less than a day before it fell. They went in specially chartered buses and by train to Santander.[39] Of the fifteen hundred whose parents elected not to send them, many had to flee within days, and joined the colonies later.

The successive expeditions of unaccompanied children, however, were much less thoroughly planned than had been the pilot voyage to Oléron in mid-March.

> I was evacuated with twenty-two members of my family, from Santander, on the *Zurriola*. I remember some of the children got caught in the ship's chain and died. They threw white bread at us upon our docking in France, and gave us another horrible vaccination, one that made a huge scar. They sent me to a school for handicapped and abnormal children. Both the treatment and the food were cold and sad. I was in a strange place, with no news of my family or country, and I didn't even know how to ask for bread.

In addition to the understandable lack of careful organization of later expeditions, there was a second problem. In marked contrast to the warm reception given to the children in Limoges, the thousands of Basque youngsters arriving in May, June, July, and August were usually ignored or greeted coldly by the French people. Many of them, coming under the auspices of the Basque Nationalist Party (PNV), were accompanied by their priests. In spite of this, an intense propaganda campaign mounted by Franco and his adherents accused all Basques of being "Red-Separatists," and thus anti-Catholic. After the destruction of Guernica in late April, the official Catholic and Rightist press in France seemed easily convinced that the Basques themselves had put the torch to their sacred city.[40] Arrayed against this popular point of view were certain important French Catholic intellectuals, who believed the eyewitness account of the young Basque priest Don Alberto de Onaindia. He came to France in May to verify that it was solely the German planes and pilots in the Insurgent army who had bombed and burned the city. The official French press service, HAVAS, appeared notably unconvinced by Don Alberto's testimony. There was, in fact, a curious mélange of information printed in France regarding the Northern Campaign in the Basque country. What appeared was often seriously distorted.[41]

In the case of the evacuation of the Basque children, these same organs of the Rightist and Catholic press predictably urged against any aid being provided from France. A front-page article in the notoriously pro-Hitler *Action Française* of May 5, 1937, commented:

> We have all the luck: England is too kind, letting us lodge 120,000 Basque refugees at great expense. First, we must evacuate them, then lodge and feed them, and finally, repatriate them. Again, England is the instrument, and France pays the price.

The article continued that it would be much simpler, safer (in that no naval incidents would occur), and cheaper to take advantage of the generous offer of Franco to have the Red Cross supervise a neutral zone within Spain for refugees. The whole evacuation was termed "ignoble propaganda from Moscow . . . promoted by the Spanish Reds for obvious reasons." As one result of this, the initial reception afforded many of the refugees in France was the coldest felt in any host country.

Boatloads of fleeing Basque women, children, and the old continued to arrive in June, July, and August. One eyewitness reports:

> As Bilbao fell, many arrived by sea, in small fishing boats, to take refuge here. I was in Bassie D'Arcachon, a summer sailing resort then. I'm ashamed to say most were badly received, not even allowed to come ashore, because they were "Reds," and therefore dangerous: exhausted, hungry, thirsty women and children. A few of us managed, unseen by authorities, to bring them food: bread and milk, during the days they remained anchored outside the harbor, until they finally were allowed to land.[42]

In interviews with the children, now adults in mid-life, many of the PNV-Catholic children spontaneously recalled their icy welcome at French ports. This appears to be most typical of those who came to the French-Basque regions just over the Pyrenees when the stream of refugees became a flood during the summer of 1937.

> All the French in the little towns were hostile: they called us "Little Basque Pigs," "Scum of Spain," "Red-Separatists," or simply "Refugees," in such a tone I would cringe and want to hide.
>
> The people there wouldn't speak Basque to us, only French, which we didn't understand. They were a different type of Basque: cold, suspicious, mean.
>
> We even had to sit in a separate section at Mass in the village, and take Communion after everyone else, as though we children would somehow contaminate the good French families.
>
> The mayor was pro-Franco and despised us. He always complained of the amount of water our little colony used, saying that the pigs they raised deserved it more than we did.
>
> The priest said we had to sit upstairs—no room for us downstairs in *his* church. We even had to pay extra for our old benches up there. The villagers did nothing for us: even at Christmas, we orphans received nothing from them. An unfeeling people.

These successive expeditions were an ordeal. By mid-June, Insurgent forces had already reached Bilbao. The *Habana* carried 3,738 children on May 31; it was packed with 4,600 on June 14.[43] The children invariably became very seasick on the short voyage to France, and the ship was also by now badly infested with body lice. All had to be deloused and submit to having their heads shaved upon arrival in France. About half the passengers, the "lucky ones," were families: mothers, children, and old relatives, traveling together to the colonies being rapidly set up in France by the Basque government. When the "unlucky" ones left the ship, they received the obligatory revaccination, and were given long French loaves and hot milk. For the quarantine period, they were taken to vacant summer resorts in Capbreton, St. Jean, Landes, Oléron, Dax, or Guethary. They lived in hastily improvised dormitories in buildings vacant since the previous summer, or in tents.

Little was organized except for daily Mass in the Catholic PNV colonies. No classes were held, and the long days at the beach soon became monotonous. For many of the children no luggage ever arrived, and they were without fresh clothes for weeks. It was a cold, wet summer; the buildings were damp, unheated, the gardens overgrown and unweeded. When donated clothing finally appeared it only added to their misery:

> They gave us old rope-soled sandals, dirty pants, shirts striped in muddy colors. In our cast-off clothes, with our shaved heads, how did we look? Why, it would make you cry.

The Basque staff took care of the children's personal needs as best they could. Without soap (there was none) they washed and dried their few clothes, while the children were sent to bathe in the cold sea. The staff found it nearly impossible to beat out the thick dust falling from the huge cork oaks ringing some colonies, or scrape the pine resin dripping from groves of pines behind the pavilions of the resorts from the children's sparse clothing.

Some of the children remember the welcome visits of anchovy fishermen from Ondarroa on the Spanish-Basque coast, though the news these men brought was frightening. Rumors constantly circulated:

> One day, a rumor ran through us that Bilbao had already fallen. We could see our teachers were worried. Finally, they told us the truth. The boys in my pavilion cried for the first time, inconsolably, until we could cry no more. We were crying for our parents, our baby brothers and sisters, at the mercy of an enemy who would massacre civilians: first in Abyssinia, now in Euzkadi.

It was by now late June. The PNV-Catholic colonies were ready at last to receive their Basque guests.

The official response of the Catholic church of France to the nearly simultaneous appeals of Msgr. Múgica and President

Aguirre in late April had been positive, but concrete help was much slower to materialize than was that of the Popular Front. It was not until early June that the Comité National Catholique de Secours aux Réfugiés d'Espagne (CNC) was formed.

The impetus for its formation came from members of a Committee for Civil and Religious Peace in Spain, founded late in 1936 by a number of French Catholic liberals, Academy members, the Catholic Youth Action, and the Catholic Teachers' Union. It was headed by Jacques Maritain. Such prominent intellectuals as François Mauriac, Emmanuel Mounier, and Claude Bourdet were members. The committee published articles and open letters in the press urging humanization of the war. After Guernica, as the Civil War entered a more devastating phase for civilians, they publicized the plight of the Catholic Basques. When refugees began to enter France, members of this committee contacted the Catholic hierarchy in southern France, urging the formation of the CNC.[44] Cardinal Verdier was approached, and agreed to be Honorary Head.

The actual working directors were Msgr. Feltin and Msgr. Mathieu, of the archdioceses of Bordeaux and Dax, respectively. A network of representatives was formed throughout the dioceses of France, with the help of the Society of St. Vincent de Paul. Appeals were printed in all diocesan papers for funds, for adoptive homes, for clothing, blankets, and for buildings and furniture suitable for lodging the refugees in colonies. By mid-June, a reception committee had been formed in Bordeaux, where a majority of the shiploads of evacuees disembarked. A large reception camp was opened in late June, near Bordeaux, in the barracks of an unused military installation. Orphanages, boarding schools, and private mansions were also donated to house the Catholic PNV Basque refugees.

According to the first report published by the CNC in June of 1939, more than 1,800 adult refugees from Bilbao were assisted, for periods ranging from a few days to nearly two years, with an average stay of about four months. The committee also arranged for the care of a shipload of 550 Basque children, who came into France in transit to Belgium. When arrangements to receive them in Belgium could not be made they were placed in French homes until they could be repatriated.[45] In all, some three million francs were spent by CNC in Spanish and Basque relief from 1937 to 1939. A list of donors shows that every diocese in France sent help, ranging from one thousand to forty thousand francs.[46]

There was, however, sympathetic coverage of the evacuation of Basque refugees in only a few portions of the French Catholic press. *Le Petit Jour* printed a long article on April 30, headlined "Save Us," detailing the pressing need to evacuate ten thousand children from Bilbao. In this interview with Sr. Izarriueta, Basque delegate for evacuation in Paris, the mission to save Basque children from famine and bombs was described as "sacred." He was quoted as saying,

> Since we Basques are 90 percent Catholic, the church cannot abandon us. As Christ said, "Suffer the little children to come unto me."[47]

Another press report in July commented:

> The enchanting, sweet naiveté of the graceful Basque refugee children is remarkable. They talk to everyone, demonstrating a feeling for friendship. I have never seen any other children wear their filth with such nobility. Many here call them "Reds," as though children could be so labelled, and work to send them far from home: Russia, the Scandinavian countries, such a strange exile.[48]

Within the CNC, the Bishop of Dax gave perhaps the greatest assistance. He provided space in Catholic institutions in several departments in the French-Basque region for refugee families and for unaccompanied children. The children's colony at Poyanne, in Landes, and the institution at Cadajuc, for example, were his former diocesan seminaries. Through the auspices of Msgr. Mathieu, these were made available until late in 1939. He was himself Basque, and he proved to be a faithful friend to the Basque refugees in France. He visited every refuge and children's colony in his region, and administered the sacrament of Confirmation to many children there. Msgr. Mathieu made continual appeals for funds to his Catholic flock, and prodded the conscience of his fellow prelates to do more for these "most Catholic refugees." His relations with the exiled Basque priests were excellent.

Msgr. Mathieu was greatly disturbed by the indifference and even animosity shown to the Basques by most French Catholics. Convinced that this heartless treatment of fellow Catholics could only be put right by the Pope, he arranged a private audience with the Holy Father in December of 1938. Reportedly, he challenged Pius XI to help rectify the "scandalous neglect and disdain shown to the Catholic Basque refugees." The Pope replied that he was confident of the strong faith of the Basques (the highest per capita number of vocations to the priesthood in the world came from a little town, Ceanuri, in Vizcaya). According to reports, the Holy Father reached into his drawer and pulled out one thousand pounds sterling, which he gave to Msgr. Mathieu for the Basque refugees. The Monsignor used it for the children's colonies.[49]

La Citadelle

One of the colonies merits particular attention as best reflecting the work of the Basque government in caring for its children—La Citadelle at St.-Jean-Pied-de-Port. St.-Jean-Pied-de-Port was the largest colony expressly intended to carry on the work of the schools of Euzkadi in exile. Its first director in fact was Vicente Amezaga. The evacuation of its pupils from Spain was delayed by the escalating Northern Campaign, so that the children, their twenty-three teachers, two cooks, and auxiliary personnel were first taken to Santander to await passage to France. Groups from *batzokis* and *ikastolas* throughout Vizcaya (Bermeo, Guernica, Munguía, all the areas of greater Bilbao) converged there and were lodged in requisitioned rooms in the Hotel Real or in schoolhouses. The two cooks for this expedition were delighted to find in Santander two items unavailable for months in Euzkadi: white bread and condensed milk. A special meal was immediately prepared of the bread and Santander cheese, followed by the beloved pudding of rice and milk, flavored with cinnamon, served cold as tradition demands. The children were ecstatic.[50] Then followed days of waiting for the Basque ship *Habana*. It never arrived. This period was memorable on at least two counts:

> We tried to go to Mass there but it was terrible: all the statues in church were headless; the altars were ruined.
>
> The big Santanderino boys would dash toward us girls and rip off our gold crosses on chains that we'd worn since our First Communion. Godless ruffians.

Clearly, in anti-clerical Santander, being Catholic meant being pro-Franco.

Finally, part of the expedition boarded a French coaler; others took whatever cargo ship would carry them to France. Once ashore, the obligatory revaccination occurred, coupled with delousing and head-shaving. All those sent en route to St.-Jean-Pied-de-Port remember the two kilo loaves of white bread given them by the sailors, their "rifles." These were to sustain them on the train ride to the colony. They arrived in the late afternoon of the feast of Saint John, when bonfires were traditionally burned in every village.

The children walked from the station into town, carrying the remnants of their loaves and a small sack of clothing. They were led by a priest, and all were reciting the Rosary. But the villagers shut their windows and doors to them, and called them *Gorriak* (Reds) in Basque. They then climbed up to the old seventeenth-century fort, La Citadelle, overlooking the town it had guarded in earlier centuries.[51] This massive grey stone fortification had been last used during the Great War to house German prisoners. Abandoned for years, it was dirty, waist high in weeds, unlighted, and infested with bats. The children spent their first night there, sleeping on the stone floors. To raise their spirits as the sun set that day, the resourceful cooks produced the first hot meal the children had enjoyed in some time, consisting of garlic soup, French bread, and boiled eggs.

The next day it was even clearer that nothing was ready;

everything would have to be improvised. The children milled about, waiting for order to emerge. They recall trampling down the grass in the plaza in a week of unsupervised play, and rolling in the mud hole the summer rain had made of the former turf. The adults quickly rallied, organizing two kitchens, an infirmary, boys' and girls' dormitories, classrooms, and a simple chapel. The interior was swept, washed, and then covered with whitewash; outside, masonry was repaired, windows reglazed, and roof leaks repaired. Very primitive toilet facilities were improvised. In spite of these efforts, La Citadelle was never to be comfortable or homelike. It housed a spartan existence, a "splendid poverty."[52]

> What I remember most about La Citadelle was that it was always so cold except in full summer. Our dormitories were unheated; we had few blankets; the damp from the river seemed to hang about us, like a perennial fog. There was enough food, but everything else was always scarce.

The education of the children was begun as soon as the classrooms were ready. All were first classified as Basque-speaking (nearly 60 percent, mainly those from rural areas) or non-Basque-speaking (the urban children). Each group was educated in its native language. Basque speakers recall being confined to quarters or fined if they were heard to speak Spanish. In the mornings, classes in the traditional school subjects were given at the primary level; afternoons were devoted to art, music, dance, sports, excursions, and daily religious services.

One group of older boys, directed by the former pastor of Our Lady of Begoña parish in Bilbao, Don Fortunato, frequently went to the river Nive flowing through town to catch trout with their hands. Others cut wood, or acted as gatekeepers. Another group of older boys, supervised by Don Pedro (known as Don Pello), had the responsibility of descending the steep path to the town below to get milk for the kitchens. They started picking up stray cigarette butts from the cobblestones, thereby eliciting disapproving comments from the townspeople. Don Pello had the habit of taking his class of boys at sunset to the drawbridge over the old moat of La Citadelle, just to talk over the day, their lives, anything. He discussed the butt-gathering, and proposed that he ration his own purchased cigarettes with them in place of the surreptitious fag ends. So the sunset dialogues were enriched by a few puffs of good tobacco.

> Don Pello cultivated our lives there in an elegant and loving manner. In every way imaginable, he helped us become men: a most exemplary mentor. He kept us so busy with class, work, sports—he played soccer alongside us—that we had no time to think of the girls. Thanks to him, I rediscovered I was Basque.

> We received an excellent formation as Basque youth. In spite of the isolation we felt, and our austere surroundings, we were content, being surrounded by our own people. We had a full cultural program, as well as good education.

Basque culture and folklore were an explicit emphasis in the program. The colony was fortunate to have well-trained artists, musicians, dancers, and singers conversant with Basque themes. A fine chorus was developed, as were dance groups, and there was a theatre. Performances were staged on Sunday for the public, and some small ensembles toured France giving presentations. Classic pageants, plays on Basque political themes, and comedy skits were staged (a mock marriage, put on by the staff, is still remembered).

The colony initially numbered five hundred children, with between seventy to eighty adults as teaching and auxiliary personnel. These included a doctor and a dentist. A large number of poor refugee families gradually trickled in to live at La Citadelle or in town. Many helped in whatever way they could, sewing winter clothes for the children, helping the cooks, cleaning, caring for sick children. At its peak, during 1938, the colony housed as many as eight hundred people, some of whom contributed little.[53] It was a totally Spanish-Basque enclave, but one that unfortunately was very costly to maintain.

The funds for the St.-Jean-Pied-de-Port colony came initially from the Basque Committee for Refugees with money from French Catholic sources. For a period, the French government provided a daily subsidy of five francs per child. Salaries for teachers came from the Basque government. Since it was the largest colony, and expected to be a showpiece, it was a financial burden that had to be shared.

As the months went by, relations with the townspeople thawed somewhat but were never particularly warm. In time, even the pro-Franco mayor was able to tolerate the new tenants of the abandoned fort. The children always came into town in groups, monitored by an adult staff member. The town priest eventually invited them to participate in the village religious processions.

> It wasn't easy to make friends with the French. Don Vicente (Amezaga) talked to the priest in Basque, but he was cold and hostile. He asked us, "If you are as Catholic as you say, why does Franco persecute you?" Don Vicente showed him our big *ikurriña,* saying, "For what this flag means, that is why we are harassed."

Life was hardest for the younger children, who missed familial warmth the most desperately. The cook in the small infirmary kitchen soon became the special protector of the littlest ones. In fall and winter, they clustered around her wood-burning cook stove, seeking both physical and emotional warmth. They clung to her, each being sure that she was really "my Jesusa." On walks with her the children held onto her legs "like chickens around the mother hen." The fort had no heating, and the river below created a penetrating dampness. Many became ill with the endemic colds, coughs, and grippe, even pneumonia. She fed the sick with special foods such as eggnogs, flans, delicious French omelets. When any of the little ones wet their beds in the dark dormitories she would excuse them, saying, "The birds did it," and no one was punished.[54]

Toilet and washing facilities were very inadequate, so that the staff had to work continually to maintain basic hygiene. Many children developed scabies. To halt the infection, rigorous measures were instituted:

> All of our clothing was boiled, and we had to use a dreadful, smelly solution of sulfur for three days running, smeared over ourselves, to cure us. Relief was often only temporary, and everyone, even the priests, got it.

The main cook performed miracles with the funds set aside for food. Meals were hearty, and very Basque: codfish stew, lamb with various beans, thick soups, potato omelets, and Basque sausages. Since, unfortunately, there was no land for a garden, the colony was always dependent on the local market for all supplies.

This colony, envisioned as a model Basque educational community, had its share of drawbacks and detractors. Given, however, the constraints of the site and the subsidy, La Citadelle performed well its function of being a nucleus of culture and language. Many children learned to speak, read, and write Basque there. The emphasis on folklore and culture permeated the lives of those who attended, as evidenced by interviews over forty years later. Some recalled visits by Aguirre:

> Whenever our *lendekari* [president] came to visit, he made us fully aware that we must cooperate to demonstrate, before the whole world what we, as Basques, were capable of doing.
>
> Our teachers and priests dedicated their lives to us. We had a full program for our religious, cultural, and educational formation, in a totally Basque atmosphere. All our teachers were more than mere educators; they were like fathers and mothers to all of us.

There was a less positive side. The colony had a succession of directors. Just six months after arriving in France, Amezaga was called to Barcelona to supervise the education of the children in the Basque colonies in Catalonia.[55] In the archives of the Basque Government-in-Exile there is an unsigned report on the colony during its first winter. Temperatures dropped to −8° C in the unheated buildings. There was a chronic shortage of books, pens, even ink. In the dining room there were so few plates and spoons that two sittings were the rule, the second using the hastily washed dishes of the first. The report noted that though there were only 440 children enrolled, the census count totaled 780. In spite of the plethora of adults, buildings were dirty, and children were reportedly forgetting their Basque, though three teachers were singled out for performing valiantly.[56]

A report by a French correspondent the next summer was much more positive. At this point, there were 550 students using thirteen classrooms, plus a series of workshops for sewing and art. The writer commented on the profusion of flowers inside and outside the old buildings, and on the stark chapel with its windows opening onto the huge trees on the fort's ramparts. One child with whom he spoke told him her father was in Barcelona, her mother in Bilbao, her little sister in Savoy. When asked the first duty of a Christian, she replied, "To forgive crimes." He wrote:

> In the simple dormitories the tragic story of the children's plight was apparent. At the head of each bed, a cheap suitcase, perhaps a ridiculously fine fur coat, one photo of the faraway parents: a child's entire fortune.[57]

Don Fortunato Unzueta, the spiritual director of the colony, showed unusual strength of character and forthrightness. In his former post at the cathedral shrine to a most important Vizcayan patron saint, Our Lady of Begoña, he had already distinguished himself for both piety and politics. In Begoña, he was custodian of a considerable treasure: the gold and jewels that had accrued as gifts of thanksgiving to the shrine over the years. When the Basque government was at the point of going into exile, he reportedly entrusted it with this collection to prevent its falling into Insurgent hands. The Basque government sent it to Switzerland for safekeeping. A few weeks after the fall of Bilbao, he was visited at La Citadelle by the papal representative of Spain, Msgr. Antoniutti. According to several who were present, Msgr. Antoniutti was not at all interested in the newly opened chapel, nor did he wish to attend the daily Mass or the Rosary, recited in Basque each afternoon. He came expressly to locate the Treasure of Begoña. He opened by commenting that certain hands had profaned the treasure.

> Don Fortunato was stung by this accusation, and being of an impetuous nature, he shoved his hands in Msgr. Antoniutti's face, shouting, "These, then, must be the profaning hands, because they are the only ones in this affair." Msgr. Antoniutti, a bit frightened, backed away, murmuring, "You should not forget to whom you are talking: to the representative of the Holy Father." Don Fortunato strode forward again to shout, "Precisely for that reason, because I *am* speaking to the Pope's emissary, do you have an obligation to hear me." He then reiterated that the jewels and gold were not profaned, but in safekeeping.[58]

That closed the incident, though conjectures as to the treasure's location were printed for some time in the Spanish Insurgent press.

Don Fortunato worked diligently to improve the colony and its relations with the village. When it became clear that isolation was to be a way of life, he devised activities to engage the children's interest. He secured a film projector and showed movies in inclement weather. He allowed the big boys to explore all areas of the ancient fort, the oblong series of buildings, the passageways surrounding the central court, and even the underground tunnels connecting many of the structures. (These tunnels became the site of a few quite innocent trysts with the adolescent girls.) When one late-arriving student brought some Parisian magazines with him, showing men and women together, Don Fortunato found out at once. He calmly destroyed them, telling the abashed boy that they could be disruptive to the life ordained for the colony. This former student noted:

> It was a delicate and difficult task to care, night and day, for five hundred children. I was used to being with girls; here, everything was segregated. There were platonic friendships, notes were passed in the lines, but nothing more. This was the way it had to be, and we all understood.

Don Fortunato carried on an extensive correspondence with the scores of Basque priests who accompanied the children to England, Belgium, or France, and served as the unofficial scribe of the priests in exile. He was an ardent Basque Nationalist, and his nature was sorely tried by the Insurgent propaganda against the Basque children abroad.[59]

During 1938–39, when the older boys had finished the secondary level, those who showed most promise, some 120 in all, went on to a smaller colony at Ciboure for advanced work. Since at that time no texts on Basque history in the language existed at that level, Leizaola himself wrote a monograph which became their text. Basque anthropology was taught by the renowned Miguel de Barandiaran; geography by Sr. Ugarte, each the most eminent in his field.[60]

In February of 1939, the colony at St.-Jean-Pied-de-Port was asked by the French government to vacate the fort. The Second World War was by now imminent—Alsace was already occupied by German troops—and the old structure was to be again used as a barracks. The French government requisitioned many Basque colony buildings for French refugees from Alsace-Lorraine, or for orphaned children from this zone. The St.-Jean-Pied-de-Port colony had already dwindled through repatriation, immigration of children to join their families in the Americas, and through graduation. When the site was vacated at the end of March, only three hundred children were still living there. The boys and teaching staff were moved to Cagnotte, the girls to Poyanne.[61] Reportedly, these colonies reflected some of the general demoralization resulting from the final defeat of the Spanish Republic, the precipitate Republican withdrawal from Catalonia, and the precarious hospitality offered by the French. By now, too, the Basque government was drained of funds, though still committed to help its most desperate citizens.

> We in Cagnotte witnessed the eve of the Second World War, the mobilization of France. We were the remnants of La Citadelle: everyone who could emigrate already had; others had been repatriated. Our teachers were scattered, and the French government was anxious to requisition our colony. We hung on until mid-August, improvising classes and meals. Our only bright spot was the rowboat Don Fortunato had managed to find somewhere. He took us out in groups, to fish and row, on a little lake there.

At Cagnotte, the older boys were given the choice of repatriation, general farm labor, or work in the grape harvest.

In spite of growing financial problems, the Basque government saw to it that its children were well fed. Early in 1938, it prepared a detailed booklet concerning the various colonies for children in France, listing the entity providing the funds, staff members and their political affiliation, facilities, education, sanitation and medical supervision, and an extraordinarily complete section on the food service including the daily menus, of which the following is an example.

> *Agen* (33 children, under CGT patronage)
>
> | | | |
> |---|---|---|
> | *Monday*: | Lunch: | Potage, Beef stew, Pudding |
> | | Dinner: | Soup, Potato salad, Peas, Apple |
> | *Tuesday:* | Lunch: | Soup, Ragout of lamb, White beans, Rice pudding. |
>
> All other days are similar, with lunch having a meat plate, but not the evening meal. Older children are supplemented with appetizers and wine.[62]

Spanish Republican Government and Basque Government Activities in France

Throughout 1937–40, the Spanish Republican government provided slight help to the Basque child refugees. By August 1937, it had established a Delegation for Evacuated Children to assist in the education and inspection of Spanish youngsters. A decree was published to ensure that the children would not forget Spanish, and Spanish textbooks and teachers were provided to the colonies. By mid-1938, some eighty-five Spanish teachers had been assigned to colonies, and each colony was given two hundred textbooks covering the literature, history, and culture of Spain. The delegation also began a census, and tried to provide coordination with the CAEE, the CNC, and the Basque Government-in-Exile.[63]

The Spanish delegation consciously promoted a policy of encouraging the placement of all evacuated children in colonies with Spanish teachers, rather than in private homes, to prevent the "Frenchification" of the children. In the colonies where Basque children predominated, the Basque government exercised a parallel vigilance, sending in Basque teachers or directors. The first census of the Basque government, in October 1937, indicated that two thousand children had been placed in fifty-eight colonies, each headed by a Basque director or directress. In other colonies, where Spanish and Basque children were mixed, at least one teacher was usually Basque.[64]

After the fall of Bilbao, many of the functionaries of the Basque bureaucracy fled Bilbao to take up their portfolios in France, forming part of the Basque Delegation in Paris or Bayonne. Others, including the cabinet of Aguirre, followed him to Valencia, then to Barcelona. There, they assisted in the Popular Front government on a very reduced level. The Basque government also aided the Basque Gudaris and families who fled to Catalonia via France. This latter group of approximately sixty thousand persons found several thousand Basque refugees already there since the Republican defeats at Irún and San Sebastián the previous August and September. Though this was a larger segment of the Basque population than that still in France by late fall in 1937, the role of the Basque government was that of an unpopular partner in the assistance activities of the entire Popular Front government. Basque politics of separatism and its fervent Catholicism were intolerable to Popular Front leadership.

Clearly, it was to be in France that the Basque government would make its most concerted and conscious effort to continue the autonomous Basque Republic, its language, and its culture in exile. There was no alternative. The Basque government was impotent to intervene in the case of children to be sent to the USSR and Mexico. The Catholic hierarchy in Belgium and Britain, as well as the Leftist groups in both countries, would expressly refuse any collaboration with the Basque Delegation. Their role in each country was to be purely token in that they were consulted as a courtesy after decisions were already made.

The hegemony still possible for the Basque Republic was forced by circumstances to be exercised through its refugee citizens in France. There, the Basque delegation reconstructed and administered a system of social services, including welfare, education, and health, as well as certain economic and governmental institutions analogous to those organized earlier in Euzkadi. Though the cabinet of Aguirre officially acted in the Spanish Republic in Valencia and Barcelona until the very end of the Spanish Civil War, the luxurious offices of the Basque Delegation on Avenue Marceau in Paris became a major focus of the Basque nation's government until 1940. The collapse of the Spanish Republic, coupled with the outbreak of World War II in 1939 and the German invasion of France in 1940 ended what had been, for nearly three years, a remarkable French interlude in the history of the Spanish-Basque nation. Citizens were housed and fed, their children educated, the ill and maimed were tended lovingly, demonstrating the tenacity of the Basques with respect to their culture and values.

The Basque government, through the Basque delegations in France, also mounted a series of traveling musical and dance troupes, as well as an international soccer team. The former groups toured Europe; the sports team also came to the United States. All presented concerts or matches to raise money for refugees.[65] One musical group, Elai-Alai, was made up of the students of a noted musician in Guernica. This troupe of forty boys and girls, aged six to sixteen, was named after a black songbird, noted for its sweet strains in springtime. After Guernica was destroyed, the director, Sr. Olaeta, took the children first to Rigoitia, then to Bilbao, then on to two large homes in Santander. From there, they were evacuated in mid-June to France. They lived in St.-Jean-Pied-de-Port at first, helping in La Citadelle. After a few weeks, a large house was arranged for them in Paris. Soon, they were giving concerts of Basque songs and dances all over France, dressed in the traditional severe dark blue, black and white costumes, with rope-soled sandals on their feet. But they frequently encountered prejudice from the French audiences:

> On tour, people called us "Communists," and we always had to eat separately. People all over France believed Franco's propaganda about Guernica, so they

> were suspicious of us. A French-Basque priest accompanied us, to explain the songs and dances, and tell what had happened to us at Guernica.[66]

This cultural group remained together through half a dozen changes of residence until France was invaded in 1940. As the fortunes of the Basque government declined, the cost of maintaining the troupe exceeded the revenue earned by its concerts. By 1940, it was being maintained by the French government. An American social worker who visited the colony late that year wrote:

> The Basque colony, near Paris, was located in a villa which had fallen into a sad state of disrepair and had not been repaired. The interior of the house was shabby and battered. There was very little furniture. About fifty children and adolescents ranging in age from one preschool child to those in their late teens were present. All the refugees in this colony were students of a Basque music and dancing teacher, some of whom were resident in his school when evacuation became necessary. Measured by American standards, this colony would fall far short of even minimum requirements.[67]

At least two members of the troupe became internationally famous singers, Lidia Ibarrondo, and Luis Mariano.

In *Euzko Deya* on October 12, 1938, the work of the Basque government was summed up thus:

> Dante speaks of the "Bitter bread of exile," and the Basque refugees in France know well what he means. Just as hard is "to go up and down the stairs of others": to be far away from your own home. Thus, it is heartening to see the work of the government of Euzkadi here, which organizes institutions where Basques can feel at home, eat their own bread, and be with their own. The greatest number in France are living in the Basque Pyrenees, where fraternity, language and customs break down the homesickness a bit. Each colony, and every colony is a living evocation of Euzkadi. The Chapel is a humble sanctuary. Games, melodies, dances, reunite the Basques in healthy joy. Education is one of the principal preoccupations of the Basque government, and

excellent teachers are found in the many colonies of the government.[68]

Behind the charity and solidarity exhibited by the Basque government in France, its leaders grappled daily with real and formidable problems. These included an acute shortage of funds, the very human difficulties which arose in many refugee colonies when people were forced to live closely together, and a series of external events which brought new and Herculean tasks to the Basque government.

The chronic lack of resources was due to many factors, but certainly the very lavish governmental offices in Paris and Bayonne, and the showpiece medical facilities at Rosarie, Cambo, and Berck-Plage were expensive to equip and maintain. These, coupled with a payment of a subsidy, based upon "sacrifice to the cause of Euzkadi" were a constant drain on the treasury. This stipend, which ranged from two and one-half to five francs daily, was paid to those who could no longer pay for their lodging and meals in the refuges, and further, had no desire to go on to Catalonia.[69] From the onset of this aid, available monies could assist fewer than half of those who requested assistance.[70]

After the fall of Bilbao, emissaries from the Basque government traveled to South and Central America to solicit funds and assistance for the Basque refugees from prosperous Basques in the well-established enclaves there. Money poured in but was dispensed even more rapidly. Another source also grew niggardly: French Catholic donations gradually diminished.[71] Across the channel, the work of caring for a large contingent of Euzkadi's children had also become onerous. Early in 1938, Sr. Azcarate, the Spanish ambassador in London, insisted that one thousand of the refugee children there be shipped to France, to be the responsibility of the Basque delegation. He was dissuaded by Sr. Gracia, who described the identical waning support of Catholic organizations in France. Gracia noted that the Basque government would shortly be expected to finance a budget of one million francs monthly for the care of refugees. This would, he lamented, exhaust all current funds in about three months. The financial situation was critical.[72]

Within the colonies, particularly in the "mixed" ones, which included both Basque Catholics and Spanish citizens of the Left, political differences frequently gave rise to serious disputes, preserved in the reports found in the voluminous archives of the Basque Government-in-Exile:

> Refuge in Mande: the 28 in this old convent were expelled from Cherbourg for having joined a Communist demonstration and insulted the nuns, and are awaiting a judicial process. The two Basque Catholics wish to leave.

In others, solidarity prevailed:

> Refuge in Calvados: Here are 20 refugees, with five children, most from the Popular Front, but good people, who mix well with the Basque Catholics. The latter, for their superior capacity, administer the colony. The townspeople give them gifts of cider and milk in abundance.[73]

Finally, as we shall see was the case in other host countries, the older boys created a special problem in France. After a "riot" over food and conditions in the camp at St.-Cloud, which generated much unfavorable publicity both in France and abroad, twenty-one teen-age boys were sent by the Basque Delegation to Catalonia.[74]

Among the difficulties faced by the Basque government as a result of outside occurrences were the issue of the repatriation of unaccompanied children, political changes in the French government, and the promulgation by Franco of the "Decree of Responsibility."

A campaign for the immediate return to Bilbao of all Basque children in France under Catholic patronage was launched by Franco and the representative of the Pope, Msgr. Antoniutti, just two months after the surrender of that city. A good deal of time and energy had to be expended by Asistencia Social, the Basque Evacuation Committee, and the Ministry of Justice and Culture to counteract the intense pressure from the Pope and Franco for repatriation. This issue will be discussed in the detail it merits in a subsequent chapter.

In the political power struggles in France, a drift to the Right had begun a few months after the Popular Front victory in 1936, a trend that was anti-working-class and vehemently anti-Communist. The Right saw Bolshevism as the greatest immediate danger to the nation. France moved toward fascism, while officially pressing for peace in Europe. Three governments came and went over an eight-month period; Socialist Léon Blum was defeated and Daladier rose to power.[75] He was extremely unsympathetic to the plight of the Basque and Spanish refugees, who were by now costing his government one million francs daily. By mid-August 1937, the French government had informed Britain, whose ships carried most of the evacuees, that no more refugees would be accepted in France. The forty-five thousand Basques already there were straining French resources. A series of policy changes followed, among them an order that any refugee who could not pay his maintenance would be repatriated to either Republican or Insurgent territory. Children in colonies were excepted, as were the sick, the wounded, those with French relatives, or those engaged in work considered essential to France.[76] Though refugees in transit to Catalonia were later allowed to land in France, the French government made sure all adult males did not tarry by sending two trainloads of them daily to Catalonia.[77] As a result of these edicts, most of the provisional refugee camps organized a few months earlier by the Ministry of Interior were liquidated. By 1938, only two thousand refugees from Spain were cared for with monies from the French government, notably a grant of seven francs daily paid to evacuees residing in the remaining colonies. This was a subsidy identical to that available to unemployed French workers, enough to buy food, but little else.[78]

Because of the forced repatriation of thousands of Basques to Catalonia, a major part of the slender resources of the Basque government were shifted back to peninsular Spain. Families were now dispersed over even more distant territories. A common pattern was that of the Gudari father in Catalonia, the mother and babies in Vizcaya, and the other children scattered in France, Great Britain, Belgium, or the Soviet Union, in children's colonies or adoptive homes.

Another external problem surfaced with the Decree of Responsibility enacted by Franco early in the war. Only children under fourteen years of age when the conflict began were exempted from "criminal responsibility in the Civil War," with its attendant penalties.[79] With this decree, repatriation to Euzkadi for most Basque refugees became a dangerous option. To her credit, France never placed undue pressure on women refugees, the children, or the old to return. She thus remained a haven for those for whom life in Insurgent Spain would be politically dangerous.

To all, emigration began to seem the most feasible alternative. To this end, the Basque government belatedly began to assess its human resources more carefully, even as its financial resources dwindled daily. A series of censuses were taken, the first completed in mid-October of 1937. In this, 581 refuges were located and 115 were actually visited personally by government officials. About a half of all Basque refugees in France at that time, some twenty thousand people, were thus counted by the official census team.[80]

A second, more detailed census in December of 1937 found only twenty-four thousand Basques in France, after repatriation by French authorities. The majority were children living in adoptive homes (seven thousand) or were families living on their own (six thousand). Substantial numbers were in colonies sponsored by the Basque government or maintained as families by the PNV, or in the French refugee colonies.[81]

A third census by the Basque Delegation in Bayonne early in 1938 noted that there were at that point a total of about fifty-seven hundred Basque children living either in forty-nine colonies or in adoptive homes in ninety-five locales.[82] Just a year later, at the close of the Civil War, only 645 children were in colonies maintained by the Basque government, though several thousand were in adoptive homes, with family members, or in colonies sponsored by other organizations.[83]

At the time when the Basque government went into exile, as the Republic completed a formal surrender, a dozen refugee colonies under their patronage counted 3,878 citizens of Euzkadi, representing a range of political affiliations. The majority were PNV members, but a large minority claimed affiliation with the Socialist party or its union, the UGT.[84]

By the following January (1940), with the Second World War under way, the Basque government was spending over 900,000 francs monthly to care for its citizens in France. Six colonies were still operating, with 205 evacuees; three others cared for only forty-three children in all. The largest outlays by far were the subsidies paid to officials, which still totalled 415,000 francs per month.[85]

To expedite emigration, the Basque Delegation finally began a serious appraisal of its refugee citizens. For the first time, a census in mid-1939 listed the professional and work experience of some 8,500 men and women. Industrial occupations were well-represented, such as printing, building trades, metalworking, and navigation. Only 146 were classified as "peasant farmers," an indication of the predominantly urban makeup of those in forced emigration. The women were trained as teachers or in the clothing professions, such as millinery, with a minority having secretarial or clerking experience.[86] However, the escape through emigration, the dream of many, was to be denied to all but a small minority of the Basque refugees in France.

Still, the Basques who stayed in France were better off than those who had gone to Catalonia. By early 1938, of the approximately 100,000 Basque refugees from the Northern Campaign, plus perhaps twenty thousand Basques from Guipúzcoa, over three-fourths were in Catalonia.

Catalonia

As early as May 22, 1937, groups of Basque families from Vizcaya began entering Catalonia, joining those thousands already there since the 1936 battles in Guipúzcoa near the French border. From June through the end of the year, thousands of Basques made their way via France to the Republican capital and surrounding countryside. In October 1937, at a reunion in Barcelona of the town councils of Guipúzcoa, a compilation of local censuses yielded a file with the names of nearly 4,700 Basque refugees who were living in Barcelona, the majority from San Sebastián or Irún.[87]

In November 1937, Asistencia Social of the Basque government began the payment of a two-peseta daily subsidy for each family member, thus assuming responsibility for their maintenance. Asistencia Social also provided free clothing, medical help through the three hospitals and one sanitorium it organized, and a system of fifty-five free dining rooms.[88] A later census, in 1938, counted over sixty-five thousand Basque citizens in Catalonia. By this date, there were eighty-three colonies, housing over ten thousand Basques, and three children's colonies, educating 236 children. One of these was maintained by Socorro Rojo of Euzkadi. In addition, a network of dormitories (*centros*) was begun all through urban Barcelona, so that 149 were sheltering people by mid-1938. Of the sixty-five thousand Basques in the census of 1938, only fifteen thousand were males of military age. Nearly six thousand were under four years of age, and another fifteen thousand were between four and fourteen years old.[89]

In Catalonia, there was little real coordination between the Republican government and the autonomous governments of Euzkadi and Catalonia in the care and education of refugee children. This mirrored the continuing lack of cooperation among the groups comprising the Popular Front government of the Spanish Republic. Each took care of its own. In 1938, for example, each Catalan refugee child in an infant colony was costing its government about three and one-half pesetas daily, while the Basque government was only able to pay two pesetas daily for its children. Some Basque children were enrolled in the Barcelona schools and the Basque government arranged for Basque teachers, and for the Basque language to be taught there. However, for most of the Basque refugee children from the Northern Campaign, school had ended forever in the spring of 1937.

The Fall of the Republic: 1939

The thousands of Basque children who, in 1937, had become part of the stream of refugees from Santander and Asturias to France, were taken almost immediately by train to Republican-held territory in Catalonia. Early in 1939, with the impending final collapse of the Spanish Republic, most walked or rode back over the border to safety in France. A relief worker wrote:

> After this epic rush across the border early in 1939, the problem of caring for the 300,000 women, children, and old men was immense. They were arbitrarily tagged for a destination, and herded into trains. The *préfets* [provincial heads] of the various departments of France were notified by telegram to expect a given number of refugees on a given date. Each *préfet* was expected to make whatever arrangements he could for their care and shelter . . . abandoned buildings, sheds behind stores, old barracks, cellars. . . . Women could not find their children, who were jostled in the crowd.[90]

At first, everyone was housed in makeshift camps in the sand dunes. As soon as possible the children were moved into colonies or placed with adoptive families by the Basque Delegation, the French government, or by one of the range of other humanitarian committees now involved in the care of refugees. One Basque, then a child of twelve, recalls:

> Our family—we were fourteen in all—fled from Euzkadi to Santander, then to Asturias, then to France on the *Thorpebay,* later sunk in Valencia. They gave us bread and chocolate squares in France, and put us on a train to Barcelona. There, the Basque government gave us clothes, and put us in a convent in Casserras, with forty other Basques. We were always hungry; we had bread only every two weeks. We lived on cabbage, chickens dead of disease the farmers gave us, boiled wheat, pine nuts from the trees around us, mushrooms, and cooked weeds. My uncle and I worked night shift in a shell factory in Gerona, and got a meal of rice and lentils there. When the war was lost, we went by foot over the Pyrenees, like mule teams through the snow, in February of 1939. Over the border, they took our picture, made us take showers, shaved our heads, and vaccinated us. They gave us shoes and clothes of whatever size, and straw mattresses to sleep on in barracks, no blankets. The Basque government helped only at first. The French soon gave us the choice: work or back to Spain. Neither the Republican nor Basque government could help us now. I worked, first breaking rocks, then for a farmer with twenty-three cows, doing everything in exchange

for bad food. The Second World War began, and we were ordered to return to Spain. I had two days of interrogation, then was ordered to report to the *cuartel* [Civil Guard] weekly. I had no further education. The war for me had totally negative effects. But better than my brother: he was killed while in battle with the Sabino Arana Gudari battalion.

In addition to the CAEE, the CNC, the French government, and the Basque delegations, a number of international organizations came to work in France with the Spanish Republican refugees. This became particularly true early in 1939, when Franco's victory seemed imminent. Even earlier, several of these groups had assisted the Basque children, usually by their sponsorship of children's colonies.

The Communist Socorro Rojo Internacional (SRI) provided the funds for a Basque colony at Gurs, France, near the Spanish border, where two hundred were housed and educated, including eighty-three children. The site was an ancient convent, set in a large wooded park. A smaller SRI colony, with twenty-five children, was located at Bois Guillaume.[91] Already noted was the sponsorship of six Basque children's colonies, housing 240 children, by the Swedish Committee for Republican Spain, and one colony, with thirty children, operated by an analogous Dutch committee. These were all functioning by the end of 1937. The International Red Cross played a minor role in France, being concerned primarily with locating children and arranging for correspondence with parents, and secondarily, with the provision of inspection of the colonies for children.[92]

Late in 1937, the International Commission for the Assistance of Spanish Child Refugees (ICASCR) began its work in France. This commission, begun as a result of a CAEE international conference, was a collaborative effort of the American Friends Service Committee and the British Quakers. Funds were collected from twenty-four countries to relieve the suffering of Spanish children. Among other works, the commission took over the sponsorship of two Basque children's colonies, presumably for orphans of the war, located at Enghien les Bains, housing 110 children, and at Cagnotte, with eighty children. (The latter became the final home for the remnants of La Citadelle). By early 1940, the ICASCR was maintaining eleven colonies for over six hundred children, most of whom were Basque. In addition, extra food, toys, clothing, and books were distributed to the children's colonies sponsored by the French government, as well as sewing materials and bedding.

One of the colonies has been described by the ICASCR director, an American, Mr. Kerschner, in some detail, as his wife was its director. A visitor in 1940 noted that it was housed in a large, airy, elegant villa, set in ample grounds near Paris. Though both indoor furnishings and outdoor equipment were sparse, the children seemed happy and well cared for. This colony moved to southern France, then to the Free French zone, with its clientele changing from Basque children to Jewish ones as the Second World War progressed.[93]

Of all the international groups involved in the Spanish Civil War, the Quakers performed the most extensive and most efficient humanitarian work. Their policy of assisting civilians of both sides was followed scrupulously. Throughout the war, in Spain and in France, and after the Republican defeat, the ICASCR fed, clothed, and housed thousands of Spaniards. They worked effectively in the provisional concentration camps in southern France from 1939 to 1940, where tens of thousands of Republican soldiers and civilians were quartered. They worked quietly, never for propaganda purposes. According to the director, "More than a dozen organizations were at work in France, but many were committed to furthering a political ideology, and would not join in a coordinated effort."[94] A spontaneous comment by Leizaola, then Minister of Justice and Culture, sums up their work with Basque children:

> Of all groups, the Quakers helped the Basques most effectively: every month we received their check until the German invasion.

In 1939, the ICASCR was besieged with offers of help from child guidance workers from the United States. The director invariably refused these offers. Kerschner noted that passports and visas necessary for such volunteers were very difficult to obtain. Further, none of those who applied could speak Spanish, so that an interpreter would be required, thus removing a needed staff person from his post. Finally, he commented:

> Nor in my opinion would the child guidance expert have found much use for her talents. The problems we faced were elemental. Refugee children had been living on sand, in fields, in cellars, abandoned buildings, in whatever shelter could be found for them. When the struggle is to get food, clothing, and warmth enough to keep life going, the immediate problem is not one for psychological solution.[95]

Another international humanitarian agency was the International League for Basque Assistance (LIAB). This was an outgrowth of the Catholic Committee for Civil and Religious Peace in Spain. The LIAB adopted a consciously neutral political stance, in contrast to the highly politicized work of many other organizations of the Left working in France with refugees. After the CNC was well launched to care for the immediate needs of the Basque refugees of 1937, the LIAB sought to bring international attention to the unique situation of the Basque Catholic refugees.[96] Besides coordinating immediate help from the Catholic hierarchy, the LIAB facilitated the emigration of Basques to the Americas, encouraged the employment, training, and formation of businesses by Basques, the exchange of prisoners, and the presentation of cultural activities, such as the folklore concerts. Since many members of LIAB were well placed in the French government, visas and other official papers could be expedited. Initially, this agency had ample funds, from Basques abroad, certain Jewish sources, the Basque government, and from French Catholics. A great deal of favorable publicity was distributed, which detailed the heroic efforts of the Basques themselves to care for citizens in exile.[97] One pamphlet noted that, in contrast to other groups of Republican refugees, French governmental resources were not utilized in caring for Basques, an assertion that was only partly true:

> Unlike Spanish refugees who were cared for by the French government, Basque refugees are supported by the LIAB and the Basque government, which assure their control and maintenance. They are NOT a charge on the French government, an important economy. By their own resources, the Basques opened 13 refugee camps, hosting 3,300 compatriots; four children's colonies, with 700 children, and care for 350 wounded and sick. Twelve of their priests came to France with them.[98]

Testimonials to the excellent deportment of Basques in the various departments of France from mayors and prelates ended this document.[99] One LIAB member noted:

> Our publicity antagonized most French Catholics, then 100 percent for Franco, but it did provoke rethinking.[100]

The LIAB was effective in expediting correspondence, in helping to reunite some families, and in securing visas for Basque children in England and Belgium en route to rejoin parents in the Americas or France. As an example, one of the many memoranda in the Archives of the Basque Government-in-Exile notes:

> 5/4/39 to LIAB from Landaburu, Asistencia Social: Iñaki A., rifleman, refugee in San Cyprien concentration camp, wishes news of his wife, Doña Begoña U. in the Basque colony at Poyanne, and of his children, A. and P. in the Red Help children's colony at Puigcerda.

After the fall of Catalonia, LIAB coordinated help to refugee Basques among the multitude of groups then operating in France. One project aiding Basque children that LIAB coordinated was the Foster Parent Plan, using funds primarily from the United States. Five colonies of Basque children were sponsored in the Biarritz area in 1939–40. Each child had an American, Australian, or British foster parent, who sent nine dollars a month for care, as well as food parcels, clothing, and letters.[101] LIAB also opened a second large camp for families, together with the CNC. The LIAB secretary, interviewed in 1980, remarked:

> After the fall of the Spanish Republic, there was no point in being so precise. The moral situation in the French

Catholic world improved: now even the children of "Red" Catalans could be helped.[102]

Two interesting assessments of the relative assistance given to Basque refugees by citizens' groups from the Left and from Catholic sources both indicate that the former were more generous:

> Clearly the CGT and the Communists helped more than anyone else: they had enormous funds from union members and weren't hampered by prejudice. Our participation (CNC, LIAB) was symbolic: we raised thousands of francs to the CGT's millions. But our help was absolutely vital to the Basques: it created the image that not all the Republican government was Red, and liberated it from the taint of being dominated by the Spanish Left.[103]

> A group of friends and I began SIFERE in 1936, to send supplies to Republican Spain. We soon joined with the CGT committee, who were an effective organization, able to get permits and facilities through their means and influence. We saw we would be ineffective as a group apart.[104]

The Catholic press in England, France, and the United States were solidly pro-Franco, a situation which certainly hindered the level of assistance received from Catholic sources for Basque and Spanish refugees. In England, for example, the appeal of the Catholic bishops for the National Joint Committee for Spanish Relief netted only 11,000 pounds of the 375,000 raised in England. This was only half the amount raised by the British Quakers.[105]

In France, the Popular Front, through the Committee of Help and the Committee of Coordination, as well as Red Help, raised and spent over three million francs in its first year of operation. This was the grand total spent under Catholic auspices during its full two and one-half years of operation. A prominent British historian of relief efforts for civilians reports:

> Ever since the beginning [of the Spanish Civil War], the response of the CGT and associated bodies to care for all Spanish Republican refugees has been magnificent, and this effort has not been relaxed, but is stronger today

> than ever. When it is remembered that the majority of those who have offered hospitality to the children are not themselves well off, it will be realized that this work has been prompted by a real spirit of altruism and self-sacrifice.[106]

The country which next offered refuge to the children of Euzkadi was Great Britain. The British Isles played host to nearly four thousand unaccompanied children, who arrived from Bilbao just two months after the first children's expedition reached France.

CHAPTER THREE

The Basque Refugee Children in Britain

Within Britain, as in France, popular sympathies were with the Spanish Republic. In spite of this, most Britons, even including the Left Labourites, were inclined toward pacifism when the Insurgent coup began. As the opposing forces in the Civil War coalesced, British business, financial, and diplomatic interests clearly favored the Insurgents. The governing Conservative party soon came to view the Popular Front coalition within the Republic as a social revolution based on bolshevism, and decided an arms embargo was the most prudent course to limit the war to the Iberian Peninsula.[1]

After the Civil War began, the Basque government officially discouraged the terrorism, destruction of churches, and anarchy that had surged throughout Spain after the Popular Front electoral victory. To those in the British Isles who were aware of the Basque Republic as autonomous, Euskadi perhaps seemed an oasis of Christian good sense. Early in 1937, for example, *The Tablet*, a Catholic periodical, printed a long article by an anonymous Basque official which carefully detailed the reasons why the Catholic Basques were fighting *against* Franco. The article closed with a call for "intervention to enforce humanitarian behaviour" on the part of Christians in Europe.[2] There was, as well, a special relationship which had existed for a century between the British Isles and the Basque country, based upon the exchange of English and Welsh coal for Basque iron ore. As a result, there had been intermarriage, and bourgeois Basques frequently sent their children to England to be educated. During World War I, too, Basque shipping firms had continued to supply British ports in contravention of Spain's professed neutrality. In the process, a number of Basque lives and vessels were lost.[3]

It is doubtful, however, whether the British rank and file were really aware that the Basque nation was quite distinct racially, culturally, and linguistically from the rest of Spain. Evidence for this view comes from the Basque refugee children, who recall being stopped in the street in 1937 in Southampton and asked why they weren't small and dark-skinned, as other Spaniards were. Dr. Richard Ellis, a Scottish doctor who came to Bilbao to give physical examinations prior to evacuation, wrote:

> The group is not strictly speaking, exclusively Basque in origin, though the majority are of an obviously different physical type from the southern Spaniard. Many have light brown or even red hair, and very few could be described as swarthy. Their facial colouring would usually pass for that of a sunburnt English child.[4]

It is clear, however, that British political leaders were aware that Basques are distinctive. Foreign Minister Anthony Eden was quoted as saying in Parliament on April 20, 1937:

> If I had to choose in Spain, I believe that the Basque government would more closely conform to our system than that of France or the Spanish Republic.[5]

The Basque Children's Committee (BCC)

In London, as early as February of 1937, the group coordinating civilian relief efforts in Spain, the National Joint Committee for Spanish Relief (NJCSR), discussed the possibility of offering refuge to Basque children.[6] This was quite unprecedented. Though France, Belgium, Italy, and Greece had accepted Armenian refugee families during and after World War I, Great Britain herself had no such tradition. Nevertheless, at the NJCSR meeting, Captain James MacNamara, a Right-wing Tory, suggested that the children be brought to England and housed in hostels until they could be adopted. Another member, Lord Listowel, a Left-wing Labour member of the House of Lords, replied that he thought it ill-advised to bring children to "cold and Protestant England"; better to consult with the French, who had already begun to receive Spanish children.[7] The matter was dropped, but reappeared a month later, with a formal request from the Basque government in Bilbao that the NJCSR send medical supplies and food into Euzkadi. This appeal was tabled, as the committee temporized, agreeing to wait until the return of *Times* correspondent George Steer from Bilbao with a full report on the situation there.[8] Two weeks later, just after the launching of the Northern Campaign in Vizcaya, the British consul in Bilbao, Mr. Stevenson, acting on his own initiative, cabled Eden in the Foreign Office, proposing that a large-scale evacuation of Basque children be undertaken. He noted that he had already received assurances from the French consul that his nation would assist, and he had found President Aguirre eager to accept such a humanitarian project, so much so that he would have the requisite passports issued "without political discrimination."[9] But this unusual diplomatic overture received no official acknowledgment.

At April's end, with Steer's return to Britain, Guernica had been firebombed, and most of its population evacuated. The London *Times* gave front-page coverage to Steer's dispatches, publishing them verbatim. Much of Britain was made aware of the great devastation visited on Basque cities by the German Condor Legion. The correspondent's eyewitness accounts of wounded and bleeding children fleeing the burning town that Vizcayans venerate galvanized British public opinion.[10] This sense of outrage prompted the British cabinet to agree at last to help Euzkadi's young refugees. The Royal Navy was now to be allowed to escort ships carrying refugees from territorial waters outside Bilbao to French ports, in disregard of the objections already lodged by General Franco.[11] On April 30, the Home Office acceded to the request of the National Joint Committee that Basque children be brought to the British Isles. Three conditions were laid down: that no cost to the Treasury be entailed for their maintenance; that private funds be gathered for their education and care; and that only noncombatants of all political parties be allowed to come. A note from the Foreign Office to the NJCSR with these stipulations arrived the next day; by May 15, the Basque Children's Committee (BCC) of the NJCSR had been hastily formed to plan for the care and housing of the pending expedition of young refugees from Vizcaya.[12] Committee members from the NJCSR traveled all over England, Scotland, and Wales to establish small local branches of the fledgling BCC to raise funds for the children's care. The Home Office had ruled that ten shillings per child per week had to be guaranteed by the BCC, and that all the children had to be housed and educated in private institutions, rather than in British homes. These were extraordinary financial obligations for the committee in a country suffering the effects of the worldwide depression which still counted two million wage earners as unemployed.[13] The local BCC branches were soon to be asked to provide housing, food, and medical care to the children, after a quarantine and transition period in a reception camp outside the port city of Southampton.

In Euzkadi, Leah Manning, a well-respected British educator, arrived to begin the arrangements. Originally, two thousand children were anticipated, but, prodded by Mrs. Manning's graphic accounts of the bombing of Guernica and the gravity of the situation, the BCC sponsored double that number, necessitating an immense effort marked by constant improvisation.

The Basque press reported in detail on the progress of the British expedition, noting the conditions set by the British government, and that the cooperation of the French government had been secured, with a reception area for the refugee children bound for Britain being set up just over the border in St.-Jean-de-Luz.[14]

In Bilbao, Mrs. Manning met frequently with President Aguirre and British and French consular officials to accomplish the physical evacuation of the refugees. She worked indefatigably to publicize the plight of the children to the British public, and found support in many quarters. An example is a letter published in full in the *Times* of London which noted the tragic bombing of Guernica, and appealed to the British people to donate funds for the coming expedition of children. Affixed to the letter were the signatures of a broad spectrum of prominent political figures: Conservative M.P. Irene Ward; Tory M.P. Harold Nicholson; Liberal M.P. Megan Lloyd-George; and Left Labour M.P. Ellen Wilkinson.[15] This public letter had a tremendous effect, which included the raising of some seventeen thousand pounds for the NJCSR in a few days. In an interview in Bilbao on May 10, Mrs. Manning reported this good news, adding innocently:

> We will get money from the United States too, as it is a rich country, where many Catholics live. They would be delighted to help the Basque people.[16]

In both her own country and the United States, however, the political mood of each government toward the Civil War in Spain, and, by extension, toward the plight of the Basques, proved to be much more pro-Insurgent than Mrs. Manning believed. In England, the new Prime Minister, Neville Chamberlain, was committed to appeasing Hitler at any cost, be it the democracy in Spain or other small nations of Europe. The national British Fascist movement, under Sir Oswald Moseley, was gaining momentum daily. Only the Leftist Labour party and a few prominent newspapers (the *Times*, the *Manchester Guardian*, and the *News Chronicle*) presented a more balanced view of the issues of the Spanish Civil War and the Northern Campaign in Euzkadi.

The Evacuation to England

In Euzkadi, the plans for the evacuation of Basque children to England proceeded, oblivious of the polarization of opinion in that country regarding the Civil War in Spain. Lists of children to be sent to England began to appear in the Bilbao press in numbered groups of five hundred. There was the greatest competition for vacancies in the expedition, the press noted, since the Basques "have always had an unlimited admiration for and faith in England, and feel they can place their children in English hands with complete confidence that they will be cared for and returned to them under happier circumstances safe and well."[17] The same article reported that twenty thousand children had been signed up for the four thousand places within two weeks.

In Bilbao, the required medical examination of each child was begun by Dr. Richard Ellis, his wife, Dr. Audrey Russell, and two nurses. It continued in spite of very difficult wartime conditions, scheduled on a fifteen-hour-a-day basis.[18] Dr. Ellis wrote:

> We learned from Mrs. Manning that the medical examination of the children bound for England had been planned to start the following day. We took the opportunity of visiting what had been the Civil Hospital, and it was perhaps the best introduction to Bilbao we could have had. Clearly under normal circumstances an up-to-date and well-run institution, it was working against impossible odds. It was bankrupt of equipment, dressings, and drugs. The X-ray apparatus was useless for want of one small part. In the casualty department, fractures were being set, and even a smashed pelvis and sacrum probed for bullets, without anaesthesia, for there were no anaesthetics to be had. Whilst we were there a little boy of five was brought in from a neighboring village with eight machine-gun wounds in his belly. He died a few minutes later. It was a relief to move on to one of the several homes for the orphans of militiamen which have been set up by the Asistencia Social. . . . Next day we were to learn the difficulties of any consecutive work. We had hardly got a group of children stripped to the waist and begun examining them when the sirens sounded and the children scattered. It was forty minutes before we could begin again, and when this had happened four times in quick succession, there were no children—and no morning—left. It was finally found necessary to work during the day in the garden immediately outside a *refugio* so that the children could be promptly reassembled, and to continue the examinations until the small hours of the morning. It says not a little both for the Basque child and the Basque mother, that even under these circumstances and often after hours of waiting, there were not a dozen out of the whole four thousand who cried or made any difficulty about having their throats examined![19]

As preparations for the English expedition proceeded, other evacuations departed every few days. A second expedition to France left Santurce, in the Bilbao harbor, on May 5, this time using two Basque ships, the *Habana* and the *Goizeko Izarra,* which were to carry many thousands of women, children, and old people to safety. The *Habana,* a vessel of 10,800 tons, was built during the reign of Alphonso XIII. Acquired by Basque shipping interests in 1931, it was the pride of Euzkadi. The *Goizeko Izarra,* a lovely yacht of the wealthy shipowner family de la Sota, was donated to the Basque government. It was placed under the safeguard of the International Red Cross and the British Navy to evacuate civilians from Vizcaya. After the May 5 children's expedition, the *Goizeko Izarra* was utilized again on May 16, and finally, on May 20, for the children's expedition to England. Then she was sold to an English shipowner, and reappeared as the *Warrior* on June 11, carrying tubercular Basque children from Gorliz Sanatorium on the Vizcayan coast to France, and on a final humanitarian voyage June 19, carrying refugees to France. She was later used for patrol duty during World War II and finally sunk by German aviation near Portland, England, in 1942.[20]

Mrs. Manning and the NJCSR had expected that the proposed expedition of four thousand Basque children to England would have been on the ships leaving May 5 or 9. Unfortunately, the Home Office had stipulated only children between five and twelve could be evacuated. Only two thousand of the children met this requirement, and Basque families able to care for their own sustenance in France or children en route to CGT colonies there went in their place. Dr. Ellis later wrote:

> We want the older children to come, especially the older girls, for if Bilbao is taken and filled with foreign troops, these are exactly children of the age we want out of the place. It should be remembered that the Basques are fighting very largely against foreign troops, being bombed by German planes from the air and attacked by Italian and Moorish troops on the ground. It will hardly be arguable that the Moors are pretty fighters or desir-

able occupants of a captured town. It is not many years since a victorious Moorish regiment marched past the General [Franco] with every bayonet decorated with enemy genitalia, and already appalling outrages have occurred in captured [Basque] villages where the Moors have more or less deliberately been allowed to get out of hand for twenty-four hours.[21]

On May 17, Mrs. Manning cabled Dr. Richard Ellis from Bilbao, to urge that Wilfred Roberts, M.P., of the NJCSR, contact the French Embassy to allow two thousand additional children to remain in Bordeaux. Permission was forthcoming from France.[22] After strenuous negotiations, aided by the publication of Msgr. Múgica's appeal letter, the Home Office relented, allowing chidren up to age fifteen to enter the British Isles.[23] Years later, Leah Manning summed up this hectic period in her humanitarian labor for the children of Euzkadi:

> In Bilbao the preparations had to be telescoped into a few weeks. They were made under heavy aerial and earth bombardment and under threat of the fall of the city. Evacuation was by sea to foreign countries, and therefore liable to frequent interruption as the policies of the receiving countries changed. No country was more guilty of these cruel changes than our own. The Basques had no sympathy either from the Home Office or the Foreign Office. Both regarded the whole thing as a nuisance and myself as an officious busybody. They changed the ages; they changed the policy of receiving family groups; and they demanded that the London Committee should guarantee ten shillings per week per head for each child—this at a time when they expected the children of their own unemployed to survive on five bob a week.[24]

The British expedition, first scheduled for May 5, finally disembarked on the vessels *Habana* and *Goizeko Izarra* on May 21, carrying 3,889 children,* 219 women teachers and aides,

* Some 263 children who were signed up did not actually join the expedition.

and fifteen priests.[25] Once aboard, the children tasted food they had not seen for months:

> I went with my two sisters, one only eight, to the harbor at Santurce. Franco's planes came over about mid-afternoon, just to watch. On board they gave us wonderful food we hadn't seen for a year: chorizos, white bread, and we all ate too much, filling our stomachs to the top. Within an hour, the whole shipload was seasick: we vomited over everything.

The trip was universally described as a nightmare: over four thousand bodies for 1,500 berths; a thousand had to sleep on mattresses on the decks. The ship was hastily scrubbed and disinfected following its most recent expedition to France, and children slept wherever they could; the berths saved for the youngest were soon commandeered by the older boys. Children were herded in the ship's public rooms, rolled up in blankets everywhere, even in the drained swimming pool.

As the ship neared land that Sunday morning:

> I was awakened by the sounds of thousands of feet on deck, and going out was greeted with cries of "*Rubio*," "*Hombre*," and asked perhaps five hundred times when we should arrive and whether they would really get white bread—and milk—and even meat, in England. Soon the boys were lined up dancing to the sound of a flute, when suddenly the whole ship listed to one side as four thousand children crowded the rails and deck and rigging to wave frantically to a blue strip on the horizon.[26]

The children were very excited as the ship pulled into the harbor at Southampton. All the elaborate decorations and bunting for the coronation of King George V had been left up in the town to greet them by order of the mayor. They were ecstatic at their warm welcome, thinking all the decorations were created in their honor.

> Our arrival: it was unforgettable, surprising, and very loving. When we entered the bay of Southampton, we thought we had entered a wonderland. Every little

> house lining the bay had its own pretty garden, well-tended, and all decorated to celebrate the coronation. Everything was bunting, flags, music playing, people waving their handkerchiefs at us, so that we thought we were awakening from a nightmare or dreaming, and that the world to which they had taken us wasn't real.
>
> In Southampton, there were thousands of people to welcome us, newsreel cameras, cakes and candies, buses to carry us, all the streets filled with fine decorations. They gave each of us a cup with the pictures of their new king and queen. It was wonderful.

Another medical examination was endured upon berthing in Southampton at 8:00 A.M., Sunday, May 23. Special attention was given to possible trachoma cases as Lord Lloyd had raised this possibility in the House of Lords on April 25.[27] None was found. Heads were inspected for ringworm, lice, their eggs (nits), and the skin for scabies. The children's tags were stamped, and a ribbon tied to each child's wrist. White meant "clean," red was "verminous," and many children were deloused with a strong red disinfectant soap they still recall after over forty years. Blue meant "infectious" or "contagious" and these were isolated in a hospital set up nearby.[28]

On reaching the camp those with "clean" white ribbons were separated from "unclean" red ones. The latter, on arrival, were bathed and disinfected. Their clothing, including that in their suitcases and bundles, was destroyed. New clothing was issued them. These clothes had a uniform institutional look, and immediately set apart the three hundred or so who had received a red label from the majority. This segregation, which in many cases separated brothers and sisters, created in the children's minds an immediate mistrust of the camp's administration.[29]

Life at Camp Stoneham

The camp at North Stoneham at Eastleigh, a few miles from Southampton, had been improvised in less than three weeks. On open land surrounded by woods, it had been donated by a local resident for the three or so months the reception area was expected to be in use. Though there was a small local committee collecting funds to aid Spain, sympathies were neither pro-Republican nor pro-Basque. In spite of this, before and throughout the coronation holiday, a crew of over two hundred (including Boy Scouts and Girl Guides, professors and plumbers) worked to prepare the site and raise the hundreds of tents necessary to house the children and their services. Water was piped into the site, incinerators built for burning rubbish, and cooking facilities constructed.[30] A clothing tent was raised to house the tons of used clothing which poured in, as well as a huge donation of new clothes from Marks and Spencer, the British department store chain. Other gifts included twenty thousand oranges, innumerable dozens of eggs, and a daily ration of free chocolate from Cadbury's.[31] A large estate house, Westend, with twenty-seven acres of ground, was donated and put to use as a hospital.[32] Everyone seemed willing to help. Even the mayor was seen serving spaghetti in his shirt sleeves to a line of Basque children.[33]

However, many problems arose. The food lines were far too long. Older boys soon learned to line up four or five times a meal—and still take food from the youngest ones. A system of colored armbands was instituted to check repeaters, but those assigned yellow bands refused to line up and went without their meals: yellow was the color of Franco's flag! Soon mess tents holding 250 children each were operative, and meal times became much happier events.[34] At first, much white bread was hoarded after the margarine was scraped off. One boy remarked "I never knew there was so much white bread in the world. We are going to eat *all* of it!"

The food seemed strange to the children, not well seasoned and indifferently cooked, both at Stoneham, and later, in colonies:

> At first, there were a lot of problems with the food they gave us in camp. Our first meal was beans, served with whole boiled Spanish onions. The volunteers had prepared what they thought we would like, but none of us ate it, just bothered the bread and milk servers to get something we were familiar with. Then they asked why

> we threw away the onions. Well, they may have been "Spanish," but none of us had ever eaten them prepared that way.
>
> The British serve small meals, smaller than we had eaten in peacetime. Their bread was soft and without body, and they always spread it with margarine, a substance strange to us. We never got used to the tea, served at every meal, but it was a black tea, served with milk. We only used herb tea when we had stomach aches or felt sick, with a little sugar.

The camp's basic organization assigned eight same-sex children to a tent, with rotating duties for each. There was daily inspection by the Boy Scouts. The children rose to loud-speaker music at eight, had breakfast in the large mess tents, occasional classes outdoors, and passed time reading and letter writing in the tents after lunch. Afternoons were also free, with periodic excursions in groups with an adult to town or local points of interest.[35] One woman recalled awakening to:

> "Good morning, children" on the loudspeaker. We woke up every morning to happy music, breakfasted, and then went to classes in the open air. Afterwards, we each had our daily assignment. They inspected our tents, and we always kept our tent cleanest of all, except when the jealous Nationalist (PNV) boys came and spoiled it.

Regrettably, the same lack of a planned program for the weeks and months in the transition camp which was reported by those sent into France marred the lives of the children at Stoneham. They had far too much time on their hands. Washing anything in sight, including small brothers and sisters, became a passion with the girls. The boys clustered around staff and visiting adults, watching them work. All cajoled the constant stream of visitors (which one day included the King and Queen of England, with young Princess Margaret Rose). They begged for pennies, which along with food and candy, were bartered for cigarettes. Even the younger boys smoked, to the dismay of the British personnel. The older boys took everything available apart, and removable objects were quietly pilfered from visitors' cars.[36]

Trust within the expedition of children was strong, however, and the solidarity among family groups impressive. Again, slightly older siblings acted as parents to three- and four-year-olds, often assuming full responsibility for their care.

At first, political differences among the children were ignored, but the strong cleavages in the Basque country were soon apparent among the children. There was considerable internal Basque political heterogeneity reflected in the camp population. The children had to be strictly segregated shortly after arrival, depending on the affiliation of their parents in registering them for evacuation. The PNV children, about half of those registered, received preferential treatment, in part because this party's leaders included the Basque president, finance minister, minister of justice and culture, and the minister of the interior.[37] Their bourgeois family background also made them particularly acceptable to their British hosts. All the classes in Euzkera and Basque folklore were given to the PNV contingent. This group was very well staffed, as all fifteen Basque priests and the Roman Catholic chapel were based in their part of the facility.[38] A few of the children in this group were reputed to be pro-Franco. At one point, they were set upon by children of Leftist parents, and beaten with a hammer. The next day, this small contingent was segregated, and slept in different tents each night so there could be no further reprisals.

> They put us in three groups: Basque Nationalists (PNV), the "Reds" (those on the Left), and the older boys. That was a result of the bad propaganda, for the "Reds" were very good people, really our salvation. I was in the PNV camp, but not because I rejected the "Reds." But this made for rivalry and resentment, and set the groups apart from the beginning.

> Within about two weeks, things were better organized. But they made a mistake in separating the PNV Catholics from us on the Left. The PNV children had chapels, priests, movies, dancing, everything you could think of, but we savages had almost nothing.[39]

The children consciously identified themselves as the "Basque children," never as "Spanish children." The significance was lost on the British camp personnel. "To us they were simply Spaniards from the north," noted Eric Pittman, one of the camp staff interviewed.[40]

The most difficult problem was the wide mental gulf between children and organizers. The children, between five or younger and fifteen, had lived for months through a civil war full of political implications. Even before the conflict, politics were very much a part of everyday life in Spain. The children were therefore aware of the double-talk and unsavory dealings of the European powers in relation to the Republican government.

> Unfortunately, almost none of the British personnel could speak Spanish at all fluently. This language barrier helped to create an atmosphere of misunderstanding and mistrust. There were few interpreters, and of these, none could understand the children who spoke only Basque. There were sporadic attempts to start classes in English, but they rarely continued beyond the third lesson. Enthusiasm waned since each lesson began with the conjugation of the verb "to have." The whole operation had been prepared as if it was some sort of Scouts and Guides jamboree, with all knowing camp drill and ready to cooperate. But we Basque children were not Scouts and Guides: we had been in a war and separated from our parents unwillingly. Most had a political awareness uncommon in England even among adults. Since psychology was not in fashion in 1937, no one analyzed the reason for our mistrust of our hosts.[41]

Medical problems were surprisingly minor. The children, though semi-starved for several months in Spain, were not in poor health upon arrival. After completing the medical examinations, Dr. Ellis wrote:

> Perhaps the most surprising feature of the examination was the good health of the group as a whole, in spite of the conditions of deprivation, anxiety, and overcrowding in which they had been living for many weeks. It was evident that even the poorer peasants have a high

> standard of care for their children, and that before the blockade almost all the latter were well developed and well fed. It was impossible to weigh and measure the whole group at this time or to apply any strict standards of nutrition, but the impression was definitely gained that although the majority showed loss of subcutaneous fat, the period of malnutrition had not been long enough to cause permanent damage or muscular weakness, and that recovery under proper conditions should be rapid and complete. A few of the smaller children, however, showed really severe marasmus, and were immediately recognizable, even before being stripped, by their blank apathetic faces, their slow movements and whispering speech, and their distended abdomens. . . . No gross evidence of vitamin deficiency was found with the exception of hyperkeratinisation around the hair follicles, which was relatively common, giving the skin a peculiarly rough feel. It was unfortunately impossible to test for night blindness. The very high incidence of dental caries, however, is probably attributable at least in part to the deficient diet.[42]

As children gained weight in camp, the only medical problem surfacing was a small outbreak of five cases of typhoid. In preventing the spread of this disease, the hygienic measure imposed ran counter to the children's cultural training, as they were told to dip their hands in a common basin of disinfectant before eating. Their reluctance to comply, based on the knowledge imparted from their mothers that it was dirty to touch water others had washed in, was overcome by dripping a bit of disinfectant individually on extended hands. In the matter of latrines, still being built as the children arrived, a Spanish-speaking visitor, native of Birmingham, implored the diggers to consult the children regarding their customary toilet facilities. The construction was therefore completed to the children's satisfaction.[43]

Everyone remarked upon the children's fear of airplanes. Since the camp was located near a private airfield, pilots had to be cautioned not to "buzz" the camp, for many children cowered or ran for cover when an airplane appeared. One prominent Basque visitor, Manuel Irujo, commented that, on a visit to Stoneham with the Duchess of Atholl, airplanes appeared, doing their maneuvers, and the children simply "disappeared into the ground as though by instinct."[44] They were clearly traumatized by their experiences in Euzkadi, and Irujo felt the fear had become part of their nature. This perception was shared by some doctors, who found the older children had more difficulty ridding themselves of this neurotic symptom. Many children were so frightened, they urinated spontaneously when airplanes approached, just as they had in Bilbao, where the most popular shelters had been the underground latrines.[45]

On June 19, an event occurred that shook each child in exile: the fall of Bilbao to Franco's troops.[46]

> News about Spain and the position of the war in the Basque Country was scanty. About twice a week in the evening, bulletins were read, in Spanish, over the loudspeakers. They consisted of brief information about counter-attacks of the Basque Gudaris and their successes. Most of the children knew the relative distances between Bilbao and places mentioned in the bulletins. To many of them it became apparent that Franco's troops were gaining ground daily. The biggest blunder was the news read on the evening of the 17th of June when it was stated that the Gudaris were counter-attacking in Bolueta and that the Iron Belt, as the defences around Bilbao were optimistically called by the Basque government, was holding all attacks! Almost everyone knew that Bolueta was *inside* the Iron Belt! Some of the older children gleaned information from English newspapers, either by borrowing them from camp staff or picking them from waste bins. In this manner some learnt late in the afternoon of the 20th of June that Bilbao had fallen to Franco the previous day. They found a copy of the *Daily Mail* with a front-page headline ANTI-REDS ENTER BILBAO. There was no need to know English to understand that headline! The words are so similar to Spanish that the meaning was clear. For good measure, there was a map showing the new front line to the west of Bilbao! The camp authorities did not know how to break the news. It was acknowledged that sooner or later the news

of the fall would be known by all. In fact, there was a suspicion that a few children already knew.[47]

When the fall was announced at camp over the loudspeaker by one of the Basque priests, a collective shriek went up, followed by wailing, hysterical weeping, and cries of "Madre" that went on for hours, until the children cried themselves to sleep. The children had been hearing bits of rumors from visitors for several days that the end of their country was near, and were nervous and jumpy. Some older children, in impotent fury, broke away through the guards at the gate, but all were rounded up by patrols. A British eyewitness remarked on the event and its unfortunate aftermath:

I never saw anything like it—can you imagine four thousand Basque children and señoritas crying right through the night? It was an extra-ordinary experience. There was complete hysteria. The PNV kids from middle-class families were completely prostrated. Gone was the last hope. Their parents were being butchered as well. This was a crisis point, too, because some 300 of the older boys reacted differently too—they didn't lie down and weep about it—they *marched* down to Southampton with the intention of getting a boat back to help their parents. Now this played right into the hands of the pro-Franco press and from that moment, they had a handle on destroying the sympathy. They said, "These red anarchists and communists are marching on Southampton—they're likely to do a lot of destruction"—that kind of propaganda, and immediately, donations began to drop off. People who were politically neutral stopped helping us. Our funds then depended entirely on those sympathetic to the Republican cause; a turning point. That was when the BCC got cold feet and brought in 13 army officers to run the camp, playing right up to the publicity. "This undisciplined mob of anarchists, we've got to hold them down." A gross injustice: as one Basque boy told me: "It's all right. You bring us here and feed us, but you don't give our parents weapons. You make us orphans."[48]

Dispersion to Colonies

A full-scale campaign to send the children to more permanent colonies in the various communities where local BCC committees were active was launched shortly after the refugees arrived in May. Appeals were made to the Salvation Army, the Catholic church, and other religious groups, as well as to Leftist political and trade union organizations. The immediate response was very good. Some ninety colonies were opened in England, Scotland, and Wales during 1937.[49] This number dropped rapidly to forty in mid-1938,[50] and only five were still open two years later.[51] Everyone, including the NJCSR leadership, Basque parents, and the children themselves, had expected their stay in Britain to last only a few months. In fact, however, only 265 children had been returned to Spain by the end of 1937.[52] Donations to the committee, which had ranged from hundreds of pounds from the Trades Union Council to pennies donated by British children, fell abruptly after the fall of Bilbao. A sponsor of the colony at Birmingham remembers:

> We could always get a lot of publicity for the Basque children in Birmingham, since Babcock-Wilcox and Guest, Keene and Nettleford (large multinational corporations) both had branches in Bilbao. But as soon as Bilbao fell to Franco, it became impossible to get any coverage or help from the press at all.[53]

Minutes of the BCC just two weeks after the children arrived indicate that press criticism of Stoneham Camp had already begun. Its administrative deficiencies and the potential health hazard posed by the refugees to British boys and girls were publicized, sharply contrasting with the tender human interest stories from the camp heretofore printed. As a result, dispersion to colonies was accelerated.[54] That same week, when the Basque Delegation in London requested that an additional three to four thousand Basque children be received in Britain, the BCC voted unanimously to reject the appeal.[55] Soon, the Catholic hierarchy complained that Catholic boys were being sent to secular colonies, and that too few Catholic girls had been sent to fill available places.[56]

The Salvation Army Colonies

The first group to leave Stoneham was that sponsored by the Salvation Army, some four hundred boys. Taken to London just three days after their arrival in Britain, they were greeted by General Evangeline Booth, and installed in Clapton, an old officer training site, formerly used as an orphanage. Their director there, Major W., "has been for many years in South America, and understands the Spanish character."[57] Soon, other children left for colonies at Birmingham, the Isle of Wight, Southall, Tunbridge Wells, and Carlisle. By June 4, 1,093 were gone.

This initial group to leave the camp were those boys who answered the call on the loudspeaker earlier that week: "Who wants to go to London?" To a Basque boy, it sounded as exciting as a trip to Madrid, and on May 26, the group arrived in London. They were housed at Clapton for a few days, until they could be dispersed to the farms at Hadleigh, Brixton, and Ramsgate. These were adult alcoholic rehabilitation centers directed by the Salvation Army.[58]

Clapton looked old, ugly, dirty, and badly cared for to the boys. It was the donated former palace of a rich Briton, and had a tradition of being haunted by the ghosts of previous owners. This fact, spread by the staff, simply terrorized the younger boys. All were immediately placed under quarantine, because of the typhoid cases back at camp. The first meal was a disaster:

> When we arrived at Clapton, they served us a stew of sorts, nothing identifiable. We all sat there, unable to eat it. Reproaches as "We'll see if you eat or not," "How many British children would love to eat this food," began. The same food reappeared at lunch and dinner; again, no one ate. A hunger strike!

That night, the older boys rebelled, throwing all the mattresses down into the garden below. One boy escaped. He was quickly found, put in prison, and beaten with a whip, a punishment then current in Britain. The police were called in to quiet the boys at Clapton. The pro-Franco British press, as well as the Rightist press in Pamplona and Salamanca, had a field day. The Basque boys were described as "savages, rebels, beasts." The consul from Euzkadi in London rushed over and spoke to the assembled youngsters, now quite subdued. He had tears in his voice as he described the bad examples they were setting. They were much affected by his talk, and sobbed along with him.

One man from Clapton remarked:

> At Clapton, I experienced all the petty tragedies of an undersized, somewhat precocious eight-year-old among older, rougher boys. I was teased, robbed of my clothes and few possessions, and so on. It was a place given to strict discipline, closed off from normal society. But I had my own small triumph. Because I was middle class, and had been educated, I quickly rose from the first level to the fourth class. For this I was given a prize for scholarship. But it was, to me, a most original prize: the magnificent sum of one shilling. It was a surprise to me, for at home, no one gave money to reward aptitude.

Some two hundred adolescent boys from this group were dispatched, half to Brixton, the balance to Hadleigh.

> [Hadleigh] was a dismal, dreary place, run like a military camp. Our companions were middle-aged drunkards, who hated the place. There was absolutely no program for us when we came, just working along with the alcoholics. Some of us were put to making bricks; others worked in the camp's laundry; I had to work with the chickens every day. We were simply unpaid labor of the most menial kind.

Some of the older boys rebelled against the army-like discipline, and they were taken to Scarborough. This camp became known as the "penal colony" of the Basque boys, and, throughout England, staff disciplined refugee children by threatening to send them there.

At Hadleigh, conditions worsened and the boys staged a work stoppage. Representatives from the Basque consulate in London investigated the situation and informed the camp administrator that the boys had rights as refugees and minors. The delegation proceeded to arrange an allowance of six shillings a week for each boy and soon classes in English began. When books arrived from the Basque government, Don Julio Briones, a refugee poet from Madrid, began teaching excellent classes in Spanish literature and history. Theatrical productions were staged for Christmas. The atmosphere at the Salvation Army colonies remained, however, "very English" and very strict.

The Salvation Army soon found the care and feeding of four hundred boys onerous. By July 28, Colonel Gordon had to request that Clapton be returned for Salvation Army use.

Few funds had come in response to their appeal for the Basque children. The last 114 children were sent to other sites or repatriated and the farm colonies closed early the next spring.[59]

Catholic Colonies

The initial response of the Catholic church in Great Britain to Msgr. Múgica's appeal was wholehearted and generous. Britain's chief prelate, the archbishop of Westminster, Arthur Hinsley, agreed to accept responsibility for twelve hundred Basque children who were practicing Catholics. He assigned Canon Craven to the BCC as his representative, as requested by the parent NJCSR.[60] Hinsley wrote to each archdiocese in England, Scotland, and Wales, giving an assigned number of Basque children as its quota. Every parish was expected to assist:

> I have to ask your help. As you know, a great number of little children have been brought to England from Bilbao. We did not bring them and many of us think they ought never to have been brought. However, they are here now. Not one of us, surely, can dare to turn them away. They are helpless and desolate in a strange land and in your name I have offered to shelter 325 of them in our Diocesan Homes. . . . A few weeks ago I also made an appeal to you through your Parish Priest and in your own homes you offered to shelter 430 children. Your response was prompt and generous. . . . For the present, however, I am informed that the Government do not intend to allow the children to live with private families.

> . . . No financial help, I am now told, will be given to me by the Government or the National Fund which has been raised for the children. . . . To find a sufficient income to maintain them (I propose) a scheme of adoption. It is estimated it will cost at least ten shillings a week to maintain each child . . . in our Diocesan Homes. . . .I ask this of you in the name of Him who said, "He that shall receive one such little child in My name, receiveth Me."
>
> Bishop of Hexham and Newcastle[61]

In addition to housing children in the diocesan orphanages, a number of excellent Catholic boarding schools also offered places. Other colonies were opened in estates donated for this purpose by wealthy Britons. As these thirty sites were readied during the summer months, the children in Stoneham Camp were carefully being screened regarding their religion and their political beliefs. The fifteen Basque priests accompanying the expedition closely questioned each child possibly eligible, essentially those in the PNV section of the encampment. To most of the Leftist children, "Catholic" had come to mean the army of Franco, in which even the Moors marched with the emblem of the Sacred Heart of Jesus on their tunics, while wreaking violence against Euzkadi. Very few, therefore, from the non-PNV parts of Stoneham chose to be classed as "*Catolica Practicante*."[62]

In contrast to the alacrity of the archbishop in accepting the child refugees, in Britain, as in France, the Catholic clergy was generally pro-Insurgent. This was overwhelmingly true of the Irish nuns (Nazarene Sisters of Charity) and priests who made up the majority of the staffs assigned to Catholic institutions throughout Britain. Some, according to interview material, were rabidly pro-Franco, reflecting the large contingent of blue-shirted Irish volunteer soldiers fighting in his army under General McDuffy against the Republicans. Propaganda broadcasts from Insurgent spokesmen even questioned the faith of the Basque priests who went into exile with the children in Britain, culminating in the assertion that these men were, in truth, *Protestant* clergy.[63] As a result, these priests had minimal relations with the nuns and priests who staffed the Catholic colonies. Although the Basque clerics had received the express authorization of the Vicar General of Bilbao to emigrate, whenever they presented themselves to their counterparts in local British parishes where Catholic colonies were located, they were received with suspicion and some rudeness rather than being welcomed as colleagues. Many were denied documents needed to serve as priests.

The major Catholic weekly, *The Tablet*, commented editorially that the offer of a neutral safety zone made by Franco in May should have been accepted, thus making the evacuation to Britain unnecessary.[64] Community hostility to the children and their Basque priests quite naturally emerged and was encouraged by the Catholic press. It became more difficult than expected to provide homes for the twelve hundred PNV children Hinsley had agreed to sponsor, and a number had to enter colonies where Leftist children predominated.[65]

In the Catholic colonies, the Basque priests arranged the religious instruction for the children housed there. In many cases, they also assumed the responsibility for teaching the language, arts, and folklore of Euzkadi. In this, they were aided by several dozen Catholic women teachers assigned to the girls' colonies. In addition, the priests also visited all Catholic children in the "mixed" colonies, thus extending their labors to the Leftist children as well. A number of conversions to the Catholic faith were the result of these apostolic endeavors.[66]

Since Catholic training in 1937 precluded education of boys and girls together, ostensibly to safeguard morals, brothers and sisters were separated and sent to single-sex colonies, boarding schools, or orphanages. This was a fearful added wrench for the children, so recently exiled from their parents and country, and one not experienced by Leftist children who were sponsored by unions and political groups.

Weston Manor

The very first Catholic contingent to leave camp was that composed of 114 girls, aged four to fourteen, from staunchly PNV families from Bilbao and its environs.[67] Late in May, the girls—accompanied by four Irish nuns, a young orphan girl who had been reared by the nuns and who did kitchen work, three Basque teachers, two Basque aides, and a Basque priest—journeyed to the Isle of Wight, to Weston Manor. There, a mansion donated to the church by a Protestant sea captain became home for a year to the refugees. The manor house was huge, many-towered, with gracious leaded windows, set in a lovely park surrounded by well-tended gardens. The converted dormitory rooms, however, were crowded with beds the children were forbidden to sit upon. Moreover, a certain nun from Ulster was a Francoist and often unpleasant.

Very soon, though, Fr. Benito came to Weston Manor:

> There was always a long line in front of his confessional. He knew and loved us all. Unlike the other priest, he always gave us absolution when we confessed to filching apples or pears from the gardener's fruit trees. Sometimes, we tried to disguise our voices, but he knew us inside out, and what we were up to. He taught us Basque, the folklore, the dances and songs. We celebrated every Basque holiday, and sewed our blue and white costumes by hand for the dances. We made our own *ikurriña*, too, to use for our performances and our holidays.

When the girls became aware of growing anti-Basque propaganda branding them as "Red-Separatist Atheists," they bade him request of the local monsignor an examination in Catholic doctrine to demonstrate their knowledge of the faith.

As committed Basque Nationalists, they recall the spontaneous pilgrimage they made to nearby Tennyson Down, some on their knees, when the fall of Bilbao was rumored. There, they prayed for their parent's safety and fasted all day, refusing the chocolates and other rarely offered sweets the staff offered to calm them.

Within a few weeks, the girls found acceptance and welcome throughout the island. Sundays were spent in private homes, drinking tea, enjoying sweets and a respite from group life. Some recall taking turns wearing the one smart striped jersey one girl had been given whenever they were invited to tea in the village. The clothing the colony received as donations was sometimes curious, particularly boxes of old boots, fastened by rusty hooks that none could manage. The refugee children always consciously presented themselves as "Basque," not "Spanish," in their by-now close association with the surrounding community. As in other host countries, this included sports, folklore performances, and holiday celebrations: Basque, English, and Irish.

During their only Christmas season there, the girls placed their shoes outside their rooms in preparation for the gifts expected on the Day of the Three Kings. The Irish nuns were baffled by this practice, but Fr. Benito explained the custom. The good sisters hurriedly made or gathered little gifts and filled each shoe with special candies. Everyone was happy and felt loved.

Already, the colony was dwindling. Some girls had returned to Bilbao in November, part of the first repatriation. By the following June, the colony was closed. Other Catholic colonies had similar histories.

The Older Boys

From the time they arrived at Stoneham, the boys aged twelve to as old as sixteen were viewed as troublemakers by much of the camp staff and the BCC.[68] These youngsters who had done the work of men during the hard months of civil war, cleaning rubble, digging trenches, reinforcing bomb shelters, acting as the man of the house, had also seen war at its worst. Machine-gunned women and children piled into trucks for burial, lorries of wounded soldiers coming to hospitals, people blown to bits, were sights etched in their minds. In rural England, they were confined to a peaceful camp overrun with small children and managed by calm, apolitical adults. As a stopgap, the boys were given a section of camp they could run to some extent themselves. They cooked their own food, cut their own wood, policed the encampment, and did other odd jobs for a small wage, two pence a task, enough for a chocolate bar or a pack of Woodbine cigarettes. After the fall of Bilbao, these boys became almost uncontrollable, breaking quarantine, stealing fruit, throwing stones at visitors. To counteract the very bad press such incidents seemed to spark, immediately reflected in a drop in public donations, Mrs. Manning took fifty of the most rebellious boys to a special colony at Diss, in Norfolk, as a well-publicized experiment. If this stabilized the youngsters, perhaps the growing campaign to repatriate the children, now that Bilbao was lost, might abate. One of those selected recalled:

> For us, it was a paradise, in a beautiful area by a river, with trees and fields. We were to govern ourselves, and, in a democratic election, chose boys to be Minister of the Navy, to guard the river and prevent drownings—he couldn't swim either!; Minister of Justice, to handle robberies in the kitchen and the storerooms—he didn't lack for work; Minister of Labor, to plan the work details and assign jobs—we picked the boy known to be the latest to get up in the morning; and Minister of Government, to deal with the British—a boy who knew English already.

It was now mid-August 1937, and nearly 350 children were still living at Stoneham. All were verminous from the straw used as bedding in the tents, and scabies was becoming epidemic. The great majority were boys in their teens, always hardest to place. About one hundred of the most troublesome were placed in Ministry of Labour camps, which were actually reformatories. Scarborough, a seaside Yorkshire town, and the Welsh town of Carmarthenshire housed these boys under the hard supervision of men trained at Borstal, the infamous reformatory. None of their jailers spoke Spanish. A final contingent of Basque boys, always referred to in BCC minutes as the "Black List," was made up of twenty-three of the most delinquent adolescents. They were shipped to France, to the custody of the Basque Delegation there, and were sent on to Catalonia in August.[69]

The Basque children immediately became a target of politicians and journalists who, covertly or overtly, applauded the Rightist rebellion in Spain, and its Fascist allies. Accounts in the Rightist press of car stealing by these boys, of their pilfering from shops, window breaking, and threatening staff with a knife fed the pro-Franco sentiment of much of the public. A photo captioned "Basque Hooligans Climbing Fence to Escape" showed two youngsters who had only gone to retrieve a ball. A current British joke of the time went:

> Why has your child become so unruly?
> Oh, he's been playing with some Basque children.

An article from the *New Statesman and Nation* compared press accounts with the reality, e.g., the car stealing was simply three boys releasing the brake on a parked car, which traveled a yard away; and the knife threat had been on the cook's part. The blacklisted youths were

> Nineteen small boys ranging from seven to fourteen. Without any difficulty they were taken to the Hotel Royal, and displayed such a regard for table manners that the guests and staff commented on it. "Who are they?" a man asked. When he was told that these were the Basque desperadoes who were terrorizing Wales, he burst into a hearty roar of laughter.[70]

One of the older boys, today a successful architect in Britain, comments:

> All the delinquency the pro-Fascist press blamed us for consisted of normal boyish pranks. Children have been picking fruit from the trees of others since the Garden of Eden, and any unruliness could be traced to some misunderstanding. But the press had a field day.

The Concerts

Within two months after arrival, the Basque children had asked permission to give concerts in the communities where they were living. Permission was immediately granted, and a most important cultural phenomenon then began.[71] Throughout England, traditional Basque dances and songs were presented to the British public. Most were small gatherings of fifty to one hundred townspeople, who paid a few pence to see a group of small boys and girls spontaneously and artlessly sing the *Boga-Boga* and dance *Las Hilanderas,* the *Jota,* and *Espatadanza*. Their simple traditional costumes of dark blue, black, and white were hand sewn, as was the *ikurriña,* the Basque flag, which usually graced the performance. A local committee member made the fund appeal, and the performers themselves passed the hat to collect money. There were larger performances in the bigger cities—Paul Robeson joined the Basque children at a benefit concert in 1938, at which the Lord Mayor of London presided.[72] Many concerts brought youngsters together from different colonies. The program notes from a Brixton concert in 1938 remark that

> . . . The purely Basque dances, like the *Ikurriñera* and the *Purucalda*, or the Weavers Dance from Biscay, have never been seen in London before. All the performers are self trained and have organized their dancing or singing on the genuine folk traditions handed down through many generations and guarded with conservative zeal. Unlike our own children, they have no self consciousness in their performance; for what they dance and sing is a true expression of a very real culture, untampered by academicalism. The children take great pride in their performance of a folk art that no war must ever be permitted to destroy.[73]

A very impressive list of patrons, including the Earl and Countess of Antrim, the Duchess of Atholl, Viscount Cecil of Chelwood, the Marchioness of Donegal, the Viscountesses of Hawarden and Hastings, the Earl of Listowel, Lord and Lady Marley, Lord and Lady Noel-Buxton, eminent churchmen, and diplomats, graced this concert. On the program cover was a depiction of the Oak Tree of Guernica. Proceeds were good; BCC minutes note: "This was a most successful way to raise money."[74]

Problems of the BCC

From the beginning of the dispersion, adequate staffing for the widely scattered colonies was difficult. Trained Spanish–speaking personnel were scarce, and other staff, who re ceived only board, room, and a few shillings for weekly pocket money, soon moved on to better jobs in the improving wartime economy as soon as their initial enthusiasm waned. The Spanish señoritas and aides were not always cooperative, and issues of religion surfaced in some of the secular colonies when strongly Catholic women were put in charge of the Socialist and Communist children. The señoritas received a half crown weekly as pocket money from the BCC, since the currency of the Basque government quickly became valueless.[75]

As problems multiplied in the management of the Stoneham Camp, and as the dispersion to the countryside began, the division within the BCC itself became more marked. The drama of the evacuation was over; now, the day-to-day problems of Stoneham seemed to exacerbate the conflicts among the various members of the BCC, whose personalities reflected most of the hues of British public opinion.

In the chair was the Duchess of Atholl, an aristocrat of ancient Scottish Highland ancestry, whose rank entitled her to a private bodyguard. An avowed Tory in her ancestral seat in the House of Lords, she had been nicknamed the "Red Duchess" by the British press for her spirited espousal of the Spanish Republic. Mr. Tewson, Labour representative of the leftist Trades Union Congress; Wilfred Roberts, a Liberal M.P.; and a Communist M.P. from the Labour Party, Eleanor Rathbone, were balanced by Right-wing Tory Captain MacNamara, Canon Craven from Roman Catholic Archbishop Hinsley's office, and the Salvation Army's militaristic Colonel Gordon. Two Quaker ladies, Miss Pye and Miss Anderson, maintained an apolitical stance.

The marked differences among British political viewpoints were to be clearly reflected as the issue gradually shifted from giving haven to the Basque children to reuniting them with their families.

Soon after Bilbao had fallen, both Britain and France had sent "unofficial" trade missions to Burgos, the seat of Franco's government. Baldwin resigned in May 1937, and the prime ministership passed to Neville Chamberlain. Foreign Minister Eden resigned shortly thereafter, to be replaced by the overtly pro-Fascist Lord Halifax. Sir Oswald Moseley, an outspoken and committed Fascist, mobilized immense pro-Hitler marches throughout London during 1937 and 1938. Chamberlain articulated the doctrine of "Peace in our Time" which captured the mood of the British populace quite faithfully. As the Spanish Republic struggled against Franco's forces, and as Hitler's territorial plans became unmistakably menacing, British leadership vacillated, appeasing the Fascists to buy time to rearm the nation for the coming world conflict.

Even as the political panorama of Britain shifted to the Right just prior to World War II, the fortunes of the Basque Children's Committee began to drop alarmingly. Throughout the first three months of the refugee children's stay, ample money flowed in. The first appeals of the parent NJCSR and large meetings in London raised over seven thousand pounds in June alone.[76] This amount, and an additional three thousand pounds from the National Joint Committee, was gone by September.[77] In a matter of weeks, the "Basque Babies Project," as the press called the evacuation, had become the paramount concern of its parent organization, absorbing over three-quarters of the NJCSR treasury. All meetings were by now set to accommodate the schedules of BCC members.[78] The energy and funds required to house, clothe, feed, educate, and provide medical care to thousands of refugee children dispersed all over the British Isles was enormous. The adoption scheme in which individuals paid the weekly costs of a Basque child was largely unsuccessful, so that a minimum of 750 pounds had to be raised each week for the balance of the unadopted children.[79]

Nevertheless, the NJCSR did begin other projects to aid Spain as the Civil War shifted to Catalonia, the Levant, and the Madrid area. Colonies for children were begun in Catalonia; the Milk Fund was expanded. Convoys of food, clothing, medical supplies, trucks, and ambulances were sent to Republican Spain, and an Eastern Spain Fund was initiated early in 1938.[80] Though the focus of the war was changing, the needs of the Basque children continued paramount. Of the £71,042 raised by the NJCSR between December 1936 and December 1937, its first year, well over 65 percent went into the BCC during its scant seven months of existence.[81]

By the end of January 1938, there were less than three thousand pounds in the NJCSR treasury, and past and present debts of the BCC would "require every shilling of this."[82] A special appeal bulletin was sent out in March 1938, which noted that 1,220 children had already been repatriated to Spain, with another sixty sent to parents outside Spain. The remaining 2,546 would, it stated, have to remain until the Spanish Civil War conditions changed greatly.[83]

But English public opinion seemed dedicated to Chamberlain's appeasement. The Spanish Republican cause became more unpopular as it became more desperate. Capitulation to Hitler continued, and he marched into Austria in March 1938. The pact at Munich gave him Czechoslovakia in September of that same year. The by-now monthly meetings of the BCC were more and more involved with the vagaries of local committees no longer able to maintain colonies, and with children coming from Catholic and Salvation Army homes no longer able or willing to care for them.

Nearly every colony that closed also incurred heavy expenses for dilapidation of the property. The BCC secretary, who visited the colonies, frequently reported very low morale, and staffing problems.[84] It was necessary to economize at every level and the NJCSR cut half its office staff as an example. The children had to live as best they could under these circumstances. Their folklore performances became more frequent, the appeals more wrenching. Money was always raised by these concerts. In contrast, the sale of Spanish war pamphlets by the NJCSR was discontinued in 1939 for lack of sales. Football matches between local teams and the Basque boys also raised money. Records of Basque songs, made by the children, were sold, as was a commemorative stamp featuring a picture of the youngest Basque refugee child. Other informational pamphlets intended to educate Britons—and raise funds—were published: "The Martyrdom of the Basques," an "Adoptions Leaflet," and "The Basque Children in England."

The major help now came from labor groups. Roman Catholic help became minimal, and the Salvation Army reported that there was no response to their appeals for the children.[85]

Sending the children back became more and more appealing to the BCC as the only feasible alternative. A resolution to do this was introduced in February 1938, producing a tie vote. The Duchess, as chair, cast the vote in favor of "sending back children to those parents known to be in Insurgent Spain and at liberty, with the Spanish Ambassador's being consulted and with assurance someone accompany the children to bring back any not reunited with their parents."[86] (This complex issue will be discussed in detail in Chapter VII.)

There were many very positive aspects to the BCC sponsorship of nearly four thousand youngsters. Consistently remarked upon during the entire sojourn of the Basque refugee children were the quite robust health exhibited by the children, the almost complete absence of diseases which could be communicated to British youngsters, and the quite spectacular weight gains made by many. There was only one death reported for the first years, from an advanced case of tuberculosis which the child clearly suffered from upon arrival. One potential suicide was given constant nursing care until her depression lifted. Dental problems were numerous but not severe. The BCC also processed a number of requests to observe the children and view their drawings and writings. These inquiries came from medical and psychiatric researchers interested in learning the effects of modern warfare from this first group of youngsters to experience its consequences fully. Though it appears these requests were granted, no published material has been located.[87]

Personal care was still given to individual children. One was provided private art lessons—today he is an internationally known sculptor. Three children were sent to their mother in the Soviet Union in December 1937. And, as an ominous portent of child refugees to come, the BCC received a request from the International Committee for Jewish Child Refugees that a number be placed in the Basque children's colonies.[88]

Other Colonies

Not all the Basque children experienced the many vicissitudes catalogued above as occurring in England. On the contrary, the small colony at 121 Kingston Hill, London, was a stable one, continuing from August 1937, until early 1940.[89] It came into being in response to an appeal made to West Londoners to look after the children of the Spanish Republican soldiers. A committee was quickly formed, with a Methodist clergyman as chair, a Church of England vicar's wife as secretary, a well-traveled international banker as treasurer, and two local borough mayors as members. Lady Layton, wife of the owner of the Liberal paper, the *News Chronicle*, and Isobel Brown, a leading Communist spokeswoman, were patrons.

A large old house in poor repair, formerly used as a private school, was rented and furnished to receive its guests. Financial support had been promised by various trade union branches, cooperative societies, the "Round Table" (a social club of local small businessmen), and individual donors.

The house itself, built a century previously, stood in a secluded park of grand houses in fine gardens. It became at once a small island of the Basque country, noticeable as soon as one entered the small wicket gate. No attempt was made to change this. The daily routine and education were left to the Basque señoritas, the food was prepared by a Spanish-Basque cook, formerly employed on the French Riviera. He had given up his job to work at Kingston Hill. A short, heavy man, he insisted on wearing the classic tall chef's hat, always immaculately white, although his kitchen reeked of burnt olive oil and was never cleaned. The children nicknamed him "Cebollas" (Onions) and dearly loved to tease him. This he bore patiently, as he was devoted to them. He prepared the potato omelets, green beans, garbanzos, white beans, whatever little meat there was, with wonderful flavor and to the children's taste. To seek out Spanish and Basque foodstuffs, he traveled all over London. Once, the local cooperative sent over a side of bacon, the first such meat in a long time (the food budget per child was seven pennies per day). When the director came upon the cook pounding the meat with a small knife—to kill the maggots in it—she insisted he throw it out. "You are a Fascist," he shouted. "They've had no meat at all for so long."[90]

About two dozen volunteers from a broad political spectrum came regularly to take the children on walks or excursions, as they could not be left unsupervised. Some "adopted" a child by paying the ten shillings weekly needed for housing, food, clothing, and medical needs. Volunteers also helped plant a large vegetable garden, which supplied much of the fresh produce eaten during the summer and fall. One volunteer, a London fishmonger, supplied fish once weekly, and the local cooperative donated some staples and, occasionally, meat. This help from the community was invaluable:

> They [the volunteers] were exquisite: a Cockney window washer who organized a splendid summer camp for the children; a young Jewish Communist, very friendly—and modish—who brought sweets and whom the children called "Papagayo"; an old lady who took each of the older boys on individual outings. They organized sports teams: local boys versus the Basque boys in soccer, a real challenge in which the Basque boys usually won. The community volunteers came mainly because of their sympathy for the Spanish Republic rather than for humanitarian reasons, I think. All in all, there was tremendous solidarity in the home.

There were three dozen children at Kingston, ranging from four to fourteen years of age upon arrival. Brothers and sisters were kept together in the secular homes, and there were two families of five children each at Kingston. The young refugees were extremely warm and affectionate with each other, always walking about holding hands. There was little formal education, as the home had no teaching supplies and very little play equipment. Some books in Spanish were finally made available by the Basque Delegation, and children did maintain their reading and writing skills. Some of the older girls attended evening classes in English. Most, however, made little effort to learn English. In the words of one informant,

> this was a more or less passive, unconscious resistance. I believe that the same factors which made for happiness and cohesion in the home hampered that interest in the

outside world which would have been the main incentive for learning a foreign language.[91]

In spite of poor heating (one inefficient fireplace) and worse sanitary facilities (there was only one bathroom, and the washwater in the tub became black after a few children had been bathed), the youngsters were healthy and happy. When all children were compared, in mid-1938, to their photos upon arrival, all had gained weight and were developing normally. None regressed in toilet habits, and there was no stealing. Only at first did they hide small treasures, as well as their shoes and toothbrushes, under their pillows. The expected "separation trauma" made only one appearance: at the summer camp on the seashore, a full year after arrival, a few of the older boys relived the evacuation. Their memories were triggered by being once again by the sea, and they sat apart, silently staring at the moon and the water.

Typically, in this colony, also, the children themselves organized concerts, giving many in drafty church halls in west London. Such spontaneous presentations were a complete novelty and the concerts were very popular. A small entrance fee and an emotional collection appeal earned a great deal of money.

There was not one child or Basque staff person whose parents or family in Spain or France were living a normal life. Many fathers were killed in action, or in prison, or shot by Franco's troops. Many mothers were refugees in France, or in prison, or under "house arrest" in Spain.[92]

Kingston Hill home existed until well after the start of World War II, always self-supporting, never a drain upon the slender finances of the BCC. The last appeal letter, dated November 20, 1939, asked for fifty pounds for the last children who were to have been repatriated in October:

> There has been a delay, however, due to difficulties in arranging transport under present conditions. . . . We are faced with at least another month of existence without any financial reserve and a weekly expenditure of £25 which will be only half covered by our income. For most of our children who have refugee parents in France, and

> who cannot go back, we have been able to find private homes. Can you help us support, for these few weeks more, those who are soon to go back?[93]

Money was forthcoming; but the home closed early in 1940. Its existence long after the BCC had committed itself to repatriation was a triumph of will, and of the persistence of the children's concerts. Donations raised nearly half the costs, but the concerts raised a good third for over two and one-half years.[94] The utilization of Basque folklore for survival was a strand in the experiences of children in each host country. It was most consistently used in England, whose refugee children gave concerts as far away as Switzerland.

The Spanish Civil War ended in March 1939. As Barcelona fell, a massive stream of refugees poured into France. The NJCSR responded by setting up offices in Perpignan and Narbonne to help refugees in both major staging areas.[95] The British government, once again, gave no official help. Though the BCC still was given office space in the NJCSR central office, all funds were now needed for more pressing humanitarian work in France. Some sixteen hundred children still remained in colonies, in hostels for older children, or with adoptive parents. Just over one hundred lived scattered among eleven Catholic institutions. In all, well over two thousand children of Socialist, Communist, Left Republican, or Anarchist parents were cared for from their arrival in late spring of 1937 until their repatriation late in 1939. In spite of the fact that England herself had finally declared war on the Axis powers in September of 1939, and faced staggering difficulties in the ensuing long conflict, some six hundred of the original contingent of Basque children were allowed to remain. By war's end in 1945, exactly 410 were left, most of whom live in Britain at present.[96] Those who stayed on were usually over fourteen, and most had no family living in Spain able to receive them. Forty years later, their lives form an unusual mosaic of events and experiences, some of which have been captured in an ensuing chapter.

CHAPTER FOUR

Belgium: Flemish and Walloon Hospitality

Political forces in Belgium in 1936 on the eve of the Spanish Civil War had formed a stable coalition government which was dominated by the Socialists, the Catholic party, and, to a smaller extent, the Liberals. Trade unions were strong, and social legislation was far-reaching. Though there was unemployment, due to the aftermath of the worldwide depression, the Benefit Fund for Family Allotments, dating from 1930, served as an economic cushion for the unemployed, those with families, and those disabled or otherwise unable to be employed. In Belgium also, Catholic Action, the great modern movement of lay Catholic progressivism, was well nurtured and effective. Communists were a tiny minority, able to work collaboratively with the Socialists.[1]

Late in 1936, following the Italian invasion in Africa, the German reoccupation of the Rhineland, and the conclusion of the French-Soviet Pact, Belgium reasserted her traditional neutrality. She saw her future as best safeguarded by maintaining independence from the alignments of the power blocs in Europe—the German-Italian Axis and the British-French alliance were moving toward a confrontation. However, when the Insurgent coup positioned the Right against the

Spanish Republic, both trade union and Catholic organizations strove to assist the civilian population, particularly those with allegiance to the Republic.

Of the very first expedition of Basque children evacuated from Euzkadi, about half were sent to Mas Éloi (near Limoges, France), or to private homes in that country. The remainder, 230 in all, stayed on in Oléron until May, living in the great beach house in the dunes. They were told that they would soon go to live in Belgium with families who were waiting to care for them.

Help from the Left

The Belgian Socialist press had reported President Aguirre's appeal for help in evacuating women, children, and the old from Euzkadi, after the destruction of Guernica.[2] On April 30 *Le Peuple* quoted Basque officials in Paris as saying that the civilian population of Bilbao would be evacuated in merchant ships already in that harbor. The officials urged the assistance of the French navy in this humanitarian work, noting that England was already evacuating such civilians. By May 14, news of a more concrete, domestic interest appeared on page one—a lengthy appeal to the Socialist mothers of Belgium. The article noted that already some 630 homeless Basque children were en route from Oléron to Belgium. A home for each child had been promised by Belgian Socialists, but a serious problem had arisen. The majority of children even now on their way were boys, aged eight to twelve, but sixty-seven out of eighty requests from adoptive families were for little girls:

> Belgian women are saying it is more pleasurable to dress a little girl. But tragedy cannot serve to satisfy caprice or vanity. The lodging and care of a homeless child requires human solidarity beyond age or sex.

The lead article asked Belgian women to contact their regional Socialist committee that very day and state: "I admit my preference for a little girl. I am also disposed to take a boy of 6–12 years." By doing so, the article closed, "They would be assured of the kisses of thousands of small Basque children."[3]

The arrival of the first expedition was reported the following week, as well as news that more would arrive shortly.[4] In late May, some 230 children of the 450 who had left Euzkadi in mid-March took buses from Oléron to Paris, where they were greeted with flags and music. All then went on to Belgium. After crossing the frontier, they were given lemonade and a strange cheese, shaped like a squash. It was found to be very rich and good, though none of the children had ever seen anything like it before.[5] The children went to the shore at Ostend, fronting the North Sea, for another, shorter quarantine period, after yet another vaccination. As other expeditions with children destined for Belgium left Bilbao,[6] the press reported that M. Spaak, the Belgian Socialist Minister of Foreign Affairs, had agreed to participate at the cabinet level in the Basque evacuation. Though the form of collaboration was unclear, as Belgium had no fleet to participate in actual transport, financial help and the lodging of refugees were expected.[7]

Immediately, hundreds of children already in France were made ready to be sent on to Belgium. Cardinal Van Roey of Belgium, rumors said, was willing to take ten thousand into Catholic homes. The Socialists, Communists, the Committee for the Defense of the Spanish Republic, and the Belgian Red Cross would take others. In all, Belgium did care for nearly 3,200 children from Euzkadi, most remaining there until the outbreak of World War II.[8]

That spring the Belgian Communist press also published reports almost daily on the progress of the evacuation of Basque children. Within Belgium the Committee to Aid the Children of Spain had been formed by a group of Socialist women at about the same time as its counterpart, the Comité d'Accueil aux Enfants d'Espagne (CAEE), in France, in August of 1936.[9] Other groups were gradually added to the committee. Within weeks, the Socorro Rojo International (SRI), the Friends of Nature, the International Friendship League, and the Brussels Federation of Unions became active members. Initially, money was collected after lectures and concerts to provide food and clothing for Spanish children. Over 125,000 Belgian francs was raised in the first few months of the committee's existence for this purpose.[10] After the April appeal of President Aguirre for homes for Basque children, and entreaties from the Popular Fronts of first Euzkadi, and then Santander, the committee turned its attention to the enlistment of adoptive families. Front-page articles appealing for more adoptive homes appeared frequently, and one Belgian woman was lauded for taking in ten refugee children, certainly a heroic response.[11]

By the beginning of July, *La Voix du Peuple* commented that, though already thousands of Basque children had found adoptive homes in France and Belgium, additional thousands were on their way from the ports of Santander, and the transition centers of France were already overflowing.[12] The arrival of four hundred children was reported on July 1, with a distribution to waiting parents being accomplished in a mere ten minutes. The children, coming from Santander, were described as "very ill and tired, but well disciplined and arriving singing the *Internationale*."[13]

Problems arose in coordinating the dispersion of children with four different organizations in operation. A coordinating committee was formed in Paris among the groups offering shelter in both France and Belgium. To channel aid more effectively, the coordinating committee established liaison with the Spanish Republican authorities, with both Flemish and Walloon leaders, and with the various aid organizations.[14] However, in July, Belgian Minister of Foreign Affairs Spaak attempted to stem the flow of Basque children by refusing to admit a contingent of 550, newly arrived in France. *La Voix du Peuple* commented:

> We must disclose the revolting attitude of the Belgian reactionary-clerical press, who try to convince the people that these miserable small Basque refugees, among whom are several amputees from Fascist bombs, are from the Popular Front, and that the border should, therefore, be closed to them. Yesterday, the Belgian Embassy in Paris told the Belgian Committee that Spaak had

> decided to refuse authorization into Belgium. We know why: the arrival of refugee children profoundly impresses public opinion; seeing thousands of children fleeing the "solicitude" of the German and Italian forces in Spain. . . . The recent incident of the colony Val D'Or, in which 240 Basque refugee children in France became riotous, was actually provoked by the mobile guard giving them Fascist salutes. And here, both the Minister of Hygiene and the Central Police have no opposition to the arrival of the Basque children, and we understand the authorization will arrive soon for their coming. However, we will not relax our vigilance.[15]

The Socialists had begun to care for children in May, at the holiday resorts at Ostend, Newport, and Heyst, with halcyonic names such as "Mon Repos," "Happy Age," and "Peter Pan." The Socialist press commented that the children were "wrenched from their parents to save them and give them back their pink cheeks."[16] Anecdotes about the children appeared regularly in the press. Their fear of airplanes was remarked upon in Belgium, as in every host country. "When an airplane passed overhead, the children were overcome with panic, and disappeared into the cellar, coming out only with much cajoling."[17] A paragraph of sensible suggestions for adoptive parents to help assuage this fear appeared in May 22 on the front page of *Le Peuple*:

> Since the Basque children do not understand our languages, and gestures may not convince them that our airplanes are harmless, tell them: No hay que tener miedo cuando entendeis [*sic*] un motor de avion: no es Fascista, sino un avion de tus amigos Belgas.

After Bilbao fell, more Basque children arrived, as did many adult refugees. They had come via Santander, or Asturias, and were reportedly a "pitiful spectacle":

> Ten carloads arrived July 2 in Belgium: children like hunted animals; skeleton nursing mothers, feeble old men and women, a long procession of misery.[18]

All the unaccompanied children were sent to adoptive homes, the older men and women to a former military sanitorium near Malines, and the others to a large chateau set in a park within Marchin, now renamed the "Belgian-Basque Home." The expedition was welcomed by a huge crowd of townsfolk, which included the Mayor of Marchin and the Belgian Minister of Foreign Affairs. One reporter commented:

> In these Basque refugees, we see the profound grief of a people obliged to leave their country, a people martyred by Fascist aggressors. They greet us with the clenched fist, demonstrating their attachment to liberty.[19]

The nearly two thousand children placed by the Socialists, Communists, and the Committee for the Defense of the Republic were usually assigned singly to private homes. The majority were working-class families with children of their own to care for. One boy from Guernica found himself to be number thirteen in the family of a factory worker; a girl from San Sebastián was the eighth in a carpenter's home. Most found themselves with at least two adoptive sisters and brothers:

> My family was poor, but very affectionate. There were three sons, and I immediately became the "Princess," the mascot. Though the boys sat at table by age, I jumped into the chair next to "Father" and he let me stay. I spent all my allowance on sweets—what wonderful chocolates.
>
> It was like heaven in my family. I had three children to play with, be my confidantes, go on trips with. It was a high-class Communist family, very loving. My education was excellent; I got a prize when I went to school back here [in San Sebastián]. And the Christmases there; not just a little *turrón* [almond candy] and maybe a chicken, but such sweets, toys, presents such as gold chains, clothes, books.
>
> I gained twenty kilos in two years. We had wonderful Christmas celebrations—huge cookies, Papa Noël, candy, chocolates. My adoptive mother used five kilos of sugar weekly, "one for each."

The largest secular group, well over one thousand children, was the responsibility of the Socialist party. They were distributed all over Belgium and Luxembourg, with the majority housed around Brussels, and others in Malines, Antwerp, and Rexousart. The Communist Socorro Rojo cared for 320 children; the Grupo de Defensa, 312; and the Belgian Red Cross, 192. Of this last group, many were placed in orphanages and in the Basque refugee camp in Marchin. Over 1,200 children were placed under Catholic patronage.[20]

Catholic Help: The Baskische Kinderwerk

In southern France, provisional camps were being emptied of unaccompanied children as rapidly as possible, for by August hundreds of new youngsters were arriving from the evacuation of Santander and Asturias. Those departing under sponsorship of the PNV were to be sent on to the Catholic homes and institutions being arranged by Cardinal Van Roey of Malines. They were to be accompanied by a number of Basque priests in voluntary exile from Euzkadi. Already, delegates from the cardinal's new organization, Baskische Kinderwerk (Basque Children's Project) had arrived in France to select children from the various quarantine colonies.

As with the prelates in England and France, the Cardinal was responding to the appeal sent to him by Msgr. Múgica. The cardinal had the letter printed (in both Flemish and French) in the diocesan newspapers throughout Belgium, for Msgr. Múgica had added to each letter this handwritten request:

> I dare to ask your eminence that this letter be published in the Catholic press.[21]

Cardinal Van Roey added his response:

> I acknowledge a deeply moving appeal to help in this lamentable situation. Christian charity obliges us to do all possible to help the Basque children.[22]

The cardinal immediately began to organize a staff and send emissaries to France to locate and visit Basque children in the refuges and colonies. These scouts soon chose 1,265 children, three dozen of whom were aged two, three, and four years of age, with an additional 141 being only five or six years old. These children were noted on a 43–page "First

List: for the Basque Children's Project."[23] Curiously, a second list exists which contains 2,367 names of Catholic families who responded to the cardinal's appeal to offer shelter.[24] It appears that well over one thousand more Basque children could have been accommodated under Catholic auspices in Belgium than were ever actually assisted. According to teachers and priests interviewed, children who were not Basque-speaking were selected for transfer to Belgium.

The cardinal set three preconditions to his charitable offer: (1) that his proposed project for the care and education of Basque children work autonomously, without any official Basque intervention; (2) that an entity be designated as responsible for the transport of the children; and (3) that each child have a certificate of good health. The cardinal's personal secretary, Msgr. Le Clef, was placed in charge of the central administrative committee of the project, which had representatives from each of the three Belgian dioceses: Brussels, Antwerp, and Malines.[25]

The tradition of welcoming refugee children into Catholic homes in Belgium was frequently referred to in the Catholic press coverage of this new humanitarian work:

> We hope those who gave help to the Armenian children after the Great War, and later, the Hungarian children, will respond once more. The children will be aged 6 to 14, from all social classes. You need only to indicate what you prefer, and pledge to provide care for six months. The Committee is also caring for Basque priests and teachers who will act as translators. Let us also warn the public: don't request only girls.[26]

Within two weeks, the Basque government in Paris received word from Msgr. Le Clef that children aged five to twelve could be sent to Belgium, given that certain additional conditions be followed.[27] Sr. Izaurrieta, a young vigorous Basque heading the Commercial section in the government's office in Paris, responded that all conditions would be rigorously met. Much correspondence then ensued. Msgr. Le Clef requested that each child's Baptismal Certificate accompany him; Sr. Izaurrieta responded:

> Without exception, in a country such as ours, Baptism is administered to all children; but, because of wartime conditions, these documents cannot be located.[28]

He did agree that rebellious children would be returned to Spain, and that the Basque government would cover all travel expenses to Belgium, using the reduced price tickets made available to his government by the French government. Izaurrieta urged that the same concession be granted by the Belgian government. He assured Msgr. Le Clef that the Basque priests would need no salary, that the Basque teachers and aides could be housed in religious institutions or inexpensive pensions, and that together they would take the responsibility for the children's spiritual and material needs "in their own tongue." He added, in closing, that the priests would also prepare Basque-French vocabularies for the children.[29]

The next round of letters, only days before the collapse of Euzkadi, dealt with a new series of conditions laid down by Msgr. Le Clef. Sr. Izaurrieta wrote that, of course, the Basque government would do its best to send teachers with enough French to be effective, but it would be impossible to find any with perfect French. All personnel sent would be strictly instructed to make no political demonstrations, "in order not to wound the feelings of the country receiving them with such hospitality."[30]

A final letter went from Paris on June 17. Izaurrieta wrote that Msgr. Le Clef's second list of requirements had been received, but it was presently impossible to arrange to meet those until the children arrived in France:

> The events of the war are escalating rapidly. Today Rebel troops are at the door of Bilbao. Civilians are evacuating en masse: the roads to Santander are filled; the evacuation from that port will be more tragic than ever.

His letter closed by stating:

> I doubt that we can satisfy each family in the matter of the sex and age of the child desired. We will care for the unloading of the children in France. Please contact us

> directly at Bordeaux. If I can get away, I will visit you to inform and thank you personally.[31]

Most of the children selected by Cardinal Van Roey's emissaries left their camps with little regret.

> We were glad to leave our austere, unfriendly camp. But one of the teachers deceived us, promising us we were going nearer home. In Bermeo, though, I had studied French, and knew that Belgium was even farther. A few tried to run away home when I told them the truth.

Some sang as they crossed an indifferent or hostile France:

> Padre Arrue taught us a song he composed that we sang whenever our train stopped. He led us from the platform, and we leaned out the windows singing:
>
> Agur [name of town] maitia
> Kristin biotz duna
> Euzkaldun artia . . .*
>
> Some French people we passed would salute us with the clenched fist, not realizing that wasn't the ideology our parents taught us.

Their welcome in Belgium was warm and happy:

> It was like a honeymoon to go to Belgium. They brought us mountains of nice clothes; people brought us cakes and candy. We had quarantine in a castle in a beautiful park; so many came to welcome us.
>
> We came the day of St. John (June 24) to Brussels. Everything was in perfect order for us. At our first stop, people came to greet us, with big signs of welcome. They gave us sandwiches and mineral water; some of us didn't like the taste.
>
> Our children came looking like lepers—heads shaven, with mange, poorly dressed. But the people of Belgium took them in—thousands of compassionate Socialists, Communists, Catholics.

*Hello, beloved [town]; We are Christian and Basque-speaking.

Before leaving France, most children had been given numbered labels with the name of their adoptive family, and a color (red, green, or white) to indicate the diocese and corresponding town and rail station where each would be housed. Family groups were kept together until the final separation. This took place in the various parish halls, train stops, or town halls en route from the border to their destinations. For many children, it became a dreadful ordeal:

> They called out numbers; not our names. We were auctioned off like animals. I spoke only Basque and understood nothing.
>
> We were divided by numbers, like pieces of meat. Everyone was claimed but us. My sister was crippled, and no one wanted us three, so the Red Cross had to put us in a Belgian orphanage.
>
> It was like a meat market: the youngest and most tender went first. No one wanted the older ones.
>
> I was left off in Amberes, the Flemish zone. I thought they were speaking German, and Germany to me was evil—Guernica, the Condor Legion, bombs. I was terrified.
>
> It was the first time our little group was separated. My friends from childhood went to another town. I never saw any of them again. Our solidarity since Santurce was broken.
>
> Here came the tragedy—families would take one child only. My brother was taken by a rich-looking family; I clutched my little sister's hand to await our luck. My father was dead, my mother in France. I was her sole protector in the world. But she was led away sobbing.

A minority were able to stay together:

> My brothers and I were taken to a charity boarding school for children of canal bargemen. To us, a boarding school had always been my parents' greatest threat for bad behavior. But the nuns were wonderful to us four. Years later, I asked the one who chose us why she did so. "I was told to bring back two girls and two boys—for which

we had space. But seeing you four, looking so abandoned, I disobeyed the Mother Superior for the only time in my life and took you all."

The Catholic Adoptive Homes and Colonies

Some seven weeks after the Socialist and Communist Basque children were settled in Belgium, the first contingent of children to be cared for by the cardinal arrived. They had left the provisional camp in Capbreton the day before, accompanied by two Basque priests. Their coming to Belgium was described in the Catholic press as "From a spot in Hell to a place in Paradise." The feature article on June 30 remarked:

> These poor little ones were so attached to one another that brothers and sisters were placed in the same locale in order to make this second separation as painless as possible, especially after the cruel one from parents and country. Though it seemed impossible to keep families together, as charitable persons who had asked for one couldn't accept two or three, the magnanimity of Antwerp is always evident. Some accepted three instead of one, all arranged so that children left each other knowing addresses of brothers and sisters.[32]

The first four hundred Catholic children were dispersed—160 around Brussels, 90 around Malines, and 150 in the Antwerp area. The magnanimity noted in Antwerp was displayed throughout Belgium in caring for the 1,265 Catholic-sponsored children. Some 134 families took two children from the same family, and three families took three children each. About a third of the Catholic sponsors in all took more than one child of a family.[33]

It is difficult to conceive that the second separation in Belgium could be more traumatic for the children than the initial one in Euzkadi, yet many interviewed remarked that this was indeed the case. In Euzkadi, their parents had clearly chosen the best alternative—evacuation. It was to be a few weeks' respite from war, a summer vacation abroad with friendly people. Such attractions as the promised abundance of white bread, sweets, and an opportunity to see new sights ameliorated the sense of loss for many during the first leavetaking, especially for the older ones. During the voyage, such excitement and anticipation were reinforced by discussions with siblings, friends, and their mentors, the Basque teachers and priests. But by now, Bilbao had fallen, and most had heard nothing from families still in Euzkadi or in flight. And here, finally, in Belgium, the somewhat desperate camaraderie built up in the "centres de triage" was ruptured. Adding to the woes of some, the separations in Belgium came to be an explicit disobedience to parental instructions to care for younger siblings, a disobedience they were powerless to avoid.

In parish halls, political party social rooms, train stations, and municipal reception rooms, the distribution of children went on through May, June, July, and August. Many of the older boys, the most difficult to place in each host country, were sent to live in Catholic parish houses in groups of half a dozen. Some were placed in secular boarding schools, public orphanages or their Catholic counterparts, in groups of from a dozen to thirty, thus becoming a small minority among the Belgian children already there.

About a quarter of the children under Catholic auspices were housed and schooled in over fifty different Catholic institutes, boarding schools, convents, pensions, and parish rectories.[34] Those twenty-five children, for example, in Duffel in Brussels, the forty in Koningshof in Antwerp, and those who lived with parish priests, tend to have very positive memories of their stay in Belgium.

> Our handful of Basque boys lived with a phenomenal parish priest. He always carried his breviary and a French-Basque dictionary; sometimes he mixed them up and prayed from the dictionary. Besides his parish work, he was carpenter, mason, and painter to maintain our rooms—how he would sweat. He began by buying enough silk to make us, himself, an *ikurriña*, which hung from his balcony until we left. Until his death in the Belgian Congo over 20 years later, he wrote to me. A saint.

> Don Mateo was an authentic father to all of us. When we explained that we didn't write our parents for not know-

> ing the proper introductory form, he sat us all down and dictated, "Here there are many trees . . ." and four more lines. After we went to the zoo, each of us wrote, listing the animals, all exactly alike. The Belgian priest cut our hair badly: like the steps to the castle; Don Mateo trimmed it so we looked smart.
>
> My sister and I, six and seven, lived with wonderful motherly nuns for nearly three years. Since we could barely write, they wrote letters home for us. We went to school with Belgians who are still our friends; their homes are open to us.
>
> My brother and I, eight and nine, lived in a boys' school run by a small American order. Brother Robert was our father and mother, kind and loving. His every sentence began with "O.K., boys." Everyone else was Belgian in the school. I remember fighting with Jacques Brel, later to become a famous singer.

Visiting among brothers and sisters was encouraged:

> After we were separated, the priest I stayed with gave me a bicycle. I went right after breakfast with him to visit Iñaki. He had been chosen by a rich family, unlike me. But his eyes were swollen shut from crying. His family only spoke Flemish, and didn't even know what his name was. I calmed him, then went to visit Maria, who was content with her family.

Other children, almost invariably taken from among the very youngest evacuated, were placed in childless "adoptive" homes. The following accounts of three interviewees gives the flavor of this experience:

> My "family" was rich, high-class, rigid. I was very spoiled and sheltered from the street children; the family doll, with beautiful clothes and white gloves always. I lost my own personality, even my own family. I called my adoptive mother "Muke," I assimilated completely. I would see my sister—she was with a very poor family—only on her birthdays. I once told her I couldn't play with her, because she was "de la rue." Once I broke a tooth at school. I was terrified my family would turn me out, as

> everything had to be perfect in their house; all was appearance there.
>
> The couple was rich, childless. She suffered from nerves. She insisted I call her "Mother." I couldn't: my mother lived in Guernica. I was always sad and lonely. I tried to run away, but at seven it was hopeless. I remember the whole boiled potatoes, everything with mustard, such fatty bacon. I forgot how to speak Basque in the Flemish school. To this day, I am afraid of strangers who speak other languages.
>
> My family was poor and lived simply. He worked on the railroad, would drink heavily, and they would quarrel. She insisted I call her "Mu," but I didn't. I stayed "home" as little as possible. Soon, I was moved to Duffel.

The labors of the twenty-three (out of thirty-three) Basque priests in Belgium with the Basque children under the cardinal's auspices were fruitful. This group included most of the younger priests, some just ordained. As a group, they were strongly Basque Nationalist in political sympathies. Recall that at this time some of their colleagues had already been imprisoned or shot for active espousal of Basque autonomy. This cadre of priests contained talented musicians, including the organist and composer from Bilbao's famous chapel of Our Lady of Begoña. Priests renowned for their work with youth in Euzkadi, linguists who prepared the Basque-French-Flemish-Spanish dictionaries and catechisms, experts in folklore who could teach and demonstrate Basque songs, dances, play the *txistu* (flute) and drum, and tell the stories of their heritage, as well as highly trained educators—all taught the children in Belgium.

A chorus of ninety trained voices was formed to tour the country; smaller choral ensembles were formed in each diocese. Many parish events soon were graced with a demonstration of traditional Basque music. The cardinal himself arranged programs for the children under his care, bringing the many small groups in each diocese together for a day of singing, dancing, and music. The younger priests were also active in promoting athletic events, particularly soccer.[35]

Nor did the spiritual field of endeavor lack emphasis. One priest interviewed recalled giving religion classes for a variety of age levels to over three hundred children in the Brussels region. In a letter written in 1937, he described the system of Catholic boarding schools in each diocese, attended by Basque priests, with other priests visiting the diverse centers of refugee children, each caring for the spiritual needs of about forty children. From this, many hundreds of First Communions resulted, including "many from children under Socialist or other auspices."[36] The Basque priest attached to Koningshof wrote:

> Our daily religious life is as follows:
>
> Upon arising, a pledge to the Virgin; immediately followed by daily Mass in our chapel, in which almost all participate; then blessing before and after each meal; daily Vespers, solemn exposition, the Rosary, and Benediction, with liturgical songs. All this is exclusively for our Basque children. On going to bed, another pledge to our Virgin.
>
> Those cared for in adoptive families also have our help, that of us refugee priests. We meet with them each Thursday. We don't limit ourselves to children of the PNV, but have many instances of children of Red or abandoned parents who have made their First Communion with us; in our case, seven in all.[37]

The importance of the symbols of Basque nationalism and of their homeland were reported frequently by those interviewed. Several, for example, mentioned that the weekly visits by Basque priests to their group in the village where they were living were of great importance in affirming their identity as Basques. These visits in several cases were held under a large tree near the parish church or town square. In every case, this tree became their own Tree of Guernica. In Castresana's autobiographical novel *El Otro Arbol De Guernica*, a tree in the orphanage-boarding school where he lived became the center for the handful of Basque boys there, as well as the motif of his book.[38]

In a similar manner, the *ikurriña* came to have great symbolic importance to the children of Basque nationalist homes in exile. The group at St. Norbert House in Duffel had theirs, designed by their Basque priest, as did the Koningshof colony. All the folkloric presentations displayed this banner, an integral part of the singing of patriotic hymns. The indigenous flute and drum accompanied the children to Belgium. Younger boys were taught to play by the Basque priests. Clearly, one of the necessities for ethnic survival in the Flemish- and French-speaking Belgian society was the cultivation and display of the rich musical gifts of their own country.

A final important symbol was the major soccer team in Vizcaya, the Atletico de Bilbao. During interviews, descriptions of the spontaneous formation of sport teams by the Basque boys was frequent, including one which was formed by youngsters en route to their destination:

> We stopped for lunch at a Belgian orphanage. I remember that as soon as we saw some Belgian boys, with gestures we invited them to play soccer. It was the first of many matches, Euzkadi vs. Belgium; we, of course, being the Atletico de Bilbao.

Castresana's book recounts the tremendous importance of the striped red and white jersey of the "Atleti" to the enclave of Basque boys in his school.

As part of the cardinal's Basque project, some two dozen young Basque women, trained as teachers, were placed throughout Belgium. One woman, in charge of those working in Brussels, recalls that all were volunteers who received no salary beyond board, room, and small expenses. They visited children in adoptive Catholic families. The group under Srta. Carmela's direction visited each family weekly, to teach Basque, Spanish, and some catechism, while monitoring each child's adjustment. In spite of these informal lessons, some children forgot their native tongue (especially the youngest), exposed as they were all day to French or Flemish at home and school. In addition, the only books available were catechisms and some dictionaries, but no textbooks. One of the director's assistants described the important role of safeguarding the child's happiness in his adoptive family. In a few cases, it became necessary to change the child to another adoptive family.

The most frequent problems were with the childless families expecting that the child call them "Mama" and "Papa" (Muka, Mu), and with a very few families who requested a child simply to help with farm work. The women workers in the former case suggested alternate terms, as "Aunt," "Uncle"; in the latter, the child would be taken and placed in a non-exploitative family. But the vast majority of children got along very well, especially those in families with children about their own age. They received ample affection, good food and care, lots of sweets and chocolates, good clothing, and an education in most cases superior to what they would have experienced in Euzkadi. The girls in Catholic boarding-houses were especially petted. There were few signs of typical regressive behavior—bedwetting, thumbsucking, or stealing—though some of the younger children reportedly cried a great deal at first.[39]

In contrast to France and Britain, rebellion among the older boys had been defused at the outset by placing them with parish priests, under the maternal care of the priest's housekeeper. Both teachers who were interviewed reported that the children in their care only became violent when Franco was praised in their presence; some tore down posters with his picture, others fought Belgian boys who praised him. Great effort was made by the priests and teachers to find the whereabouts of the children's parents after the fall of Bilbao, so that correspondence could be resumed. The fatherly and motherly support of such Basque mentors was clearly invaluable to the adjustment of the children in Belgium.

The Family Allowance

An advantage enjoyed by the Basque children living in Belgium was that most of their adoptive parents were eligible for a national family allowance dating from 1930. The Socialist Belgian government was unique in providing this subsidy to many of the families caring for a Basque child. Though the regulations were clear that only when the natural parents were dead, ill, or had "truly abandoned" their child was the allowance to be available, this was interpreted so broadly that funds were disbursed to many host families. The Minister of Labor had a letter distributed in January 1938, stating:

> Families who care for Basque children have asked me concerning the Family Allowance. I have answered that families can [receive] benefit for children that are really abandoned or [where] their natural parents are absolutely incapable of exercising parental responsibilities. It is possible that the Minister of Social Planning may extend the 1930 requirements, given the present troubled situation in Spain. Either the Belgian consul or Spanish authorities could attest to the natural parents' abandonment due to circumstances. It is desirable that the Pay officer [of the allowance] expedite this in each area.[40]

Clearly, some impetus for this unprecedented help came from the office of Cardinal Van Roey, as did pressure from the secular political parties. Van Roey's office continued efforts to ease requirements. In March, it circulated a letter with sample statements attesting to the "abandonment of Basque children," noting that, at present, only those families already receiving allowance for their natural children could be granted a stipend for their adoptive Basque children, which ranged from three to four hundred francs each month. His office then initiated inquiries with the Tax Minister regarding families claiming Basque children as tax dependents, but found only "total orphans" could so qualify a host family.[41]

The Basque government, by now in exile in France, apparently had very minimal relations with the thousands of Basque children in Belgium. Telesforo Monzón of the PNV acted as the representative for a period, though no one interviewed recalled his work there on their behalf. At the outset, as noted, the cardinal had set the pre-condition that there be no official Basque intervention. Interview material indicates that the cardinal's secretary, Msgr. Le Clef, was decidedly pro-Franco, and the cardinal's own politics were unclear. Certain tensions developed as a result. These are well summarized in a long letter sent to Leizaola in Paris from the Spanish Republican ambassador in Brussels, Sr. Mariano Ruiz, in January 1938:

> In matter of the 1,500 Basque children sponsored directly by the Archbishop of Malines [Cardinal Van Roey], my inquiries have brought only disdainful and indirect responses, always by the secret channels of his Eminence. To date, I have been unable to obtain the addresses of the families caring for them. When Sr. Monzón came as your delegate, my soul was quieted. The cardinal himself received Sr. Monzón, but would still not release the list. I have tried to locate this information in other ways, but it appears the cardinal's jurisdiction is total. Even the Socialist party secretary was no help.[42]

As a result of such a thorough lack of cooperation, there was no role for the representatives of Aguirre's government. Though both his own mother and younger brothers took up residence in Brussels, and did visit the Basque children and attend their folklore presentations, there was no official presence.

The Casa de España, attached to Sr. Ruiz's consulate in Brussels, was somewhat more effectively involved. All the children who were the responsibility of secular groups were visited periodically by personnel from the Casa. Problems with host families and correspondence with parents were handled in this way. There was little or no emphasis on regional Basque folklore or maintenance of the language for this large group. Religious practice was left to the Basque priests and to the host families. However, the Casa did help to maintain contact among the Basque children under secular auspices. Concerts and films of the Civil War were presented to the large contingent of Basque children in the Brussels area. Some books written in Spanish were also distributed, especially to the secular boardinghouses, and a library was organized for the use of the children.[43]

The issue of language was more complicated in Belgium than in other host countries, since there are two official languages—Flemish in the north, and French in the center and south. Since both languages are required for normal life in the north, and Flemish is considered provincial by the French-speaking south, a number of the children became quadrilingual. This included about half of those in Catholic settings, since seven of eleven colonies and adoptive homes were in the Flemish area.[44]

For these children, the Basque personnel prepared vocabularies and catechisms in the four languages: Basque, Spanish, Flemish, and French. Such language facility acquired in natural use in everyday situations is not unexpected.[45] Most of the children of Europe are at least bilingual, and many Belgian children learn to speak three languages. The Basque children, in every country, learned to use the languages of their hosts.

The experiences of the Basque youngsters in Belgium were quite uniformly positive. This fact was highlighted by a number of interviews with Basques who, as children, spent weeks or months in France before going to Belgium, or by those who left Belgium to rejoin parents who had fled to France. In every case, the Belgian years were those remembered with most pleasure.

CHAPTER FIVE

Basque Children in the Soviet Union: The Sovieticos

Just as was the case with the "Democratic" (non-Fascist) countries already viewed, the Soviet Union signed the Non-Intervention agreement in 1936. Thus, for a time, its help was limited to shipments of food and clothing for noncombatants in the Spanish Republic. Throughout the Soviet Union, meetings which demonstrated solidarity with the Spanish people were conducted. Pledges of aid were printed in *Pravda*, as were complete texts of the speeches given at such rallies. Trade unions within the country sponsored fund drives, raising over two million dollars in less than a month for the Republican cause. Soviet leaders were elated by the revolution, a vindication of their political beliefs, while the Russian people felt a genuine fraternity with the proletariat fighting in Spain. As we have seen, the Socialist- and Communist-assisted organizations in many nations also raised money, and sent in food, clothing, and needed medical supplies. Estimates range as high as fifty million dollars for the value of the food shipments sent in from Popular Front and union groups internationally.[1]

After the battles throughout Spain during July, August, and September of 1936, as the full extent of Axis military support for the Insurgents became apparent, Stalin began to ship war materiel into the Spanish Republic. The International Brigade was also conceived, and recruitment of its soldiers began. Though headquartered in France, its genesis and organization was directed from the Soviet Union. Stalin's fear of a Fascist victory in Spain was related to the security of the Soviet Union as well as his desire for a Popular Front victory. Stalin saw clearly that an Insurgent success would isolate France, now an integral part of Soviet external security.[2]

In Euzkadi in the early spring of 1937, Stalin and the military help his country was sending to the Republican cause were well publicized in the Leftist press. There had been Soviet planes and aviators in Bilbao since the previous October.[3] La Pasionaria,* a Basque Communist, was known and respected by many Basques. It was not surprising, then, that when, in Euzkadi in early May, it became known that Russia had offered to host Basque children, working-class Basque parents eagerly signed up their children for the expedition.[4] A few even had relatives who had escaped to Russia after the Asturian miners' revolt was crushed by the government in 1934.

> We all knew a great deal about the Soviet Union from letters my cousin sent us. He had a good job there, after he fled for his life from Gijón late in 1934. He had been involved in the strike in the mines there, and had been one of the leaders, so the authorities were after him.[5]

Others had relatives who had visited Russian ports as sailors.

The First Two Expeditions

The first contingent of Basque and Spanish children to arrive in the Soviet Union, however, were twenty-one sons and daughters of Republican pilots and Communist Party officials. They had left the Madrid area for Valencia, then sailed for Odessa from Cartagena on the ship *Gran Canarias* on March 17, 1937.[6] Coincidentally, they arrived in their host

*The name given to Dolores Ibarruri, the leading spokeswoman of the Spanish Communist party.

country the same day the first group of Basque children evacuated from Bilbao arrived in France. The "Sovieticos" were housed immediately in a summer camp in the Crimea, ordinarily used by the Pioneers, the Soviet youth organization.

All of them were upper middle class, as the children of officers and officials, and included Amaya, La Pasionaria's daughter. They had some trouble adjusting to the sons and daughters of Basque miners and laborers and factory workers who joined them in the Soviet Union a few weeks later. Some of these early arrivals, when interviewed in 1979, remarked upon the terrible language and poor manners of the refugee children joining them in June.

> Our small group had known one another for some time. We all played on the beach in Valencia together. With increased bombardments, our parents decided to send us to Russia, just for a few months, until things looked better in Spain. We were kept apart there until summer, when a very large group of Basque children arrived. They were unschooled, hungry, and were wise beyond their years. Their fathers were miners, factory workers; they were all from the poorest class.

The second expedition was composed of 1,745 children from sixty Basque towns and villages. The largest number came from around Bilbao (446), and there were 122 refugees from San Sebastián. Most of the balance were from Eibar and other industrial areas of Euzkadi. A few children were refugees from Navarra and Alava, whose parents had fled these Franco-held zones shortly after the Civil War began.[7] All their parents were Leftists—Socialist, Communist, Anarchist, or Left Republican. When these children arrived in Leningrad, they were all singing the "Internationale" and giving the *puño*.

Though the Basques pride themselves on being Europe's oldest democracy, class consciousness certainly exists among them. These children were from the very poorest sections in Bilbao—the industrial belt, laced with rows of old decaying six-story stone apartments, surrounded by the noxious steel mills lining the filthy miles of the city's harbor. The constant fog and rain there mixed with factory smoke to stain the roofs and walls with dripping grey muck.

Basque families, rich or poor, were large. Many of the children evacuated had two or more siblings with them, and a baby or two left at home with their mother. Some fathers worked in the iron mines in nearby Gallarta, the village where La Pasionaria had been born and reared. She had experienced personally the exploitation that for generations had been the lot of Basque miners. Others worked on the docks, in the mills, in shipbuilding, or in transport.

The growth of the Communist Party in the Basque country since the beginning of the Civil War mirrored its phenomenal growth in other parts of Spain. Its membership in Euzkadi had risen from a couple of thousand in 1932 to perhaps twenty-two thousand by June of 1937.[8] The major strength of the party in Euzkadi was in the working-class neighborhoods of San Inazio, Sestao, Zorroza, Baracaldo, Portugalete, and La Peña, and in the industrial towns, such as Eibar, near the Guipúzcoan border. Parents from these areas knew that there was little or no chance that their children would have better lives than their own or a decent education. Many felt certain that salvation for their families lay in the unification of the proletarian masses against their capitalist bosses.

The Basque Communist leadership which emerged was strongly committed to autonomy; it was "Red-Separatist," a position that was anathema to the Spanish and International Communist Party leadership. Another feature distinguished Basque Communists from Communists elsewhere. Many remained at least nominal Catholics, or allowed their wives and children to practice the faith. For the first deviation, his Basque separatism, the Basque Communist Party leader, Manuel Astigarrabia, was quietly deposed after the fall of Bilbao.[9] His removal and the ideological climate encountered in Russia were to deprive the Basque child refugees there of the opportunity to practice their faith. Regional differences were de-emphasized also, though some opportunities to celebrate their Basque culture and folklore were provided. However, the Basques were usually lumped with the Leftist "Spanish Republican" children and all were treated alike.

In Euzkadi, as the Northern Campaign was being planned by Franco, the Communist newspaper *Euzkadi Roja* had achieved the largest circulation in the country, some forty-four thousand copies being sold daily in the late winter of 1936 and spring of 1937.[10] When small groups of Republican children began to be evacuated to Russia, it was reported in this periodical's pages, beginning April 2.[11] A month later, word came that the Russian ambassador in Valencia had begun arrangements for a ship to transport Basque children to Russia.[12] At the same time, a representative of the Russian government contacted Sr. Gracia with the offer to care for fifteen hundred Basque children, aged seven to twelve, with preference to those whose fathers had died in battle. Gracia accepted the offer which came with a clear set of conditions:

1) Only those children whose parents voluntarily gave permission in writing could be evacuated;
2) The Soviet government would care for all the children's needs in Russia, placing them in colonies or with families;
3) The children would be educated by Spanish teachers already sent by the Republican government into Russia;
4) Asistencia Social was to correspond continuously with the children, as well as keep the parents informed, using a file on each child, made with three copies;
5) The children would be repatriated when their parents wished.[13]

By means of posters, radio announcements, and articles in the press, the Russian offer was publicized throughout Euzkadi.

Only those who had signed up their children in the Communist Party headquarters could be taken. The head of Asistencia Social had assured the public that the largest possible number would be sent, and that they would be educated with other Republican children from Madrid, Valencia, and Barcelona.[14]

By June 6, lists of children numbered from 1 to 1,745, along with their teachers and aides, were published in the Communist daily. A special commendation was printed, welcoming the large contingent from Eibar, Guipúzcoa, sponsored by Comrade Gracia from that city. All had come to Vizcaya when Eibar fell to Franco some weeks earlier. It was also reported that Spanish textbooks and recreation books would accompany the children on their trip to Russia, so that their language would not be forgotten. In addition, the Ministry of Justice and Culture sent in several sets of schoolbooks. With the children went a director, a doctor, four nurses, and a number of Basque teachers.[15]

The expedition set sail for France on June 11 in the early morning, just a week before the fall of Bilbao. Upon arrival in France, the 1,745 children destined for the Soviet Union were separated and sent on to Leningrad, while the balance, some 2,855, remained in France. Pictures and stories appeared in the Bilbao press, along with word that an additional 3,000 would soon be sent to Russia under auspices of Red Help International.[16] *L'Humanité* in Paris, and other Communist papers, reported the event.

The separation of children in Bordeaux, France, went smoothly, though a few very young children destined for France became confused and almost ended up in Russia. All were assured that they would be home for Christmas, as their parents and everyone involved believed. Throughout the evacuation, the wishes of the parents were scrupulously respected by the Basque government. As an example, correspondence in the Archives of the Basque Government-in-Exile indicates that some pressure was later placed on that government that Basque children already in England or France be sent on to the Soviet Union. Leizaola responded to these suggestions by writing that all political groups could send their children to any host country "without fraud." He, himself, with six expatriate children, alone had the right to determine where to send his children, just as did every parent. He recommended that the Delegation for Spanish Children Abroad, established late in 1937 under Sr. Ormas and Communist Minister of Education Jesús Hernández, stop such tactics.[17]

The Basque children who were to become the Sovieticos

were put aboard the *Sontay*, a coal ship, carrying an all Indo-Chinese crew. On board, the children were given tea, a beverage they were to become fond of during their years in Russia. At this time, however, they threw the cups of tea overboard. All slept crowded in the hold. Many were frightened by the strange crew with whom they were unable to communicate. Since the ship usually carried coal, it was dirty and ill-kept. The children were given little food, and even then, with the rough passage, they vomited onto the mattresses. The voyage was in every sense a disaster.

The citizens of Leningrad had been well prepared by the press for the arrival of this contingent of Basque child refugees from the Northern Campaign. Dispatches from the *Sontay* were printed daily, as well as several ingenuous notes to Russia from the children en route:

> We pioneers from the Basque country are touched by the affection and care you manifest toward us. We are very thankful and will try to justify your help.
>
> In defense of our country, we send you our best greetings.[18]

In contrast to their miserable sea voyage, the incredible reception has been etched in their memories. At the wharves in Leningrad were thousands of Russians waving their handkerchiefs. Sirens were blowing and bands were playing. The children were taken off, and bathed carefully by "jolly nurses in such clean big white aprons." They were deloused if necessary, and had their hair combed and pomaded. Each was given four suits of new clothes; these light green uniforms were to characterize the "Spanish Children" throughout the Soviet Union for months to come. They were then escorted by Young Pioneers to a special program organized in their honor. It was held in the Palace of Young Pioneers, an immense and ornate palace of the tsars. There, they were the guests of honor at a huge banquet.

> It was a fabulous reception they gave for us. There was a love for Spain expressed by the people in every way. They gave us a dinner, with our nearly 2,000 small selves

> as the honored guests. Such meat, fishes, breads, everything. And for dessert, the best of the best cakes and cookies. It was unforgettable.

They recall eating voraciously after the dreadful sea voyage. It was during the season of the "white nights" in Leningrad, close as it is to the Arctic Circle. The strange and luminous day into night both excited and frightened the children.

Their arrival in Leningrad was reported in *Pravda* thus:

> Large buses roll up to the Palace of Pioneers, with dark children's heads looking out, waving red flags, calling, "Viva Russia." . . . In two ranks, hundreds of young Lenin Pioneers are ranged; music of the Pioneer orchestra, with its girl drummer, sounds; bouquets of flowers fly to greet our Basque child refugee guests. They ascend by marble staircases through gilded state rooms. The Basque children are struck by the wealth and splendor: "Such palaces appear only in fairy tales, and besides, belong only to the king." Friendships are quickly made as the young Pioneers give scarlet ties, the badges of Pioneers, to their guests. Older Pioneers carry the little three- and four-year-old Basque children to stroll among ancient trees in the lovely garden outdoors. Later, the "Internationale" is sung in Russian and Spanish. The Basque children are invited to rest, be happy and learn, by the Pioneer secretary. Francisco Arnaiz of Bilbao spoke in return saying, "Our fathers are fighting in Republican Spain. When they have won, we will create a Spain without abandoned children, with palaces such as you have here."[19]

The children were taken on sightseeing tours of Leningrad and then by train to Moscow, some four hundred miles away. From there, they were dispersed to sanitoria in the district to rest and recuperate. Most were sent on to Pioneer summer camps at resorts in the Odessa area at Artak on the sea, near vineyards, in beautiful green parks, or in the Crimea. Well-equipped buildings had been carefully readied:

> Everything was sparkling clean. There was snow white linen on the little beds. Canopies had been built over the spacious terraces. Small tables and chairs had been in-

> stalled. An abundance of toys, bicycles, dolls, balls, and cars awaited. Posters and pictures on the walls will remind children of their homeland. Local Pioneers were impatient for their Basque guests, and brought bouquets of flowers to welcome them. Basque sailors in Odessa, from a ship carrying lemons, excitedly embraced the children when they arrived. One Basque child showed bullets and shrapnel from Guernica from his house, destroyed by German and Italian bombs.[20]

The news of the Basque children was reported daily, in human interest stories written in *Pravda*. Some of their diary entries were published, as were excerpts from their letters written home to parents. There were interviews such as:

> I never expected anything like this. They give you as much food as you wish; I've already put on 1½ kilos. It's especially nice in the evening, when we organize songs and dances. I am embroidering Papa a military bag. Mama, what happiness.
>
> I have here my own real bed. Everything is cleanliness. We will soon be meeting Russian children, and I am making a gift for my future comrade—a model air plane.[21]

A film on the Basque children's arrival was prepared and shown in both Leningrad and Moscow.[22]

When summer had passed, the children left their Pioneer camps and returned to Moscow to begin classes. They had, indeed, been able to rest, regain their health, and be happy. Reports published in *Pravda* noted that José Barrárez had gained 8.5 kg, Francisco Navarro, 5.3 kg, and that the children had sent Comrade Stalin a note of thanks.[23] The children found the climate near the Black Sea much more pleasant than in Euzkadi. Their health returned; even those with running sores from malnutrition improved. Several with scarlatina or tuberculosis, however, went to hospitals. All remarked that they were treated like princes, with their own special beach, ample food (six meals a day), and many trips to nearby points of interest.

The expected interchange with Russian children did not

materialize. Apparently, it was decided that, in order to accustom the children to collective life, and to preserve their language and culture, they should be educated separately, and reared apart from Russian children. According to La Pasionaria:

> We, the Spanish, were like an island, independent of the fact that we had close ties with all the Soviet organizations. We Spaniards considered ourselves always united, and our politics were Spanish and oriented toward maintaining the children so that they might not forget their language and accustom themselves to think of their country, to which they would return and where their lives would continue. To this end, every help was given us by the Soviet authorities, including bringing Spanish teachers, organizing schools for the children—everything we needed.[24]

The Third Expedition

As the Civil War progressed and the situation became increasingly desperate for the Republican cause, more refugee children arrived in Russia. In late September, after the fall of Bilbao, Santander, and Asturias signaled a complete Insurgent victory in the Northern Campaign, two ships from Gijón arrived in Leningrad after a stopover in England. They were the *Cooperatizie* and the *Njersinski* bearing 1,061 Asturian and Basque children. With them came twenty-six teachers and sixty-one nurses and aides. Many of this group were reported to be orphans. Most were from very large families, with as many as five coming from one home. A toddler of three, one of many three-years-olds in this group, was described in the press as arriving brandishing the Communist *puño,* and saying "Tovarish" to all. Most were children of miners, and were reported as having loosed some "hot Spanish curses" when they glimpsed an Italian (Fascist) ship in the harbor at Leningrad.[25]

Another smaller group arrived the following March, seventy-two in all, child refugees from Madrid and Valencia. They brought with them three Spanish teachers and their own Spanish textbooks.[26] Other very small groups arrived throughout 1938, and after the war's end in 1939, but they were no longer reported in *Pravda*. In all, it appears that between three thousand and five thousand children from Spain went to Russia. Jesús Hernández, Communist minister of instruction in the Republican government, gave the higher figure in 1953, ten years after he had left the Soviet Union.[27] Others, including historian Comin Colomer, and Rafael Miralles, a Cuban diplomat in Moscow from 1944–45, report a total of four thousand.[28] One Basque teacher, who taught the children in both Kiev and Moscow, contends that about three thousand children arrived from Spain, well over two-thirds being Basque.[29] Valentín González, who lived in Moscow from 1939–49, uses the figure of 5,863 children and adults, with some 1,700 Basque children arriving in 1937.[30] Whatever the actual totals, all the Basques interviewed agreed that they spent four years "living like princes and princesses, being educated in the best manner possible, like being in a Paradise."

Education

Their education took place in a series of Children's Houses and youth boarding schools, mainly in the vicinity of Moscow. There were fourteen schools in all, ranging in size from about 100 to 350 children. In Moscow there were five Children's Houses, as well as the boarding schools Pravda, Petrovska-Numovski, and Krasnovidov. Others were set up in Leningrad, the Crimea, and in the Ukraine.[31]

The children were enrolled in the two youth groups all Soviet children joined, the Pioneers for those eleven through fourteen years of age, and the Komsomols, for those 15 years and older. Their education was according to the Soviet plan, with a primary course of four grades, followed by a secondary through grade seven. After this, most attended the state schools, completing grades eight to ten there, before going on to further training in the university, a technical school, or in a factory.

The children enjoyed the close friendships formed in collective life, which took the place, they report, of familial love. They were happy, and were being educated in a very careful and well-planned way. These children enjoyed rich cultural experiences—theatre, ballet, art museums, excursions, the circus. All these would have been unattainable for them as children of poor miners and factory workers in Euzkadi. Though the schools were large institutions, the youngest children were educated in small groups of about eight, each with a special nurse in charge. These nurses were especially trained and were described as unusually supportive and loving with the three-, four-, five-, and six-year-old Basque children. The older children also had very fine teachers who dedicated their lives to them.

> There was never a lack of affection in our schools there. The Russians always treated us with a love and sympathy that is unforgettable. I think it was better than that our own parents showed us when we returned here. I can't say more than that.
>
> We arrived in Russia more savage than civilized. After all, our families were all large and poor. We were totally uncultured, without any academic preparation. The experience in Russia changed our lives. We became educated, thinking persons.
>
> The Soviet Union and its government has its vicissitudes, its defects, certainly. For example, one would expect that, by now, people would have a little more. But in the matter of its relationship to the Spanish people, when we were there, we can only feel gratitude.

The son of a Basque pilot, in the Republican forces, from the upper middle class commented:

> After us, the sons of miners and workers came from the north, foul-mouthed, badly behaved, destroying the toilets, making extra work for our teachers. But all learned, little by little, thanks to these teachers.

The daughter of a worker from Bilbao, who came with her four brothers:

> Our own parents only gave us slaps on the cheek and complaints, but the teachers there were so incredibly patient and helpful and loving to us.

But one of the Sovieticos, a professor of Spanish in the Soviet Union, notes:

> The collective life both forms and deforms. The formation is wide, far-ranging, but in a certain mold. The deformation is in the lack of richness of ideas; we were more like robots. Nothing was ever "mine," always "ours." It was necessary for the struggle to fight as a group. As a result, I'm a realist, perhaps a bit cold. But I could never be a fanatic for any ideology.

One of the very youngest to go to Russia:

> When I was four, I, with my brothers, was evacuated, first from Bilbao, then Gijón. I left Gijón as my mother was giving birth to my baby sister. But, in spite of lacking my mother's care, in the Children's Houses of Russia the nurses cared for us lovingly, just like real mothers, and we were happy.

All children enjoyed the sport program, which included skating, skiing, and water sports. There were classes in photography, ballet, and sewing. There were few discipline problems despite the fact that the children came to Russia after months of enduring war, and from very poor neighborhoods that were often chaotic, with children living "in the streets." Corporal punishment of Spanish children was not permitted and teachers patiently calmed many children who had been neglected. Little by little they interested them in learning. Everywhere the children went, always accompanied by their teachers or nurses, they were greeted warmly by the Russian people:

> In lines for the cinema, or the buses, Russians stood aside to let us go first, or relinquished their seats to us. In the country, people approached to give us fruit, or sweets or flowers.

The children were glorified just as the heroes of the Spanish Revolution were. Modesto, Lister, El Campesino, and La Pasionaria were all well known in the Soviet Union. One of the Basque teachers who lived in Russia for eighteen years felt that the Russian people romanticized Spain as the country of the sun, so lacking in much of Russia. Russians, according to him, are very predisposed to read Spanish literature; many classics are well known there. Spanish themes are common in Russian classical ballet. According to a British historian of dance, Douglass Kennedy, masters of the St. Petersburg Ballet came to Euzkadi in the nineteenth century. As a result of seeing the Basque folk dances, they incorporated many of its elements into the classic Russian ballet repertoire. The Russians were amazed at the energy, grace, and aesthetic sense displayed by these unschooled Basque dancers.[32]

During the period of the Civil War, many popular Soviet novels had as their hero a brave and heroic Spanish Republican fighter. In the theatre, plays about the war in Spain were frequently staged. This keen interest in the struggle of Spanish democracy against the Fascists even extended to popular dress, with the Republican Army cap, in its Soviet version, becoming a fad, worn by men and women alike. Though the average citizen of the Soviet Union was not aware of the actual Russian military involvement in the Spanish Civil War during its opening stages, they were enthusiastic about welcoming its child refugees. Photos of the Basque youngsters appeared in the popular *Literaturnaya Gazeta*, including one of Amaya, La Pasionaria's daughter, who arrived in the March expedition. In June, photos of the Basque children in their summer camp appeared, along with a sentimental poem of tribute to these brave children of the struggle.[33] While any personal interchange was minimal after the initial greetings and welcomes, the Russian people attended the many folklore presentations produced by the children.

Each colony of children had both a chorus and a dance group, which appeared at Soviet festivals and other events, always garbed in handmade regional costumes. The Basque children were taught the traditional songs and dances by their teachers and the older children. A few Basque sailors visited the children during their summers near the port of Odessa, and taught them the Weavers Dance and the Sword Dance. The Catalans and Asturians, other major regions represented, also were part of these presentations. Several Basque children achieved some national acclaim. For example, Maria Escogarria sang Basque songs on national radio, and Aurora Aguirre from Bilbao received the Order of Lenin for her dancing. *La Jota Vasca* was presented by the Bolshoi Ballet, and David Oistrakh made a recording of Basque songs, which he arranged and played. A ballet troupe of Basque girls and boys also toured Russia. And even before their arrival, a Basque soccer team had toured Russia in 1936, leaving as champions.[34]

The textbooks and courses of study the children used were all in Spanish. Russian was introduced gradually. A special anthology of Spanish literature was prepared and edited by the Soviet Commissar of Culture. This spanned the major works produced in Spain from the twelfth to the sixteenth century and included Cervantes, Lope de Vega, and even "La Celestina." Mathematics and geography were also specially designed courses of study. Geography, particularly, had a focus on Spain and its colonial period. Children recall that the day the war there was lost to Franco, the map of Spain was turned to the wall.

The friendships between boys and girls reared together and collectively was very different from that experienced in Catholic Spain. It was described by those interviewed as "more rational and healthy, based on comradeship, as boys and girls were treated [in Russia] much more as peers working together for common goals." The youngest recall being separated from older siblings, as colonies were made up of children grouped by age. Brothers and sisters kept in contact by letter and visits all through the year, and especially at the summer camps. A Russian woman reared in Kharkov described the Spanish children she summered with in a Young Pioneer camp in 1938:

> They were always separate, their Spanish teachers always with them. They seemed dark to us, but very well dressed. Their teachers looked very stylish—we had so little in those days—and some were very blonde. They presented their songs and dances to us in camp. They always behaved very correctly, and had their own sec-

tion of beach. Later, we heard a rumor that the Spanish teachers had been arrested and were in prison.

The Stalin Purges

During this period, Stalin was purging presumed deviationists in Russia. In Spain, also, the Communist Party, as a member of the Popular Front, was imprisoning members of POUM, a Marxist revolutionary party. Within Russia, many foreigners were imprisoned or worse, and this is reported to have been the case with some of the Spanish teachers.

Valentín González, better known as the Spanish Republican war hero El Campesino, wrote briefly concerning the children from Spain in his memoirs of life in the Soviet Union prior to his expulsion. Arriving in 1939, after the Republican defeat, he reports that 60 percent of the teachers who had accompanied the children from Spain had already been liquidated. Some, he wrote, were arrested and detained in Lubianka prison. Others were sent to factories or condemned to hard labor in the infamous correctional camps of Stalin. The most outspoken of the Socialists and Left Republicans were shot. He writes:

> During the Civil war, the children and their teachers were well treated. With the end of the war, everything changed completely. The repression against the teachers began in 1939. The majority of them maintained their spirit of independence regarding Communism, a grave crime for the fanatics of the Moscow committee and the NKVD. They were accused of being "Trotskyites" and sent to be punished.[35]

Jesús Hernández, formerly minister of education in the Spanish Republic, echoes these charges in a book written after his own expulsion:

> The first lessons the Spanish children received were edifying, as long as the Civil War lasted. After the defeat, Stalin knew the children could not return to their country. The Spanish teachers were removed; Russian ones were substituted, as were Russian textbooks. The children were forced to cut wood and harvest crops, alternating with their classes. The norms of labor exhausted

> the children and their studies became a myth. I protested to the Commissar of Education to no avail.[36]

The expatriate Soviet writer, Aleksandr Solzhenitsyn, in his monumental *Gulag Archipelago*, notes that "The international camp at Kharkov—there was such a place—[was] full of Spaniards [from their Civil War]." Regarding the Spanish children, he writes that many of them, after World War II, were also imprisoned:

> They were [classed as] 7–35—SOE—Socially Dangerous Element. And those who were particularly stubborn got 58–6—espionage on behalf of America.[37]

Comin Colomer, a pro-Franco historian of the Civil War, describes the Spanish children in Russia as being forced into labor camps after the Republican defeat, suffering throughout World War II, but benefiting from the intercession of La Pasionaria afterwards.[38]

The two Basque teachers interviewed in Spain in 1980 did not report such purges and imprisonment. However, they were not questioned directly about such political matters. The few Sovieticos interviewed in Mexico and the United States, when questioned specifically about such a liquidation, did not recall it. On the contrary, all could remember the names of their teachers from Spain, who followed them to the east in 1941 in wartime, after four years of study in their special schools. Another source, one of the Basque Sovieticos, whose story forms part of a book recently published in Barcelona, *Los Niños de la Guerra*, recalled every stage in her education in Russia before 1941:

> Begoña hasn't forgotten her teachers from that period: Herraiz, wounded in the Civil War, and rejected for service as crippled when volunteering for the Soviet army; "Cerezo," nearly blind, but always loving; the lawyer, Sanchez, converted into a teacher, and others, whose names she can no longer recall.[39]

Perhaps the comment of a Sovietico interviewed in Bilbao in 1982 best sums up the issue:

> There was no wholesale purge or liquidation of our teachers at any time. What did happen, or what we heard rumors of having happened, was that a few who spoke out against the government there, immersing themselves into internal politics, were detained.

Overall, what emerges from the interviews and archival materials is that the Basque and Spanish refugee children lived and studied in their special schools, quite separate from the Soviet citizenry, from 1937 until 1941. By mid-June of that fourth year, however, this life changed abruptly. The refugee children from Spain became refugees once more, along with millions of Soviets. Overnight, the Nazi invasion of Russia destroyed the security they had known and mingled their fate with that of their Soviet hosts.

The lives of the Basque refugee children during and after World War II in each of the host countries of Europe will be described in Chapter 8, "Aftermaths." Their experiences in three other countries offering hospitality to very small groups of youngsters from the Basque Republic prior to the Nazi invasions shows once again the variety of assistance given to them.

CHAPTER SIX

Switzerland, Denmark, The United States, and Mexico

fter the appeal of President Aguirre to the countries of Europe to offer hospitality to the Basque children, countries besides France, England, Belgium, and Russia also offered their help. As early as mid-May, *Euzkadi Roja* published the news that Switzerland had offered to care for Basque children and to provide them with an excellent education. A spokesman indicated that two hundred could be accommodated.[1]

As the children arrived in France, the committees of both the French Popular Front and the Catholic church encouraged their analogous assemblies throughout Europe to sponsor colonies in their own countries. Sweden tried to participate but ultimately followed the example of Holland by helping to sponsor the six colonies in France already noted. The two additional European countries who became actual hosts to small numbers of Basque children were Switzerland, where 245 children were housed under Catholic and Socialist auspices, and Denmark, where the Danish Committee of the Popular Front sponsored 102 children.[2]

Switzerland

The children who were to be sent on to Switzerland arrived in France on the last such voyage of the *Habana*, in mid-June of 1937. After a period of quarantine, they were sent on to Geneva and to the Lucerne area. There, Caritas had arranged for forty-five children to be placed in Catholic adoptive homes.[3] The rest were allocated to homes by the Socialist party of Bordeaux office in cooperation with its counterpart in Switzerland.[4]

One child who was among those sent recalls:

> My older brother and I came to Geneva in August at the time of the harvest. They brought us to a big banquet, with everything prepared beautifully. Then they called out our names. It was horrible, horrible! We were taken by different families living some ten kilometers apart. We both cried and cried. My big adoptive family treated me like a pet doll; my brother's, a childless one, exploited him, expecting him to do the work of a man in their vineyard. We spent Sundays together, but that always ended in tears when we parted. We were only nine and eleven, and had promised our mother to stay together. We went to French school and learned quickly. All that time we had no news of our family. My mother had fled to Santander; my father was already a prisoner in Euzkadi.

Many of the children sent to Switzerland under Catholic auspices were repatriated quickly—thirty returned after five months, though eleven did not return to Euzkadi until mid-1939.[5] Those under Socialist auspices were returned to France in 1939, where by then many of their parents were themselves refugees from Catalonia. The few Basque children in Switzerland never became a domestic political issue.

Denmark

In Denmark, a Committee for Spanish Refugee Children was formed in response to President Aguirre's appeal. Members included the head of Copenhagen's municipal hospital, and a Socialist member of parliament. Its director was the civil governor of Copenhagen. The committee reportedly had very strong ties to the Popular Front in France, ties that included being the recipient of funds from an anti-Fascist society in Paris, the Matteoti Club.[6]

It was not until August, however, that the first and only contingent of children arrived from Santander and were welcomed into Denmark.[7] They were divided into two groups, and taken to vacant summer worker camps in Ordrup, and in Odense, near Copenhagen. Here, they passed a pleasant autumn and a bitter Danish winter. The directors of the larger colony at Ordrup, with seventy-two children, and the smaller one, with thirty, were both highly trained state teachers who supervised the children's education. The Danes reportedly showered the children with new clothes, sweets, and gifts. Funds to maintain the two colonies were collected from throughout Denmark. The Minister of Public Instruction for the Spanish Republic, as well as the Basque government, was kept informed of the children's progress.[8] Correspondence with their parents was reportedly well organized. The register of the 102 children in Denmark shows a majority came from Santander and Asturias; only twenty-three were from the Basque provinces.[9]

Within weeks of the children's arrival, the Insurgent government in Burgos expressed interest in repatriating them all to Spain.[10] Since at this time the Franco government did not have diplomatic recognition from Denmark, the German ambassador, Alfred Tveede, acted as the emissary. Tveede first proposed that a neutral camp in Insurgent Spain be opened for the children, to be supervised by the Spanish Red Cross. It appears that some funds were made available for this proposal.[11] However, when a list of the children and other data were requested by Tveede from the Danish foreign minister and the officials from Burgos, none was forthcoming. The camp did not materialize.[12]

By early April of 1938, the continued presence of the children had become a heated political issue, soon to generate "the most violent incident in the contemporary history of the Danish Parliament."[13] Since Denmark continued to recognize only Republican Spain, Tveede worked to assure the government that both repatriation and recognition of Insurgent Spain were necessary. He wrote to the foreign minister of Burgos:

> I attribute the difficulties in repatriating the Basque children partly to the handiwork of the Ambassador of Red Spain, and partly to the profound ignorance concerning

> Nationalist Spain that reigns here, creating the impression that returning the children would expose them to terror. It would be opportune to have information about the situation of Basque children now in Spain, as well as about those being repatriated from England.[14]

By early 1938, he had converted at least one Conservative parliament member, Mr. Purshel, to this view. In parliament, Purshel engaged in an acrimonious debate concerning the delays in repatriating the children with two other members, Larsen and Hancroft (Communist and Socialist, respectively). The latter two defended the continued stay of the children as reflecting the desires expressed by their parents as well as being consistent with the history of Denmark in always offering the right of refuge. Purshel attacked this, maintaining that the Spanish Republic's days were numbered. Denmark, he said, should concern itself with establishing relations with General Franco and the Burgos government, as had England, France, and other countries:

> The Basque children have nothing to do with the right of refuge. The majority of them are enemies of society. . . . Bringing the children in was solely for Communist propaganda purposes. I, personally, sincerely hope General Franco wins, and imposes order in Spain.[15]

Tveede's account continued: "this frank declaration so enraged the Reds that a scandalous round of shouts, insults, and threats to throw Mr. Purshel out ensued, so that the session had to be terminated."

By mid-May of 1938, however, the Danish committee had reconsidered its commitment to house the children on Danish soil. The price for the site at Ordrup had risen sharply for a proposed second year, and its director was anxious to return to his former employment. For the summer, this teacher took the entire group to a remote seaside resort on the island of Fionia. Such isolation seemed necessary to allow the political upheaval occasioned by the children's presence to die down. It was a beautiful setting, isolated from the mainland and reached only by an hour's ferry ride.[16]

A widely printed interview with the director, Mr. Neilson,

made it clear that the colony was keeping a very low profile. Neilsen indicated repeatedly that any information about the children could come only from the minister of foreign affairs. He also repeated this statement when questioned about Msgr. Antoniutti and his reported attempts to obtain a list of the Spanish children in Denmark.

> In the case of any inquiry from Spain, whether from those living in areas captured by Franco, or governed from Valencia, it must be handled by the Minister of Foreign Affairs. I have never heard any talk about Monsignor Antoniutti, who is mentioned in rumours as the person attempting to obtain information regarding the children's names. As I said before, an official inquiry will be answered by the Minister of Foreign Affairs.[17]

Neilson did state that the children were to be sent to southern France in October. When asked about the cost of maintaining the colony until that date, he commented that the daily cost for each child was two kroner, and the total until repatriation would be 424,000 kroner—to be supplied by the committee.

In mid-August, Ambassador Tveede reported this interview to Franco in Burgos. He commented that at a recent meeting of the Danish Committee, Dr. Carl Brantling, committee member and president of the Danish-Spanish Association, as well as a corresponding member of the Royal History Society of Madrid, had stated that the offering of refuge to the Basque and Spanish children "had built a bridge between Spain and Denmark." He personally disagreed with this viewpoint.[18]

In early August, the committee met with the Spanish Republican delegate in Denmark to decide the future of the children. It was agreed to follow the example of Sweden and Norway by sponsoring colonies in France. Funds to transport and maintain the children for a full year would be raised by the committee. Among reasons cited were the increased cost of sites in Denmark. The money raised could be more effectively employed in France, where living costs were lower. The similarity between the languages of Spain and France, as well as the future utility of French for the children, and the similarity in climate were also advantages. Finally, there was the fact that repatriation to Franco Spain as a political issue would not be as problematic in France.[19]

By September's end, the committee reported that a site, a large castle near Paris, was ready for the children. The final report noted that, during their year in Denmark, the children had lacked neither food, clothing, nor the attentions of the Danish people, so that their stay had been very worthwhile in spite of the difficult separation from their parents.[20]

The United States

In the United States strenuous efforts were made to permit admission of refugee children from Euzkadi. A campaign was organized for this purpose shortly after President Aguirre's plea to the world. A Board of Guardians for Basque Children was formed, with such influential members as Albert Einstein; Mary Woolley, president emeritus of Mt. Holyoke College; Dorothy Thompson, the well-known columnist; Congresswoman Caroline O'Day; William Dodd, son of the ambassador to Germany; and others. Mrs. Eleanor Roosevelt became very interested in the plight of the Basque children, and offered her support. Upon her insistence, the ambassador to Spain, Claude Bowers, was made the honorary head of the board. Its able secretary was Dr. Frank Bohn, who was the son-in-law of then-Secretary of Commerce Roper. Overall, the board had excellent contacts in Washington.[21]

An appeal for two thousand adoptive homes was launched, and by mid-June over 2,700 American families had responded. There was help from at least one Basque enclave as well:

> The Spanish chargé d'affaires informed under-secretary of State [Sumner] Welles that a group of Spanish Basques who owned a large Mexican hat factory in St. Louis had made known their desire to care for some of the children should they be permitted to enter the United States.[22]

Dr. Bohn was quoted in *Euzkadi Roja* in Bilbao on May 23 as offering to sponsor five hundred Basque children immediately, place them on board the liner *President Roosevelt*, then in Bordeaux, and guarantee their maintenance in the United States. This offer had been made by cable to Don Manuel de Irujo, in Barcelona, who was then minister of justice in the Popular Front government under Dr. Negrin.[23] According to Sr. Irujo, when interviewed shortly before his death: "After that, nothing more was ever said in any manner about any Basque children in the United States."

Clearly, the board's humanitarian gesture became a political issue immediately after it became public. To understand such a response in the secular, pluralistic United States, we have to examine the attitude of the Catholic hierarchy here and abroad, for there have been few events which so polarized public opinion along religious lines in this country.

The Papal State in Rome supported the Italian invasion of Abyssinia, and Pope Pius XI was convinced that the Spanish Civil War was caused by the "Communist menace," a threat he felt outweighed all other perils to the Catholic faith. His successor, Pius XII, thought the same, and both were supporters of General Franco. Pius XII encouraged the Spanish hierarchy to prepare a joint pastoral letter which labeled the Republican government as "Communist, Anarchist, and Atheist." This letter, reprinted in translation throughout the American Catholic press, was widely accepted by American Catholics. Most believed that General Franco was fighting to save Spain from Bolshevism. This "unfamiliar religious passion" on the part of American Catholics was poised against a generally pro-Republican stance on the part of Protestants in the United States. It was primarily the Catholics who first accepted the now-common tactic of branding any generally Leftist government as "Communist" whenever its program posed a threat to the religious, economic, or political interests of the establishment.[24]

By early June, the Catholic press was filled with discussions of the pros and cons of allowing Basque children to find a haven in the United States. In a typical article entitled "Fate's Hostages: Basque Child Refugees are Political Football in Muddled Washington," the array of pressure groups, both pro and con, manifested close parallels to those in Europe. Strongly against any immigration was the Catholic hierarchy, led by Cardinal O'Connell, Archbishop of Boston. The major Catholic weekly, *America*, effected a curious change of position within two weeks to reflect his views:

> *The Tragic Plight of the Basque Children* . . . Bilbao is doomed. . . . Upwards of 200,000 civilians are trapped behind the battle lines. . . . A Board of Guardians seeks to bring 500 of these children to the United States. They are mostly Catholics. It will be a crime crying to God if we Catholics do not use our united powers to care for the bodies and souls of these little Basques.[25]

> *Comment*: Genuine sympathy for the privations and hardships that have fallen to the lot of the some 6000 Basque children evacuated from Bilbao has been rather dramatically expressed in newspapers and newsreels . . . but the doubt still lingers as to the actual motive behind the government's insistence on their removal to other countries. . . . It is quite evident that the purpose was not merely the safety of the children. The aim quite apparently seems to be to put Franco and the Nationalist [Insurgent] cause in the light of a ruthless aggressor.

> The Basque children, kidnapped from their homes in and around Bilbao, are still being made the playthings of designing Leftists. Balked in its effort to bring 500 little Basques here, the self-elected Board of Guardians tenaciously grips the hope of distorting the destinies of these children. It first announced that it would seek to collect $500,000 for the purpose of supporting Basque refugee camps in France, and England. Then came the announcement that the Board was transforming itself into the Joint Committee to Aid Spanish Children, which had for its aim a campaign to raise $3,000,000 for the establishment in France of camps to care for the Basque children. The strategy of all these inhumane efforts is obvious: these children are kept in exile from their native soil in order that they may be indoctrinated with ideas hostile to Spanish unity.[26]

By the following spring, a writer for this weekly did an on-the-spot appraisal:

> *Basque Children Exiled While Basque Mothers Weep*: Saddest

> Tragedy and Greatest Crime of Spain. . . . When I went to Bilbao, I had every belief that I should find it in ruins. Actually, I had the greatest difficulty finding any mark of war at all in the city. As far as I could discover, no child was killed in Bilbao by Franco's fire. . . . There had been unquestionably a serious food shortage as there always seems to be under the Red regime.[27]

A number of congressmen led by Representative McCormack of Massachusetts, joined the Catholic church in opposing the acceptance of the children. Immigration laws posed an initial barrier, until the State Department waived both the regulation mandating individual visas and the posting of a five-hundred-dollar bond for each child. The child welfare groups also opposing the expedition were reminded that they had not opposed the entry of some 250 Jewish children from Germany since 1935.

The proposal of the Board of Guardians for Basque Children was shuffled from the secretary of labor to the State Department to President Roosevelt. He reportedly informed the board that if it could "enlist the support and collaboration of some prominent Catholic welfare society the plan might be engineered successfully. This would show its good intent."[28] He returned it to the labor secretary who returned it to the board. The Catholic church was not willing to support or collaborate in the proposed project, and one spokesman, the Supreme Knight of the Knights of Columbus, commented:

> The attempt of the American Board of Guardians for Basque Children to bring 2,000 Basque children to the United States is an unholy exploitation of children for Communist propaganda purposes.[29]

Though the writer heard reports in Mexico from the Basque children sent there that some were actually admitted to the United States, a widely traveled Basque-American, Jose Eiguren, notes:

> To my knowledge, no Basque children were allowed in the U.S.A. After the various countries received their quotas, there were about 2,700 left, homeless, with no place to be sent. When the Basque government asked the

U.S.A. to accept these children, it was rejected as possibly discriminatory, as the U.S.A. was not going to give asylum to other children from the Iberian peninsula. (No others had requested this.) These 2,700 children were later accepted by the USSR. Any Basque children who came in, came under regular immigration quotas, or as priority cases, i.e. those with relatives in the United States who were citizens.[30]

A second result of the position of the American Catholic church that Basques were Communist-led was that the American Basque colony in the West felt it was unwise to offer overt assistance to the Basque Autonomous Government. In addition to individual funds sent to kinsmen privately, this colony sent one thousand wool blankets for Basque women imprisoned in Spain. This was their only collective assistance.[31]

Mexico

The Basque children who were to be evacuated to Mexico were refugees from the battles in Guipúzcoa in August and September of 1936. All remember their flight across the border to France, where they found refuge for a few days to a few weeks. The newly elected Socialist government in France was not yet mobilized to help them, and its official adherence to the policy of "Non-Intervention" made their presence an embarrassment. They felt unwelcome in France, so the majority recrossed the border to enter the Republican territory around Catalonia.

> In 1936, we were bombarded from the air and from the sea. Everyone lived in the basements in Irún all through the battles. Then we crossed into France; all, save my father, who stayed on to fight. In Bordeaux, a Spanish family took us in. Soon, my father came to get us. We crossed again, a family of refugees, and went on to Lerida, where Father went to work again as a mechanic on the railroad. Food was very scarce: there were lines for bread beginning at 3 A.M., until it ran out. And the bombing began there too. One thing I'll never forget: in a magazine there, called "Pages of Blood," was a photo of our very own house in Euzkadi, but only the four walls

> were left standing. By May [1937], our parents thought it best to send us away. We all wanted to go to Mexico, near the land of Tom Mix. We imagined Indians with feathers, cowboys, adventures. Everyone thought we would be home for Christmas.

The Basque children were to make up a very small part of the expedition to Mexico, invited there in the spring of 1937 by the president of Mexico, Don Lázaro Cárdenas. In Valencia and Barcelona, the ambassador to Mexico, Sr. Gordon Ordaz, arranged for the registration of children in the embassies, requiring the usual health check, parental consent, and photos. The proposed expedition to Mexico was quite popular, due, no doubt, to the lure of the Americas, the fact that Spanish was spoken there, and the known presence of a large Hispanic colony already resident in the capital. The proposed evacuation was quickly subscribed to by parents from the Left. The majority were Catalonians, with large minorities who were refugees from Málaga or Madrid. In all, little more than two dozen Basque children from Euzkadi, hailing from Irún and San Sebastián, went along with 430 others. The children were accompanied by four nurses, two doctors, and eight teachers, all members of the Anarchist CNT or socialist UGT unions.[32]

The stated age limits, from six to twelve, were not observed. Several dozen boys between thirteen and eighteen were in the group. At the other end of the age spectrum were a half dozen toddlers, some not yet walking or talking, and carried in the arms of their older sisters. In all, sixty children were under six years of age.[33] The expedition left Valencia by train on May 20, with 156 children who had come to that city from Alicante, or who were in flight from Málaga and Madrid. In Barcelona, the balance of the expedition, including the Basque children, joined the group. The majority of the children were of the laboring class, with parents who were affiliated with the Socialist, Communist, or Anarchist parties.[34] They were pleased to send their offspring to a country so clearly committed to Socialism as was Mexico under Cárdenas. In contrast, the small contingent of Basque children were middle class (the parents of some were doctors or other professionals). They had lived in relatively comfortable circumstances before the war.

A number of the oldest boys had been sent to evade military service; others were reportedly incorrigible, and "their parents wanted to put an ocean between them."[35] These boys were to bring the expedition to Mexico international ill fame for their delinquency. Their first escapade took place at the Hotel Real in Barcelona, where all were gathered for a leavetaking. The older boys broke into the kitchen and threw the fruit and vegetables about, causing a near riot. After this episode, they were all put on board a train to Bordeaux. During the journey they were given a cold lunch of hard-boiled egg, rolls, fruit and, according to the French custom, a quarter liter of red wine. The bigger boys snatched this wine from the younger children and were soon all drunk.[36]

In Bordeaux, the group was housed in small hotels until the *Méxique*, a French ship, arrived to take them to Mexico. Once on board, seasickness attacked them all. By the time the ship touched land at Havana, however, all were recovered and eating immense meals to make up for months of insufficient rations.[37] Some of the teachers tried to divert the younger children with games during their fourteen-day voyage; but the older boys again banded together to roam the ship. They stole food, especially the canned milk stored in the lifeboats, as well as equipment secured there.

In Havana, the government was decidedly pro-Franco, so the expedition's time ashore was very brief, being limited to a tour of the city. In spite of the official policy, the Cuban people welcomed them with cheers and music, and threw sweets and money to them as they passed in their fleet of rented taxis. A Mexican correspondent, who was returning home on the *Méxique* after volunteer service in the Republican army, went ashore with the refugees. Through a mishap, he was delayed in returning. The captain gave the order to sail. The children, many of whom the writer had befriended, tried to prevent the casting off:

> A tumultuous demonstration ensued, in which the children shouted Socialist slogans deafeningly, and roved the ship from stem to stern. They accosted the captain,

> called him "Fascist," and held onto the cables to the docks until their hands bled. Then they threatened to burn the ship. As they were about to do this, word came that the writer was coming on board.[38]

A few days later, the children glimpsed the Mexican coast, ringed with palm trees that they found enchanting. Awaiting the children at the port of Veracruz were thousands of Mexican citizens. The full leadership of the Committee of Help for Spanish Children and of the Popular Front of Mexico were also there. Many people offered the children slices of exotic fruits they had never before tasted, such as mangoes, pineapples, chirimoyas, and "bananas that were tastier than those in Spain."[39] Money, gifts, sweets, and toys were also showered on them. All the major papers had front page articles, with photos, about their arrival.

They were immediately taken by train to Mexico City. Here, again, the citizenry greeted their coming enthusiastically. The children were officially welcomed by President Cárdenas, his wife, and son. The latter, Cuauhtemoc, was later to be a classmate of a few of the children at preparatory school and the university. The Spanish children responded to this welcome by singing the "Internationale," giving the clenched fist salute, and, unaware of his position, addressing the president as "Comrade."[40] The following day, they were taken by train to Morelia, Michoacán, where Cárdenas had ordered two old former Catholic seminaries to be renovated for their use.

The Mexican Committee of Help had been formed some months earlier by a group of prominent Mexican women, including the wife of President Cárdenas, and was directed by the wife of a respected educator. It functioned as a branch of the French Popular Front Committee of Help. These women had organized a very successful campaign to raise money for the five hundred "orphaned" children from Spain that they planned to sponsor. During the winter of 1936, they raised over thirteen thousand pesos, much of which came from union groups in every state of the Republic of Mexico.[41]

The "Niños de Morelia," as the children soon came to be known throughout Mexico, have been unusually well documented. There are two theses on the experiences of the Spanish children in the social experiment that their school, the Escuela España-México, represented.[42] The school's only permanent director (1938–40) has written his memoirs.[43] A magazine series has recently been published by a Catalan who was a refugee child in the school.[44] All of this published material reflects very faithfully the responses gathered in interviews. Finally, a 1983 Mexican television series on the "Niños" also corroborates earlier material.

It is clear that Cárdenas, and those who organized the project, were influenced by the reports on the collective education being offered in the Soviet Union to all children, including those of the lower classes. The refugee guests from Spain's revolution were expected to enjoy the benefits of such a new training, the first in the hemisphere. Consequently, no expense was to be spared in educating the children. The staff was especially selected and numbered over sixty. Special shops for the teaching of various trades were installed. Swimming pools and other amenities were envisioned, all to prepare the children to return to build a new and democratic Spain after the forces of Franco were defeated.[45] In order to assist the Spanish children in their initial adjustment, fifty children from the Morelia area, offspring of the very poor, were also enrolled. This idea was only partially successful:

> Instead, what was normal occurred. The Mexican children learned our customs, assimilated our way of speaking, our idioms, even the "th" instead of "s"; our games and songs. And forty years later it is our Mexican fellow students who remember most faithfully the songs and games we of Spain have forgotten.

Some peer learning, of course, did occur:

> They [the Mexican students] taught us how much to pay for fruit, tacos, jicama at the food stands, so we weren't overcharged for long. We also learned that what looked like jelly was a very hot chili. We learned that right away.

The Escuela España-México was to have a well-publicized few years. A number of visitors from the United States came to see it, and most wrote positive comments in the guest book. Those closer to the school, however, have reported that problems seemed to be constant in its brief history. These were identical to those experienced by the Basque children in other host countries. They were exacerbated by the trauma the children had already experienced in their flight from Guipúzcoa, and by the absence of any Basque or Spanish personnel in Morelia.

In Mexico, by Cárdenas's orders, the Spanish teachers who had accompanied the children from Barcelona were immediately replaced by Mexican staff. This caused some rumblings in the Republican government in Spain, but the Mexican personnel stayed on, while the Spaniards were sent back to Mexico City.

> A few days after arriving in Morelia, the Spanish teachers were made to return to the capital. This change was received with anger by the children, who had lived some time with these people, and had come from the same country and suffered the same conditions, which made them united. Their relationship was so intimate, it at times resembled that of parent and child. Much affection was expressed between teachers and children. The Mexican teachers remained only educators, and did not become personal friends, making a different situation.[46]

Some of this new staff proved to be very anti-Spanish. The porter and certain teachers openly displayed their feelings against the children. They associated the refugee children from Spain with the conquest of Mexico by Cortés over four hundred years earlier.

> On the part of General Cárdenas, there was warmth, certainly. But the rest of the Mexican staff, the majority, didn't like us, that was clear. They seemed to resent us being there, and clearly preferred the cadre of children from Morelia enrolled with us. . . . When a new director, Sr. Reyes-Perez was put in charge of the school, he had to face several problems, among them, that of "Hispanophobia." A number of the teachers simply disliked the Spanish children solely on account of their nationality. Reyes-Perez was obliged to dismiss them.[47]

Thus, "Los Niños de Morelia" found a unique barrier to their acceptance into the Mexican culture. This very pervasive prejudice against Spaniards, especially pronounced since the Revolution of 1910, with its glorification of indigenous Mexican blood and culture, was one which labeled every Spaniard as a *Gachupín*.[48] The refugee children were identified as the beginning of a new Spanish economic conquest, hardly more benign than the genocidal conquest of the sixteenth century. Rather than being refugees from a failing revolution, and the young guests of Cárdenas, they were viewed, as were the adult Spanish refugees who came later, as arriving in Mexico to exploit, once again, its material wealth. This prejudice was widely shared by many Mexicans:

> Some of the young men in town tried to bother us because we were from Spain, and they tried to get others to torment us. They still blamed us for excesses committed during the colonial period. Once, I almost got beaten up by some ignorant peasants, whom a ranch owner's son had incited with tales of a movie about the Spanish conquest. The workers must have thought it had happened just the past week, for they chased me, and wanted to lynch me.[49]

This barrier became more pronounced after the Civil War ended, and shiploads of adult Spanish Republican refugees began coming into Mexico. Rubio notes:

> The Spanish immigrant in Mexico, especially since the revolution, has suffered from a governmental and social conceptualization that is unenviable: the ridiculous, despised Gachupín. This characterization included the perception by Mexicans that the immigrant had come to enrich himself at their cost.[50]

The prejudice soon surfaced in some of the newspaper publicity critical of this project of Cárdenas. Editorials commented that the children of Mexico, rather than their Spanish counterparts, deserved such a fine school and that poor Mexican children suffering from disease and malnourishment should be helped first.[51] It also became well known that this school cost more than the usual state school, and that its orientation was of the Left.

There was yet another segment of Mexican society that felt antipathy to the Spanish Republican refugee children, a segment made up of much earlier immigrants from Spain, most of whom had by now become wealthy. They were in the main solidly Catholic, and usually pro-Franco. These Spaniards, very different in background and affiliation from the vanguard of Civil War refugees, formed a very cohesive group in urban Mexico, calling themselves the "Honorable Spanish Colony." They had, by themselves, established a number of social clubs and sports centers, as well as a fine private hospital. Some of these facilities were in operation well before the Mexican Revolution of 1910. The wealth of this colony was enormous.

In 1937, when the children arrived, these descendants of earlier Spanish immigrants owned 60 percent of all land in Mexico, over two-thirds of the textile factories, and had a monopoly of the publishing trade. The Basques—and the majority of the old immigrant Spaniards were from the north of Spain—had been concentrated in northern Mexico in their early years, and had developed extensive mining and cattle interests. Spaniards thus controlled commerce, heavy industry, and had huge real estate holdings. They were seldom found employed in menial labor, but tended to own their own businesses. As a result, the majority of bakeries, groceries, hardware stores, and breweries—the latter, extremely profitable—were Spanish owned. The natural jealousy felt by indigenous Mexicans towards these successful immigrants was reinforced by knowledge that much anti-social enterprise (bars and brothels) was also under Spanish control. There were, as well, strong elements of class and color operating in this pervasive prejudice against Spaniards present in Mexico. A further element was that the Spaniards who came to Mexico, and particularly the Basques, arrived with little capital but a will to work and succeed.[52]

Clearly, this anti-Spanish feeling was reciprocated in the social and business associations of the Spanish entrepreneurs, both on a formal and informal level. It was also faithfully reflected in the endogamous marriage patterns of this caste-like strata of Mexican society. Politically, the "Honorable Spanish Colony" had weathered the Mexican Revolution with notable success. It felt no affection for the Second Republic in Spain, and even less for the Popular Front.[53] The Basques in this colony, among the very richest and most powerful men in Mexico, were not attracted to Basque Nationalist aspirations. Neither, as we have seen, were their wealthy counterparts in Euzkadi. What these cleavages were to mean for the Spanish children was soon apparent in the press treatment of the social experiment in Morelia, an experiment underwritten by the Mexican government.

Editorials chastising the Leftist orientation and lack of religion exhibited by the children appeared. These were fueled, as in England, by the wayward behavior of the older boys. They soon provoked a crisis when some of them broke into a chapel adjoining their dormitory, defaced the religious statues, and threw rocks and garbage around. A battle with the townspeople ensued, which necessitated the intervention of the police. This melee was widely publicized in the Rightist press in Mexico, and republished in the Spanish equivalent in Burgos.[54]

It is noteworthy that the major Mexico City papers no longer printed reports on the children within a very few days after their arrival. In *Excelsior,* for example, articles on the children had shifted to the inside pages within a week of their arrival in Veracruz, and disappeared altogether two days later.[55] Other papers did the same. The later flurries of news were quite negative in tone. In all the publicity, the Niños de Morelia were usually labeled as "orphans" and were also very frequently identified mistakenly as Basque. An excerpt from Cárdenas's speech of welcome is one example:

> Most of the children are Basque, and are sons and daughters of the Basque soldiers who defended Bilbao. We plan to give them hospitality until the war in Spain is over.[56]

Another source, a report from the International Red Cross, states,

> We were apprised by the delegates of the Mexican Red Cross of the arrival of 400 children, all Basque, accompanied by their teachers and administrative personnel.[57]

The role that Cárdenas played in the school was quite important. Although his memoirs make it clear the original impetus for the expedition was the women on the Committee of Help, he visited with some frequency, and "made sure to speak to each child as he shook hands."[58] When the expedition was first being planned, a number of wealthy Rightist Spanish families offered to take a child each into their homes, but he wished to try the model of the Socialist training school. He planned certain improvements, one being a bakery on the premises. This was built after the children complained about the tortillas served at every meal rather than the French bread to which they were accustomed.[59] Another improvement was the construction of two swimming pools.

In 1937, the president was in the middle of his six-year term, one marked by a commitment to actual agrarian reform, the nationalization of the petroleum industry, and other Socialist reforms. Though he was adored by the *campesinos* and workers, he was limited to one term by law. In 1940, he was replaced by a quite different leader, Avilo Camacho. Though the school existed until 1943, it did so in a very changed form.

Cárdenas had been able, during his six-year term, to offer both material and moral support to Republican Spain. In the matter of armaments, Mexico sent whatever it could; in foodstuffs, particularly the garbanzos that were to sustain the Basques, Mexico's help was vital.

Politically, Cárdenas also did all that was possible. In the League of Nations, Mexico was the only open and stalwart ally of the Spanish Republic. But within Mexico, powerful interests were covertly pro-Franco. These interests included the Catholic church, the Rightist press, the army, to a large extent the Spanish colony, and international commercial interests. These elements damaged the educational project for Spanish refugee children that Cárdenas supported in every conceivable way.

But, clearly, the internal problems of the school were also

damaging and difficult to solve. In Morelia, in 1937, the children experienced frequent changes of staff. Three directors came and went within the first six months. These and other problems were reported both in Mexico and Insurgent Spain, to the point that the International Red Cross felt it necessary to request that the Mexican Red Cross inspect the facility. The Spanish Republican government also sent an inspector, who reported on shortcomings. Both recommended certain improvements in the facilities, particularly in sanitation.[60] The grim buildings were two centuries old, and therefore difficult to clean or maintain. They had been constructed to serve a self-sufficient community, with cultivable land, livestock, and orchards. The cell-like rooms opened onto wide, space-wasting corridors. Plumbing and lighting were primitive. The presence of a cemetery in the patio of the larger structure, where the youngest children were housed, did nothing to improve the environment. In fact, the bones that periodically worked their way to the surface caused many nightmares among the children. A great deal of dust was also generated by the ancient graves, which soon made respiratory illnesses common. When the children complained to Cárdenas, he had the area paved for a playground.[61] Unfortunately, a child was killed during its construction, one of the eight who perished, in part due to insufficient supervision, and to deficiencies in the slow renovation of the old buildings. An example of the latter was the electrocution of a child who was locked out one evening and tried to enter by climbing the wall, and touched an exposed wire. The child had been very popular; his death frightened and depressed the children.[62]

At about this time, early in 1938, Cárdenas hired a new director to bring order and peace to the troubled school. Dr. Reyes-Perez, a young teacher and active Communist, also envisioned the institution as a model Socialist pilot project. After observing the chaos of a typical school day, he began anew. He first stopped the curious mixture of military discipline (at least in theory) coupled with almost complete anarchy on the part of students and staff. Thefts, runaways, and adolescent amours had become common, the first on the part of staff as well as students. Reyes-Perez fired many employees and replaced them with Communists who also were committed to the idea of the school. From these, he formed "Shock Troops," who carefully planned an intensive program of study and work.[63] Initially, he had tried the notion of utilizing some of the older boys who were natural leaders as a disciplinary force, but he found them unjust and overly punitive. Another step was to send thirty of the most troublesome boys on to a military school, and some of the budding young women to a convent boarding school in Puebla. These steps considerably diminished the number of love affairs.

The "Shock Troops" helped the director to enforce rules on class attendance, and he curbed runaways by having bedchecks nightly. In a comprehensive health examination, the first since the children's arrival, Reyes-Perez found that most of the children were anemic and that many had respiratory diseases. Some 20 percent still had scabies, and another 20 percent had conjunctivitis. He noted that psychological illnesses were nearly epidemic.[64] These he attributed in part to the trauma of their wartime life, but also to a different psychological make-up of the Spanish children. He characterized the Spanish "*blancos*" as exceptionally stubborn, and unable to accept domination, but quick to learn (though not profoundly) and with a talent for synthesis. They also seemed to him passionate and, at times, brutal. The "*tostadas*" in the school, the Mexicans, were more malleable, passive, good at analysis, slower to learn, but more accurate, less dynamic, less exuberant, and uninterested in domination. Perhaps with some justification, he related the Spanish children's perception of themselves as having preferred status in Cárdenas's project with their unconscious arrogance toward the staff and their Mexican classmates. He was accurate in noting that the most neglected were the very youngest, who attached themselves to anyone nearby, "calling 'Mama' without the least idea of what this word meant."[65]

Some of the psychological problems the "Niños de Morelia" recalled in their interviews were clearly based in the wartime years. All had been terrified of airplanes. Months later, in Morelia, an airplane passing over could send some into convulsions. Other examples abound of the timeless quality of the child's unconscious which cannot reflect the secure present reality. Many children regressed in their toilet habits, and bedwetting, even for children of eight years and more, was common:

> Those of us who wet the bed were segregated by day and by night. By day, no one wanted to be near us, as we smelled so foul. By night, we were made to sleep on the cold stone floors, on old woven mats. The only toilet was far away, down a long passage, unlighted, and filthy with urine and feces. We didn't often make it in time. We were shunned, teased, punished; our dignity as children was erased, exterminated.

Stealing was rampant, from the school, townsfolk, and from each other:

> We youngest were the targets of everyone. They took our allowance, our clothes, our food, even our one blanket.

The sexual episodes characteristic of boarding school life when supervision is lacking occurred:

> They brought me an eight-year-old boy [a Basque] and the sixteen-year-old who had abused him. The little one was sent to our doctor; the other, I sent to a reform center.[66]

This same incident, reported by a fellow student:

> One day an incident occurred inside the boys' dormitory from which the director created a great scandal. It was really only a joke—a youngster, half-aroused by an older boy, with others watching. At that age, both masturbation and homosexual play are normal.[67]

Perhaps as a result of this occurrence, this one family of Basques did return to Spain, the only one to do so out of the ten families there. Another event, this with a fatal aftermath, occurred near the new swimming pool. The children had discovered a wall that was so weakened it would sway when pushed. This became their impromptu swing for several weeks, with no adult comment. Further weakened by this play, the wall collapsed, burying a seven-year-old Basque boy under it, where he died.

There were many other incidents, less tragic by far, but of sufficient importance to be recalled over forty years later by the children as adults. An example of these was the celebration of the first Christmas in the school. On the Day of Epiphany, as was the custom in Spain, the smallest children put out their shoes and awaited the gifts sure to be there the next morning. But the staff provided nothing. Again, some of the older boys made the occasion memorable by putting feces in the shoes. Another came into the children's dormitory with an erection protruding from his opened trousers. Displaying this to the embarrassed youngsters, he shouted, "Here is what the Three Kings have brought for you."[68]

Reyes-Perez worked untiringly to improve the school. When he surveyed the children's educational accomplishments, he found three-quarters of the children were nearly illiterate. He began intensive remedial programs, giving rewards for good marks and an allowance each Sunday for those who had fulfilled their norm of accomplishment. He instituted a "Stakhanovist, work-intensive, rational, and authentically Socialist education."[69] Reyes-Perez was able to institute many reforms during his two-year tenure, with the help of his Shock Troops.

He was less successful when he turned his attention to other aspects of the children's lives, such as the food service:

> We have already mentioned that the children did not like the food. . . . It seems that the most objective explanation is that the Spaniard is accustomed to eat larger meals than the Mexican, and above all, more bread. Doubtless, the school only offered three meals a day, with tortillas rather than bread, as is the custom here. And the style of cooking is different. All this contributed to the feeling that the food was both poor and insufficient.[70]

> We never really had enough to eat: Breakfast was beans, tortillas, coffee and milk; lunch, soup, beans, bread; Merienda, bread, coffee and milk, with an egg and a kind of cocoa on Sunday. We stole food, begged food, bought

> tacos at the food stands with the little money we had, and visited the families in town as often as we could. The dining room was often a riot, with bad food and plates flying. Once, when an early director struck a child, he had hot coffee thrown in his face.[71]

Reyes-Perez also was unable to improve the sanitation of the school:

> The floors were black with fleas, which were burned off twice a year, for only temporary relief. The lice we brought with us. They were loyal and never left in spite of halfway measures, such as our wearing caps saturated with alcohol to kill them. You'll notice that pictures show us with shaved heads or wearing these caps. These problems were terrible for us children, but ignored by the staff. Why, we had louse races and bet on flea jumps all the time.[72]

The Basque Children

Reyes-Perez did not encourage any regionalism whatsoever—all the children as citizens of the new Spain of the future were identical. In the environment of the school, the small Basque contingent of children became indistinguishable from their classmates, at least to outsiders. Among the twenty-odd children, few were Basque-speaking:

> We all lived in border cities, devoted to tourists. Though our parents spoke it, it wasn't of much use to us. In the farms, in the country, though, all spoke it.

There were no Basque mentors, no one to teach the language, folkways, songs and dances—no reminders of Euzkadi. Some lost contact with their families until after World War II. Yet, within the school, both staff and fellow students who were interviewed in 1979 remarked that "everyone knew which children were Basque because they stayed together."

Of those who were born in Euzkadi, twelve were less than five years old when they fled with their families from Guipúzcoa.[73] Much of what they now remember appears to be reconstructed from stories told by older siblings. All the children recall a lack of affection in their childhoods spent in the Escuela España-México.

> Naturally, we suffered an immense nostalgia for our parents, and our country. We would hide ourselves and cry and cry. I cried for weeks under the covers; there was no one to kiss me "good night."
>
> The lack of affection marked me psychologically. I vomited for months in Morelia. The Mexicans didn't like us, that was clear.
>
> I have always felt a lack of security in my life, a consciousness of being abandoned. I didn't marry until I was thirty-nine; until then, I felt alone.

The older Basque boys were sent on by 1940 to military and other secondary schools in Mexico City or, in one case, Durango, and in another, to Orizaba. They found themselves mixed in with the most rebellious Spanish boys. They were all badly treated. Some ran away; others recall being taught nothing; at least two were turned out into the street.

> In 1939, at fourteen, I slept in a dining room for Spanish refugees, and worked for my meals there. Then, a Sr. Miaja, from JARE [a refugee aid organization led by the Socialist Prieto] sent me to Chihuahua as a sheepherder. Later, I worked as a fisherman, then a sailor, traveling all over the world. All of us had to fight to survive.
>
> After Morelia, I came to Hijos del Ejercito #2 [a military school], here in Mexico City. It was worthless, only punishment, not in the least a comprehensive education. Cárdenas was out; Camacho wasn't interested in us; there were no funds for us. By 1940, the refugees had organized some big farms and shops, which later failed.* But I became an apprentice machinist and worked my way up, from age fourteen on. Now I have my own machine shop.

*The Santa Clara Project in Chihuahua, funded by SERE, contained 150,000 hectares of land and 450 Spanish colonists. It was a failure and was dissolved in 1944. See Fagen, p. 55, for a discussion.[74]

> We were truly forsaken. At thirteen, I worked in a hotel for a few months. Then I went to the U.S.A., without papers, and herded sheep in Idaho. I served in the U.S. army, then was deported to Mexico. Here, I've worked for the same company, first as a salesman, now as manager, until today.

Most of the six Basque girls, in contrast, lived in hostels subsidized by the Spanish Republican government until they completed their secondary education or training.

> The *casas de hogar* were good. We were thirty girls from Morelia, living together, having only to work, study, and care for our clothing. We were invited out a great deal. I worked in perfume stores and married early. My twin worked for a photographer; she married early, too.

There were a half-dozen of these pensions, which lasted until World War II and helped perhaps a fourth of the Niños de Morelia. At no time did the Basque men and women who came to Mexico as refugee children receive any help from the Basque colony already entrenched in Mexico.

> Not one of us girls was invited to attend their Colegio de la Vizcaina [an exclusive school begun in the 18th century]. In the Basque colony here, no one took the least interest in us. They are the richest of the rich, in Mexico, but they didn't worry themselves about us.
>
> Nobody helped us after we left the school, least of all the Basque colony. Not even to give us a peso piece! Only the Quakers helped us or were interested.

In spite of this, several have strong ties to the Basque country today, especially those who have married Basques. About half have visited their hometown; many correspond with relatives there, and one family has a daughter who is working in Euzkadi.

Within the group, extremely durable friendships have grown. Nearly half of those still living belong to a social club, the Club Asturiano, and meet there in family groups on weekends. They have attended each other's weddings and funerals. A couple of the men commented that the males in the group are closer to one another than to their blood brothers, born after they left Spain. They keep in contact with all the Basques in the group, except one family who moved out of Mexico City. None has ever attended the now-yearly reunion of the Niños de Morelia, held in Michoacán. On the other hand, they have clear reasons for not joining the Basque Club (Centro Vasco) in Mexico City. It has no sports program, and is much more expensive to join than the Club Asturiano. One also remarked that their presence in the Club Asturiano gives that club a touch of class (*algo de categoria*).

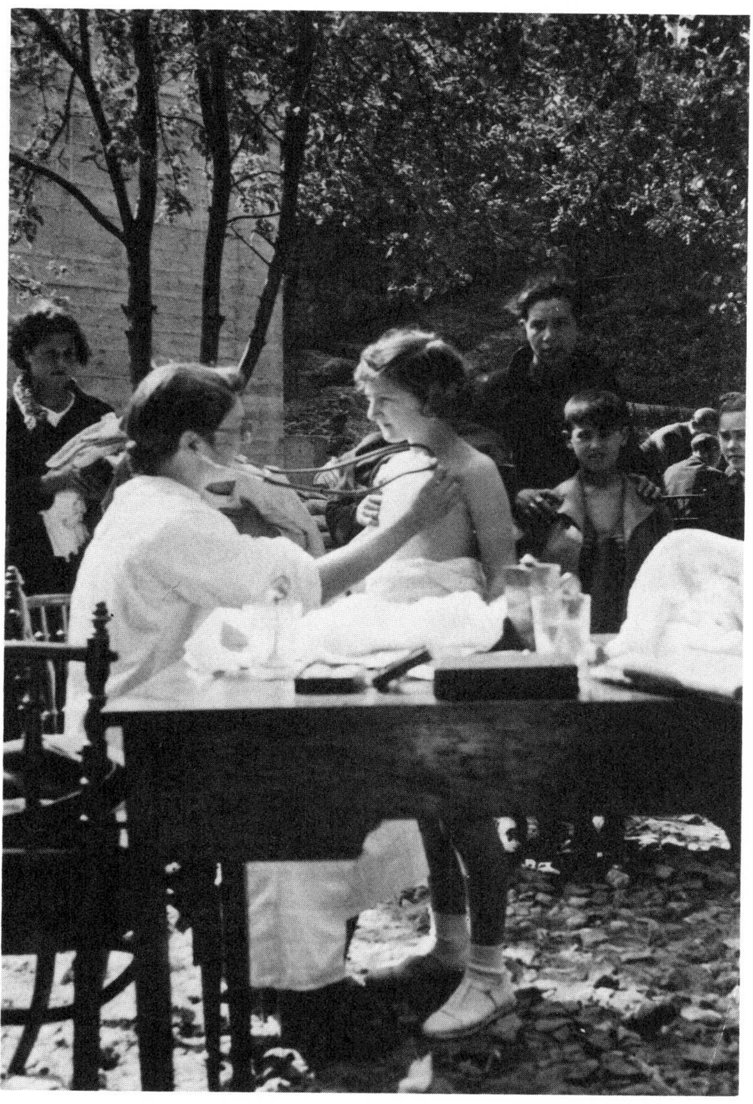

Medical examination of Basque children, by Drs. Audrey and Richard Ellis, in Bilbao, prior to their evacuation to England, May 1937. (Photo courtesy of Stephen Ellis)

Basque children with their priests, being evacuated to France on the *Habana* during the Spring of 1937.

Aboard the *Habana*, bound for Great Britain, May 1937. (Photo courtesy of Stephen Ellis)

Basque government colony at St.-Jean-Pied-de-Port, France. A group of the older boys flanked by Don Fortunato and Don Pello, their mentors. (Photo courtesy of Jesús Pascual Eraso)

Southampton, England. Basque refugee girls devise an outdoor laundry in the provisional camp in June 1937. Note tents in the background, which housed children for some months. (Photo courtesy of Stephen Ellis)

The Basque colony at Jatxu, France, for children of Gudaris, underwritten by Manuel Inchausti. The child on crutches was wounded at Guernica. (Photo courtesy of the director, Miren Barriola)

Basque Government-sponsored colony at Poyanne, France. Basque girls improvise a tea party in the garden. (Photo courtesy of Piru Ajuria, Partido Nacionalista Vasco)

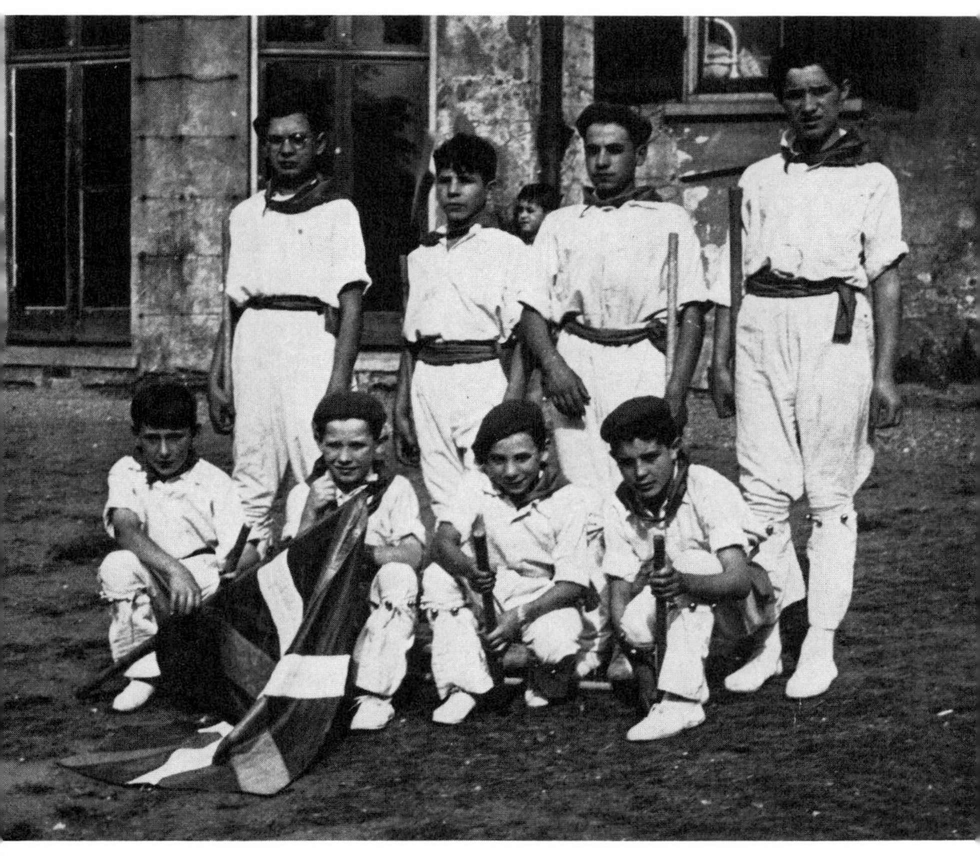

Kingston Hill Colony, London. Basque boys dressed to perform folk dance at a local church hall, with the Basque flag. (Photo courtesy of Eric Pittman)

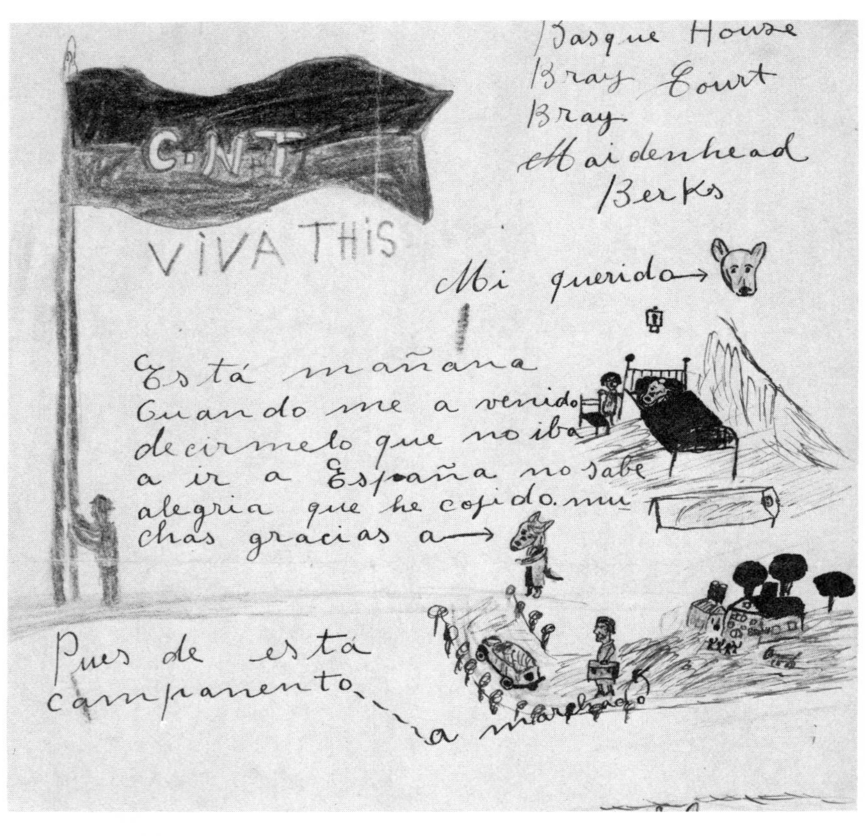

Basque House
Bray Court
Bray
Maidenhead
Berks

C.N.T.

VIVA THIS

Mi querido →

Está mañana
Cuando me a venido
decirmelo que no iba
a ir a España no sabe
alegria que he cojido. muchas gracias a →

Pues de está
campanento
a marchado

Letter from a Basque boy to his friend, Dr. Richard Ellis (the "bear"). The boy is overjoyed to learn that he does not have to return to Spain. The flag is the Anarchist pennant. (Photo courtesy of Stephen Ellis)

Colony at Theydon Blois, England. Basque children enjoy tea with a Member of Parliament. (Photo courtesy of Isabel Balzategui)

Souvenir stamp sold in the British Isles, bearing a likeness of the youngest Basque child evacuated to Great Britain. (Photo courtesy of Leonor Munoz Prieto)

Belgium. First Holy Communion of Basque refugee children at St. Norbert's House, Duffels, in 1948. (Photo courtesy of Esteban Urrien)

Child refugees at the Escuela España-México, eating their first Mexican-style tortillas. (Photo courtesy of Dolores Pla)

Basque children arriving in the Soviet Union, being greeted by Young Pioneers, 1937. (Photo courtesy of Piru Ajuria, Partido Nacionalista Vasco)

Soviet Union, after World War II. Basque girls in a sewing class in Moscow. (Photo courtesy of Juanita Unzueta)

Switzerland. Basque refugee girl (at left) with her adoptive family in their vineyard near Geneva, 1937. (Photo courtesy of Emma Santin)

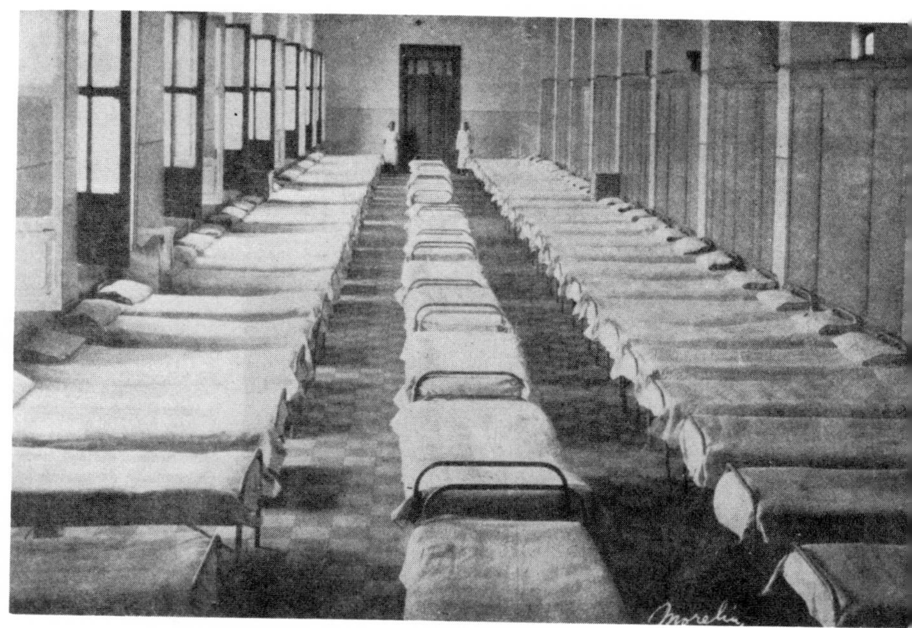

Austere dormitory quarters for the Basque refugee children at the Escuela España-México in Morelia, Mexico.

San Sebastián. The author interviewing the president of the Basque Republic in Exile, Jesus Maria de Leizaola, upon his return to Spain. (Photo courtesy of Jesus Legarreta)

CHAPTER SEVEN

The Repatriation to Euzkadi

The repatriation proceeded in very different ways in France, England, and Belgium. To those children sent to Russia and Mexico, and to their parents, repatriation became an often bitter illusion. The children matured into adolescence, then adulthood, in exile. Most have never returned to the Basque country to live.

In Bilbao, the Rightist press reappeared less than a month after the defeat of the Basque army; the *Gaceta del Norte* resumed publication on July 11, 1937, followed by *El Hierro* and *El Correo Español.*[1] *Euzkadi Roja* and *La Tarde* had gone out of existence shortly before the fall of Bilbao, the last issues appearing on June 15, 1937. The reflection of the new regime in these publications was apparent—great attention to the remarks of General Franco, often pictured on page one astride a great white horse; scrupulous reporting of the myriad religious events and activities of clerical personages; warm thanks to those citizens donating their jewelry or money to the cause; and, more ominously, daily columns of names of those who had completed prison sentences, those whose liberty from house arrest had been approved by the military government, or those ordered to appear before the Delegation of Control to be considered for the required Safe Conduct card.[2]

Shortly, reports on the Basque children evacuated to foreign countries began to appear in the press. The first item, on July 23, noted that the Red Cross had received word from the French government that any Basque child evacuated "by the Red-Separatist government of Vizcaya" would be brought to the border for repatriation whenever the parents wished to reclaim him.[3] The first of many lists to follow of evacuated children appeared four days later. There were ten names, with their respective host towns in France, followed by the request that parents report to the Falange office "to inform themselves of a matter of interest to them."[4]

One week later the Vatican recognized Franco's government. In early August, Msgr. Hildebrando Antoniutti was sent to Spain to supervise the repatriation of the Basque children.[5] The campaign for repatriation gathered momentum everywhere, aided most particularly by representatives of the Catholic church in Rome, Spain, and the non-Socialist host countries. The Pope sent 300,000 lira as a token sum to aid the repatriation process.[6] Msgr. Antoniutti, as the pope's apostolic delegate (personal representative) pressed the higher hierarchy throughout Europe for reclamation. Early in August, Fr. Roca Gabana arrived in Euzkadi to direct the day-by-day work of organizing the repatriation in a special office hurriedly opened in downtown Bilbao.[7] The Rightist European press—*L'Osservatore Romano* in Rome, *L'Action Française* in France, *Le Métropole* in Belgium, and the *Daily Mail* in England—urged repatriation at once.

Within Spain, the new archbishop of Vitoria, Msgr. Lauzirica, the replacement for Msgr. Mateo Múgica, published a pastoral letter in mid-October to all the faithful in his archdiocese, including Vizcaya. In it, he urged the immediate repatriation of all Basque children. He called the evacuation of children a "horrible crime," stating that they were

> dragged violently from their homes by an unjust order, and taken in foreign ships far from their parents by these enemies of God and country for vicious reasons. The

> presence of the refugee children serves to provoke general compassion towards the Basques.

He noted further that "the voices of nearly five thousand parents have risen powerfully to reclaim their children. These parents were exercising their sacred right, for Christ and country, in this time of peace open to all Spaniards." He charged that the Basque children "were in danger of losing their faith, especially those in countries controlled by Moscow or the Popular Front." The letter closed by saying, "After having perpetrated this, they [the Basque Government-in-Exile] attempt to extend the exile, raising all possible obstacles to impede the Christian work, which the Pope and Spain have begun, toward the rapid repatriation of these unfortunate children." The missive was published in its entirety in the Bilbao press, on page one, under headlines saying, "Suffer the Little Children to Come Unto me."[8] Forty-three years later, a Basque evacuated to England at age fourteen commented in his home in Begoña, Bilbao:

> I suppose the Fascists thought that prolonging our stay in democratic or socialist countries would mature the seeds of future enemies.

In Bilbao, to be sure, there was no danger of bombing as the battlefront had shifted east and south. Thousands of its citizens returned from Santander and other short-lived havens. Public dining rooms and nurseries were soon in operation under Insurgent supervision; rebuilding began, and factories reopened. The first 1,700 citizens to return were given a "splendid breakfast" and another four thousand persons were expected to arrive home shortly. The Auxilio Social housed ten thousand returning refugees in one week. During September alone, 8,400 returned from France, and 13,560 from Santander.[9] But political reprisals increased in severity. Prisons and convents soon overflowed with Basque men and women who were of questionable loyalty in Insurgent eyes. Hundreds more were shot to death, and thousands suffered the confiscation of their homes, farms, businesses, and valuables.[10]

The press in Bilbao carried uniformly unfavorable stories regarding the evacuated children: "Crimson children are terrorizing every part of England"; "The forgotten children sent to Mexico to an old building, without sheets, blankets, clean clothes, given too little food, and that, repugnant, are reduced to begging or public charity";[11] "The problem of 20,000 Basque children in France grows, as the Red Spanish Embassy reduces its subsidy";[12] a pathetic photo was published of a toddler, no more than three years of age, wearing Identity tag #2476, unknown to anyone in Belgium;[13] and reports were printed about food riots in Russia by the Basque children.[14] By the end of October, the announcement of the coming repatriation of the first group of British children was published in Bilbao, with a warning against those parents who had not yet come in to request their children's return—"They will lament this bitterly."[15]

The politics of repatriation were clearly expressed that same day in an article entitled "The Basque Children in Foreign Countries." It noted:

> The presence of our children in England, Belgium, France, and the Soviet Union . . . serves to defame the New Spain, our army, and the glorious Caudillo (Franco). The absence of the children is a sword nailed in our hearts; the evacuation, a political farce. The Holy Father has already sent representatives here to help in the reclamation. It is therefore required that all parents of expatriate children, especially those in England, immediately reclaim them, through a request sent to the Falange Provincial office.[16]

In a position paper prepared on the Basque children by the Insurgent Ministry of Interior in Salamanca, the change in public opinion in Europe due to the evacuation was detailed.

> Though the refugees from Guipúzcoa in 1936 were unwelcome in France, the Basque children of 1937, arriving with their priests, singing their Catholic songs, and without the clenched fist salute, have strongly affected public opinion. People ask, "Why does Franco persecute such good people." Even those on the Right say this. Basque officials scrupulously visit all the Catholic hierar-

chy in each country. Already, political repercussions against our cause have appeared in all countries, as special trains of Basque children are organized and received triumphantly. We will lose a generation of Basque youth to Communism unless we give the world the idea of Franco's humanitarianism. At present, we have only the one offer from Franco for a neutral refugee zone. If we repatriate the children, the pretext for this calumny will evaporate. We urge a process through neutral hands, say the International Red Cross, and diplomatic personnel, with a decree signed by Franco, carried by a respected ecclesiastic, but no one like Cardinal Gomá, to the prelates of France, Britain, Denmark, Switzerland, and Belgium. Ethically, parents, not the state, are in charge of their sons. The state's enemies spread the rumor that the repatriation requests are forced by us, the victors. Rarely is such force recommended. Persuasion, yes, since the Spanish state has a supplemental interest in these children. Thus, the state may *stimulate* action on the parents' part for the children's good. Thus, visits to colonies by *"hombres de confianza"* to our cause are necessary. In every possible case, it is now required to intervene with parents and tutors of these Basque children.[17]

In spite of threats and exhortations from press and pulpit, the cooperation of the International Red Cross, and the new British consul in Bilbao, parents in Vizcaya were resisting repatriation. In early September, the press became strident. Headlines on page one of the major papers in Bilbao proclaimed:

> Parents of expatriate children: Come to the Repatriation Office, bringing all the data you can. Don't let us think that some of you aren't Catholic. The grandeur of the Church and the limitless love of the Pope know that you parents will come and let us help return your children.[18]

In the press, the conduct of Basque children already enrolled in the Black Arrow and Pelayo, Falange youth groups, were contrasted with that of the refugee children, the "scandalous ones" in England and France. Other articles about the Falange youth groups sent to Germany and Italy rhapsodized regarding the training they were receiving there, how "Mussolini, with our children, sang the Hymn of Spain."[19] There were daily columns of the many activities of the Fascist youth groups, illustrated with drawings of children in their new uniforms, with glowing descriptions of their work for God and Country. Still, parents did not hasten to the offices of the Falange or the Apostolic Delegate. Without the names and addresses of the over nineteen thousand children evacuated the preceding spring and summer, the Papal Nuncio and the Falange could do next to nothing.

Then an unexpected treasure was discovered in Santander by the victorious Insurgent army as it entered there at the end of August. Officials discovered a complete list, compiled by Asistencia Social, of the more than fifteen thousand children sent to France, England, and Russia from Bilbao. Reports in the press celebrated a "Transcendental Recovery of Documents from the so-called Red-Separatist Government of Euzkadi." This file, one of the four scrupulously prepared earlier by Juan Gracia, was of inestimable value to Franco's repatriation campaign.[20] Had it not fallen into his hands, the repatriation would have been prolonged and perhaps unsuccessful. The files on the many Basque children sent to Russia were of particular curiosity to the press, as was the fact that the last expedition sailed exactly a week before Insurgent troops entered Bilbao.

By the end of September, the necessary administrative machinery was in place in Bilbao for total repatriation of the children. A special committee of the Provincial Office for the Protection of Minors was at once formed, called "Section Five: Repatriation of Children Abroad." It was charged with "the responsibility of reclaiming children evacuated from Spain by the so-called Red Separatist government, and with the coordination of all necessary data which will be transferred to this junta, including the 1,479 files of children in Russia." Don Luis de Llaguno was appointed as its president; members included representatives of the Falange, the Juventud de Ofensiva Nacional Sindicalista (JONS)—a Fascist youth organization—and Auxilio Social.[21]

With this, the repatriation campaign began in dead earnest. Day after day, lists of fifty names of children were published in the newspapers, with the admonition that their parents report immediately to the Section Five office located behind the provincial government building in downtown Bilbao. These lists were conspicuously placed next to the column of "Edicts of the Day" of the Insurgent Army of Occupation. The latter consisted of announcements ordering new groups of citizens to report to the Civil Guard "without excuse or delay."[22]

A further prod to Basque parents who had sent away children was the message contained in two large public presentations in Bilbao sponsored by the office of the Papal Nuncio. The first took place in the Buenos Aires theatre on November 28. Fr. Gabana, recently returned from his tour of certain children's colonies in France and England, lectured on the moral care of children in both countries. He recounted that over fourteen hundred Basque children were under Protestant auspices in England. He further stated that, in the colony operated by the Salvation Army in London, some four hundred took Holy Communion the first Sunday there, but only thirteen the second. The press reported that "an audible gasp of disbelief and outrage shook the assemblage."[23] Gabana also noted that, in France, many Catholic children were in the adoptive homes of Communists, and that the French Popular Front was determined to educate these children to be adherents of this secular faith.*

A second gathering, early in 1938, in the immense Arriaga Theater, found the Falange leader, Oriol Urquijo, explaining forcefully the importance of repatriating the Basque children. He appealed, "Give them to us, for our formation."[24]

*Fr. Gabana's expressed concern for the morals of the young refugees was somewhat singular. According to a Basque priest, well-placed in the Aguirre government, Gabana had an unsavory reputation for a morals charge involving minors in a previous post. An appeal was made to the Pope by the Basque clergy for his removal, but it proved fruitless.[25]

French Repatriation

France, host to the great majority of refugee children from Spain, became an immediate target of the repatriation efforts of Msgr. Antoniutti, the Falange, and the Section Five organization. Pressure on the French Catholic hierarchy from the Papal Nuncio took the form of requests of the St. Vincent de Paul Society to expedite the return of all children in colonies, and alleged pressure to extradite the Basque priests who had gone into exile with the children. Personal visits to La Citadelle, coupled with calls on members of the Comité National Catholique (CNC) and the preparation of material favorable to repatriation published in the French Catholic press, were undertaken by the monsignor. One Basque recalled:

> Msgr. Antoniutti came to visit us that fall. He spoke to us of Franco's wish that we return to our homes in Spain. He visited our little chapel, but seemed in a hurry, and declined to stay for our service in Basque. A rumor started that he had had a row with Don Fortunato.

The official stance of the French government, through its minister of interior, was to leave the issue of repatriation essentially to the private organizations sponsoring children. Whatever pressure was used reflected the cost of maintaining each refugee, which soon totaled some fifteen francs daily, shared by the national and provincial governments. It appears, however, that the Popular Front was able, even after its electoral defeat, to exercise enough influence to limit the expulsion of refugees to those of military age. However, after the French government shifted to the right, in mid-1937, a special envoy was sent to Burgos to open unofficial diplomatic negotiations with the Franco government.

The repatriation procedure as adopted by the French government was initiated only by a reclamation request from parents. The child was then awarded a visa by the French consul in Republican Spain, which was sent on to the Spanish embassy, usually via the Spanish consul in Bayonne. He, in turn, signed off on the request and sent it to the French minister of foreign affairs, who transferred it to the Ministry of the Interior. This office alerted the prefect of the police in whatever department the child was being housed. The prefect contacted the child's caretakers, who arranged transport through the St. Vincent de Paul Society to the border. In this careful process, children would leave in very small groups, and often singly, ostensibly to avoid any political demonstrations.[26]

When the first such requests from the French ambassador in Spain arrived (for nine children from La Citadelle), the Spanish consul in Bayonne forwarded them without comment. This alacrity moved the Basque delegation to send an official protest to the Spanish (Republican) ambassador in Paris:

> This requires a diplomatic intervention on your part with the French government, and also with your colleague, the French Ambassador to Spain. The Rebels employ every means to exact requests, and it is important to make the French government see that it doesn't become an instrument of this coercion.[27]

From early August onward, the Basque Delegation used every means at its disposal to countermand the pressures for repatriation. Diplomatic channels were employed whenever possible. Perhaps the strongest weapon was use, once again, of the concept of the "free will of the parents." This was coupled with the Basque government's right of education of Euzkadi's children expressed by the Spanish Republic in October of 1936.[28] A careful campaign was begun to obtain letters from Basque parents living in refuges in France, stating that their children, living in colonies in France, England, or Belgium, were not to be repatriated. Over 650 parents responded to this appeal during the first government census by agreeing:

> I, parent of x, now residing in y, exercise my parental rights by giving, freely and spontaneously, to the Basque Committee on Evacuation, the responsibility of education and Christian-Basque instruction in the way they judge best. I promise to receive my children when the cited committee judges this to be appropriate. (1937 Census Form: Archives, Basque Government-in-Exile).[29]

The Basque delegation prepared a position paper that was circulated widely. It included documentation which indicated that many requests for repatriation were fictitious or signed under pressure, that there was no guarantee that those repatriated would not be persecuted, and that the children repatriated would be enrolled in paramilitary groups of a totalitarian type repugnant to Basques. The paper noted that all gestures for repatriation were generated by Catholic sources. Throughout the document, the specifically political nature of the repatriation was addressed clearly.[30] These efforts by the Basque Delegation had some apparent effect, as the Franco Ministry of Information noted in late October that the French Ministry of Interior, "inspired by the Red ambassador of Spain in Paris," had ordered that no child be reclaimed.[31] When Msgr. Antoniutti demanded of the French hierarchy that all children of La Citadelle be repatriated, the Basque government established that, in fact, at least 156 of the children (over one-third) had parents actually living in France who were naturally opposed to their repatriation to Bilbao.[32]

From its new office in Burgos, the International Red Cross, (IRC) tried to expedite the process of repatriation. It designed a simple form requiring only three signatures: a parent, an IRC representative, and the French consul in Insurgent-held San Sebastián.This was intended to circumvent the lengthy, prudent process used by the French government.[33] In spite of all these efforts only ninety-five children were repatriated in 1937, and a total of only forty-three in 1938.[34]

The two groups leaving in 1937 were made up of children from La Citadelle. As they crossed the border into Spain, they were welcomed by Msgr. Antoniutti and given Rebel flags, "which the little ones received with great emotion."[35] At least one remembers their crossing the border as traumatic and frightening:

> None of us wanted to return, but we were powerless. We felt at home in La Citadelle, but we were coming back to the unknown. At the border, they tried to make us salute Franco's flag, but we just stared at them.

The Bilbao press headlined the return of these first children as "rescued from an anarchist-separatist kidnapping."[36]

Repatriation from England

Even earlier than in France, articles had appeared in two Catholic journals in England, the *Universe* and the *Catholic Herald*, pressing for the return of the children. Thus, in the case of the 3,889 children sent to England, repatriation became an issue shortly after their arrival, beginning immediately after the fall of Bilbao. Even as the children landed in Southampton, the Catholic *Tablet* editorialized,

> There is no question now of the wisdom or of the necessity for bringing in this large company so far from its native land. Highly reasonable proposals were put forth in General Franco's name, to provide a neutral area in which refugees could live securely outside the fighting zone around Bilbao. . . . It is greatly to be hoped that no attempt will be made to use them as propaganda, but that they will be enabled to live quiet and healthy lives through an English summer, and that they may be repatriated before very long.[37]

The day after the children arrived, a sympathetic article in a Labour-oriented paper commented that children of the British unemployed, well over 1.7 million in 1937, were also suffering. The ten shillings per week the NJCSR had to guarantee for each child was, in fact, higher than the allowance per child on the government dole, though wayward British children in boarding homes were allowed ten shillings five pence, or up to fifteen shillings weekly in exceptional cases.[38]

When the *Universe* and *Herald* articles appeared, both noted that Franco was anxious to receive Basque children in Bilbao, and that Catholic authorities were willing to repatriate all of the children in their care. The BCC met three days later, and discussion of repatriation occupied half of the minutes taken. Canon Craven, the representative of Archbishop Hinsley, disavowed the two articles at once. But Captain MacNamara stated that he had received repatriation inquiries from all over England. He suggested that an office be opened in Bilbao to begin the process. Instead, a press statement was prepared emphasizing that "until the children's parents were in a position to take them back under conditions of safety, the BCC would continue to offer them refuge."[39]

In opposition, the Duke of Alba, as Franco's personal representative in England, urged formation of a repatriation committee forthwith. This was quickly formed, under the leadership of Sir Arnold Wilson, a member of Parliament, and a staunch supporter of Insurgent Spain. Through a press campaign, including a series of "Letters to the Editor," public speeches, and other events, the members of this group, known as the Wilson Repatriation Committee, were able to slow the fund-raising efforts of the BCC. One of its members, in a speech reported in the *Manchester Guardian*, made the position of the Wilson Repatriation Committee very clear:

> I don't mind telling you that I am on the Repatriation Committee about these little Basque devils and it is very difficult to get them back. Don't pay a penny towards the upkeep of these Basques. . . . they are a pretty expensive cup of tea.[40]

Very soon after the formation of this committee, word came via the Foreign Office that the new British consul, Mr. Pears, had received repatriation requests from parents in Bilbao.[41] (Mr. Stevenson, referred to as "El Consul Rojo" by Franco's supporters, had been replaced after the fall of Bilbao.[42]) If these requests were genuine, the BCC knew that its policies were in serious trouble. Added to the growing interest in repatriation after the Insurgent victory in Bilbao was the bad press concerning the behavior of the Basque youngsters in certain areas of Great Britain.

Both the staff and leadership of the BCC mobilized to counteract the work of the Wilson Committee. First, to defuse the negative reports regarding the "outrageous" actions of the refugee Basque youngsters in the British press, they immediately took the steps previously noted. That is, the BCC replaced the director of the Stoneham Camp with "an experienced military officer just retired from active service";

it shipped twenty-three of the boys on the "black list" to France; and it opened the camp at Diss for fifty of the remaining most troublesome boys.[43] A *Times* correspondent, after visiting the colonies in response to the wave of horror stories about "savage Basque children," wrote: "The high pitched whirr of axe-grinding which has been the Basque children's career in this country has drowned out the still, small voice of truth."[44]

Thus, within two months after the children's arrival, the BCC was under heavy pressure from the Foreign Office, the Home Office, the Catholic and Right-wing press, as well as from many of its own members, to send the children home. Since they had actually received no repatriation requests, the committee decided to send representatives to Bilbao as soon as possible to survey the situation and verify the authenticity of the requests others were receiving. It was reported at the BCC meeting in July that at the London colony, Theydon Bois,

> One of the boys received a letter from his parents, saying that everything in Bilbao was now normal, and food was plentiful, and he must come back and join the Black Arrow Regiment.* The child became highly excited upon reading the letter, and said he knew his father would never wish him to join the Black Arrows. He pointed to a small tear at the corner of the letter which he said was a pre-arranged signal from his father that nothing in a letter with a torn corner was to be believed. Mrs. Manning submitted that pressure was being brought on Bilbao parents to write such letters by Bilbao authorities.[45]

Other instances of questionable requests began to appear, particularly among those Father Gabana brought to England in September. He carried with him both a card index of parents who had requested repatriation, and a stack of presumed letters from the parents. The first had many inaccuracies, and many of the parental letters were on typed forms.

*Falange Youth Group.

Of the nine hundred children listed, in only 493 cases did the individual's number correspond with those entered in BCC office files when the children arrived. Fr. Gabana, when asked about the list, said that half had been supplied by the Falange office, and the rest by his office, but that both were reliable. He thought that after this first group was repatriated, Franco would allow an investigative group of the BCC into Bilbao. He also would allow the committee to view the parents' letters.[46] Canon Craven added the official Catholic view on the issue, as of October 1: It should be speedy, he said, as the support of the one thousand children was costing between five and six hundred pounds weekly. "We, the Catholics, took them out of charity, but did not think they would be kept longer than absolutely necessary, and the money is nearly exhausted. If the BCC declines to send the children back, my people will be forced to consider other methods. . . . We want to see the whole four thousand back as there is now no danger in Bilbao."[47]

The Basque Government-in-Exile mobilized its representatives to counter, or at least delay, the repatriation. From London the Basque consul wrote to Gracia in Paris, urging that letters from parents not wishing to reclaim their children from England, France, or Belgium be encouraged. Consul Uranga wrote,

> Fr. Gabana states his requests for repatriation come from tearful mothers in Bilbao. He is a cold, cautious man who hides his feelings well. I acted as interpreter with the BCC, though his English is good. He repeats his proposal to repatriate 900 children in a correct but aggressive manner, stating that 500 children are already arriving from Belgium, and a priest in Bayonne is arranging repatriation of many of the children in France.[48]

Consul Uranga noted that the BCC was sending a neutral fact-finding group to Bilbao, before agreeing to any repatriation. The consul added these frank comments:

> I think personally that some sent to Bilbao would be no worse off than at present in Catholic homes, though the rest are doing well and don't wish to return. Those in Catholic homes are not well-treated; they are objects of

> special persecution ever since Bilbao fell. Catholics here are not contributing, the children are badly fed, and the object of constant insinuations on the part of the nuns.

His letter ended with an anecdote:

> I also have word from the teachers of a Catholic colony that was visited last Sunday by the aforesaid Gabana. . . . The envoy told the children that he came in the name of Catholic Spain to apprise them of General Franco's desire that they return to Bilbao. Upon hearing the word "Catholic" the girls especially, all Basque Nationalists, made a general uproar. The envoy, Gabana, not content with this response, then spoke of Guernica, saying it had been burned by the Reds. The indignation of the children was such that the envoy had to leave the colony very hurriedly.[49]

The Basque representatives in France quickly gathered letters from forty-three parents, refugees in France, who did not want their children in England repatriated. A number of their children's names had already appeared in the lists published daily in Bilbao. When parents there did come into the offices, they were told to write letters requesting reclamation.[50] It was clear that many requests were signed by parents under duress, and that the lists, published without investigation as to the condition or location of parents, were being used as a pretext for pressuring parents still in Vizcaya.[51]

The BCC was fully aware of this tactic by Insurgent authorities anxious to eliminate a source of international embarrassment to their regime. The BCC commission of three neutral observers which accompanied the first repatriated 163 children was charged with verifying other requests submitted by Fr. Gabana. Additionally, the BCC had invited three prominent attorneys to advise them (as in loco parentis guardians of the children) on the legality of the repatriation requests of Fr. Gabana, as well as its own legal position in the process. The attorneys met six times in October of 1937 to examine the 387 repatriation letters (many for two, three, or more children from the same family), to discuss the repatriation process thoroughly, and to hear testimony from those involved with the children. The attorneys made their report in late October, stating that the applications were genuine and that the eight hundred children should be repatriated at the earliest possible date. They recommended that a neutral commission appointed by Fr. Gabana and the BCC accompany the first group of children to Spain and arrange for the return of subsequent groups.[52]

The BCC had no choice but to accept the findings. Mrs. Lydia Gee, a fluent Spanish speaker who had visited Spain previously for other humanitarian groups, was appointed to the commission. She was totally non-political, and her devotion to children was well known, so it was felt she could accomplish this delicate mission. Accompanying her was a British doctor from the League of Nations, Norman White, as well as a former member of the Ministry of Health, Dame Janet Campbell.

Newspaper reports of the Basque children's leavetaking, as well as Mrs. Gee's personal journal, detailed the mournful parting. The *News-Chronicle*, staunchly anti-Franco, published a long article, contrasting photos of the destruction of Guernica, Bilbao, and Santander with "Happy Basque Children at Rowley Lodge, Barnet." The author, Phillip Jordon, described the press campaign against the children, called "Reds, savages, even cannibals, and thieves," and noted that the Falangist press in Bilbao was printing threatening messages to parents to reclaim their children.[53] The *Times* described the departure with the headline "They Cannot Understand Why They Must Go Back," and quoted Leah Manning as saying that "some boys threatened to throw themselves into the sea rather than go back to Bilbao."[54]

The group, gathered from Catholic colonies in Dundee, Liverpool, Cardiff, and Wight, had yet another medical examination and a "final English breakfast—cereal with raisins and milk, bread, butter and jam, a banana, and cups of coffee." After a bus ride to Victoria station,

> They descended pathetically from the buses, clasping dolls, teddy bears, picture books, or bright new cardboard attache cases. They were newly washed, spic and span, labeled with their names. Some cried, some were

> silent. Almost all have noticeably put on height and weight since they arrived.[55]

They sailed on the SS *Brighton* to Dieppe, and went on by train to Hendaye on November 12.

> In ten minutes the children were filing over the International Bridge and, on arrival at the centre, where Spain officially begins, all, rather pathetically and uncertainly, raised their hands in the Fascist salute.[56]

The children were then lined up for hours while speeches extolling Franco were given by Falange officials. Dignitaries, including Msgr. Antoniutti and the governor of Guipúzcoa also spoke. Mrs. Gee wrote,

> The parents were waiting behind a barrier, and all were harangued for hours, as though they were bandits. The children were finally given black bread and ersatz coffee, while we, as visitors, were given white bread. We only had a four day safe-conduct, and if we overstayed, we would be imprisoned. The children went to Irún, to a dinner, and we went on to Bilbao.[57]

The Bilbao press reported this arrival much more copiously than the two preceding repatriations already completed in October—sixteen children from Belgium; seventy-eight from France. Articles began, "As the Spanish flag was flying, and the Carlist Requete band was playing the 'Hymn to Spain,' the children gave rigorous Falange salutes." Accounts in the papers contrasted this with the clenched fist salute and the "Internationale" sung when the children left Spain. After a round of speeches, the youngsters were taken to church, fed, and sent by train to Bilbao.[58] Their arrival in Bilbao was noted in the [London] *Times*:

> A Falangist band headed the children's march from the stations last night through specially illuminated streets crowded with cheering people. For escort there were many small boys of the new Bilbao in dark blue uniforms, and each carrying either a torch or a model rifle. Each was obviously eager to show off to new arrivals the transfiguration of Bilbao since Gen. Franco's forces took

> Bilbao from the Basques . . . It is proposed that children be taught in schools to think of themselves primarily as Spaniards, rather than as Basques. They are to be enlisted in the Falangist organization known as the "Arrows," similar to Germany's "Jungvolk" or Italy's "Balilla." An eight-year-old boy told me in Guernica yesterday that 100 village boys are already enrolled in the Arrows, and their own anthem is sung to the air of the Horstwessel song.[59]

In Bilbao, the children were served a "splendid supper" at ten in the evening.[60]

Mrs. Gee worked rapidly in Euzkadi to verify a number of the requests pending for repatriation. Her rough notes indicate that, of one thousand applications on the forms in the British Consulate in Bilbao, many did not bear the mother's signature. Many parents, when she contacted them personally, wanted their children to remain in England. In other cases, request letters were fraudulent, as parents were in France, refugees themselves. One parent, interviewed in 1980, remarked:

> I, like so many others, did not request my children's return. I was in a concentration camp in France when they were sent back. Almost by chance, an aunt heard of it, and kept them until I could return.

The neutral commission soon left because the safe conduct of the group was only extended to six days. The second contingent of children to arrive from England, fifty-six in all, were met only briefly at the border before the observers departed the country.

The commission from Bilbao reported to the BCC at a special meeting on November 23. This meeting was closed to visitors. Mrs. Gee noted the poverty of many of the parents. Another observer stated that parents were afraid of the consequences of not reclaiming their children. Mrs. Gee emphasized that General Franco wanted every child back. The BCC moved to request of the Duke of Alba that a permanent representative in Bilbao be approved to supervise the repatriation. A form devised by the BCC would now be used by both the office of the Apostolic Delegate and that of Section Five. The group felt that it was safe to send children back, as the situation in the Bilbao area was apparently normal, with free meal service and child welfare institutions operative. The BCC voted another three hundred pounds to help defray repatriation costs.[61]

The repatriation process continued slowly in England as only 265 children had left by the end of 1937.[62] Though the theater of the Spanish Civil War had by now shifted to the Madrid and Barcelona areas, and air raids by Insurgent planes became daily occurrences to the civilian populations there, the needs of the Basque children continued to be paramount in the NJCSR. Early in 1938, eight hundred remained a direct charge of the BCC. Another six hundred remaining in Catholic colonies soon became the responsibility of the BCC, as was the case with the children housed in Salvation Army institutions. Of those on Fr. Gabana's original list, 174 could not be repatriated,[63] because their parents were dead, missing, or refugees themselves.

The Catholic press in England continually exerted pressure to repatriate every child. *The Tablet* editorialized:

> The Auxilio Social in Bilbao is a very efficient and vigorous organization, which provides for the wants of all those who are suffering need today. It circularizes every house with a form on which the householders are invited to say what they will give, either in money or kind, every week. The responses vary. Few people in Spain today have much in the way of a money income, but there is no one who does not give, if not in money, then in kind. The vans of Auxilio Social go from house to house and collect the resources. With these resources the free dining rooms for children are maintained. The children who benefit from these meals live with their parents, but their parents are thus relieved of a measure of housekeeping expense. Sometimes, where there is a family of four or five, two of the children will come for their meals to the Auxilio Social. As parents find work or earn more, they notify the organization, and in the past year the numbers of people needing help have in fact halved.

> We drove out to a day playground and children's restaurant in the high hills, in what used to be part of the iron belt, and saw a great number of children who came out to spend every day there, returning to their own homes to sleep. This continued residence at home is part of the policy of Auxilio Social, which is very anxious not to separate families or needlessly to weaken home life. Looking at that playground, and the extremely capable and pleasant young Spanish women who were running it as volunteers, it was hard to enter the mentality of the people in England who consider themselves better guardians for Basque children than their own compatriots. The Spanish view of the refusal to return the children still in England is quite simply that they are kept here to be used for propaganda. But they did not greatly mind. The terrible thing that has happened, and the fate from which being brought to England has undoubtedly saved many of these children, was their kidnapping and despatch to Russia with no prospect of their eventual rescue or return. Several thousand children suffered this fate from this part of Spain alone.[64]

By the end of 1938, another group of child refugees was arriving in England—Jewish youngsters from Germany, Czechoslovakia, Austria, and Poland.[65] Some were taken to Bray Court colony and placed with the Basque children there. Others were housed at Southampton. One woman interviewed in Bilbao recalled their arrival:

> My three sisters and I stayed in England for three years. When Weston Manor closed in 1938—only eighteen Basque girls were left then—we went back to Southampton, to Nazareth House. In 1939, the Jewish children were coming to England, refugees from Germany and other places. We were then in our teens, and we helped bathe the littlest Jewish children, little more than babies. One little six-year-old boy, very serious, followed us to Mass. He sat with us, knelt with us, and told us, "I love you."

Another woman, interviewed in a Hutterite community in upstate New York in 1981, spoke of her years as a Jewish refugee child in England:

> At thirteen, I attended a boarding school in London in 1939, and remember being taken to an international dance exhibit in a concert hall there. I'll never forget the dances a group of Basque children performed for us—they were incredible. I was born in Germany, and had first escaped to France, and later lived in South America. I've never seen such dancing before or since.

At this same time, the BCC made a case-by-case report on the Basque children, 1,054 in all, who had not yet been repatriated. This analysis, from the files of the BCC, dates from mid-1939.[66]

Analysis Showing Total Number of Basque Children in England with Full Particulars of their Parents' Circumstances

1. Total number of children in England		1,054
2. Categories which in the view of the Basque Children's Committee, and subject to individual investigation in all cases, can be repatriated		
1. Both parents in Spain		145
2. Father dead, mother in Spain		69
3. Father in Spain, mother dead		21
4. Father abroad, mother in Spain		47
5. Father in Spain, mother abroad		50
6. Father's whereabouts unknown, mother in Spain		43
7. Father in Spain, mother's whereabouts unknown		13
8. Father dead, mother's whereabouts unknown		16
9. Father's whereabouts unknown, mother dead		17
10. Both parents dead		56
	Total:	477
3. Categories which in the opinion of the Basque Children's Committee should remain in England because it is impossible to restore them to their parents under existing war conditions		
1. Both parents abroad		164
2. Both parents unknown		76
3. Both parents prisoners		26
4. Father in prison, mother in Spain		135
5. Father in Spain, mother in prison		1
6. Father prisoner, mother abroad		35
7. Father abroad, mother prisoner		2
8. Father prisoner, mother dead		8
9. Father dead, mother prisoner		1

10.	Father in prison, mother unknown	14
11.	Father dead, mother abroad	50
12.	Father unknown, mother prisoner	14
13.	Father abroad, mother dead	13
14.	Father abroad, mother unknown	6
15.	Father unknown, mother abroad	34
	Total:	577

By the end of 1938, nearly two thousand children still resided in England, and by February 1939, when war in Spain ended, 1,600 remained in the country.

Less than six months later, England herself was at war. At this point, the BCC listed 1,155 children as living in England:[67]

Report on Repatriation

Children brought to England	3,889
Lost by decease	8
Lost by repatriation	2,726
Left in England	1,155
Señoritas repatriated	95
Señoritas left in England	122
Priests left in England	10

With the beginning of World War II, the position of the Basque children in England became more precarious. The BCC had few funds to spend for their care, and it was difficult to justify their continued expatriation within a country at war. In spite of this, the BCC did everything possible to continue to offer hospitality to those who could not return. A letter from its secretary to an adoptive family made this position clear:

> Since the outbreak of war, considerable pressure has been brought to bear on the Basque Children's Committee by the Foreign Office, who are asking us to return to Spain immediately all children who are orphans, or have one or both parents in Spain.
>
> The BCC has given very long and serious consideration to the Foreign Office request, and has now agreed that as a general principle children in these three categories

> should be returned, since they are probably safer in Spain than they would be under war conditions in this country. The Committee is however prepared to consider individual objections and representations on their merits. At the same time, the Committee feels obligated to point out that it is unlikely to be able to accept financial responsibility for the Basque children for more than another month or so.
>
> The BCC also feels, and the Foreign Office agreed, that children who have parents in France should not be returned to Spain since this might mean a lifetime separation of families. We should therefore be glad to know whether you would be prepared to consider offering hospitality to one of these children if the child you now have should be returned to Spain. As the matter is urgent, we should be glad to have your reply at the earliest possible date.
>
> We would like to emphasize that many children will remain in England and we do request you very urgently to give hospitality to another child if the one you have at present is returned to Spain.[68]

The BCC continued to repatriate children only after the most scrupulous investigation. Since Franco would not permit BCC members in Bilbao, all inquiries regarding repatriation had to be routed to a Dr. Byloff of the "Save the Children Fund" who was then based in Bilbao. She carefully investigated each request and made a recommendation based on parental ability to support the child. Dr. Byloff noted that any help (food, clothing, medical care) was only available through the Fascist channels—even Quaker help had to be channeled through the government—and some Basque parents refused to apply for political reasons. She also verified that a number of repatriated children had to be placed in the Falange orphanages, as they had no living parents. Many parents of children in England were reported to be in prison (235), in exile abroad (164), dead (72), or unknown (76). In all such cases, their children would have to remain in England. She noted that some mothers were ashamed to tell their children that their father was in prison; when children arrived in Bilbao, the family could hardly survive.

In her reports, Dr. Byloff discussed the issue of forced claims for repatriation. These were most prevalent in small communities, "where everyone's business is known to everybody, and the authorities or priest have forced the parents to claim." In such cases, she felt that recent letters from parents would be valuable.[69] One such parental letter has survived:

> June 1939
>
> My dear children, Adela, Joaquín, Fernando, Enrique, Javi, and Rosa,
>
> I am without job, and therefore, if you are obliged to come to Bilbao, I cannot maintain you. Just do say to your friends and protectors that they help you. Can you not find some families who would shelter you? Can you gain some money. *Don't listen to nobody but me.*
>
> That the good families protect you,
> Your father[70]

In retrospect, after the fall of Bilbao the hospitality provided in Britain became generally strained.

Sir James Cable's appraisal of the sojourn of the Basque children in Britain notes:

> Throughout their stay, moreover, the political climate was changing to the children's disadvantage. . . . The children now [March 1938] belonged all too obviously in the camp of the defeated: . . . an obstacle to the future of Anglo-Spanish relations. . . . It is, however, an interesting indication of the widespread diffusion of ideological prejudices in the thirties, that the presence in England of this dwindling number of Basque children should have continued to command so much attention, even to excite actual animosity, among the officials of a Government whose avowed policy of Non-Intervention was interpreted to exclude assistance in their maintenance, but not opposition to their presence.[71]

Repatriation continued slowly through the spring and summer of 1940, the strange period of the "Phony War," when France could still be crossed safely. The last official reclamation occurred after the fall of France. On July 10, 1940, twenty-six children returned on a Spanish cargo boat from Manchester. A total of 2,805 were officially returned to the Basque provinces.[72] Hundreds more went to France to rejoin parents, also refugees. Small groups went to Mexico and South America to rejoin parents there. And eight had died in England.

Belgian Repatriation

Repatriation of Basque children from Belgium did not become the political issue characteristic of certain other host countries. The Belgian government left the process of repatriating its over three thousand young guests entirely in the hands of the five organizations responsible for them. Cardinal Van Roey was the first to begin sending children back to Spain. He responded to the strong pressure placed by the Pope through Msgr. Antoniutti on the European Catholic hierarchy, but he did so in a very careful manner. He quietly named a Repatriation Commission, headed by Msgr. Janssens. He sent Janssens to Bilbao to confer directly with Msgr. Antoniutti; he arrived near the end of August 1937.[73] A few weeks later, the first article in *Le Métropole* appeared, urging immediate repatriation of all Basque children. Heading the article was a poignant drawing pressing for the return of all children to the new Spain.[74]

Msgr. Janssens brought with him a packet of letters written by children living under Catholic auspices, as well as the list of the 1,265 children in their care, with the names and addresses of their adoptive family or school. He announced to the press that parents should contact him if they had lost contact with their children and suspected that they might be in Belgium.[75] The response to this offer was minimal. So few parents came to the office of Msgr. Antoniutti, that within two weeks the Bilbao papers were publishing the names of twenty-five children in Belgium each day along with the instructions that parents come in to sign reclamation forms for their return.[76] Successive lists of Belgian children appeared on September 11, 12, 14, 15, 16, 21, 24, and 25, always on the same page of the Bilbao papers. From the 21st forward, the original directive to parents was omitted. Instead, the text read: "These expatriate children are begging for news of their parents."[77]

Yet, in spite of the energetic efforts of the Apostolic Office of Repatriation and the new official Junta for the Repatriation of Children, very few parents signed the required forms. The very first children to arrive in Bilbao, however, came from Belgium, a group of only sixteen.[78] They came in mid-October, accompanied by the Belgian consul and Msgr. Janssens. The children were enthusiastically greeted by Msgr. Antoniutti, and widely feted. Their attendants were given tours of the brand new Falange orphanage and other programs of assistance to children, through the Auxilio Social.[79] A second group of forty-nine children came from Belgium early in November, and forty-eight more on November 24.[80]

In Bilbao, additional measures were begun to ensure the reclamation of expatriated children:

> Basque children left Brussels by train, accompanied by Monsignor Janssens, and other religious. Many were sobbing, though this emotion was not echoed by the religious. They will go direct to Paris, and cross the border at Hendaye. The jurisdiction of His Eminence [Van Roey] now appears to be international in scope.[81]

By the time this third contingent arrived in Bilbao, however, the campaign for reclamation had lost much of its credibility. Though initially it had seemed that the repatriation would go smoothly and rapidly after the lists became available, and the Pope, as well as his Papal Nuncio, lent financial and moral support to the effort, an unforeseen event occurred. Upon the arrival in Belgium of Fr. Gabana, as emissary from Msgr. Antoniutti, a list he brought with him was circulated. He claimed that the nine hundred names on it were bona fide requests for reclamation from anguished parents in the Basque country.[82] The list, however, contained so many inaccuracies as to be highly suspect. The most glaring, perhaps, was the presence on it of the children of the Basque secretary of the Catholic Committee in Malines itself. Since she had her children with her, the error or falsity was obvious.

This incident was widely publicized by the Basque Government-in-Exile, appearing in England, France, and even in South America. Curiously, Fr. Gabana returned to the Archbishop's office with an amended list of only about three hundred names, but again the two children of the secretary were on it.

> The priest [Fr. Gabana] brought a list of 900 names, assuring the Cardinal that their parents, residing in the Franco zone, wished to reclaim them. The members of the Belgian Committee questioned the list; the priest withdrew. He returned with a shorter list, with only 300 names. But again, the name of M.A., secretary to the Belgian committee, as desiring her two children returned, appeared. This woman is very disturbed by the insolence of this maneuver.[83]

Perhaps as a result of this occurrence, the Cardinal began to require that the validity of each reclamation request be attested to by the Belgian consul. The repatriation process for the children of Belgium moved even more slowly after this. During the entire next year, until the end of the Civil War in Spain, only 256 children under Catholic auspices were returned.[84]

Of the children cared for by secular groups, which were immune to the appeals of both the Pope and Franco, nearly everyone remained. But as the hostilities of World War II moved closer to Belgium in 1939, its government began to consider the future safety of the more than two thousand remaining children who had been there for two years. A neutral governmental commission was set up to activate the repatriation process by alerting adoptive parents throughout Belgium of the urgency of the situation. Parents still living in Spain were notified, and invited to request that their children be repatriated. The Spanish consul in Belgium was enlisted, and a series of expeditions were planned and organized.[85]

The first group was scheduled to leave the port of Antwerp by the end of April 1939, with expenses paid by the Belgian government. The International Red Cross facilitated the process by arranging the notification of parents in Spain of the day of arrival of their children. Forms were arranged, and temporary visas procured for those children whose parents were refugees in France.[86] According to one Basque priest interviewed, more children could have been sent on to parents already in South America, were it not for lack of cooperation of the French government. Many sources also commented that at least some children were repatriated when there were no parents to receive them in Spain. These children ended up in the Falange orphanages. Several of those interviewed who had been sent as children to Belgium had found upon arrival that their parents had not requested their return. Others commented on the great fortitude their parents showed in resisting the campaign for repatriation launched by religious and civil authorities in Spain. One of the children sent to Belgium wrote as an adult:

> The repatriation of the majority of the children to Spain began in October 1937, ending in 1939. Msgr. Antoniutti, Papal Nuncio in Spain at that time, appears to have taken a very active role in the repatriation, and the pressure of the new Spanish authorities manifested itself in certain of the interventions and decisions imposed on certain families.

Still, by November of 1939, with Belgium embroiled in the war hostilities, some seven hundred children still remained in the country.

An interesting historical footnote is that José Antonio Aguirre, the president of the Basque Government-in-Exile, arrived clandestinely in Brussels as the last of the children were leaving, in mid-1940. He was fleeing the German occupation of France, which had caught the Basque government by surprise. According to several Basques interviewed, he was hidden in a Jesuit school which had earlier housed Basque children, and was sent on to Antwerp. Here, he was able to arrange false papers and alter his appearance with glasses and a mustache. He and his family found eventual sanctuary in South America.

The Repatriation From Mexico

The repatriation of the Niños de Morelia was initiated by the Insurgent Spanish Red Cross in Burgos in June of 1938.

The repatriation project was undertaken by the International Red Cross, using the standard procedure of requiring a request from each child's parents or the guardian. Negotiations were begun with the Mexican Red Cross and with the Cárdenas government. This latter did not recognize the new Spanish regime, and the negotiations proved to be both protracted and ultimately fruitless. Another strong factor was that, by 1939, a large group of Republican refugees, including many politicians and intellectuals, had been given refuge and, in fact, been welcomed by Cárdenas. They, naturally, were strongly opposed to the repatriation of any children to Franco's Spain.[87]

When Camacho came to power, the project was resumed, with more success. Early in 1941, the secretary of foreign affairs for Mexico informed the press that a new policy would be effected, by which children who had been properly requested for reclamation by their parents would be returned to Spain. At this point, there were requests for 137 of the children. A second, smaller group was also scheduled for repatriation just prior to the outbreak of World War II. This return was generated by the Spanish ambassador to Guatemala, and acceded to by Camacho.[88]

By 1952, however, of the 348 children located in one study, a total of ninety-five had returned to Spain.[89] Perhaps those not locatable included some of those who had been returned in the early forties.[90] As already noted, children from only one Basque family returned to Spain. Indeed, of the nine families who did not return, three were able to induce one or both parents to effect reunion by coming to live with them in Mexico.

The Soviet Union

In marked contrast to the position regarding repatriation of children from France, England, and Belgium, the Basque Government-in-Exile itself began to initiate reclamation of the children sent to Russia as early as 1938, well before the Republican defeat. Basque parents who were refugees in France were advised to contact the Spanish Republican Embassy in Moscow to request that their children be repatriated to France. A continuing series of diplomatic overtures followed, as attested to by the file of diplomatic correspondence in the archives of the Basque government in Paris. These even included negotiations to return Basque children to parents in Franco's Spain.[91] It appears that the government of Aguirre shared the view of Franco that an extended sojourn of its children in an avowedly atheistic country was undesirable. In the case of the Basques, the peril to the child's faith and morals clearly outweighed even the political hazards of living in a Fascist Spain.

By the following spring, Franco's victory and the imminent outbreak of World War II allowed little attention to be devoted by international humanitarian groups, or by the governments involved, to the repatriation of the children. President Aguirre sent a personal letter to Joseph Stalin, asking that he facilitate the return of children requested by their parents.[92] Leizaola began a series of actions with the International Red Cross, requesting that they try to arrange an exchange of Basque children in Russia for a group of 150 Russian sailors interned in Mallorca by the new government of Franco. Negotiations were begun in April 1939, but by the following June, the sailors had been repatriated in exchange for a quantity of Soviet gasoline delivered to Bilbao, at Franco's behest.[93] Clearly, this product was more necessary to rebuild a "new Spain" than were the children.

All the International Red Cross was able to facilitate was correspondence between the children and their parents. Its representative in Russia managed to obtain the addresses of the two colonies near Odessa where many of the Basque children were being educated. In June of 1939, two thousand messages with the parents' addresses were sent to the Russian Red Cross, to be distributed to these children as a first step in restoring contact that might possibly lead to repatriation.[94] There was little immediate effect: only three children were authorized to leave Russia that August. They returned to their parents in France.

At the same time, the archbishop of Malines, a great friend of the Basques, intervened by offering to pay the cost of repatriation. Shortly thereafter, 130 Basque children were repatriated, 123 to Vizcayan parents and seven to parents now refugees in France.[95]

The Basque government went to some pains to explain that the alacrity with which they had sent children to Russia in 1937 was consistent with their willingness to assist parents in recovering these children. There were long articles in *Eusko Deva* to clarify this issue and reply to critics, citing the preeminence of the "free will" of the parents in both cases.[96] In a letter to the Basque Delegation in Bayonne, Aguirre noted that, though there were prominent French Catholic women urging that the children be reclaimed, which the Basque government was anxious to do, they were also abiding by the wishes of parents who wanted their children to stay in the Soviet Union. Finally, he noted, his government had so few resources, that this committee of French women needed to provide the required funds for such repatriation. He, however, had written again to Stalin about the matter, and hoped for a favorable reply.[97]

By 1940,* the International League for the Friends of the Basques (LIAB) prepared a summary of the situation, noting:

> In spite of attempting on numerous occasions to expedite the reclamation of Basque children from Russia, it appears to be impossible. Since the expulsion of S. from Russia, the avenue of the Red Cross is closed; diplomatic avenues thru the United States are now closed; the Ambassador of France in Moscow is not interested, nor is France itself now disposed to allow the entrance of a large group of children who have received a communist education. Finally, the lack of courtesy of the Russian authorities and their representatives makes negotiation impossible.[98]

Little was accomplished during World War II, though efforts were continuous, using every feasible means. The first problem in the postwar period was, of course, simply to lo-

*The Non-Aggression Pact between Hitler and Stalin was now in effect.

cate the children, now six years older. Many had traveled over many parts of the Soviet Union, and their personal odysseys during Hitler's invasion had made any communication with parents impossible. To restore contact, the good offices of La Pasionaria were enlisted by the Basque Government-in-Exile. At a dinner in Paris, in 1945, attended by this personage and the Republican and Catalan presidents-in-exile, Giral and Irla, Leizaola brought up the matter of the Basque children. La Pasionaria told him that all that was required was a letter requesting their return directed to Comrade Stalin personally. This he did immediately, but Leizaola never received a reply.[99]

Appeals were made to the headquarters of the Spanish Communist Party in Paris. Leizaola was told that parents should write to the address enclosed and they would receive a reply in a month. The address, handwritten, since the Paris delegation had no typewriter with Russian letters, was that of the Soviet minister of instruction. This was done.[100] Then diplomatic problems began, particularly the necessity of obtaining French visas and passage money for children to be repatriated. The International League of the Friends of the Basques (LIAB) took the initiative to obtain the required visas, and prepared a standard repatriation form for Basque children living in Russia.[101] At about the same time, *Eusko Deya* published letters from parents in France, South America, and Mexico wishing to reclaim their children in Russia.[102]

The feeling that perhaps repatriation of the children was about to begin was nourished in 1946 by the arrival in New York of twenty-one children, many of whom were Basque, en route to their parents now living in Mexico. This group of parents included several pilots of the Spanish Republican Air Force, as well as prominent Marxist intellectuals. They had paid for their children's trip from Odessa to Mexico. The Soviet government had given each child new clothing, about seventy dollars, and transportation to Odessa. The Mexican ambassador to Russia, Luis Quintanilla, had helped arrange the repatriation, as had Jesús Hernandez.

The first group to be repatriated after the close of World

War II was described by press accounts as totally bilingual, rather immature in appearance, but bright and obviously well educated. The press in Mexico commented that many other Spanish Republican parents whose children had not been repatriated were very anxious to be reunited.[103] One of those repatriated notes:

> After the war, we all were brought to Moscow. Some of us were to be repatriated to France, Mexico, etc. They gave us new clothes, and we sailed off to rejoin our families. None of us had lost our Spanish but some had a hard time adjusting to the life of the family, after years of separation. Our small group who came to Mexico has kept some of the camaraderie we had in Russia.

Soon after this harbinger of possible success, the Basque Government-in-Exile wrote to the Communist Party of Euzkadi, now in exile in Bayonne, to get details of the repatriation to Mexico. The reply was several weeks in arriving and very vague. It stated only that the arrangements had been made through Russian diplomatic personnel in Mexico, with mediation through Spanish Republican or Basque officials.[104] Another letter to the International Red Cross brought the suggestion that perhaps requests directed to the Russian ambassador in Paris might be effective.[105] The LIAB had already filed twenty-five visa requests for repatriations with the French Ministry of Foreign Affairs.[106] With this groundwork accomplished, a formal letter was sent to Ambassador Bogomolov in Paris in early December. The letter requested that the Soviet minister of public instruction, Section for Spanish Children, send a complete list of children, their addresses, and present situation. If this were not feasible, would the minister then respond to inquiries from individual parents, including those living in Spain? The replies would be handled with absolute discretion. Furthermore, the issue of repatriation to Basque parents in France, Chile, Venezuela, and Mexico should be addressed, especially as the French government would grant entry visas to children whose parents were residents of France.[107]

In February of 1947, four children from the LIAB list of

twenty-five arrived in Paris via Prague. When interviewed, they told of malnutrition and a precarious existence during the war, and stated that half of the Basque children had died or disappeared.[108] In their capacity as being responsible for Basque children entrusted to them by their parents, the Basque Government-in-Exile immediately pressured for further repatriation, particularly of an additional forty-nine children whose requests were pending, including some with parents in Chile, Cuba, Argentina, Venezuela, and Mexico.[109] The concern for the safety of the Basque children in Russia was not assuaged when an account of a Cuban diplomat's ten months in the country was published in Madrid in 1947. Rafael Miralles indicated his belief that Stalin was preventing the children from leaving so that their poor treatment would not become known.[110]

In 1947 the Spanish Republican Government-in-Exile also made a series of diplomatic overtures to initiate the repatriation to France of the Spanish children still in the Soviet Union. These efforts by then-President Llopis were unavailing.[111] Later that same year, Santiago Carrillo came to Paris from Moscow, to present a talk on the Spanish Republican children in Russia on the tenth anniversary year of their arrival there. He extolled the training and education that they were receiving, but did not refer directly to their possible repatriation.[112] At this point, parents in Spain could not even receive letters from their children in Russia without danger of visits from Franco's Civil Guard. There appears to have been no further repatriation during the "Cold War" period which then ensued in international politics.

In 1956, after nearly twenty years of living as expatriates, the Basque children, now all young adults, began to hear of a projected repatriation.

> There were notices in Spanish and Russian posted on the board of the Spanish Club in Moscow, which we all frequented. They instructed us to contact the Red Cross if we wanted to return to Spain. Those of us who had maintained close contact with our families faced a decision. And those who had married Russians had the hardest one.

The political situation in both the Soviet Union and Franco's Spain had changed markedly since the end of the Civil War. Stalin was now dead; Franco had been invited to join the international forum of the United Nations. In exchange for permission to construct and man large United States military bases on Spanish soil, President Eisenhower pressured the Allies to admit Spain to the United Nations Security Council. Relations between the two countries had become increasingly cordial since Eisenhower took office, and culminated in this international rehabilitation of the Franco regime. Once admitted to the forum of the United Nations in 1955, Spain alleged that thousands of children of Spanish Republicans evacuated to the Soviet Union during the Civil War were dead or in the prison camps in Siberia. Russian diplomats replied that most of the children were living and working around Moscow, and that any who wished to return to Spain could do so.[113] Within Spain, Franco had declared an amnesty for Spanish Republicans in exile, and the end of the Decree of Responsibility. The way seemed clear for a full-scale reclamation.

In Russia, those who decided to return contacted their families, and applied for help from the Soviet Red Cross in preparing their exit papers. The Russian press was completely silent on this pending repatriation. Though nearly twelve hundred Basque and Spanish men and women, with the children and in some cases, Russian wives, who now comprised their families, emigrated in a few weeks, the fact was not mentioned. The arrival of the children had been described in glowing detail, but in the two intervening decades the style and content of the Russian press appeared to change. Political news supplanted human interest stories in large measure. Normal during wartime, this focus seemed to continue, so that the only news from Spain appearing in *Pravda* in all of 1956 was a report from a Tass correspondent in Córdoba, who wrote that Russian aid to the Spanish Republic was still remembered, albeit secretly, by the citizenry.[114]

In Spain, however, press accounts of a projected repatriation of the last group of Basque children evacuated in 1937—as well as the Spanish children evacuated in 1938–39—began in late July 1956. The Bilbao press reported on a press conference called by the Spanish foreign affairs minister, quoting him as disclosing that the Soviet government had approved a request from the Soviet Red Cross for the repatriation of those Spaniards sent to Russia who wished to return. The report continued by saying that an expedition of five hundred repatriates was already in the planning stage, with the assistance of the French Red Cross. To expedite this repatriation, the minister requested that anyone having relatives in Russia communicate with the Spanish Red Cross, supplying names, personal data, and the date and their embarkation point on leaving Spain.[115]

Thus, after an exile of nearly twenty years, about twelve hundred young men and women returned to Spain, bringing with them perhaps six hundred children born in Russia. This total included sixty-five Russian-born wives, who had married Spanish or, in a few cases, Basque men. From an analysis of the passenger lists and other sources, it appears that just under five hundred of the Basque children sent into Russia in June and September of 1937 returned, or fewer than a quarter of those evacuated. That September, in Valencia, the first group of 532, nearly three hundred of whom were Basques, arrived from Russia on the vessel *Crimea*. The press commented that 157 Vizcayans, 88 Navarrese, and 54 Guipúzcoans arrived, all of whom spoke fluent Russian and Spanish, as did their childen (some 147 in all). Many of the group had advanced university degrees, and all, including the women, had been employed in Russia.[116]

Three more expeditions from Russia arrived: 324 adults and 137 children on October 22; 400 on November 24, and 418 on December 19. Included among these were twenty-seven of the teachers who had emigrated with the children in 1937.[117]All had new clothes, and cameras, purchased upon leaving. Nearly a hundred of the men had married Russian wives, who accompanied them. However, no Russian husbands had been permitted to leave, "since Russia lost twenty million men in the war." One Basque woman gave birth on the way to Odessa.*

Nearly half of those repatriated were from the Basque country. When interviewed, many stated that they had returned primarily for reasons of family. Twenty-four years later, all said that their dream of returning to Spain had been sustained through nearly twenty years in exile. They arrived eager to be part of Spain.

In 1956 Spain was only just beginning to become industrialized after a slow recovery from the years of civil war. Consequently, much of the technical training many had received in Russia was useless in Spain. The degrees of those who had finished university and post-graduate courses were not recognized, though the course work had been far superior to that offered in Spanish institutions. Revalidation of professional credentials in Madrid was necessary—a long, complicated, and expensive process. To survive, nearly all were forced to take jobs as laborers. Respected economists became factory workers, marine engineers worked as stevedores, and pilots became miners.

> I came because I always received letters from my parents begging me to return. But it was a terribly disillusioning experience to come to Franco's Spain. My *carnet* was the wrong color, and I needed special papers to travel outside my town. I just couldn't get work. After all my education and training, I was back where my poor father had been, a stone cutter and polisher.

> It took me nearly four years, three trips to Madrid and many courses to revalidate my degree. And this in spite of the fact that Russia was technically far ahead of Spain in its professional education.

All of the women interviewed also found it impossible, at least initially, to resume their professional careers. Basque women doctors, chemists, professors, architects, and engineers, found their specialties closed to women in Spain.

*That child is now a university student in Bilbao.

Their years of experience counted for nothing. The child care facilities they had utilized in Russia did not exist in Euzkadi. By necessity, they adapted to the only way of life open to them, that of homemaker. Some of the women reported great difficulty in taking on the expected role of *ama de casa*, the only possible occupation for women in Spain in 1956:

> I found it very difficult to be a mother and housewife when I returned. I knew nothing of child-rearing. I was employed in Russia as a chemist. I couldn't sew or clean a fish. We had to eat in restaurants here at first, until I educated myself. Many of us had such problems. My sister, for example, was educated very theoretically as an economist. We had had no experience in a family atmosphere. All was in a collective model, very unique. The discipline there was implicit; I found it difficult to provide explicit discipline to my four children. And I had hoped to continue my work, but it was impossible here.

Another factor in the Spanish economy added to the problems of adjustment of the Sovieticos. Most couples were forced by the acute housing shortage to live with one or another set of Basque parents. Since no one had been married by the Catholic church, the parents now insisted upon this ceremony, years after the fact. Worst of all, they had departed as children, and their parents expected dutiful children back. Unpleasant quarrels broke out. The children had seen much more of the world than had their parents. The majority of parents were still very poor, uneducated, and uncultured. Their children had adapted to another way of life, and had the advantages of education and an exposure to culture.

Many Sovieticos soon returned to Russia, unable to adjust to Spain, a Spain much different from their illusions and dreams in exile.

> I would say that a good percentage of those who returned here, especially those with Russian wives, ended up back in Russia. My brother, for one, returned, as he had more opportunity there. In fact, most of those who stayed are better off than we in Spain. Except for my wife and her family here, I would have gone back myself.

Some were forced to leave. About twenty families were expelled without passports, to France (which refused to admit them). They returned to Russia. About thirty, including two who were interviewed, spent years in the state prisons in Burgos or Madrid. All were continually harassed by the police, "hunted like bugs." Their *carnets*, or identity papers, were the same yellow as those of prostitutes and criminals, and had "Repatriated from Soviet Union" stamped across them. Employers were wary of hiring them despite their superb qualifications. Family and friends were sometimes uneasy about being seen with them. Each had to report weekly to the Civil Guard headquarters, and were not usually permitted to travel. Their papers relegated them to third class transportation for approved journeys.[118]

A curious episode transpired when a great number of Basque Sovieticos were sent to Madrid soon after their return. They were put up in good pensions for two weeks, all expenses paid, for each of three such sessions. They were interrogated daily there, by fluent Russian speakers who were obviously not Spanish. Questions about the location of armament factories, the Russian telephone system, the defense system, even their neighbors' work, were asked. The men identified themselves as members of the Central Intelligence Agency of the United States.[119]

The harassment continued for years, though the Sovieticos were careful to maintain themselves as completely apolitical. In spite of this, they were always suspect, especially when labor unrest broke out periodically in the industrial north. In Bilbao, to this day they frequent a Russian-Spanish friendship club, to which Russian sailors in port frequently come, but "solely to practice their Russian." They report intermittent police surveillance. Recently, in a national magazine, some commented that their harassment by the police in Spain was a policy "made in America."

> The country we found again was that of Franco. We suffered constant interrogations, we had to go periodically to report to the Civil Guard; and often had problems obtaining our own identification. In addition, as is usual in these matters, they didn't recognize our professional

training. Brilliant engineers with specializations that could have been useful here had to work as laborers. The majority of us lived marginally, unable to rise above the trauma of our life in a country that never accepts us . . . . We formed a Soviet Friendship society, with no political overtones, that is constantly monitored by the police, and we are unable to carry on a normal social life. Every labor problem in Asturias or Cataluña was seen as the work of spies in Moscow's service, though Franco never actually produced any proof. They even blamed ETA on us.[120]

CHAPTER EIGHT

Aftermaths

In all of the countries of Europe which offered hospitality to the Basque child refugees, the gathering war clouds signaling the outbreak of an international conflict forced the host nations to reconsider the future of the children expatriated in 1936–39. In each case, their exile became increasingly problematic as the clash between the Allies and the Axis drew closer.

The Basque Children in France

As the war neared, the number of Basque refugees—soldiers, families, and evacuated children—who stayed on in France totaled about sixty thousand. Some five thousand were Gudaris who had fought in Catalonia.[1] In 1939 most of these were quickly interned by French authorities in the infamous concentration camp of Gurs, with others going to provisional camps at Argeles, St. Cyprian, Bancaré, or Bram.[2] Also fleeing Catalonia in 1939 was a large group of women and children, with old relatives, who had fled Euzkadi in 1936–37. These contingents found nearly twenty thousand women, children, and aged relatives who had already spent nearly two years under French auspices. The latter group still included some five hundred of the unaccompanied children evacuated in 1937.[3]

At this point, French hospitality was further strained by an overall total of 475,000 refugees from Spain, the high point of the evacuation being reached in mid-February of 1939.[4] In March there was a strenuous debate in the French Chamber of Deputies which resulted in a series of measures enacted into law concerning them. The French government also issued an appeal to the countries of the Western Hemisphere to take in refugees.[5]

The first program open to adult male refugees in good health was recruitment into work brigades engaged in fortifying France. Though this arduous employment paid only one-half franc per day, men were given quite adequate food, clothing, shelter, tobacco, and, most important, a family subsidy. This last benefit made enlistment a desirable option, as did the opportunity to leave the horror, distress, and inactivity of life in the hastily improvised camps.[6]

Another option for men and women, as well as for the children of working age, was to labor in the harvest, in agriculture, or in factories. France had had a long history of "guest labor," much of it traditionally from Spain. In the months before the stunning Nazi invasion in 1940, the need for such labor warmed the chilly welcome given earlier to the predominantly Basque refugees from the Northern Campaign in the spring of 1937.* The birthrate in France had been especially depressed all through the thirties. Many hands were needed now that could not be found in the French citizenry. Thus, in the case of the evacuated children, those who had reached their mid-teens were now given the option of working in France or returning to Spain. By early 1940, even refugee families headed by a mother and with the father residing in Spain were encouraged to stay.[7]

A third option for the boys in their late teens, and for the soldiers from Spain, was to enlist in the French Foreign Legion or in the French armed forces. By late 1939, the commander of the camp at Gurs had the names of 1,200 men, nearly all Basque, who wanted to join the French forces to

* Only a few months earlier, in 1939, the French had ordered the repatriation of *all* children, orphans or not, unless this would impose grave risk on their parents.

continue their fight against fascism. Aguirre wrote, at the outbreak of World War II, that "Basques have been fighting in this war since the beginning."[8]

A fourth option for the refugees was emigration to the Western Hemisphere. A great deal of attention was given to this possibility by the French government, as well as by the Spanish Republican and Basque governments now in exile in Paris. To the initial appeal of the French government, the Republic of Mexico, still headed by Republican Spain's staunchest friend in the West, Don Lázaro Cárdenas, gave the first and most generous reply. In April, Mexico sent both the Spanish Republican government and the French government a set of criteria for admission of Spanish refugees. Noting that some 300,000 Mexican workers were unemployed, the letter stressed the importance of sending in only qualified workers who could be employed in specific occupations. Singled out was "the need for experienced fishermen, preferably of Basque, or Galician birth, to exploit the maritime resources of the Gulf of Mexico."[9] Since almost no Galicians had sought refuge in France, Basques were to fill this demand. Further, the request gave preference to those with relatives in Mexico.

A few weeks later, the Republic of Chile offered to receive 130 orphan children, the majority of them to be Basque, from the colonies in France. Both the French and Spanish authorities declined this proposal as one offering insufficient safeguards for the children's welfare.[10] Later that month, Chile again offered to take refugees, again preferably Basque, for the initiation of a fishing industry projected by the government.[11] Shortly thereafter, Venezuela followed suit, allowing *only* Basques to be admitted. This offer was reportedly generated by Basque Jesuits already in residence there.[12] The United States merely offered the remainder of its 1939 immigration quota for Spanish Nationals—two hundred slots. Santo Domingo also agreed to take some Spanish refugees, as did Cuba. By the end of 1939, the number of Spaniards (including many Basques who had left France for the New World) totaled 10,600. About 7,400 went to Mexico, 1,200 to

Santo Domingo, 1,400 to Chile, 400 to Venezuela, 200 to Colombia, and some small groups to Cuba.[13]

In order to emigrate, the families had first to be reunited. This meant, in many cases, first locating children dispersed to two or more colonies, then their mother, and finally the concentration camp in which the father was held. Initiating the request with, in the case of the Basque refugees, the Basque Government-in-Exile, at its Bayonne office was the next step. At this point, reunited families had to struggle with a highly politicized emigration process, controlled by two competing organizations, representing, again, some of the cleavages in the Spanish Republican government, now in exile.

The first to begin the work of expediting re-emigration was the Servicios de Evacuación y Emigración de Republicanos Españoles (SERE). This, the official organ of the exile government, was very tightly controlled by Dr. Negrin, leader of the Council of Ministers, now in Paris. Curiously, though there is no evidence to support his contention, Negrin declared that SERE had been created in 1937 to aid the Basque refugees from the Northern Campaign, as well as those from Asturias and Santander.[14] In reality, SERE began in early 1939, using funds fortuitously expatriated from Spain before the debacle of Barcelona. This organization was administered by the Popular Front, with Julio Jauregui sitting on its board as the delegate from the PNV.

Of the well over one hundred million francs expended by SERE in its few months of existence, very little was spent to help the thousands of Spanish Republican soldiers imprisoned in the French concentration camps. Instead, the funds were employed overwhelmingly to assist Marxist political figures and their families to emigrate to Mexico, Santo Domingo, and Chile.[15]

The second organization, Junta de Auxilio a los Republicanos Españoles (JARE), came into being in Mexico in July 1939. It was headed by the former Socialist deputy from Bilbao, Indalecio Prieto. For his organization, Prieto used government funds "liberated" from the yacht *Vita*, sent from

Spain to Veracruz, Mexico, "with a good part of the Republican treasury" (gold, jewelry, notes, and bonds).[16]

Both Basques and Communists were conspicuously absent in the administrative council of JARE. As a result of this omission, and because the actual policy of SERE was to limit its assistance only to Communists, the Basque government found itself with the major responsibility for any re-emigration for the refugees from Euzkadi. To initiate this process, a number of prominent Basques toured those countries in the Western Hemisphere which already hosted long-standing Basque colonies. It was even reported, in Mexico, that several of these officials had sailed to Veracruz on the *Vita*, along with the Spanish treasury, to scout out possible sites for the establishment of Basque agricultural colonies.[17] According to correspondence in the Basque Government Archives, a list of instructions given to the first sixty-five Basques to emigrate included the reminder that Basques already in the Americas were ill-disposed to receive them, due to Fascist propaganda which had labeled them "Basque Reds." They therefore had the important charge of changing these attitudes by their actions.[18]

By mid-1939 the Basque Bureau of Census had compiled its most complete count, listing over 8,500 adult men and women by their profession. This was circulated to possible host countries. The report noted that:

> It is fully appreciated by the Government of Euzkadi that some of the vocations analyzed in the following list might not at first sight suggest an economically useful addition to your country's population. This might apply particularly to Basque musicians, artists, authors, professors of art and science, teachers, lawyers, bankers, etc. It should be understood, however, that the Basques are a hard-working and adaptable people who have proved their qualities as settlers; and that these people would apply vigor and intelligence to any opportunity open to them in return for an opportunity to live in an atmosphere free from political persecution.[19]

Such planning, coupled with strong appeals to Basque enclaves in Mexico, Venezuela, Argentina, Chile, and Uruguay, produced results. Particularly in Venezuela and Argentina, their well-established clubs, the "Centros Vascos,"* developed special committees to aid the emigration of Basques. Formalities such as a sponsor and financial bond were waived in these countries.[20] However, by now, World War II had begun, and difficulties in obtaining neutral ships for transport of refugees across the Atlantic added to the dilemma. One woman recalls the anguish of this second diaspora:

> My father was called to Barcelona from La Citadelle in 1938; my mother and I stayed on as refugees in France. When the [Spanish civil] war ended, he joined us, hoping to stay in Europe, near Euzkadi. My sister was born the day the Second World War broke out. With war, all hope was lost, as the Germans would send anyone in the Basque government to Franco. My father went to Marseilles to get passage; we three stayed in Biarritz. He sent word for my mother to join him. The messenger was killed on his return. My poor mother went to him, leaving us, both aged less than two, with my aunt. My parents arrived in Buenos Aires after an odyssey lasting fifteen months. I didn't see them again until 1948.

In spite of the many vicissitudes experienced by all Basque refugees who chose to emigrate, their efforts met with some success. Venezuela welcomed 1,500 Basque political refugees; Argentina, about 1,400. Not one of them ever became a public charge.[21]

The final option, and the one ultimately followed by the great majority of the refugees from Spain, was that of repatriation. Early in 1940, more than two-thirds of all the refugees had already been repatriated. Another tenth had been able to emigrate; only about 140,000 of the nearly one-half million of the previous year were now the guests of France. World War II now began in earnest. The German assault

* These Basque clubs, with sports and eating facilities, are found in several Latin-American capitals.

soon penetrated the chief French defense, the Maginot Line. Forty days later, France fell. According to one source, this shameful rout caused some satisfaction among the refugee soldiers from Spain, who saw it as justly deserved for French lack of hospitality toward them.[22]

But, with the German victory, the Nazi occupation of Paris and the North began. Next came the installation of a collaborationist regime, the Vichy government, in the rest of France. Spanish refugees were once again an unwelcome burden. The Spanish Republican and Basque governments-in-exile had to evacuate precipitously as the Nazis entered Paris. Their official assistance networks evaporated overnight.

By the date of the French armistice, in 1940, about 4,400 of the nine thousand Basque children living in adoptive homes or children's colonies in France had been officially repatriated, with the last contingent of five arriving in Irún on August 21, 1940.[23] Others had been reunited with their families and had emigrated. Only forty-three children were being cared for in the three small colonies the Basque government still operated early in 1940.[24] These remnants, and certainly many other thousands, were now in a situation of considerable peril. The Vichy government wanted them to leave at once; however, Franco's Decree of Responsibility was menacing.

The French concentration camps for Spanish Civil War refugees were emptied rapidly. Fewer than five thousand prisoners remained by year's end. The adult males, about forty thousand in all, and including many Basques, were sent into Germany. They were placed in factories, work camps, and the infamous extermination camps of Dachau, Buchenwald, and Mauthausen. Thousands died there.[25]

Within France, some of the older boys from the children's colonies found an equally dangerous occupation—they joined the Maquis. This arm of the French Resistance blossomed in the part of France not occupied by the departments to the south, and near the border of Spain. One interviewee, who had studied at La Citadelle, enlisted at age seventeen in the all-Basque battalion *Gernika,* commanded by Pedro Ordoki.

> I lived in the mountains for two years, acting as a guide, lookout, and scout. I knew every inch of those mountains. My unit helped hundreds of Resistance fighters, downed pilots, and soldiers to escape.

For his service this young Basque, barely out of his teens, received a citation for courage in May of 1945. The exploits of this famous battalion also reached Franco Spain. As a result, the young man immediately had five *condenas de muerte* (death sentences) placed on him, if he should ever be caught in Spain.

The Gernika battalion captured a German outpost, Blockhaus Y33, in Montalivet, France, in 1945. De Gaulle himself reviewed the unit the following year, and declared: "France will not forget the actions done by the Basques for the liberation of her soil."[26]

The Basque children who could neither return to Spain nor emigrate tended to remain in the French-Basque provinces where they had earlier lived in the refuges or children's colonies. Some found employment on French-Basque farms. Many of the children who were orphans were adopted by French-Basque families. Other Basque children were cared for by an American humanitarian organization, the Unitarian Service Committee (USC).

This organization entered France in 1944 to establish a project in Toulouse. Their purpose was to aid Spanish Republican refugees who had, by now, weathered two wars. First, they opened a hospital for Maquis Spaniards injured in the resistance, persons who were denied treatment in French hospitals. A dispensary was also opened to serve all Spanish refugees in the south of France. Assistance was given in emigration matters. Food parcels and a great deal of clothing were also dispensed regularly, as well as a small subsidy to families without an income.

The Toulouse Project opened a colony for eighty Basque children in St. Goin, Basse Pyrénées, early in 1945, which lasted until 1951. Two villas on the beach at St.-Jean-de-Luz were also rented for summers to house one hundred children, the majority of whom were Basque. Here, refugee children could enjoy a healthy holiday and live in pleasant beach homes named, appropriately, the "Côte-Basque." In nearby Les Andelys, a children's canteen was operated for three years by the USC, serving a hot meal and milk daily. Other USC projects for refugee children were, unfortunately, short-lived. A Boston dowager opened her summer home on the French coast to Basque children; another wealthy American expatriate distributed clothing. These last projects were clear examples of what came to be termed "chateau philanthropy" by USC personnel: the great lady of the town distributing charity to the poor Basque refugee children. What invariably happened was that the "great lady" soon tired of the novelty, and went on to other pursuits.

The colony at St. Goins, on the other hand, endured for nearly seven years, educating scores of Basque children. Folklore presentations were frequent, with the children taught by Basque dancers from Oléron. Qualified teachers instructed them in both academic and practical subjects. The colony, which was adequately funded by donors in the United States, was a success by all standards.

The USC came to be a lifeline for many Basque families who had suffered the rigors of the Civil War. Each person had to be recommended by a Spanish political organization, and only the most distressed could apply. USC records abound in lists of Basques assisted: amputees at the Cambo sanitarium, widows, mothers with husbands and sons in Spanish prisons, and Basque soldiers still in the Gurs concentration camp, their health broken, starving in their bunks.[27]

A large resettlement project was also undertaken by the USC. Some 3,500 refugees from Spain living in southwest France were admitted to Ecuador in 1940. They were sent to a new colony optimistically named "Simón Bolívar," after the famous Basque liberator of South America. The colony covered 1,140 acres near Quito, acres that were uncleared virgin forest. Income was to be generated by preparing charcoal to be sold in the capital. The majority of settlers were ethnic Basques, many with several children. They worked diligently at first to make the colony a success. The expected income from the charcoal did not materialize, and a series of problems beset the families trying a new life in the wilderness. In addition, the director of the colony was reportedly incompetent, and more and more people drifted into Quito to seek opportunity there. By 1944 only nine hundred refugees still lived in the Simón Bolívar colony. It was closed later that year, and all support was withdrawn. It is not known what eventually happened to the refugees.[28]

Other charitable organizations which were able to continue relief work during the German occupation, such as Oxfam, the Quakers, and Caritas, did not limit their help to Spanish Republican refugees, as did USC. Because most of their funds were soon being used to help Jewish, Polish, Czech, Dutch, Greek, and other refugees from Hitler, the USC became the most effective agency aiding Basque refugees in France after World War II. It was also the only organization to continue to educate the children long after the end of World War II.

In the matter of education, the other refugee children from Spain who remained in France found little opportunity to attend school. Though in 1936 the French government had ruled that all immigrant children should be educated in the French state schools, for most, formal education ended in 1937. During their most crucial years, the majority were educated only sporadically. Consequently, as adults, the youngsters from Spain could obtain only unskilled jobs in factories or work in agriculture. A study done of Spanish refugee children found that they had lost educational status relative to their own parents, as only 10 percent of the children reached secondary school in France, while 20 percent of their parents had completed this level in Spain. A final barrier was that French citizenship is required for any fellowship for university work, so the Spanish refugee children were not eligible.[29]

Today, those who stayed on in France are well assimilated into French life. They frequently cross the border for visits with relatives, to hunt doves, or to attend reunions. Their lives are almost indistinguishable from the native French-Basques.

The end of World War II brought home the reality of international politics for all refugees from Spain, and particularly for those who had volunteered to serve in the Maquis or other branches of the Free French forces. Instead of the triumphal return to build a new Spain exemplified in the popular slogan, "Hoy, Paris; Mañana, España," Allied diplomacy eventually accommodated to the Franco regime. Only until 1947, then, were the refugees from Spain authentic political exiles. With the recognition of the Spanish dictatorship, they simply became forgotten refugees.

Even their legitimate governments-in-exile, restored and once more installed in Paris, became marginal. In the case of the Basques, the still-forceful Aguirre traveled to friendly countries in South America, and both he and Pedro Beitia, Basque representative to the United States, presented the Basque issue in Washington and before the United Nations. However, they gained little attention from a war-weary and pragmatic world. The final blow to Basque aspirations was the admission of Franco to the United Nations in the mid-fifties.[30]

Today, perhaps the only exception to the pervasive assimilation of Basque refugees to the life and culture of France is the small colony of aging Basques who were distinguished for political activity during and after the Spanish Civil War. As Franco's health weakened and the end of his regime neared, some refugees returned to France from self-exile in South America to be near the borders of their beloved Euzkadi. The shabby offices of the Basque Government-in-Exile on Rue Singer in Paris served these and other remnants of the Basque nation as a political center until 1980. At that time, the Parliament of Spain of King Juan Carlos voted a statute of autonomy to the Basque region of Vizcaya, Guipúzcoa, and Alava. Shortly thereafter, the seat of the Basque government was transferred from Paris to Vitoria.

England

Of the 1,021 Basque children remaining in England in mid-1939, the Basque Children's Committee (BCC) expected that more than half (577) would stay on indefinitely. Their parents were known to be dead, in prison, abroad, or missing.

As early as March 1939, those children over fourteen years of age, who by then comprised over one-fourth of those in England, were given the option of remaining. Most chose to stay, a decision prompted by the reports of repression in Euzkadi by Franco.[31] A few months earlier, there had been a welcome change in official policy, so that some of the older children had been allowed to enroll in the British state schools. But this did little to solve the major problem of the BCC in 1939—its chronic lack of funds.

By the end of 1939, all of the children remaining in England were gathered from Catholic and other colonies still operating and placed in private foster homes or in the six colonies designated as group homes: Camberly, Carshalton, Didsbury, Carleon, Barnet, and Plymouth. The BCC arranged all the foster homes, although the organization was itself beset with difficulties. Unfortunately, siblings who had remained together in secular colonies for over two years had to be separated, one child going to each foster home.

One hundred fourteen children, out of the original twelve hundred, who were still living in a handful of Catholic colonies posed a special problem. For about a third, their parents were dead, missing, or were refugees. Nearly one-half had only one parent in Franco Spain; the other was in a French camp or was a refugee. Whenever there was correspondence, the parents expressed their desire that the child remain in England.[32] Though the Catholic authorities could no longer contribute to their upkeep, they still were very anxious that the children go to Catholic foster homes. Most of the younger ones adjusted fairly well to their respective foster families, though some still remember the loneliness of living with people very different from themselves. One child, aged only five in 1939, was misplaced in the dispersion to private homes, and lost contact with her five older siblings for many months. This particular family was scattered all over England.

In the middle of 1940, when Germany invaded France, a final group of about five hundred children still remained in various parts of England. They were, in the main, from the industrial belt around Bilbao. Their fathers had been employed as factory workers, and were generally of Leftist sympathies. The children reflected these convictions, and consciously saw their emigration as a political exile. Some engaged in extensive political activism during and after World War II, in the fight against fascism.

> For a long time, we felt we would be part of the liberation of Spain. We were a very united group, all of us with strong anti-fascist convictions. We kept our aims clear, and engaged in a great deal of political work. We had nothing in common with later Spanish immigrants, who came for economic reasons; ours was a political immigration. We had foresight of what we wanted in our lives.

They were often not at all strongly Catholic, and most had been placed in secular homes in 1937. Their expenses had been largely underwritten by the Labour party, through the Trades Union Council and similar groups. Several commented on their having been forced to attend Catholic services in certain of the various homes they had lived in "so people would send us donations." Others recalled their rebellion at Clapton on being forced to pray before meals. Here, after a note was quietly passed, the group rose and sang the "Internationale" instead. At the Cambridge colony for orphans of Socialist Basque soldiers, there was considerable disdain for Basque nationalism. The children ignored the *ikurriña* flying over the home when they arrived, and no one even knew how to sing the Basque anthem.

> They were a homogeneous group from a hostel in Bilbao, Asistencia Social organised, and financed by the Socialist Party. All their fathers were militiamen who had been killed early in the war. The children had been brought up as "children of heroes" in a very political atmosphere, and inherited their prejudices as a sacred trust. They came to us on condition that they should be under no political or religious influence. The deep cleavage between the Basque Nationalists and the Socialists was scarcely realised here, and it was a dangerous pitfall to well-meaning friends with little knowledge of politics. When, for instance a cake inscribed "Gora Euzkadi" was placed on the tea-table of the Y.M.C.A. Club Room, to

> welcome them, it was a strain on their good manners: "They thought we were Basque Nationalists!" Mrs. Ryle has told the story of the portrait of the young Basque President which had to be removed and returned to the donor with a polite note explaining that they owed no allegiance except to the President of the Spanish Republic. It was felt by the Socialists that the Nationalists, who had only come in on the Government side at the eleventh hour when Basque independence, and even speech, were threatened, had not shared with the Socialists the burden and heat of the day. In the children's minds all the picturesque trappings of National patriotism, the folk-songs and national dances, were the special attributes of the party (PNV). The use of the beautiful white Basque flag with its green cross was anathema and it was only after long and tactful efforts on the Señoritas' part that the children could be prevailed upon to learn "Boga Boga" or the "Basque Weavers" dance.[33]

All of the children in the Cambridge colony remained in England, having no parents to return to. As a group, they consciously prepared themselves to return to continue the revolution in Spain. Their dislike of Basque Nationalist aspirations was complete. Several, interviewed in 1980, commented:

> No, we had no Basque Nationalist personnel. If any had come, we would have stoned them. Actually, many of us weren't of Basque origin. Our parents had come in to work in the Bilbao factories or mines from other parts of the north. We were farther to the left than the bourgeois Basque Nationalists.

Others, when interviewed as adults, felt critical of the BCC policies. These, they said, at times mirrored the sentiments of the pro-Fascists in the BCC, or, at best, a simple expediency. Several of those interviewed commented:

> We, as children, were fully aware of the Non-Intervention policy, and for this reason, didn't believe a lot of what the British said. Basque children over age ten or so were very politicized, and understood the politics of European nations well.

They particularly resented the fact that, by and large, their education was neglected in England. Many found this to be a lifelong handicap. Most, having come to England without having completed primary school, were given only occasional English lessons, and some religious instruction for the nearly three years they lived in colonies. Those sent to the English Catholic boarding schools received a normal British education, but these children were usually the very first to be repatriated. Relatively few of those who stayed went on to the secondary level, and even fewer to the technical colleges. Only about thirty went to the university, using funds from the Juan Luis Vives trust, administered by the Spanish Republican Government-in-Exile. Of those given the university fellowships, more than half attended for only one year:

> What we received was barely enough to live on, with nothing left for movies or dances. If you failed one course, your grant was not renewed. At the same time, jobs were plentiful in the munitions factories, and paid very well, with plenty of overtime. So most of us dropped out and went to work.

One exception was the colony underwritten by the London Teachers' Association—the Leah Manning colony at Theydon Bois. The thirty children there in 1937 enrolled immediately in the local schools, and many went on to nearby Essex Technical College. Clearly, however, education was not seen as a responsibility of the BCC, nor was it mentioned in the voluminous government reports concerning the Basque children. This policy meant, of course, that the children as adults would be qualified only for factory jobs. Many indeed have spent all their lives as production workers, capable and faithful in their work but educationally unequipped for professional or administrative positions.

One of the ironies of history is that England herself inaugurated a full-scale evacuation of London and other major cities. Children and their mothers were sent to the countryside, beginning in September 1939. This evacuation, though in planning for eighteen months, was in many respects a failure. Mothers and children from London's slums could not adjust to country life, and soon returned to cities racked by German air raids in 1940–41. The British government found nearly half a million children without educational facilities in early 1940, in part due to the evacuation scheme.[34] Since the government could do so little for its own children, perhaps it is not surprising that so little was done for the Basque guests.

A perhaps more bitter irony of history and of the inequality of governmental policies also occurred in England, concerning the American policy toward the emigration of British child refugees in World War II. The children from Euzkadi who were not repatriated became aware that the response of the United States to the evacuation of British children to her shores was far different from that afforded themselves. Migration of large groups of British children, including the wholesale transfer of certain English boarding schools, began in 1940.* The United States Committee for the Care of Europe's Children, composed of over a dozen philanthropic organizations, proposed to bring in thirty thousand British children. They arranged to house them in fine private preparatory schools, such as Exeter, Millbrook, and Andover, and to enlist American families as foster parents. All would receive scholarships to these excellent boarding schools during their stay. Because of difficulties in transport across the Atlantic far fewer arrived than projected, but those who came found homes with families in very comfortable circumstances.

> Group migration of British schoolboys to this part of America, and in some instances, wholesale transfer of British schools, are being projected. Boys between the ages of 13 and 16 will be educated at the expense of the schools (Tabor, Phillips, Exeter, etc.) with the American foster parents meeting the expenses of housing and food. Half of the 30,000 children to be evacuated from Britain by August 31 will be sent to Canada.[35]

* In a recent book, *America, Lost and Found,* Anthony Bailey, one of the British refugee children, recalls his four years with an American family in Ohio.

For the Basque children who could not be repatriated, the lives of many revolved around the Socialist youth groups, of which they were ardent members. Though they may have been loath initially to master the dances and songs of their country, many became adept performers, particularly when the concerts became so profitable. These Basques continued to give their concerts during and after World War II. Some remember traveling to France and Switzerland to perform. The Communist periodical, *Mundo Obrero*, printed in Toulouse after the Spanish Republican defeat, commented on "the skill and grace of the Basque boys from the Socialist Youth (JSU) from London" in a front-page story in 1946.[36] Others recall soccer matches and other joint athletic events. Not all these were successful in joining together the Basque and British youth:

> The BCC tried to arrange excursions with a Leftist youth group, the Progressive Ramblers, who were devoted to long hikes on Sundays. We all went to the first, but only two of us showed up for the second hike: we had both been accustomed to hike every Sunday with our families in Euzkadi's mountains. Then came the Blitz, and all social life stopped for nearly a year, as we lived in air raid shelters once again, dodging the same German planes we had seen in Euzkadi, four years earlier.[37]

The BCC had seen clearly that, with the final defeat of the Spanish Republican forces, most of the children could never return home. At this point, a fortuitous change in official policy occurred. The head of the Home Office, Sir Samuel Hoare, lifted the ban on the employment of alien workers. Since so many of the children were now of working age, fourteen, the BCC saw that, with training, many could be absorbed into the burgeoning war industries.

To this end, the Basque Boys Training Committee was formed in May 1939. Representatives on the BCC from the Trades Union Council arranged apprenticeships or night school classes in agricultural or technical subjects for boys of working age.[38] The BCC rented a series of hostels in the major cities for the older children who were working or studying there. Those interviewed who had lived in the hostels recall that they were very united and maintained their political convictions. As they went out to work, they brought with them their independent attitudes. Many rebelled in the factories or assembly lines when the bosses exploited or demeaned them.

These young Basques resented the curfew imposed upon them and the regulations that made it illegal for them to change employment. Both of these wartime laws were the result of Franco's neutral position throughout World War II, coupled with their alien status. In spite of this, most of those aged fourteen or over soon found jobs in clothing factories, such as Polykof, or in other factories, as Tarran Industries, which were gearing up for full wartime production. Young women tended to work in small shops, restaurants, or the clothing factories.

The Fascist press in England vehemently objected to these young refugees allegedly taking jobs from British workers. One article referred to "Sweated Basques, conniving through the Basque Children's Committee, with 'Red' Trade unions, to give them preferential hiring." The same article noted that "Foreign Jews were inundating British employers with offers of their cut-price alien workers."[39] The BCC did what it could to counter such negative propaganda, and to improve the working conditions in the factories where the children were employed.

The BCC, through the Basque Boys Training Committee, was also the founder of a unique journal, *Amistad*, dealing with the children's lives in exile. This became an important unifying force among the several hundred Basque children still in England.

> In the middle of March, the secretary of the BCC, Molly Garrett, called a meeting of all of us in London to form a social club, in typical English style. As a first step, she urged us to put out a little magazine to send around to all 421 Basque children living in England. Perhaps she wanted to keep us together so we wouldn't succumb to the life of London streets and pubs. The first issue came out in May. I worked on every one, being editor for a

> time, but always writing articles, drawing the little sketches, and doing titles.
>
> A year later, March 1941, the Basque Boys Training Committee closed down and the International Committee for Spanish Child Refugees took over financially. By then, a number of English people had donated money, as did the Basque boys and girls, who enjoyed the magazine.[40]

The first issue was printed in two languages, with all material translated. It contained long letters of commendation from the major figures on the BCC: The Duchess of Atholl, Wilfred Roberts, and Elinor Rathbone. Announcements of interest to the Basque children, now spread all over England, were printed. New regulations on aliens were carefully explained in both English and Spanish; the announcement of a national conference of Basque children was made; the opening of a library of Spanish books open to all was reported. Appeals for the thirty shillings weekly to keep a boy in training were printed. The first issue also noted that the Basque children were the only group in Britain receiving no British help, as the cabinet had voted early in 1938 against authorizing any funds whatsoever for refugees from Spain. Several of the articles written by the children spoke of their nostalgia for their homeland:

> I think of yesterday, when I looked down at the fields from a hill in my country. But it wasn't yesterday. There, I would pass hours watching the farmers gathering the golden corn, or cutting hay from the meadows. Then it was carted home in wagons drawn by a pair of oxen, led by a farmer singing a song sung for generations past, of unknown origin, accompanied only by the squeaking wagon wheel. What an example of labor and peace. During the long winter nights, I sat with my parents near the hearth, where the logs crackle and glow, listening to the elders recite tales of long ago, handed down from father to son. We listened intently to them, making comments at the end, in complete harmony. But now the fields are sad and desolate; the road the ox wagon traveled is filled with bomb holes; the hearth where I spent long winter evenings no longer exists; only the

> walls remain in the houses in my town. Mechanized birds, black in colour, set fire and ruin all over the countryside.[41]

The first issue of *Amistad* reported that, of the 460 Basque children in England in mid-1940, one-third were over fourteen. Of these, 121 were already employed, and forty-five were totally self-supporting, being no longer a drain on the very slender resources of the BCC. Those employed had jobs in the following fields:

Engineering	50
Clothing	29
Agriculture	8
Miscellaneous (includes hotel work, catering, mining, and clerical)	34

Nearly all of these boys were living in working-class homes, as lodgers. In fact, Manuel Irujo, who represented the Basque Government-in-England during World War II, noted:

> Not one lived in a Tory home, and few in the houses of Liberals. Rather, nearly all lived in the humble and modest homes of laborers, factory workers, miners, the very best homes, really. You see, the children of the Basque middle class had already been repatriated. And the collections of the BCC had gone to nothing, and a family atmosphere was felt to be better for them. However, the British families did not all maintain enough supervision and, at times, foster homes had to be changed. But then, the English are the English. Better perhaps would have been groups, as before, but with a teacher in charge, and the boys and girls over fifteen at their workplace. We did what little we could to help.[42]

Throughout the war years, *Amistad* appeared at fairly regular intervals, serving as a link among the Basque children. The Basque Boys Training Committee also took leadership in promoting the cultural presentations throughout England. These were financially successful throughout the early years of World War II. Conferences and festivals were also organized that brought as many as 150 of the children together in London for weekends of visiting, renewal of friendships, and performance of traditional folklore. When the Basque House (Euzko Etxea) opened late in 1943 in London, some sponsorship of the Training Committee came from the Basque government, with funds obtained from the International Committee for Spanish Child Refugees.

Amistad ceased publication in July of 1944, following D-Day, the Normandy invasion. Unfortunately, however, the last issue was never actually printed:

> Everything was ready for the printer, including a feature story titled, "Basque Blood in Normandy." It was about two Basque refugee boys fighting with the British troops, who were killed in the invasion. But I had to leave to pick the crops, and it never appeared.[43]

The last issue seen by the writer was number 25, published in May of 1943, to commemorate the seventh anniversary of the children's arrival in England. It is composed almost entirely of historical summaries, written by the boys themselves. About 80 percent of the text is in Spanish. A survey of the founding of the Second Republic in 1931, the Asturian Miners' Strike in 1934, Franco's revolt in 1936, Guernica in 1937, and a recapitulation of their "English years" made up the bulk of this issue. It reported that by then nearly all the children were employed or in training.[44]

Throughout World War II, the small but loyal band of British supporters of the Basque children did not desert them. Dr. Richard Ellis personally corresponded with many of the older boys while he served as a Royal Air Force doctor. He also set up a home for six of the children in Suffolk, in the Midlands, supervised by the parents of two of the children, who had themselves fled Spain in 1939. There were about fifty Basque refugee children in the area, and they congregated on weekends at this home to have some Basque cultural, social, and gastronomic life. A number found employment at the English Electric Company in nearby historic Stratford.[45] The energetic new secretary of the BCC, Miss Betty Pickens, tried to find people to help those children with unusual talents. Those from the Cambridge colony found homes for the duration with prominent intellectuals there. One of the four colonies still functioning, Carshalton, was adopted by a committee from the United States. Clothing from the American Red Cross came regularly, and money for the children's special expenses came from donors in the States. Mrs. Eleanor Roosevelt came to visit upon one well-remembered occasion.[46]

As the war went on, young Basque women worked as domestics or in the hastily improvised system of war nurseries initiated to free English women from child care so they could work in wartime industry. Some of the Basque teachers, the "Señoritas," also found work there. A number of Basque boys enlisted in the British army, and served in Europe and Africa. One of those interviewed remembers another army some joined:

> Don Manuel Irujo came to Carshalton early in 1941. He described the Basque Battalion fighting with de Gaulle's Free French, and wanted us older boys to join as officers. Already, there were many of Basque descent from South America in the Battalion. Some of us went. It was demobilized in 1942, however, due to British pressure on de Gaulle after Franco complained to British diplomats. A sad affair.[47]

One of the over four hundred who stayed on in England wrote:

> We all became assimilated into the British way of life. The Basque character is generally dour, persistent, individualistic and hard-working. Most of the youngsters displayed these characteristics. They worked well in the factories where the majority were sent during the war years. Many took what opportunities were available to study and obtain professional qualifications, and at least four made headlines for their achievements. Ramon Aldecoa played football for the Wolverhampton Wanderers and Coventry City between 1942 and 1947, after which he went to play for Atletico de Bilbao. Pirmin Trecu was a well-known male dancer in the Sadler's

Wells Ballet in the late forties and early fifties. Marina de Gabarain became a renowned operatic singer on the Continent, and one season sang *La Cenerentola* at Glyndebourne. The last, Jose Alberdi, a world-famous sculptor, pioneered the use of plastics as a medium for sculpture in Britain. His works in stone and metal grace Oxford University, as well as banks, office buildings, and hotels in England. He is a Fellow of the Royal Society of British Sculptors. Others made their careers in scientific research, architecture, building, commerce, engineering, and teaching. Three were killed serving with the forces during the war. The children, described by a newspaper soon after their arrival at North Stoneham as "difficult, aggressive, wholly alien to English manners and culture," matured and acquired the "manners and culture" so respected by that reporter of 1937.

As the years passed, many married young British men and women; but quite a number, well over half, married within the group. Despite the forty years that have passed since their landing at Southampton, the sense of family and blood bond that united them in those early days in a foreign country still remains.[48]

The daughter born to one of the Basque girls who stayed on in England* has interviewed a number of the over two hundred Basque refugee children still living in England. She reports two characteristics these middle-aged adults appear to have in common:

1) A sense of guilt for not having shared the poverty and repression of those repatriated to Spain.

2) A total lack of common ground when they visit or meet with those repatriated to Spain, even those within the same family. This is astonishing to them, and contrary to their expectations.

After this preliminary research, Ms. Yolanda Genge comments, "Perhaps those who stayed have outwardly assimi-

* A child from Gallarta, as was La Pasionaria.

lated, while still feeling themselves to be ethnic Basques, not Britons."[49]

After World War II, Basque officials in London and Paris were able to arrange for the reunion of some two dozen children with their relatives who were refugees in France.[50]

A few of those whom the writer interviewed in England did try to return to Franco's Spain. One, for example, arranged for a visa for a visit in 1957. When he met his parents in Bilbao, he found they expected him to remarry his wife immediately in the Catholic church while on his visit. Neither he nor his wife had felt this to be necessary in Britain. In addition, he learned that he would have to petition the Spanish government for a pardon, under Franco's Decree of Responsibility, if he intended to continue to live in Euzkadi. He and his wife returned to England, and have not visited Spain since.

Belgium

As we have seen, the Basque children sent to Belgium enjoyed a generally halcyonic expatriation. Fewer than one-fifth were repatriated before mid-1939, so that most stayed for at least two years in Belgium. The granting of a family allowance to the adoptive parents who took the children into their homes was clearly one reason that the children did not become an economic burden. The political pressure that Cardinal van Roey was able to use very judiciously for the welfare of the children was augmented by the help of the Socialist and Communist parties. The extent of cooperation among those hosting the refugee children was unparalleled in other adoptive countries, as was the lack of polarization in government policy as World War II drew closer.

By the end of 1939, several months after the outbreak of World War II, over 2,500 of the 3,200 children had been officially repatriated to Spain.[51] Of the nearly six hundred remaining, some joined parents in France for eventual re-emigration to the Western Hemisphere. Others trickled home throughout World War II, some staying briefly in a *hostal* sponsored by the International Red Cross in Fuenterrabía, outside San Sebastián.[52]

After the war, more were repatriated. Others, now old enough to leave as adults, emigrated to Mexico, Venezuela, or Argentina to join relatives. Fewer than one hundred stayed on in Belgium. Of this small contingent, several were young girls who were, for all practical purposes, adopted by the adoptive parents who had already cared for them for almost three years. In most cases, the adoptive parents were childless, and certainly able to provide a more comfortable life for the child than could her real parents in Euzkadi. In some of the cases of girls being "adopted," an attempt by relatives to regain physical custody of the child through the International Red Cross was ineffective, and one "tug of war" was reported at the border in Hendaye, with the adoptive parents and an uncle, a refugee in France, both claiming the child.

By now, also, a number of the Basque children who had been twelve or more when evacuated had married Belgian men and women. All their schooling had been in the state or Catholic schools, side by side with Belgians.

The Basque government maintained a small delegation in Brussels until 1939. After the fall of France, and the occupation of Belgium, the nominal presence of the Basque government, which had been little more than a fiction, came to an end. But, again, as in other host countries, those who had shown themselves to be friends continued to help. In a few cases, the parents of children fled Spain to join their children, usually after World War II. One family of nine children, four of whom were evacuated to Belgium in 1937, is illustrative of the experience of those who stayed on in Belgium. By 1950, the father had completed his prison sentence in Spain and the parents and youngest children rejoined their sons, now in their mid-twenties, in Belgium. Simply by dint of hard work and taking advantage of whatever education they could manage while working, all the children have achieved success. The boys are now university professors, administrators of Catholic education, engineers, and legal heads of important corporations. Some married Belgian women, but most of their children have Basque names. The oldest son has kept up a relationship with all the Basque children who stayed on, perhaps fifty at this point. In 1980, when he was injured in an accident, his Basque friends were faithful visitors to his hospital bed.

Martin Aguirre comments that all the Basques are employed, are heads of families, and have integrated very well into Belgian life. Most of them visit family members who live in Euzkadi, with some having a summer home in the San Sebastián area. They receive Basque publications and send their children to Euzkadi to improve their language. Nearly all speak both French and Flemish, as well as Spanish and Basque. They remain a cohesive group with strong ties to their homeland.[53]

The Soviet Union

The Basque and Spanish children invited to Russia during the Civil War enjoyed a separate and favored life there until Hitler's invasion in mid-1941. The abrupt and drastic changes which followed are well-described in the words of one Basque girl, who was five years of age when she arrived in the Soviet Union in 1938. Ariadne Pascual has written her recollections of the war years in Russia:

> JUNE 22, 1941: AT 04:00 THIS MORNING, HITLER'S ARMY CROSSED THE RUSSIAN BORDER.
>
> I was only 8, but clearly remember that Sunday. We were having a party in the recreation room, with games and folk dancing. Like the other girls in my group, I was wearing a blue silk dress, embroidered with yellow polka dots. Suddenly, one of our Spanish teachers broke into the room in a very agitated manner and told us that the party was over. War had sought us out; it had followed us even here.
>
> Later that summer, as the Germans advanced toward Moscow, their bombers began to raid our surroundings at night. At first we took cover in the woods by the river, where we used to swim in the summer and ski in the winter. But later, as the raids became more frequent, all of us—men, women and children—hastily built shelters. On the edge of the big woods, where we used to pick flowers and chase butterflies, we dug several long

> trenches to accommodate 30 people each. We covered them with large logs, and on top, dirt and branches disguised the trenches from the planes. At first, spending the nights in those dugouts was an exciting new adventure for us children, but as the nights got colder, we longed for our warm beds.
>
> OCTOBER 1941: HITLER BELIEVES THE GERMANS WILL TAKE MOSCOW.
>
> Just before midnight on October 15, the Soviet Government, together with the foreign diplomats, prepared to evacuate from the capital to Kuibishev. Then, Mother Russia—for the second time—gathered the Spanish children in her arms. To protect us from the war, we were sent down river in boats, as if we each were a little Moses to be saved for the fulfillment of some destiny.[54]

The evacuation from Moscow, with Hitler's armies only fifteen kilometers away, was extremely well organized, quiet, and without panic. The people were well disciplined, and filed into waiting transport to move east. The Basque children in the Leningrad area were not all evacuated in time. They were part of the heroic siege of that northern city, in which 800,000 people died of malnutrition, cold, illness, and bombs. In the winter of 1941, when Lake Ladoga froze, these Basque children were the first to be evacuated to safety in eastern Russia by the rail system hastily built over its ice.

Those whom the German invasion caught near Odessa were evacuated swiftly in trucks, carrying their Spanish books and their precious sewing machines with them. All the boys and girls wore the identical sensible ski clothing for the journey east to safety. Tens of thousands of Russians were killed in the war in this area.

In general, those from the Odessa area were first sent to Moscow. Then as the Germans neared, they were evacuated to Stalingrad, the Saratov region, and to the south and east. Others went to the Urals, in Central Siberia, to the area around Ufa, where temperatures reached -40°C that winter. Others went even farther east, to Samarkand, Tashkent, and Kazakstan, in Asiatic Russia. Many went to Tiflis; others to Baku, in the Caspian region. Their odyssey totaled over two thousand miles, always moving ahead of the advancing Germans.

Some of the older boys refused to be evacuated. Many of those children, barely sixteen years old, stayed behind.

> Storming the Hall of Columns in Moscow where the 4th battalion was stationed for the night, they demanded to be sent into the fight. Like their fathers in Spain's war, they marched to the front singing:
>
> El Ejercito del Ebro
> Rumba-la-rumba-la-rumban-ban
> Se me parte el corazón
> Ay Carmela, Ay Carmela.
>
> The Armies of Ebro
> Rumba-la-rumba-la-rumban-ban
> My heart is breaking
> Oh, Carmela, Oh, Carmela.
>
> And perhaps some German veteran, now fighting on the Moscow front, recognized this song, one he had heard several years earlier on the battlefield of Spain.[55]

Others volunteered for training as pilots in the military college. Many served throughout the war, and won decorations for bravery. Though Stalin officially rejected the enlistment of Spanish children ("They were to be reserved to return to Spain"), dozens enlisted using forged papers. According to Irena Falcon, long-time secretary to La Pasionaria:

> Their Russian was by now fluent, and this helped them pass as "Ivan," rather than "José María," though Dolores urged them not to volunteer.

A great number were killed, including the brothers of two of the Sovieticos interviewed in Spain in 1980. La Pasionaria herself lost a son in the decisive battle of Stalingrad. With him also perished perhaps 90 percent of the seventy-four Basque and Asturian children, now of military age, who fought there alongside the Russian soldiers. In all, in World War II, over ten million Russian soldiers died, as did millions of civilians.[56]

By the end of November, the battlegrounds were deep in

snow. The fierce Russian winter of 1941 once more repelled the enemy. The ill-clad Germans, like Napoleon's armies of 1812, retreated frozen and beaten, and by the end of December, they were two hundred miles away from Moscow.

> Meanwhile, we docked at a small town just north of Saratov, on the Volga's east bank, where we lived until the end of 1944. The town was deserted, the crops left in the fields. Its inhabitants, Russian citizens, descendants of Germans who had settled there at the time of Catherine the Great, had been hastily sent to Siberia to prevent their defection to the enemy.[57]

This old German colony, Horjoses, was a very rich one. The wealthy farmers had great fruit orchards, fertile fields planted with a variety of crops, excellent stock, including pedigreed cows and fine horses. They had all been so quickly interned and evacuated that no arrangements for caretakers had been made. When the children arrived, the cows were in agony, their udders clogged with milk. The chickens were starving and had been reduced to cannibalism. This surreal abandoned village and open countryside without humans terrified and repelled the children. They were already disturbed by their second forced evacuation to a strange place. Here, nothing was organized to help them. They were unsupervised for many weeks, and many literally ran wild. They ravaged the melon fields and orchards to feed themselves. Nothing was harvested or stored, and acres of food rotted. Some became more and more destructive as the days passed, and groups of young thieves formed spontaneously to range the countryside, stealing and breaking into the abandoned homes. Order was gradually restored and classes began again. Many recall the water sports on the Volga, an idyllic life once again, while the summer lasted. Then, winter came.

> That fall I started first grade, and that winter, with temperatures dropping to -40° C, was the worst I can remember. We were always cold and hungry. The Franklin stove in the middle of our room, where we first graders studied and slept, didn't generate enough heat either day or night. We slept two to a bed, one on each end, holding the other's feet during the night to keep them

> warm. During the day, we huddled around the stove where we baked beets and potatoes whenever we could steal them from the kitchen. Our meals were reduced to beets, cabbage, boiled potatoes with sunflower oil, and oatmeal infested with worms.[58]

The war was terribly difficult for everyone. Hunger was widespread, partly as a result of the failure of the potato harvest that year and partly due to the impossibility of importing food during the German invasion. In spite of the food shortage, the Spanish children were always given a larger ration than that given Soviet citizens. One Sovietico, now in Mexico, has guarded her Russian ration book. Her coupons entitled her to 700 grams of bread, when Soviets received 450 or 500 grams. Even in the siege of Leningrad, when 25 grams was the ration, the Spanish children were given a larger amount. Some Sovieticos recall subsisting on carrots that winter, prepared in every imaginable way. Many, especially in the most eastern areas, were as malnourished as their Russian neighbors. All were organized to help in the harvests each year of the war. Sunflowers—hundreds of acres in the collective farms were used for their precious oil—potatoes, wheat, fruits, and vegetables were the main crops. Boys and girls cut and hauled wood all through the years of war. They learned from the Russians they worked alongside how to forage for food in the forests and waterways of the countryside.

> With the coming of spring, our food supply increased. We dug for mussels on the Volga's sandy banks. We salted and dried fish in the sun to preserve it for winter. Summers, we picked delicious wild berries from the surrounding woods, and, from the fields, herbs for soups. In the fall, we gathered mushrooms of all shapes and colors. I still remember my feeling of pleasure whenever I found a specially prized mushroom under a tree.[59]

In all the southern and eastern areas of the Soviet Union to which the Spanish and Basque children were evacuated, schooling resumed within a few months. Small groups were merged by age and accomplishment, and their education continued. There was emphasis on physical fitness. Sewing and knitting became activities important for survival. Some woolen clothing arrived from the United States, but the sizes were far too large. The children unraveled the garments, and reknit them to usable dimensions. Some were sold to the Russian people nearby in exchange for food the peasants produced privately, to augment the scanty rations. Letters no longer came from home. Parents in Spain, France, and elsewhere no longer heard from their children. But morale continued to be surprisingly high, due in large part to the Spanish and Basque teachers with the children.

> On long winter evenings, with no kerosene for our lamps, our beloved teacher, Claudia, raised our morale by telling Jack London's stories about the Yukon, and by describing Charlie Chaplin's movies. I particularly remember her recounting of the scene in *The Gold Rush* in which a hungry Chaplin boils a shoe and eats it, delicately pulling and sucking the nails as if they were juicy chicken bones, and rolling the shoe laces around his fork as if they were spaghetti. Claudia's images stayed with me until I saw the movie thirty years later in Mexico.[60]

This period in the lives of the Spanish and Basque children brought them much closer to their adoptive country and the Russian people. Many commented, forty-three years later, that the Russian love of the land is identical to that of the Basques.

> More important, having endured the war years together, we children and the teachers, both Russian and Spanish, had now become a large family. Also we had begun to know more about the outside world. Our contact with America became more direct than it had been through Claudia's tales. Roosevelt's lend lease program to aid Russia during the war brought with it American culture. We saw movies and became acquainted with American actors. I particularly remember Deanna Durbin and Shirley Temple. We saw Sonia Henie, the Olympic skating champion, in "Sun Valley." Later, I battled lines in Moscow to see Walt Disney's "Bambi," a great success with the Russians. Whenever we had a party, we danced to American jazz.[61]

After the Russian victory at Stalingrad, the Basque and Spanish children who had been dispersed throughout the eastern provinces were gathered up and brought back to the Moscow area, beginning in mid-1944. By this time the German offensive in Russia had been crushed. The fighting had shifted westward; the Normandy invasion by the Allies and the liberation of Paris were already history.

Estimates vary of how many of the children survived the more than three years of bitter warfare. Certainly many perished as a result of the bombings, exposure, malnutrition, tuberculosis, and malaria, as did millions of Soviet citizens. Rafael Miralles, a Cuban diplomat in Moscow, estimated in 1947 that about five hundred of the four thousand children—the number most authorities report as being sent into Russia—died in World War II.[62] Jesús Hernández, minister of education in the Spanish Republican government, who fled to Russia in 1939, wrote that about 750 had already died of severe malnutrition and tuberculosis even before the Germans invaded the country in 1941. He reports that, in a medical inspection he ordered early in 1941, some 50 percent of the refugee children were found to be tubercular. He notes that after the war began, conditions for the children became even worse, especially for the youngest ones. The older children turned to thievery to survive. They formed roving bands in the Urals and Siberia, terrorizing the citizens of Tashkent and Kokan, among other cities. Some of the girls, he reports, turned to prostitution.[63] Several of the Sovieticos interviewed in Mexico echoed these reports spontaneously during interviews. Very few of the children fell into German hands, although a group of seventeen were taken prisoner in the Caucasus, and were later used for propaganda purposes in both Spain and Germany by the Fascists. In all, as Hernández states, "What is certain is that more than two thousand of the five thousand children who were evacuated from Spain in 1936–37 [sic] found death in the Soviet Paradise."[64]

An even higher death toll is reported by Valentín González, the "El Campesino" of the Spanish Republican forces. His figure for the total of children and adults evacuated from Spain is 5,823; of these, he claims only 1,200 were still alive when he left the Soviet Union in 1949. He notes accurately that 1,700 of the nearly 6,000 were "children from the north, who came in during 1937." His account corroborates the banditry and prostitution among the older children, but he adds that "this was common among Russian children of the same age evacuated to the east"; and further that "such behaviour was typical only in the first few months of the German invasion, as the Spanish population was hastily moved to Tashkent, Samarkand, Ufa, Tiflis, Alma-Ata, etc." González also commented on the sad fate of several Spanish Communist leaders and their families in the Soviet Union during the war. He describes the plight of Eguilazo, Zarauza, and others from the north who died of starvation.[65]

Those Sovieticos interviewed invariably described the war years as "going from Paradise to the inferno." They were by now refugees twice over, having experienced this trauma in 1937 as well as in 1941.

The children from Spain who were again survivors were quickly regrouped for further education, either in Moscow or Leningrad. By 1944–45, even the youngest ones were in their last years of primary education. Under the Soviet system of the period, those who had finished seven years of schooling with high marks were given four additional years of academic instruction, and then entered the university. Unlike Soviet children, all the children from Spain were allowed to enroll in the university without any entrance examinations. Those who were less apt were sent to a technical college or an institute attached to a factory after the seven years of primary schooling. This primary education was clearly more comprehensive than that offered in Spain, since those interviewed who left Russia around 1946 report that they were accelerated upon entering the school systems in Mexico, Santo Domingo, and Cuba.

Some Basques interviewed had been given special training in ballet with masters of the Russian ballet; others were sent to art institutes; still others studied voice and instrumental music. During all this advanced training, Russian men and women studied, worked, and lived in dormitories alongside the children from Spain. Close friendships naturally began between the Russian and Spanish young adults since, by then, the refugee children were well-assimilated into Soviet life. Several of those interviewed remarked that, having seen the heroism of the people in repelling the Nazi invasion and having worked side by side with the Russians in the harvest or on the assembly line during the war, they felt very drawn to the culture.

These sentiments were mirrored in a series of articles published in *Alkartu*,* a Basque Communist journal published in Spanish in Toulouse, France, beginning in 1945. In one, a description of the life of the Basque children in Russia was reported, based on letters written by Araceli Sanchez, a daughter of a worker from Baracaldo, Vizcaya. She, with fifty other Basque children, was studying electrical engineering in Moscow. Araceli noted that the day victory was announced, she celebrated by dancing in the streets with her Russian friends. She wrote that in the factories the eight-hour day had just returned, after years of wartime schedules, and that Bizet's opera *Carmen* was being performed in the Grand Theater of Moscow to the delight of all the Spanish and Basque children. Already, she commented, all the refugee children evacuated from their various schools had returned, looking very grown up, and ready for work or study. She closed by remarking that all the Russian friends expected that she and the other Basques would soon return to Euzkadi, now that fascism had been defeated by the Allies.[66]

Subsequent articles and photographs regarding the Basque children in Russia were published, all in a laudatory tone. Early in 1946, an open letter to families whose children had been sent to the Soviet Union was printed, urging parents to write in care of the paper, to a Julian Gonzalez for information about their children. In spite of this invitation, fewer than 150 of the Basque children in all were repatriated following the end of World War II. Instead of the return Araceli Sanchez anticipated, assimilation to Soviet life continued.[67]

**Alkartu* means "Solidarity" in Basque.

In July of 1947, over two thousand of the children from Spain came to the immense Stanislavsky Theater in Moscow to celebrate the tenth anniversary of their arrival in the Soviet Union. In the theater lobby, their art work—painting, sculpture, metalwork, and photography—was displayed. Examples of sewing and tailoring, welding, and carpentry were also on exhibit. The many awards the children from Spain had received in their factories for exceeding the norms of production were hung on the lobby walls. Major functionaries of the Spanish Communist party were on stage to welcome them. Santiago Carrillo presented a lengthy eulogy to the accomplishments of the children. He described their feted arrival in Leningrad in 1937; the happy years before the German invasion; their evacuation to the east; and the hardships they had suffered alongside the Russian people. He then gave the statistics on their present lives:

1,500 Spanish and Basque children in the secondary schools or in the universities.
750 in factory work, with many of these also studying in courses given in institutes attached to the workplace.
327 in technical education (textiles, aviation, automotive, construction, shipping, communications).
500 of the youngest studying for a university degree.[68]

Carrillo noted of this total of 3,077, each received a living stipend; free housing in schools, worker dormitories, or student hostels; free vacations at the worker resorts in summer; free medical care; and an assured position upon completion of their education or training. He singled out a number of young Basque men for special praise as "Stakhanovites," those exceeding production norms. One, Mauricio Garrudo, of Bilbao, had completed a year's production as a lathe operator in seven months, and "proposed to complete another year's work by the anniversary of the October Revolution, only three months away." For this, Mauricio won the prize of the banner of La Pasionaria. Carrillo also singled out, among others, Basques such as Rosa Elizalde, José María Uribe, José Arribas, and Cosme G. Basqueriz for exceeding the production norms, commenting:

> We can be sure that from the Soviet factories will come not only excellent workers, but rather, workers who have a developed consciousness; revolutionary workers who, tomorrow in Spain, will not resign themselves to be exploited slaves of Capitalism. Rather, workers who will be the worthy sons of the miners and metalworkers of Euzkadi and Asturias.[69]

He also praised other Basque young men and women who were excelling in their university courses, such as Vincent and Julia Delgado of Eibar and Emilio Etchgoyen. As part of the program, the songs and dances of Euzkadi were performed by choral and dance groups organized among the children. One "son of the Basque Country," Agustín Gomez, also spoke, telling of his life in Bilbao during the Spanish Civil War, and his present career as both an electrical engineer and a star player on the famous Moscow soccer team, the Torpedoes. Gomez declared:

> Here in the Soviet Union, we have found a second country. And we have realized that never, as sons of the working class in the Spain of Franco, or in any capitalist country, could we have acquired such training and knowledge.[70]

Carrillo closed the presentation by saying that the young men and women being honored that day would be the foundation of a new Spain.[71]

The Sovieticos interviewed in Mexico, Spain, and the United States described their lives as young adults in Russia as being happy, well-ordered, and satisfying. About half of those interviewed had brothers or sisters who had not been repatriated. Some were engineers there; others were teachers, doctors, or army officials. They lived well and had little desire to leave.

Many of those who refused repatriation in 1956 had married Russian men or women. Because of the high death toll among Russian males in World War II, men were not allowed to emigrate. Those Spanish men who married Russian women frequently deferred to the wishes of their wives to stay on in Russia. Among those who chose repatriation with their Russian wives, many of the marriages were failures, according to Sovieticos interviewed in Spain. The Russian wives could not adjust to Spain, and the husbands found life quite different from what they expected. In some cases, the couple and their children re-entered Russia; in others, there was separation.

Within Russia, during the educational years of the children, the Casas de Niños, as we have seen, were reserved for the children from Spain, and certain ones were almost exclusively Basque, with some children from Asturias. But in the factories, the worker dormitories, the technical institutes, and the universities, young Russian adults were in the majority, and many romances were the natural result. However, perhaps as a result of the concentration of Basques in certain colonies, the proportion of Basque endogamous marriage seems very high, at least 85 percent among those who came back in 1956 to Spain. Of those few Basques interviewed who came to Mexico ten years earlier, in 1945–46, none of the six married Basques, though, of the four who married, two married Spaniards, one of these being Asturian.

Throughout the years of exile, the children from Spain have frequented the Spanish Club in Moscow, a center for Spanish cultural and social events. Notices of interest to them, a library of Spanish books, and other amenities have kept it as an oasis of things Spanish. It has served as an informal network since World War II, and is frequented today by the aging exiles, as well as young students from Hispanic countries being educated in the Soviet Union. It is visited as well by the Sovieticos from Spain who frequently travel back to the land of their childhood and young adulthood to visit siblings who refused repatriation. In their homes in Eibar and industrial areas of Vizcaya are samovars, vodka, Russian dolls, books, and paintings to attest to the importance of the twenty years in Russia experienced by these Sovieticos.

Mexico

The lives of the Niños de Morelia have been examined in some detail. In the work of Vera Foulkes, a follow-up interview with eight of the children was reported in 1952, as well as certain material on 340 others.[72] All, by then, were young adults, aged from about nineteen to over thirty. She noted that, after the tenure of Cárdenas as president, the school enrolled more and more poor Mexican children, and soon became indistinguishable from the usual state boarding school. A number of sources indicated that after 1940 Cárdenas continued to help the Spanish students, "out of his own pocket." The *casas de hogar* were maintained by the Spanish Comité Técnico de Fidecomiso para Auxiliar a los Republicanos Españoles (CTFARE), funded by Prieto's JARE until the mid-forties, when funds were exhausted. By then, all the children were of working age.

A few children were given fellowships to attend the university through the Juan Luis Vives Trust. Among them was one Basque who had become a boyhood chum of Cuauhtemoc Cárdenas, son of the president. Some of the more apt students were enrolled in the Luis Vives School, on the outskirts of Mexico City. It was modeled after the new progressive secular schools begun during the second Spanish Republic. Others enrolled in the Colegio de Madrid, also founded by refugees from Spain.

Ms. Foulkes writes that, fifteen years after their arrival, most of the children seemed to be leading normal lives.[73] This in itself is an important point, for the negative reputation of the Niños de Morelia had continued into the fifties. Hearsay and unpublished reports indicated that the children, now young adults, were appearing before the authorities with unusual frequency for various crimes. In fact, Foulkes found that very few had such records, and that the charge had usually been vagrancy, rather than delinquency.

In her general summary of the information on 348 children, she reports that about a quarter had been repatriated, with two and one-half times as many women as men in this group. Most were already married; over three-quarters of the males and 51 percent of the females. A much larger relative proportion of males than females had married Mexicans rather than Spaniards (70 as against 40 percent). Nearly half the men were employed as office help or tradespersons. Ten percent could be classed as anti-social; including 2 percent in prison, and 8 percent vagrants or marijuana users.[74]

A few were still studying, but a surprisingly small number (6 percent) had pursued professional careers. She noted that most had left school forever by the end of secondary training. Those who went on to the *preparatoria*, the year of study required for university matriculation, did not, as a rule, complete their university training. Lack of money was cited as the usual reason, since their fellowships were inadequate for daily necessities, especially after the pensions, the *casas de hogar*, were closed. She observes that lack of role models and counsel from adults could also be the reasons so few finished. She notes that a large number ran away from school very early, often after their primary schooling. These boys and girls, she reasons, found it hard to accustom themselves to the discipline of a regular boarding school routine after the chaotic and emancipated life in wartime.

Foulkes cites the work of Reyes-Perez as the basis of her contention that the children, as a whole, had great difficulty with any kind of discipline, and especially that first offered at the Escuela España-Mexico. This, she characterizes as ambivalent: rigid in form, but poorly and inconsistently administered. Examples she cites to illustrate this distaste for discipline include the propensity of the children to form attachments only to staff persons without authority (the cooks, handymen, maids),* the habitual running away, and frequent riotous or anarchic behavior. An interesting observation made in the Foulkes study is that many of the boys married women a good deal older than themselves. She at-

*This point is still salient. In Morelia, the writer met such a staff couple, now in their mid-eighties, who provided affection and nurture to the children and are still sought out by returning alumni. A man arrived after nearly thirty-five years of residence back in Valencia, Spain, to show his family the school in Morelia, and the two people he remembered with emotion—the seamstress and her husband, the school's former janitor.

tributes this to a lack of maternal affection during their own childhood in Morelia.[75]

Emeterio Paya-Valera, a former student who has published his recollections of the school in a weekly magazine of Morelia, has pursued the avocation of unofficial historian of the Escuela España-México and secretary of the alumni organization. As such, he has maintained extensive files on a large majority of the children, including those who were repatriated to Spain.

In summing up the collective impressions he has gathered from his extensive correspondence with his classmates, and personal visits with them during the annual reunions he has organized, he writes:

> Probably our evacuation has produced more negative results than positive in view of the final outcome: our feelings of paternal abandonment, and uprooting from our native country, damaging many of us in an unforgettable way. Collectively, it created a kind of precarious solidarity, though we felt marked by our abandonment under circumstances of trauma.[76]

Paya-Valera indicates that in his initial follow-up he found that a number of the Niños de Morelia simply disappeared from view, especially those who were in the youngest group. Several that he knows are alcoholics, to the point of delirium tremens; over a dozen are potential suicides; a large number live in a marginal manner. On the other hand, some have achieved acclaim in art, letters, business, etc. He does not necessarily agree with Foulkes's finding that most, as young adults, were apathetic politically, after an education in a strongly Communist environment. He does agree that many found their way back to Catholicism, especially the women.[77]

A third writer, historian Javier Rubio, writes that the expatriate children experienced unique difficulties in adaptation, due to their education among overwhelmingly Spanish peers. This prevented "Mexicanization," and foreshadowed their later inability to identify with either the old Spanish colony or with the Civil War refugees who arrived from 1939 onwards. He posits an intergenerational and class barrier between these children and the later adult refugees that is largely insurmountable.[78]

A fourth source, Carlos Blanco Aguinaga, a Basque who emigrated with his family first to France, and later, to Mexico in 1939, attended school with several of the Niños de Morelia who were sent to Mexico City to the Luis Vives School or the Colegio de Madrid. Now a university professor in California, he has maintained a lifelong friendship with several of them. He remarked:

> I know from them the bad conditions of their lives—poor food and schooling in Morelia, prejudice against them in the capital. When they came to school with me, they were savages, very rebellious. I know well that the Basque colony in Mexico City gave them no help.[79]

Recently, a study by Dolores Pla noted that data gathered from both interviews and questionnaires mailed to the Niños de Morelia during 1979–80 indicate general agreement with Foulkes's findings (thirty years earlier) that they had led normal lives. Many commented that their economic status was better than that of siblings who had remained in Franco's Spain. Pla did find, however, a suicide rate among the Spanish "niños" that was over twenty times higher than expected.[80]

More than a quarter century after the Foulkes's study, this writer found a rather different picture among the small subgroup of children from Euzkadi. (There were a number of other clearly Basque-surnamed children among the Niños de Morelia, but they were from outside Euzkadi.) This contingent of twenty-four formed only a small percentage of the expedition, and was greatly outnumbered by Catalans and those from Castilla. First, a much smaller proportion of Basque children returned to Spain—only one family, noted earlier, of the ten represented. A surprisingly large proportion, nearly a third, are dead, all of natural causes. Every child has married. One-third married endogamously, either within the established Basque colony, or, in one case, by returning to Euzkadi to find a mate. One-third married Spaniards from the same sources. Only one-third married Mexicans, in marked contrast to Foulkes's sample. Those males who returned to Spain to find wives followed the pattern of late marriage noted by others.[81]

The employment record of the Basque men is excellent. All are working, with half owning their own shop or business, a quarter being managers, and the rest working for an employer. All the women are housewives and involved with child-rearing. Of the ten families interviewed, there are a total of thirty-nine children, with family size ranging from two to six. All of the families were interviewed in their homes, which were uniformly very well kept and attractively decorated. From the interview, and other information, it appears that all have risen into the middle class. Three are definitely upper middle class; one is the wife of a wealthy publisher; another, the wife of a factory owner; and the third (the protégé of Cárdenas) a prominent engineer in a government ministry.

As a group, they express pride in being refugees, but no longer consider themselves to be Niños de Morelia. Rather, they view themselves as adults forced to become mature and autonomous at a young age, with little help from anyone. Most feel that the effects of being political refugees are positive, since their opposition to Franco was a just cause. Several commented on the problems of adjustment brought on by a lack of maternal affection, including difficulties in identification, lack of a sense of security, and some anger at their parents for sending them away so young. There are no suicides or alcoholics, and all are still in contact with others in their small group. In general, they note, as did Foulkes in 1953, that they are better off today than they would have been under Franco.

Euzkadi

The Euzkadi encountered by the first children repatriated from France late in 1937 was changed markedly from that they had left six or eight months earlier. Their reception at the border foretold their future:

> We were greeted by Franco's flag; with his Civil Guards, and his Catholic nuns flanking it. All our mementoes, pictures, even souvenir Bibles, were taken away. They gave us coffee and milk, but it wasn't real coffee, and there was no milk. They made us give the Fascist salute.

One Basque woman remembers the trip across France, after leaving England. As they neared the border, the children began to sing Basque hymns:

> Fr. Gabana told us to be quiet: We were returning to the New Spain, and our old songs were not appreciated there. He advised us to sing in Castilian from now on.

When the children who had been sent to France were reunited with their families, they found many tragedies. Of the thirty interviewed, five reported that their fathers had been shot in prison, as had two of their uncles. Four others had fathers in jail; the mother of another was in jail as well. Four found their fathers had gone into exile; the mother of another was a refugee in France. Three had older brothers who had been killed in battle. Again, twenty of these thirty children found relatives dead, jailed, or exiled. There were few repatriations without parental request from France, probably because all but two of the children interviewed remained there until the outbreak of World War II.

Of the twenty-six children interviewed who had been evacuated to England, eight learned that their fathers had been shot to death in prison. The fathers of another three were in jail; another was in the hospital, wounded in battle. Two mothers had died during the war, one of tuberculosis. One mother had been exiled to another part of Spain for four years because she had held a minor municipal post under the Republic; three others had chosen exile in France. Two brothers had died in battle; at least one father was in a concentration camp in France. In all, eight were reclaimed without a request from their parents; they lived with other relatives or in the Falange orphanage. Trauma thus characterized the reentry of twenty of the twenty-six sent to England.

The children sent to Belgium who were interviewed as

adults came home to perhaps less trauma. Three of the twenty-one noted that their fathers had been shot in prison (as had the uncle of another) or killed in battle; the fathers of another four were in prison; and the brother of one was in a concentration camp. Two others had either a father or mother in exile. In all, then ninė of the twenty-one came home to find a parent dead, in jail, or in exile. None of these children were repatriated until after Hitler had annexed the Danzig corridor in mid-1939, and their safety in Belgium had become questionable. Still, one person reported that his reclamation had not been requested by his parents.[82]

In the interviews, many of these Basques spontaneously spoke of their return as "from a paradise to an inferno." They experienced unrelenting persecution through the balance of their childhoods and well into adulthood. This persecution took many forms, some as basic as the denial of sufficient food and medical care. The lack of food was especially grave until well after the end of World War II. Franco had a policy of sending food to Germany in exchange for medicines and certain manufactured goods. As a result of the severe malnutrition, the incidence of tuberculosis soared in Euzkadi. One teacher interviewed commented: "It was ironic; our food went to Hitler and he sent us medicine to cure the tuberculosis the lack of food helped to cause." Food was provided to children in the Auxilio Social dining rooms, but political indoctrination was the quid pro quo. Both the Catholic church, with funds from Pius XII, and the Falange opened orphanages for those children whose parents were dead, in prison, ill, or in exile. Again, the price was political adherence to Franco.

The one-course meal, the *Plato Unico,* popularized by Franco as a wartime necessity and copied from Hitler's *Eintof,* became a cruel joke to the children who were repatriated to Euzkadi. It was rare that urban children found more than this to eat:

> In the Calle Ascao, there was a burro eating *algorrobas* [a legume fed to stock] from a nosebag. Well, I grabbed the whole sack, and ran home, so we would have something to eat.

> We came home to a total repression. We had to eat at Auxilio Social, as my father was jailed for years.
>
> When we were repatriated from Belgium, we found life very black. As in most homes, my father was in jail, and seven minor children were at home. There was no way we could earn money, but that was really unimportant, since there wasn't anything to buy, after the great conqueror, El Caudillo of Spain, Franco, declared Euzkadi to be in a state of exception. No bread, much less *tortas*. I don't know how we survived, or brought something to eat to my father in Larriñaga prison. I believe we lived in a state of amnesia because I can't remember anything except from time to time we ate, sometimes *algorrobas* we got from animal nosebags and turnips foraged from the fields. The bread ration of fifty grams looked more like mule dung passed through an oven than bread.

Even those in the rural areas suffered:

> Everything we grew was requisitioned to be sent away. What we produced—corn, beans, milk—they took, even our livestock. We had to hide something for ourselves.
>
> Those were the years we from the *caserios* carried our sausages, our beans, our *talos* [coarse corn meal] to the market wrapped around ourselves. People were desperate; they would rob to eat.

Medical care was only available to those who could pay. As a result, a number of those interviewed spoke of the deaths of their siblings and other relatives from diseases exacerbated by poor nutrition and inadequate medical care.

There was no money for clothes or blankets. When homes were requisitioned, they were totally stripped. What saved some of the children was a good supply of clothes from their adoptive parents, sent with them upon repatriation.

> My family in Belgium gave me enough clothes for two years in Euzkadi. It was a godsend to my mother, who made over my clothes for my younger sisters.

Some of the clothing was not suitable:

> When I came home, my whole family had one room, and

> the only furniture was a table and bed. They had taken our house, as my father was associated with the PNV. When my mother opened my suitcase, she found white gloves and fancy clothes; nothing warm or useful. At my school, they couldn't believe I was a charity case, because my clothes were so elegant.

The political persecution was intense. A relentless purge of every Basque connected with the autonomous government began. This was soon given a legal trapping in the Decree of Responsibility promulgated by Franco in 1938. This decree made it a crime against Spain for anyone over the age of fourteen to have helped undermine public order since October 1, 1934; to have impeded the Insurgent cause, even by being grievously passive anytime after the coup in 1936; or to have belonged to any Leftist political party, any regional nationalist organization, liberal party, or Masonic lodge. Trials were conducted by tribunals composed of the Falange and the army: there were no appeals and no due process, and torture was relied upon to extract confession.[83] Penalties ranged from execution, which ended the lives of as many as one thousand Basques in Bilbao by October of 1937, to exile in Africa, imprisonment, requisition of all property, or a form of "house arrest," involving a kind of probationary status requiring weekly checks by the police. One of these penalties was the fate of most of the repatriated children's parents, or one they themselves suffered:

> In one tragic night, in Dueso, Santoña [Santander], my father was executed, with twenty others. No one knows where they are buried. Someone told us they were put in a common grave there; not even in the earth of Euzkadi.

> As soon as the Insurgent troops entered, the denunciation began; the mayor and the city architect were shot at once. My father fled to France—he was a councilman—so they imprisoned my mother.

> The new regime requisitioned our farm, the stock, everything. My husband was jailed. My baby was a few weeks old, so I went to my aunt in Bilbao, to be nearer the jail, and to have a roof over our heads.

> I came back to my birthplace in Guipúzcoa, where my father had been the mayor. His carpentry shop had been requisitioned; a Franquista was in charge. All the employees were likewise. I knew them. The boss said he was sorry, but there was no work for me. I was now 17, and had to report each Sunday to the commissariat. I lived and supported my mother by odd jobs.

> The head of the Civil Guard here was God; a little Napoleon. A girlfriend denounced me; we had a pageant in school and I wouldn't carry the Spanish flag. At 16, I spent six months in jail with thieves and prostitutes. My family had been bourgeois, but I learned all people are really alike, in or out of prison.

Another problem faced by the children was that their *carnets* or identity papers noted that they had been repatriated from abroad, thus signaling prospective employers that they could be considered as having had parents of questionable loyalty to the cause of Franco during the Civil War. Thus, the punishment of the parents was inherited by their children.

In addition to such overt penalties, a more internal, and perhaps more profound, punishment began for the children. Anything connected with their parents' role in the Civil War had to be hidden, suppressed. Self-censorship emerged in the destruction of letters, photos, and other memorabilia. Anything relating to their lives as refugees also had to be forgotten. Any ties to adoptive parents abroad, to friends there, teachers, or priests in exile had to be discouraged. The children were made conscious of the need to guard against the *denuncios* (denunciations) from neighbors which could put the family in great jeopardy. A Basque mother, now eighty-two, reported:

> Before they came to our house, I tore up and then burned all the letters from my children in England, and anything that they might question.

A Basque priest, now eighty-six, and returned to Euzkadi from years of exile in Argentina:

> I kept a list of the Basque girls I taught in England, and I

> wrote an article about our colony while I was in Argentina. But I didn't try to bring anything like that back here.

Parents who had sent their children to the Soviet Union had to send and receive letters by circuitous routes to avoid suspicion.

There were economic reprisals as well. Heads of families who had held municipal posts in the autonomous government were blacklisted. Anyone who had served in the Basque army fell under the Decree of Responsibility and was suspect. Management of much of Bilbao's steel and other heavy industry had been put in German hands; only those who could prove their loyalty to Franco were employed. With many men dead, in prison, or with *carnets* that showed their lack of loyalty to Franco, mothers or, in some cases the children, had to keep the family together. A number of the repatriated children commented on this precarious way of life:

> With my father gone, my mother tried to operate a *merceria* [small sewing and notions business]. But no one had any money. So we traded thread for beans or anything to eat.

> My father was executed; my mother nearly blind from malnutrition and lack of medical treatment. Thus, at thirteen, I passed from the life of student to the life of work. First, I mopped the floors for a woman of the easy life, the "lady" of an officer in Franco's army. She paid me in sugar, oil, or beans. Then I sold sandwiches in Bilbao's bars, for one peseta a day. Next, seven years in a factory. Finally, in 1949, I got a job with the telephone company. But I couldn't get a police clearance as a Franco lover, since I had been a refugee in France. Through a cousin with "pull," the best I could get was classification as an "Indifferent," as I was only twelve in the war. But I could never be an official operator, as my "political background" wasn't good.

At every level of employment, the government kept a vigilant eye on its employees:

> One day, where I worked, someone wrote *Viva Rusia* in

> the washroom. A great inquisition ensued; each of us had to go singly to the boss and write *Viva España*, and he checked our penmanship. Many of us could barely write; our education stopped in 1936.

Another form of discrimination was in education. Many of the state schools were converted into jails to house the hundreds of political prisoners. The Catholic schools were costly, and scholarships went only to those with demonstrated loyalty to the regime. For most of those repatriated, their education stopped upon crossing the border. Of the seventy-seven children interviewed who had been sent to France, England, and Belgium, thirty-two had only primary schooling with no more education upon returning; thirty-five had some secondary work, in many cases in the host country; only ten had completed the secondary curriculum and gone on to the university.

The Basque language was proscribed by Franco early in 1938, being prohibited in education and public speech.[84] Nothing could be published in the mother tongue. An edict prohibiting the use of Basque first names for children was also promulgated. This even extended to the gravestones of those already buried who were memorialized by their Basque name. The inscriptions were taken off and replaced with a Castilian name. Street signs insisted that everyone "Speak the language of the Empire."

The political indoctrination required in the new Spain was anathema to Basque parents. Children were expected to enroll in the Falange youth organizations, such as the Flechas, Pelayos, and Balillas. These were para-military Fascist clubs, in which members marched with mock rifles, learned the Fascist salute, and had as heroes both Mussolini and Hitler. Their catechism was a ten-point morality program, stressing obedience to their leader, a fight to the death for Spain, and a firm allegiance to the Catholic church. A number of juvenile publications presented a rosy picture of the new Spain when the Reds were beaten. One, *Chicos*, was published in San Sebastián; others, such as *Flechas* and *Maravillas*, and a comic called *Adventures of a Nationalist Soldier*, were published outside Euzkadi. Some of the juvenile political material was at first prepared by academicians; later, more aggressive language was used in portraying heroic children fighting for God and country. Exemplary battles against Red-Separatists, Masons, Jews, and Marxists on the part of children were described. The female counterparts of the Flechas were counseled to help their brothers in the struggle and, later, to be good wives and docile Catholics.[85] An extensive system of summer camps was established in Euzkadi with obligatory attendance during school vacations. In such an environment, self-imposed constraints replaced those mandated officially. Forty years later, the writer encountered numerous examples:

> Three Basques, after being interviewed, cautiously showed me copies of Steer's account of the Northern Campaign, *The Tree of Gernika*, forbidden in Euzkadi during Franco's reign. The books had been purchased in France; two had been kept in their owners' respective desks at foreign consulates, a presumably safe place.

> A family member, whom I was unable to draw into a political conversation, told me, "Dorothy, for forty years we could only talk of weather or the crops; now we are unable to talk of anything else."

Some rebelled:

> On the feast of San Juan in Bermeo, I hung the *ikurriña* from the church spire. That was in 1959, twenty years after my return from France. Too early! They found out, and I spent months in jail. They beat me so that I still limp.

The Reunions

Perhaps the most significant indicator of the importance of the evacuation from Euzkadi in the lives of the Basque refugee children is the phenomenon of their spontaneous reunions. In the words of one faithful participant:

> All of the companions of La Citadelle maintain a constant friendship. We go yearly to celebrate a meal of authentic

> brotherhood, to recall, with deep emotion, that important part of our lives.

A complete weekend reunion is enjoyed periodically by the small colony of children of Basque militiamen who spent nearly three years in Jatxu, France. The directress of the colony, andereño Maritxu Barriola, has kept a very close friendship with the children she taught more than forty years ago. Their reunions are a source of great joy to her.

The reunions of the children of Jatxu are, in reality, a weekend pilgrimage of men and women, many now greying and grandparents, to the scenes of their childhood. At the most recent reunion, all thirty of the children were able to attend, except one who is living in Washington, D.C. and one in Venezuela. They came from all parts of Euzkadi, from Madrid, even from Paris, to visit the graves of their patron, and of others involved in Lurdes, the pilot colony at Jatxu. They assisted at special masses, were welcomed warmly this time by the town mayor, and were guests at ceremonial dinners. It was an occasion full of tears and gladness, ably arranged by their still-active directress from forty years before, Srta. Barriola.

The Basque refugee children who lived and worked at La Citadelle have been holding reunions for at least a decade. The date is fixed, the feast of San Juan, to commemorate their austere arrival at St.-Jean-Pied-de-Port decades earlier. The site shifts from France to towns in Euzkadi in alternate years, so that all who wish to attend can be accommodated. Wives and husbands are invited, and always over one hundred of the colony members are present. Cooks and teachers, now in their seventies and eighties, relive the experience with the Basques who were their charges. Stories, jokes, songs, and an elaborate dinner follow a solemn mass. The Basque priests who went with the children into exile are dead now, but they are commemorated in the recollections of those whose lives they enriched as mentors.

One tangible result of the reception of the refugee children on French soil is their dedication of plaques and crosses and their planting of oak trees to symbolize the significance of their exile across the Pyrenees. The oak trees are flourishing; and the French citizens are perhaps aware of the meaning of the Basque words on the plaques and crosses placed at several colony sites in the French-Basque provinces.

A very similar set of reunions has evolved in England for the refugee children who were not repatriated.

In Euzkadi itself, the reunions started very informally among those who had come from the same barrio, as they began to arrange to meet at a local restaurant. These informal gatherings still take place in at least three of the Bilbao neighborhoods, usually in the PNV *batsokis* in Matico, Sondica, and Deusto. Since many of the refugee children have resumed correspondence with their British hosts and friends, more and more reunions now include Britishers.

One typical colony, that of Weston Manor, has a tea yearly to fete the young orphan woman who was cook's helper in 1937. Mrs. Laura Markham plans her yearly vacation to attend this party. A dozen of the "girls from Weston Manor" gather to reminisce with her, and sing the songs they learned there: "Goodbye, my sister, Hello, Weston Manor for everyone," in Basque and English. Today, grandmotherly women from this colony also make an annual pilgrimage to Oñate. There, they lunch with their old priest, Don Benito, who returned from self-exile in Argentina at the time of the amnesty of Franco. He remembers every girl by name, and tries to keep up with the names of their children and grandchildren. He attends mass with them to commemorate the occasion, and joins them in reminiscence. Another contingent of children who were cared for in Carleon by a Basque couple who had settled there in the twenties meets monthly in Bilbao. Several from this small colony went to England to participate in the golden wedding anniversary of the couple's marriage.

In Bilbao, the first large-scale reunion, complete with a chartered plane from London to carry some 200 *niños*, was planned to take place during the writer's year of research. A mammoth banquet was arranged to be presided over by the mayor of Bilbao, himself one of the evacuated children. Charter and other difficulties prevented the grand reunion.

However, over one hundred Basques met in a London restaurant that May, as they have for a number of years, to celebrate their arrival in Britain. The Spanish restaurant serves a complete Basque meal, memories and news are exchanged, photos pass from hand to hand, wine flows freely.

These gatherings, begun about 1967, were held only every five years at first. They are now held annually, with a special committee of volunteers taking the responsibility for arrangements. The event clearly assumes more and more importance to the Basques as they reach middle age and beyond. From attendance at a recent gathering, it is apparent that the Basques have largely married within their group, as Spanish is the language of conversation. The spouses who are British seem to enjoy the event quietly; the Basques, on the contrary, are boisterous and full of joy. Their organization has, in fact, recently become quite formalized and another attempt will be made to hold a reunion in Bilbao with the compatriots who were repatriated. One of the group in England writes:

> Each May, some 160 of the Basque refugee children, now parents themselves, meet in a London restaurant to remember the events of 1937 and to renew past ties and memories. With them are about ninety wives, husbands, and children of the original "children." They sing Basque songs, dance Basque dances. There are also a few restrained tears and deeply felt emotions for some remembered only in spirit. More than forty years away from the land they left as children has not quenched the flame of their proud Basque heritage, a heritage they have upheld with modesty and dignity, often against prejudice and difficulty.[86]

The Basque children in England who were repatriated have also returned to place plaques at the site of some of the colonies, and have planted the traditional oak tree to symbolize the Tree of Guernica on British soil. The plaques usually list the names of the children in the colony, the names of their teachers and priests and, frequently, a rendering of the Virgin of Begoña.

The scattered remnants of the Basque refugee children

who stayed on in Belgium meet informally to exchange memories and news of themselves and relatives in Euzkadi. Those children who were repatriated from Belgium, more than those who stayed in any other country, have maintained closest ties with their adoptive families and staff. The writer saw innumerable photos of adoptive families and of teachers and priests in the Catholic colonies. Visits to and from Belgium are common; attendance at family weddings and baptisms is also the rule. The children from St. Norbert House also have returned in a body to dedicate a plaque in Brussels to commemorate their years there.

In the Soviet Union, the Spanish Club in Moscow still serves as a focus for the Basque children who left their homeland over forty years earlier. Its counterpart exists in Bilbao. the Club Adamis. Here, every Friday night, the Sovieticos gather to converse in Russian, to drink tea, and to reminisce. Occasionally, they are joined by Russian sailors who have put in at Bilbao's extensive port facility. The club is totally nonpolitical, according to its members, and serves only as a cultural link to their two decades in Russia.

In Mexico, an annual homage to Don Lázaro Cárdenas occurs each June in Morelia, Michoacán, at the present site of the Escuela España-México. The ceremony takes place in the town square, where a statue of Don Lázaro has been erected, and includes music, speeches, and the presentation of a wreath. In attendance are many of the Niños de Morelia, as well as their aging teachers and auxiliary staff. After the ceremony, a typical Mexican dinner is served at the school, now an institution for Mexican orphans. One of the moving sights viewed by the writer while attending the forty-third such reunion was the singing by the Spanish Republican "children" of the Spanish songs of their youth in Spain, before their evacuation. These persons, now in their fifties, relived, in a few emotional hours, the years of their lives spent in the school. One of them, now living in Mexico City, tried to teach some of the present students some of these songs and Catalan dance steps. Photos of each child and their records were brought out from the school archives for the benefit of the children and spouses who also came to celebrate the anniversary of arrival in Mexico. The program for this yearly event, organized by the volunteer secretary of the Niños de Morelia, Emeterio Paya-Valera, contains several quotes from the children on the important day, forty-three years earlier, when the *Méxique* landed at Veracruz: "Mexico is a great country. President Cárdenas is our best friend: Viva Mexico."

In all, over two hundred "children" attended, with 150 others (spouses, staff of the school, and local politicians). Those who had been the refugees from Spain showed most emotion at the symbolic raising of the original flag they brought from the Republic of Spain, which is carefully preserved in the office of the school.

According to Sr. Paya-Valera:

> Normally most of the former students return happily to Morelia, cry emotionally on seeing their friends and then visit the little corners and places frequented during their childhood. They enjoy the typical dishes here once again. Circumstances foreign to us stripped us of our parents and country. Here in Morelia, we found certain substitutes for what we had lost.
>
> Some, however, react traumatically, crying in silence, or weeping abundantly, shipwrecked by memories not always pleasant.

Curiously, none of the Basque children have participated in the annual or larger quinquennial ceremonies held in Morelia. In all, thirty of the 120 Basques interviewed participated in formal or informal reunions: nine from France; eleven from England, and ten from the Soviet Union.

In Washington, D.C., a very small reunion now takes place, with a handful of Basques who were sent to colonies in France for varying periods before their final emigration to the United States. This reunion takes place on *Aberri Eguna,* the annual "Day of our Nation" (PNV), in the home of one of the members.

Common to all the reunions is the sharing of recollections, both happy and sad. Certainly, these social events serve as an opportunity for catharsis, and a rethinking of remembered traumas from the perspective of a mature adult. In the reunions attended by the writer, there seems to have been a concentration on the pleasant aspects of life in exile, and a "working through" of unpleasant events from memories of the years away from home and family. As a result, "tragedies" or hardships are now seen as having made the bearer mature or independent. The reunions also serve to emphasize to the participants the importance of their exile that was so quickly forgotten by the world.

CHAPTER NINE

The Summing Up

There are lessons to be learned from this "modest evacuation" of nearly twenty thousand Basque children far from their parents and homeland. Seeking sanctuary from the terrors of modern warfare, they were the first contingent of such magnitude in modern history.[1] Some instructive generalizations can be drawn from their experiences in the various host countries in the settings they found, ranging from living with adoptive families to life in huge collective institutions. We know that in what has been called "The Century of the Refugee" the destiny of this young cohort has been shared by many others in the ensuing four decades.[2] We recall the Polish, Jewish, Dutch, French, Belgian, Greek, and other refugee children of World War II. Later, Palestinian, Hungarian, Tibetan, Indian, and African youngsters fled their native lands; then, Cuban children, the Vietnamese "orphans," and the "boat people" of Southeast Asia. The trauma and exile suffered worldwide by displaced children, now numbering in the millions, is foreshadowed in the Guernica generation.[3] Their history, in retrospect, is perhaps our best opportunity to understand a growing social issue—that of populations who cannot return home after conflicts are resolved.

For clearly, ever since the Spanish Civil War, and increasingly thereafter, a new element has intervened in international disputes: that of opposing world ideological systems, with closed borders. Such sealed frontiers as the "Iron Curtain" or the "Bamboo Curtain" quite effectively partition the world, excluding those who do not embrace each system's particular political view. Refugee children, with or without their families, can no longer be repatriated. They are exiled for life.

In the case of the Basque children, following the defeat of the Spanish Republic, a majority were repatriated to Euzkadi. Substantial numbers, however, were reunited with their parents, now themselves refugees from fascism, and subsequently emigrated to the Americas or remained in the host country. Those sent into the Soviet Union or to Mexico stayed on there, as neither nation recognized the new government established by Franco in Spain.[4] These groups, then, are the earliest manifestation of the contemporary issue just described. They are the most pristine, as well as longest standing, example of refugee children who by reason of their political beliefs cannot return to their birthplace. Today, the Guernica generation is in midlife. What we can learn from their experiences can help to mitigate the twin problems of separation trauma and the assimilation of refugee children throughout the world.

It is curious that although there is a substantial body of research literature on adult refugees and migrants, surprisingly little is to be found on the effects of forced migration on children. J. Donald Cohon, in his study of Indo-Chinese refugee children,[5] and Adamandia Mando Dalianis, in her retrospective study of Greek children of the 1946–50 Civil War in Greece,[6] comment on the extremely few publications on child and adolescent survivors, the lack of longitudinal follow-up studies, and the difficulty of generalizing about children from clinical data on adult refugees. The major work available until the past decade concerns children evacuated within their own country, and deals only with separation trauma. This research, by John Bowlby, Susan Isaacs, and others who studied the evacuation of children from London in the winter of 1940–41, has developed from a theoretical framework to an almost classic picture of the effects of the separation from parents on the lives of young children. After surveying the children sent from the city to the countryside to escape the "Blitz" bombing by Axis planes, Bowlby summarized the extensive interviews by postulating a traumatic process in four stages. He saw the child as moving through, first, a "protest" stage, in which he cries, becomes disruptive and aggressive; next, Bowlby found a "despair" period, in which the child conforms outwardly and passively accepts his lot; and thirdly, a "detachment" phase, in which the child withdraws, and may seemingly accept a surrogate mother. Very frequently, when the child is reunited with his real mother, a fourth phase, that of "angry rejection," will occur, with the child unable to re-attach to her, at least temporarily.[7]

During this same period, Anna Freud administered several wartime nurseries opened for the children evacuated from London. Echoing her father Sigmund Freud's principle of the pivotal role played in a child's emotional development by his relationship to his mother, Miss Freud found clinical verification in the behavior of the young children enrolled in her nurseries. She writes:

> The war acquires comparatively little significance for children so long as it only threatens their lives, disturbs their material comfort, or cuts their food rations. It becomes enormously significant the moment it breaks up family life and uproots the first emotional atachments of the child within the family group.[8]

In reviewing the wartime nurseries, she concluded that the experience of evacuation to the nurseries was as upsetting to the children as was the bombing itself. She noted:

> Although the young reared in group settings may be accelerated in skill development and early social responses, the milieu limits both the child's emotional life and personality development.[9]

In the wartime nurseries, Miss Freud found that other children were seen as a menace to whatever relationship a child had formed with a staff person. Jealous clinging and possessiveness toward the surrogate mother was the rule. Autoerotic habits such as masturbation increased, as did rhythmic behavior—solitary head knocking and rocking. She found more exhibitionism, as well, which she explained as the child's wish to be loved and admired. In the slightly older children—above five years—there were constant attempts to create artificial families. They consoled the youngest ones with love play, tenderness, and affection. Durable early friendships developed, rare among such young children, who normally tend to attach themselves to adults or older children.[10] Freud also found what she termed "marked curiosity about sex and family matters," which she saw as abnormal and due to their deprivation from the "normal intimacies of family life."[11] She concluded:

> For young children, even a mediocre family is better than the best communal nursery. So much staff is required for adequate mother substitutes that it would be better for each staff member simply to take two or so children home to rear them.[12]

The British Ministry of Health drew the same conclusion regarding the evacuation plan it supervised during World War II. The youngsters evacuated, aged seven to sixteen, after transport from their London homes to rural billets in private homes or colonies, seemed to regress in their behavior. For example, bed-wetting became common, as were such nervous symptoms as the inability to concentrate at school and simple homesickness. About a quarter showed these minor symptoms immediately, and from 1942 to 1946, fully a third of all children referred to Child Guidance clinics in London were those who had been evacuated during 1940–41.[13] Isaacs, in 1941, detailed the results in one community, Cambridge, when 656 London children were evacuated there. She noted that one out of ten showed an unhappy adjustment, a figure which was reduced to one in twenty when siblings were reunited and housed together. She also found a sharp increase in maladjustment in the adolescents evacuated, rising from 13 percent at age thirteen to 24 percent for those fourteen to fifteen. Isaacs also found that differences in intelligence among children had no effect, nor did a mismatch between the socioeconomic level of the child and that of the billeting family, rather common in Cambridge.[14] She recommended that family and school groups be kept together in any future evacuation, that there be a transition center for initial adjustment, with provision for difficult children, and that basic information follow the child whenever there would be a change in residence.[15] Freud similarly suggested that school classes be sent *in toto* with a known teacher. She proposed that children under five could attend a nursery during the day to become accustomed to the setting and the staff, and when events made it necessary, be evacuated together with any mothers who so wished, going as paid staff. (She expected few would.)[16]

It is worthy of note that each of these recommendations was anticipated in the evacuation of Basque children to the schools in France supported by the Basque government, several years prior to the findings of Isaacs and Freud.

After World War II, the Nazi concentration camps emptied throughout northern Europe. Thousands of parents of a dozen nationalities began the search for their lost children. International relief agencies and child welfare associations labored to reunite families and assist them to begin their lives anew. These immense population movements have kindled an interest in the effects of such involuntary international migrations on the individual and how these may relate to subsequent assimilation of the refugee to the new host culture.

From studies of adult refugees after 1945, it seems clear that forced migration, by itself, is so stressful that both regression and mental illness can develop in formerly intact adults.[17] Further, when persecution or danger to life precedes the flight, the probability of psychiatric aftermaths increases.[18] Mental illness is also more frequent in situations where a long period ensues between the flight and a definite resettlement, and when this period is marked by rumors and uncertainty. Basque parents in France just before, during, and after World War II would seem to exemplify these conditions. How would such stresses—forced migration and assimilation—affect their children?

A. A. Weinberg, who has done extensive research on the voluntary and quasi-voluntary migration of Jews to Israel, found a not surprising "remarkable similarity between the needs of newborn human beings and new adult immigrants: need for belonging, to be loved, understood, and supported."[19] If this is correct, the reactions of children to an experience which can infantilize adults must be profound, perhaps sufficiently traumatic to leave lasting psychological damage.

Yet, the anecdotal material gathered by Anna Freud and Sophie Dann at Windermere, England, from six Jewish children found together at the Terezin concentration camp seems to refute this presumption. The children, all of whose parents had been killed in the camp, were initially wild and restless, destroying all play materials brought to them. Each identified completely with the other five and was very aggressive toward adults. Compulsive behavior marked each of them—one scratched herself until she bled, then smeared herself with the blood; four were noisy, continuous thumbsuckers; all masturbated; and every one had an excessive craving for sugar and sweets. Constant nurturing and psychotherapy were provided for each throughout their later childhood and adolescence. All today lead essentially normal lives.[20]

What is surprising then about the sparse recent work on child survivors are the findings of resilience, coping, and apparent normalcy they exhibit. For example, Sarah Moskovitz has studied twenty-four Jewish toddlers found in the death camps or in hiding after World War II. All were also reared at Windermere. Since she found these survivors to be leading quite normal lives, she concludes that more attention should be directed at factors which ameliorate the trauma of separation and forced migration. Only one of the twenty-four had a history of mental illness.[21]

In a recent book, *War Through Children's Eyes*, some 120 essays written by Polish children deported with their families into the Soviet Union between 1939 and 1941 are collected and annotated. The preface notes:

> War, deportation, the death of loved ones, starvation, and hard labor were the life story of all the children whose compositions we read. And yet only a few of them showed in their writings signs of severe psychological and emotional disturbance. Perhaps those with less resistance did not survive; those who did had three powerful allies: family, religion, and patriotism.[22]

In a review of the literature on adult refugees and migrants, in order to identify factors which allay trauma and ease the stress of forced migration, several such elements emerge. H. B. M. Murphy, writing on the adaptation of immigrants to Canada, listed the presence in the host country of an existing "colony" or social group similar to that left by the immigrants, and the relative absence of pressure to assimilate to the culture and language of the receiving country.[23] A. A. Weinberg notes the importance of the initial experiences in the new country to subsequent adaptation,[24] and Maria Pfister-Ammende finds that adaptation does not truly begin until the refugee is convinced that there is no possibility of return to his homeland.[25]

From the foregoing, and a review of the available literature on refugee children, certain principles have emerged regarding these children of crisis. There appear to be a set of structural features which affect the extent of trauma the child will experience. These include the age at evacuation, since younger children seem to suffer the most adverse effects; the length of time the child is away from home, with the longer the absence, the greater the trauma; whether or not siblings accompany the child, and subsequently, whether they are kept together in the host country; how closely the scale of living arrangements there approach the normal family environment; and whether the people in the receiving country accept (or reject) the youngsters.

Another set of factors, which can be termed "situational," were gleaned from the literature on ethnic identity and its maintenance. These factors seem particularly appropriate in the case of the Basques, a very cohesive group through centuries of migration, and one which has managed to preserve ethnic values, customs, language, and folklore in enclaves throughout the world. These variables consist of the ethnic composition of the groups evacuated, e.g. whether they were primarily Basque; whether Basque mentors were present; whether Basque culture and language and the Catholic religion were encouraged; and whether there was a support system (clubs, sports, or governmental entities) present in the host country. It was expected that, with the children from Euzkadi, the structural factors would tend to correlate with a minimization of any trauma of separation, while the situational factors would tend to assist in ethnic identity maintenance. The presence of both sets of factors in the lives of the Basque refugee children would thus tend to promote overall successful life experience.

The summary of the interviews completed is presented in the accompanying table.

In looking at the interview material gathered from respondents in each country, some possible conclusions suggest themselves. First of all, a stay of from three to six months had no effect on the adult lives of the children. Those in each country who had been repatriated in a few months felt the experience was no more than a strange holiday, a novelty without aftereffects. A second generalization, borne out in every contingent of children, was that brothers and sisters should never be separated. Great effort was made to keep siblings from families together in the Leftist colonies in England, France, and the Basque government colonies in France. Thus, separation tended to occur most often in those children sent to live in Catholic institutions or to adoptive families. The effect of such a separation was usually devastating to the children of all ages. The youngest children lost their substitute parents, and the older siblings felt the guilt of disobedience to their parents' instructions added to the pain of dispersion of their own generation of the family. It also appears that the separation of siblings in the Soviet Union due to the system of age-grading was ameliorated in large part by two factors—the collective nature of the education, and the periodic reunions at the summer camps. The youngest children were able to find substitute nurturance in the

Children's Houses, while the older ones found that peer relationships took the place of family ties.

A third overall finding was that the children, as mature adults, still felt very sensitive about the changes in their lives brought about by the various shifts in the governments of their respective host countries. Especially pronounced in France in 1937 (when the Leftist Blum government was succeeded by a Rightist one) was their feeling of powerlessness as French policy changed towards them. Some children were sent at once to Belgium; others to Catalonia; and the pressure for their repatriation increased. Again, for those not repatriated until 1940, life under the German occupation and the Vichy regime was a series of ever-narrowing options. Those who attempted to emigrate with their families, but were halted by the barriers placed by the French or by the highly politicized Spanish Republican emigration bureaus, still feel a bitterness at the machinations of those in control. The changes in the British government had less effect than did those in France. However, Chamberlain's appeasement policies and the rise of fascism in Britain until World War II began made their presence a continual embarrassment to those who took reponsibility for their care. In Belgium, the vicissitudes of governmental policies had relatively little consequence. Their family allowances continued, and their presence never became a political issue. In Belgium, too, the repatriation process was apolitical, in marked contrast to the experience of those in England.

For those sent to the Soviet Union, the purges of Stalin had relatively little effect, while the rupture of the Hitler-Stalin Pact and subsequent German invasion completely disrupted their hitherto happy experience.

The refugee children in Mexico found that the arbitrary removal by Cárdenas of the Spanish teachers who had been evacuated with them destroyed a valuable link with their mother country. On the other hand, the end of Cárdenas's term in office removed their stalwart patron, and made their lives more problematic. In all these events, the children were impotent to intervene. Some writers trace the destruction of

Interview Summary

	FRANCE	ENGLAND	BELGIUM	USSR	MEXICO
Total Number of Unaccompanied Children	9,000	3,889	3,200	2,500	456 (few were Basque)
Sample Interviewed	30	26	21	21	11
Structural Factors					
Length of Stay	2+ years	2 years (some six months)	2+ years	20–45 years	45 years
Age at Evacuation	6–15 (4 under 11)	6–16 (6 under 11)	5–13 (14 under 11)	3–14 (11 under 11)	6–12 (6 under 11)
Siblings Kept Together	Usually not	Yes, about half were	Usually not	Usually not	Yes

Small-Scale Living Arrangements	Usually (full range) majority in adoptive homes	Usually (full range) most in small colonies	Yes, majority in adoptive homes	No, large institutions	No, large institutions
Community Acceptance	No	Yes	Yes	Yes	No
Situational Factors					
Majority of Group Basque	Yes	Yes	Yes	Yes	No
Basque Mentors Present	Yes	Yes	For about half the children	No	No
Basque Culture, Language, Religion Encouraged	Yes	In Catholic colonies, Yes	For about half the children	No	No
Basque Support System in Host Country	Yes	No	No	No	Yes

property commonly seen in later refugee children living in concentration camps to this feeling of powerlessness transformed into rage:

> We break chairs in camp because we did not have a chance of breaking Nazi heads.[26]

Perhaps the "riots" reported at the Salvation Army home at Clapton, the damage to the baths in the Crimea, and the destructive behavior at the Escuela España-México can also be attributed to such helplessness and the ensuing rage felt by the Basque children in exile.

A fourth consideration is the profound importance of the initial reception given to the refugee children in each host country. The cold, frightening lack of welcome the majority who were interviewed remembered when they landed in France colored their years of exile there. In contrast, those evacuated to England still recall with pleasure the elaborate bunting, posters, decorations, and music greeting their arrival. Though as adults they realize that these were leftovers from the coronation ceremonies of George VI, they are nonetheless grateful for such a welcome. In Belgium, as in the Soviet Union, the banquets, cakes, flowers, and candies showered upon them had a lasting effect on their memories from this period of their lives. Those sent to Mexico, however, indicate that the initial welcome became overlaid with the subsequent bitterness the experiences in the Escuela España-México engendered.

From a closer look at the interviews and other material, other instructive conclusions emerge. Some of these run counter to intuitive wisdom and the findings of those writing about the experiences of other refugee children. We will consider them in a rough chronological order, corresponding to the unfolding lives of the Basque refugee children from 1937 to the recent present.

Age at Separation

Among the first variables considered of great importance in assessing the trauma of the separation of a child from parents are those of the child's age at separation, and the provision of acceptable mother-substitutes until the child can be reunited with his parents. Whatever the circumstances of the separation, it can be devastating to the child who experiences it at any age. The conventional wisdom regarding the importance of age at separation which indicates, according to both Freud and Bowlby, that it is most damaging to children under three, next most traumatic to those from three to eight, and of minor effect in those over eight years of age,* may be reexamined in light of the Basque data.[27] Clearly, the hardest children to deal with were the teen-aged boys and, in some cases, girls. In each country, special colonies had to be devised for these youthful troublemakers, who filched fruit, vandalized neighboring villages, poached on the host country's adolescent girls whenever they could and, in the case of the Sovieticos, formed roving bands to pillage the countryside during World War II. Running away and vandalism of the institutions that housed them were also frequent in every country except Belgium. Conversely, the two countries which had the largest number of very young children, Belgium and the Soviet Union, had little trouble with them. Those evacuated at age three or four who were subsequently interviewed reported an absence of traumatic memories. In Belgium this seems to have been due to the child's ability to form an attachment with the adoptive mother; in Russia, the nurturing received from the nurses in the Children's Houses seemed to compensate.

What is pervasive in the recollections of those evacuated is the unconscious attempts to reconstitute the family unit. Older siblings, cousins, or young uncles took on the role of parents. Many of the older children recall that the youngest in the colony quickly became the "baby" to them. Staff was also used to fill the parental role. This, in fact, occurred repeatedly in the lives of certain children who were moved from colony to colony in France, England, and Belgium.

* Isaacs found increased maladjustment in children aged thirteen and over.

Scale of Setting

It is again the conventional wisdom that the smaller the scale of a setting for children and, by inference, the more the institution mirrors the family constellation, the better will be the emotional growth and satisfaction felt by those who live there. Thus, the model colonies in both France and England, Jatxu and Cambridge, had a maximum of thirty children, and a staff ratio of about one adult to six children.

However, large institutions, with from one hundred to over five hundred children were also found in these countries, and were the rule in both the Soviet Union and Mexico. It should be noted, first, that much of the extensive literature which has painted the most dismal picture of the trauma of institutionalized life for young children is drawn from material from orphanages, where staffing is minimal and most regulations are simply for the convenience of the administration. For this reason, the child development literature abounds with examples of infants and young children who suffer from various syndromes of "institutionalism," such as "failure to thrive," marasmus, depressed affect, low intelligence scores, and an inability to form any attachment in childhood or adulthood. To sum up this work, Bowlby states:

> It may be said that group residential care is always to be avoided for those under about six years, that it is suitable for short-stay children (under 6 months) between 6 and 12, and for both short-stay and some long-stay children who are adolescents.[28]

In general, however, and with the probable exceptions of the Escuela España-México and Clapton in England, the larger institutions (particularly La Citadelle in France, the Orphanage Rationalist in Brussels, the Koningshof in Antwerp, and all the boarding schools in the Soviet Union) appear to have been sufficiently staffed with well-intentioned persons so that even the youngest children, those most prone to the deleterious effects of institutional life coupled with separation from the parents, did not suffer ill effects. This was, in fact, contrary to the writer's biases during the interviews, in particular with the Sovieticos, to hear nothing but praise and devotion expressed for the experience of collective living by the Basque children in Russia. This was invariably described as "rational, natural, a treatment like that of princes, with loving Russian teachers and nurses, and with our own teachers to retain our Spanish heritage."

In explanation, it is probable that it was the intense politicization of those sent into Russia, i.e. the knowledge, consistently reinforced, that they were to prepare themselves to return to a new Spain, which helped them to adjust to their life in exile.[29] And, as already noted, the staff, both Russian and Spanish seemed, on the whole, to be nurturing and able to compensate for the absence of parents. The children invariably formed very strong friendships with others in their class, friendships that have remained strong to this day. Perhaps the most bitter comments, which may also help to explain the lack of trauma felt by some sent to Russia, was that their treatment there was far superior to whatever they might have expected in their own homes. Many of the children came from poor, large families with little opportunity for a better life, and "slaps on the cheek instead of affection."

Of all those interviewed who had been in Russia, only one felt that the collective life did not provide sufficient warmth and nurturing. Both this woman and her sister entered a convent upon reunion with their parents in Mexico.

In viewing the retrospective experience of those Basque children who found shelter in adoptive homes with foster parents, as was common in both France and Belgium, it may be useful to consider some of the current literature on the issue of family versus institutional life. Reviews in Bowlby and Hicklin indicate that, whether as a placement arrangement in peacetime or as a refuge under wartime conditions, the best solution is for the child to live with a family rather than in a boarding institution. This is especially true for children of less than six years of age. However, both note that the careful matching of the child with the prospective family is important and a trial period arrangement valuable. They suggest that care should be taken to discover the motivation of those volunteering to be foster parents, and childless couples who expect the child to become their "possession'' should be weeded out. The foster parents should encourage all possible contact between the child and his or her parents and siblings. Even in adoptive homes, however, some war-damaged children find adjustment to be difficult. Frequent illness, sometimes psychosomatic in nature, the withdrawal of affection and trust, and running away, or even stealing from one's benefactors, may occur.* A set of favorable circumstances, gleaned from work on adoptive homes includes:

1) Presence of other children, and the child's siblings if possible, in the adoptive home.
2) The adoptive parent's children should be about four years older, or younger, than the refugee child of the same sex, though children of the opposite sex, but of the same age, work well.
3) Nervous, anxious children did best in quiet, conventional homes; active, aggressive children did best in free-and-easy homes with companions.
4) Children over thirteen generally do poorly in foster homes; other children are essential.
5) Children under ten do poorly with adoptive parents aged over about forty-five years.
6) Jealousy and rivalry often result when sex and age of the refugee child matches sex and age of the adoptive parent's child.[30]

The individual experiences of the Basque children who lived with adoptive parents corroborate these latter findings. Particularly poignant was the experience of children in Belgium who were taken in by childless couples who were later loathe to relinquish them for repatriation to their natural parents. In some cases, the Basque parents were unable to retrieve the child—invariably a young girl. During their stays, the conflict induced by the adoptive parents' insistence on

* These reactions were infrequently mentioned by the Basques who supervised such situations.

the child's using the terms "mother" and "father" has already been mentioned. The number of such cases reported by Basque staff and by those sent into Belgium as children makes this a pitfall to be considered.

On the other hand, the happiness experienced by Basque children with their foster brothers and sisters has been reflected in the constancy of visits to and from the adoptive families there. The writer saw a number of photo albums, full of pictures of foster brothers, sisters, and parents; many letters from the adoptive families; and remarks such as, "in some ways, I feel closer to [an adoptive sibling] than to my real ones, because of how good she [or he] was to me when I was alone." Of the fifteen who had lived in adoptive homes in Belgium, only four found it a negative experience overall, and in each case the adoptive family was childless. In the recollections of the other eleven, feelings were overwhelmingly positive. Fully two-thirds still continued the friendships begun there.

Community Acceptance

In turning to the effects on the children of their relationship to the people in the various host countries—beyond their adoptive families or caretaker—overall conclusions are more difficult to derive. They tend to be colored by the initial reception, the subsequent changes in government policy in the host country and the types of colonies or homes the refugee children were sent into. Naturally, those living in adoptive families in both France and Belgium were easily integrated into the life of the country. Conversely, those in colonies, refuges, or large boarding institutions usually maintained an enclave status, which limited interchange with the host citizenry to such occasions as the folklore presentions and religious celebrations. In both England and, to a lesser extent, Belgium and France, however, the "adoption" of children by families or clubs did lead to a welcome amount of socializing, delicious sweets, and friendships that were very valuable to the Basque children. In France, about a third of the Basques had such pleasant experiences; in England, all but six had fond memories of individual families who had welcomed them; in Belgium, all but three recall such opportunities. In the Soviet Union, the outbreak of World War II brought an end to the separation of the Basque and Spanish children from the Russian people. In Mexico, upon graduation from the Escuela España-México, the children tended to assimilate to Mexican life, and even within the school, there were several dozen Mexican children also studying and living with them. It is clear from the interview material that the opportunities given the children in colonies to visit periodically with adoptive families were of great help in alleviating the trauma of exile.

To many, the adults in the weekend adoptive families filled the important role of *padrino* and *madrina* (godparents) in the lives of the children and provided at least an approximation of the family life the Basque children so sorely missed during certain important years of their own childhoods. Other writers on the theme of refugee life have also noted the ambiguity often apparent in looking at the role of the host country in the overall success of an individual's forced emigration. We have seen that often a dichotomy exists between the official policies of a government and the actual daily practices of its citizens toward refugees. Thus, a retrospective appraisal of the refugee experience *vis-à-vis* the host country's government or its citizens may mask what those who experienced the actual events report. A now-classic study of World War II refugees, *Flight and Resettlement*, states:

> The presence of innate latent good will towards the refugee does not always mean successful resettlement, while the presence of a certain amount of hostility may not be a complete barrier to it. The resettlement of Spanish Republican refugees in Mexico aroused intense opposition from the church party there and was carried through by the president [Cárdenas] against the opposition of the legislature. Yet this very opposition encouraged the pro-refugee party in the country to special efforts, and resettlement is reported to have been unusually successful.[31]

As we have seen, for the Basques among the Niños de

Morelia this success, apparent only in an economic sense, was at the expense of the greatest trauma suffered in any host country. Only in Mexico was their Spanish heritage a distinct handicap, consigning them to the status of *gachupines* (Spanish immigrants, come to exploit Mexico).

In reviewing the set of "structural factors" described earlier in terms of their effects on the trauma suffered by the refugee children from Euzkadi, it appears that they tend to refute the accepted judgment regarding age at separation and scale of living arrangements, while corroborating the importance of keeping siblings together, or at least providing periodic opportunities for visits, and the salience of the community's acceptance, beginning with the initial welcome upon arrival in the host country.

In looking at the "situational factors," which were expected to affect the maintenance of culture and ethnic identity in exile, the experience of the Basque children is instructive.

Were the Majority Basque?

Only in Mexico were the Basque refugee children in a distinct minority. In both France and the Soviet Union, where many Spanish Republican refugees in addition to children of Euzkadi were housed, efforts were made to keep the expeditions of Basque children together in colonies or schools. The children from Euzkadi among the Niños de Morelia did tend to form a sub-group, but they were unable to maintain any semblance of Basque culture during their school years. Subsequently, particularly among those who married Basque women, or brought their parents to Mexico to join them, some evidence of their Basque heritage persists. It is, however, quite limited, and clearly independent of the Basque support system of Centros Vascos with their sports and cultural events in Mexico City.

Basque Mentors Present?

A critical generalization is that the role of "mentors" from the Basque country was of extreme importance to the children evacuated. Wherever Basque staff accompanied the children into exile, sharing with them the upheaval and culture shock in a strange country, the children gained strength to bear the trauma of separation from parents and country. The role of the nearly one hundred Basque priests who fled with the children to France, England, and Belgium was of inestimable value. Perhaps most important for the boys and adolescent men were these role models of courage, learning, fortitude, and dedication to Basque ideals. Anecdotes, a few of which have been included in the preceding text of this book, abound as to the solicitude these priests felt for the children. This interest extended well after repatriation in many instances, since lifelong correspondence with the priests was common. In some cases, it was the non-Basque priests from the host country who parented the children, particularly in Belgium. Here, the role of the Catholic hierarchy remained relatively immune to the efforts of Msgr. Antoniutti for repatriation. The other Basque staff members, including the cooks, have also been scrupulous in maintaining the relationships begun with the children during their exile. In the evacuation to Socialist countries, and especially in Mexico, where accompanying personnel were sent away and replaced by Mexican staff, the children had fewer familiar persons to attach themselves to. This became a foretaste of the incomplete assimilation to the host countries experienced by at least some of those evacuated.

In any evacuation of young children, then, it is crucial to send personnel from the country of origin. Those writing about the refugee children of World War II make this obvious point repeatedly. One source, for example, in a careful comparison of the mental health of refugees of various nationalities who found shelter in Switzerland, notes:

> In the Swiss camps, there was a lower than expected rate of neurosis and personality disorder among Jewish refugees. They alone had Orthodox doctors with them who had also gone through the hell of persecution and internment. The doctors and patients were linked by a strong bond, and the former was a "clanarzt" (member of the tribe) in every sense of the word.[32]

The pivotal role played by the Basque priests was noted by Basques sent to each of the non-Socialist countries. Twenty of the thirty children sent into France, fifteen of the twenty-eight in England, and six of the twenty-one in Belgium commented on the importance of these men in their lives. A number of others experienced somewhat similar assistance from the native-born priests and nuns in each of these countries in the Catholic boarding schools and rectories in which they lived.

Language in Exile

A natural corollary to the necessity of sending in people who are of the same ethnicity and culture as the children is obvious in the issue of language. Acknowledged as a prime culture-bearer, language can serve as both a bridge and a barrier to assimilation to the ways of the host culture. We have seen that in the Basque colony at Kingston Hill the reluctance of the children to learn English reinforced their solidarity, as did the presence of sufficient Basque personnel to provide language and culture models. On the other hand, those in Belgium and France who lived in adoptive homes, whether French- or Flemish-speaking, and attended the state schools, rapidly learned the one or two languages necessary to survive and tended to forget their native tongues. Several Basques, however, commented on being placed initially with the kindergarten children in the state school and, in one case, with retarded children, until they learned the language. All noted that this was accomplished most easily in adoptive homes where there were host children of school age. In such situations, learning the host language is the strongest bridge to adaptation and an impetus to assimilation. One interesting artifact of this is the extensive correspondence still carried on with host families, particularly in England and Belgium. In every case, this is still effected in the language of the adoptive family in the host country, and may be the only opportunity still available to use that language for those repatriated to Euzkadi.

Given that "The most striking ethnic marker of the

Basques is their language,"[33] the maintenance and enrichment of the language in exile was of great importance to the child refugees. This was clearly most consciously exemplified in the colonies in France sponsored by the Basque government. Eighteen of the Basques educated there recalled in their interviews that at least part of their education was in Euskera. In England, by contrast, only five recall such training, though two remember learning what little of the language they know from a Basque priest there. In Belgium, only two had any training in the language. In the Socialist countries there was none of consequence.

The modest emphasis upon Euskera reflects its minimal use in Euzkadi in the mid-thirties, as well as the fact that the majority of those evacuated were urban children, while the traditional stronghold of the Basque language has been the rural folk on the farms. Exposure at any level to the language abroad, and its importance as a cultural anchor, clearly influenced the lives of some of the children. Today, a surprising percentage of the Basques evacuated after Guernica work or teach in the *ikastola* movement. Sixteen of the seventy-six interviewed from France, England, and Belgium are participants. One of these has initiated the *ikastola* movement in Venezuela; another is married to the Director of *ikastolas* for all of Guipúzcoa. Some work as teachers for pay during the day; most volunteer their services for night school classes. This finding is perhaps explained by the realization, as adults, of the transcending importance of their own language to those who were, as children, taken far away from their homeland.

Culture

The strength and constancy of Basque culture was another salient factor in the children's adaptation to their exile. The importance of their language, folklore, and folklore presentations, already noted, the Catholic religion, and the efforts of the Basque Government-in-Exile all played significant roles in the lives of those evacuated to the non-Socialist countries.

To look first at folklore, certain experiences seem to have been particularly notable to the Basque children. These included the actual learning of the songs and dances, whether from a priest, a teacher, an older refugee or, as in Russia, even a Basque sailor in port. This activity reminded them of the traditional pastimes in Euzkadi, moored their cultural identity, served as a link with their homes, and was clearly felt by all to be an activity that would be pleasing to their parents. The range and complexity of Basque song and dance has astounded many students of folklore. Further, the ease and naturalness of the presentations is also quite rare in our day. Informal presentations still take place regularly all over Euzkadi, mainly for local rather than tourist consumption. Those interviewed commented on their pleasure in preparing the appropriate costumes, which they sewed by hand, using whatever materials of the correct color could be found.

This conscious fostering of cultural traditions had a second advantage. The small admission charged for the concerts helped the refugee children feel that they were not totally dependent on the charity of others and entirely powerless so far from home. In most cases, these performances were quite lucrative. At the same time they helped to neutralize unfavorable propaganda against the children in some of the host countries.

Religion

In looking at the role played by the Roman Catholic religion during the exile of the Basque children, much of what has been described earlier regarding the role of the clergy is of obvious relevance here. Religion in the Basque country is not left to women and children. Unique among Hispanic countries is the regular observance of mass and other rituals by adult males. Historically, due to the great number of young Basques choosing the priesthood as a vocation, the clergy in Euzkadi is drawn largely from within the kinship network. Basque priests have a history of interest and activity in politics, especially Basque nationalist politics. They frequently excel at the feats of strength so important in the male life of Euzkadi. Thus the church in Euzkadi has an earthy flavor to it, one that is rooted in the culture of the Basques and which is quite unlike that of the rest of Spain. People truly believe in God, and truly revere the local saints, turning to them in grief and in thanksgiving. Religion is not an empty observance, a piety reserved only for Sunday.

As a result, the children in exile—excepting those strongly Leftist—took particular pleasure in the practice of their faith. In the host countries they adhered doggedly to their holy day processions and myriad of observances. Their regular progress through the unvarying ritual ceremonies of the church—Confession, First Communion, then Confirmation—pleased them and served as another link to their life before evacuation. Many of the Basques remarked on how conscious they were of having to make a good impression on their hosts abroad in order to bring honor to their parents. Religion was one excellent way to effect this. In certain PNV colonies then, the round of rituals each day was quite considerable, but each observance functioned positively in the lives of the exiled children.

Basque Government

A final tie to Euzkadi was the presence of the Basque government. This respected administration ceased to exist for those evacuated to the Soviet Union and Mexico; and for the children of Belgium, it was almost as evanescent. In both France and, to a lesser extent, England, however, the presence and help given by its representatives was of great importance to the children. Of those in England, five noted that they had some help from its envoys; nineteen who had been refugees in France recall its assistance, particularly those sheltered in Basque-sponsored colonies until mid-1939. Specific assistance such as food, medical help, and shelter, and the less tangible support provided through visits and participation of dignitaries in patriotic, religious, and folklore events were recalled with warmth. Certainly, the symbolic value for many tended to outweigh the extent of actual assistance the government of Aguirre, Irujo, Leizaola, and Landaburu could give from 1939 onward. For these Basques in exile, their government most effectively exemplified Basque nationalism.

Whatever its dynamics, the value of the efforts of the Basque government to maintain solidarity and Basque nationalism among its evacuated children was considerable. For those among the thousands of yesterday's exiled children who today are part of the leadership cohort in Euzkadi, allegiance to the Basque government has never faltered.

The Importance of Food

During the interviews with the Basques who had been refugees as children, the writer was struck by the large number of spontaneous comments concerning their food in exile. Though perhaps no more striking than in neighboring French, Castilian Spanish, and Italian cultures, the value and importance placed on food and the eating of large quantities of it seems to occupy a central place in Basque culture. The writer, during her year of residence with both rural and urban branches of her family, found that the rituals of growing, preserving (especially the pig-killing and making of winter sausages), preparing, and eating food seemed central to Basque daily life. As one of many possible examples, the conversation of a group of family members at the bedside of the critically ill patriarch addressed the question of who, during the previous five years, had produced the best chorizo. There was also the inordinate care and concomitant labor required to distribute fresh milk on a regular basis from the family farm to the far-flung family network.

This preoccupation with food followed the children into exile. Forty-five years later, it reappeared in the interview comments about the kind, quantity, and savor of the foods served in the host countries. In France, to cite a positive example, the instant appearance of long white French loaves, loaves weighing two kilos, enraptured the children. At the other extreme, both the tortillas* in the Escuela España-México and the black bread in Russia provoked food riots. Again, the initial meal served in the provisional camp in England—Spanish onions served whole and intended to provide a link with home—was a disaster. In England, also, the ubiquitous tea, used in Spain only during illness (and then

* Kenny notes that, in Mexico, the eating of bread rather than tortillas is an indication of middle- or upper-class membership in the official census of Mexico.[34]

made of camomile), was a puzzle to the children. In Belgium, there were negative comments about the propensity of adoptive parents to serve huge whole boiled potatoes, instead of the beloved fried ones. Few enjoyed the use of a strange condiment, mustard, on meat. Children remember being given such peculiar foods and being punished for not eating them. One commented that dinner to her still suggested the "Hour of the Potato," when she spent long periods trying to masticate the whole potatoes, whole onions, and quarters of boiled cabbage served to her.

There were also some positive comments which shed light on a way in which trauma came to be alleviated. One was the super-abundance of sweets and fine chocolates enjoyed by the children in Belgium, which many can still describe in detail after more than forty years. Wherever the children were sent, sweets, more than any other foodstuff, meant love. And when the sweets formed part of a holiday celebration, life became happier, most especially when the celebration far outshone that experienced at home.

This series of comments corroborates the findings in studies of later children of crisis, those in relocation camps following World War II. Children in such situations naively expect that the adults will provide exactly the original, beloved foods remembered from home. When this does not occur, as happened to the Basque children in England, Belgium, Mexico, and Russia, there is discontent and even upheaval. In one such study of Jewish refugee children, Margaret Hicklin remarks:

> Our real failure to supply the children with ample and acceptable food in *their own* estimation was, in part, responsible for disturbances in the dining rooms. Mealtimes, for each child, represented an emotional climax.[35]

Hicklin describes a number of observed residual psychological effects of the earlier deprivation of food on young children in Britain. These included the suspicion of strange dishes and the use of food as gifts to express friendship among the children of the colony. White bread was especially favored, and it was hoarded obsessively in spite of its availability in abundance. Such behavior was noted in interviews with the caretakers of the Basque children in exile.

Hicklin further states that food, to a child separated from his parents, has both a real and a symbolic value. Its real value as life-giving nourishment is overlaid with its potential to express the child's expectation of love. Perhaps this explains the significance to the children at Kingston Hill in London of their compatriot cook, as it can the life long love felt for Jesusa, the cook at the infirmary in La Citadelle.

The Use of Drawing and Writing in Exile

In addition to those activities already described, two in which the Basque children engaged during their sojourns in the host countries deserve notice. The first, reported by three of the writers who observed them, was the use of drawing to work through the trauma of their separation from parents and homeland. A few of these pictures have survived in the album of the Scotsman Dr. Ellis, and among the memorabilia of the children. They reflect what has been written about them. Kerschner, the Quaker co-director of a colony in France in the 1940s writes:

> The [Basque] children's singing and dancing gave them, and us, much pleasure. But in no form of art expression did they show more excellence than in drawing and painting with watercolors. . . . Some made sets of watercolors which might well serve as illustrations for the stark little autobiographies they wrote, describing their trek out of Spain, the wreckage they saw, the bombs, and other dangers. Later, the pictures were of pleasant scenes—birds, flowers, and children playing. That expression in words and pictures of the experiences suffered during their flight might well have released them from continued dwelling on the horrors of these experiences.[36]

Similarly, Jessie Stewart, director of the Cambridge colony notes:

> We had a group of adults, quite exceptional people, who gave much of their time and knowledge to teaching these children, and they were happily and fully occupied from the beginning, and very quickly, the signs of strain dis-

> appeared. The most interesting record of their development in the first six months was the series of paintings. In the first days, few of these were without an aeroplane, a burning house, or a battleship belching fire. But after a few weeks, villages and farm scenes and strange flowers appeared more and more frequently, and it became rare to see any reminder of the war.[37]

Finally, Alfred Brauner, who visited the Basque children from Guipúzcoa who fled to Catalonia in 1936, observed:

> When the children were asked to draw or describe what was most meaningful to them, they drew pictures of the homes they had left behind them, but always burned or destroyed. They wrote about their homes now requisitioned by the Insurgents. But only a handful spoke or drew their toys. When I asked what they hoped in the future, they replied, "My parents in my home, bread, and a job."[38]

As noted, art was frequently presented to the children in tandem with writing about the tragic experiences they had endured. Several of the Basques interviewed had written fairly extensive autobiographies of their evacuation and sojourns abroad. At least two have been published, and a number of others have been excerpted and are to be found in this study. It has been observed frequently, concerning the Jewish prisoners in the Nazi concentration camps, that the need to document their suffering and persecution at times became an obsession. Perhaps the act of bearing witness to this unprecedented genocide also served to lessen the trauma, by universalizing one's individual experience. The Basque children who kept diaries or later recaptured their exile in an autobiography invariably found the task to be satisfying. Many have a photographic history of their period in the host country. Examples of this appear in this work as well.

The Summing Up

In summing up the retrospective experience of the Basques who were interviewed, a final weighing can be made of what was for some an adventure and for others an ordeal. Most of those interviewed in each country (with the exception of Mexico) felt that, overall, the experience had been a positive one. This was unanimous among the twenty-one Basques sent into the Soviet Union; and positive for all but four of those sent into France, and for all but one who went to England. Four of those sent into Belgium felt the effects on their lives had been somewhat negative. These had been the very youngest children of those sent. A great variety of reasons were given as to why the experience was felt to have been positive. Some cited the value of having been exposed to a more advanced country and new language, which in a number of cases made possible their present profession (for example, language teacher or consulate employee). The excellent education offered in Russia and Belgium was emphasized. The acceleration of maturity through having to cope with the unknown; the friendships made which have continued (at least four have sent their children to be educated in their host country); and first exposure to or training in what was to become their profession (be it priest or confectioner) were also mentioned.

Many of the Basques commented that it was only with their adulthood and parenting that they realized the true significance of their sojourn abroad. For every one repatriated from France, England, and Belgium, the extreme contrast between life in the host country and the subsequent decades of repression and persecution under Franco surely aided in whatever glorification the period of exile has acquired with time.

The importance of a retrospective look at the few years of life in a host country against the decades of harassment each experienced in Euzkadi under Franco can be better appreciated by a brief consideration of the interview data. In France, for example, nearly half of those interviewed fell under Franco's Decree of Responsibility. This was indicated on their identity papers, thus subjecting them to police surveillance for years. Their education was interrupted, so that about equal numbers dropped out of primary school as completed it, and fewer than half finished the secondary course. Half of those sent to England also were subject to Franco's decree, and their educational attainments were even lower than the French cohort. The Belgian group fared much better, as only one was old enough to be condemned under this decree. All finished the primary, and over half completed the secondary level. For many whose responses form the core of this book, then, their lives in foreign lands may now have a charm in the retelling that was lacking in the actuality of their sojourns. We all tend to rewrite our histories when we relive them in memory.

Another perspective on the trauma of exile compared to the repatriation to a Spain ruled by Franco is available in the comments of the children sent into the Soviet Union. Among those interviewed, ten of the sixteen who were repatriated to Euzkadi spontaneously noted that they should have stayed in Russia, and thirteen commented on how hard it had been to start over in Franco's Spain. All but two came back simply for family reasons to care for aging parents who, after waiting two decades for their return, wanted them at home.

For the minority of children for whom evacuation was simply an ordeal throughout, the lack of love, either in the colonies or in the adoptive homes, was frequently cited. The youngest children sent into Belgium and Mexico tended to suffer such trauma, commenting that they almost "died of fear," or suffered from a lifelong lack of confidence, or cried for weeks, or still have a feeling of insecurity, or vomited for years, or lacked parental counsel when entering young manhood or womanhood. Some few still live at home or with siblings, being unable to live independently. Three receive psychiatric care. But these are a distinct minority, overall. Rather, it appears that, unlike other later refugee populations studied, the Basque children did not suffer from either the high suicide rate (six times normal) or the high rate of mental breakdown (again over six times normal), of the various ethnic groups of refugees sheltered in Switzerland during and after World War II.[39]

In fact, all but a very few of those either interviewed or about whom material was gathered from siblings are apparently functioning at a normal level, living normal lives and, for those who are themselves parents, rearing children who seem no different from those of parents who were never evacuated.

Of the Basques questioned who had been evacuated as children as to whether they felt that their lives had been changed in any way by the experience and whether they were satisfied, the majority felt that their lives had been affected, usually positively, and that they were, in general, satisfied. Though the writer had anticipated that those most satisfied would be those whose sojourn abroad included both the structural and situational factors noted at the outset, this did not prove to be invariably so. These factors were confirmed as important in the Mexican case, but were disconfirmed in the Soviet Union, where most structural and situational factors were absent. In the other European countries where substantial numbers of children were sponsored, the factors held up more generally. Those who, when interviewed, saw their lives as being affected negatively, noted the lack of love in exile, the poor education obtained there, overly possessive adoptive parents, or inequitable military discipline in their colonies. Among those who felt satisfaction with what life had brought them, the joys of parenting and the ability always to find work were most frequently mentioned. Here again, the dismal Euzkadi to which they returned after two, three, or twenty years of exile clearly colored their statements.

Interestingly enough, several of those interviewed declined to answer such questions, saying that a simple answer to a complex life was less than useless. These Basques, who, like those who responded, were at the half-century mark in their lives, declined to encapsulate in a few words what has been a period of unbelievable changes in the human condition.

All of those who were parents were asked about their own parenting experiences. None of the men noted any problems in their own roles as fathers, some remarking that *Ser padre es toda pasta* (To be a father is all gravy). As for the women, even of those sent into Russia to life in a collective, only a few expressed any recollection of difficulty in their own child-rearing. The majority of the women described motherhood and the actual rearing of children as the greatest joy they had known. Those who were more reserved in their accolades noted that the collective experience in both Russia and Mexico had not prepared them well for child-rearing, and that, in two cases, their over protectiveness toward their children could be traced to their separation in childhood from their own parents. Several of those who found the evacuation to France, England, or Belgium to have had negative effects had neither married nor had children. Again, a few of the Sovieticos commented that the intricacies of homemaking, after their repatriation to Euzkadi, caused them some difficulty.

Two of those reporting a similar problem in Mexico have made use of the ready availability of household help to surmount such problems. Overall, then, the effects on the Basques of their evacuation were perceived as usually positive, though a small minority could trace difficulties in their own later lives and ability to function as parents to their exile.

Finally, the interviewees were asked to suggest ways in which an evacuation today, for reasons of the security of their own children (or grandchildren), could be made less problematic. There was a really surprising range of responses, from that of one Sovietico that evacuation would be useless in a war today, since, in a nuclear clash, all the world would be affected, to those (a majority) who would wish exactly the same treatment for their children that they had received. This did not vary whether the individual had been in the children's colonies of the Basque government in France, an adoptive home in Belgium, the collective boarding schools in the Soviet Union, or the Catholic or secular colonies and boarding schools in England and Belgium. About a quarter, however, thought that the opposite kind of placement from what they experienced was the better: private homes if they had been in colonies, or Basque-sponsored colonies if they had been in private homes. Those who had been in both, some ten in all, opted for the life in private homes. Perceptively enough, several men said that the question was not relevant, since refugees are not permitted to impose conditions on their evacuation circumstances. All those who remarked that private adoptive homes were the best solution for evacuated children cited the lack of love in other situations, such as colonies or large institutions, a love "that is much more important than bread and butter."

Several noted that the entire evacuation process should be made much more humane. They objected strenuously to the practice of using numbers instead of their names, to the unnecessarily frequent physical examinations, a fetish for "health," the consecutive vaccinations (with consequent large scars),* and the interminable quarantines, where they were made to feel like pestilential prisoners. The delousing routines were remembered as being utterly degrading. Later, the improvised colonies in most countries made cleanliness almost impossible, so that scabies and lice were chronic afflictions they still recall with disgust. Much scorn was expressed for the manner of distributing children to adoptive families, "like a raffle or auction, with the young tender meat going first to become the family's new 'pet,' and no one wanting the older boys and girls at all." Others stated that the lack of counsel they received as, for example, when their menstrual periods began or when possible occupations were suggested to them, would be alleviated in an ideal evacuation. A few still smarted at the military discipline and unjust punishments in certain colonies. About one in five, regardless of host country, said that they would prefer to die with their children rather than evacuate them. Nearly half stressed the importance of having the children accompanied by Basque personnel, people they, as parents, would trust to keep alive the values and traditions of being Basque.

What has emerged from the interview data with the Guernica generation is an apparent lack of traumatization as a result of the children's separation from home and parents, and subsequent exile in a foreign country. Some possible reasons for this have already been suggested, including the politicization of the children, use of staff and siblings as substitute parents, the presence of Basque mentors, salience of Basque culture, and the recency factor (the more recent per-

* Even today, exposing these scars seems, in many, to trigger some of the emotions felt so many years before.

secution after repatriation was greater). We need to look as well at certain consistent cultural practices of the Basques for further answers. These include their tradition of "lending" children, their extensive history of emigration, the early admission to adulthood in Euzkadi, and two other concepts central to the Basque ethos, *indarra*, or strength, and *sendotasuna*, or force of character.

There is a clear propensity, particularly in large, poor, rural families in the Basque country, to give children up for adoption and subsequent inheritance within the extended kinship network, particularly to childless relatives. The centuries-old history of Basque emigration to the Americas is also relevant, particularly among quite young males of the large rural or urban families. In Euzkadi, the land or patrimony is considered impartible, and tends to go, undivided, to only one child. The coupling of this economic imperative to emigrate for opportunity with the early admission to adulthood in Basque society (which defines boys of twelve as of full working age in industry or agriculture) is also of consequence here as a partial explanation of the lack of trauma perceived by the evacuated Basque children. The traditional Basque values of *indarra* and *sendotasuna* may also add some answers. These highly esteemed traits are realized in a number of everyday contexts, and they are consistently presented to the young to emulate.[40] Thus, the Basque recreational and sports events require endurance and strength as well as style and grace: the lifting of great weights, the chopping of logs, the game of jai-alai. As an example, the callouses a twelve-year-old boy can demonstrate on his palm, without comment, after days of practice hitting the ball in the *frontón* (jai alai court), would draw quiet approval from his uncles; on the other hand, the protests of a wife that she can no longer help her husband in the fields when the baby arrives draw disapproval from her aunts. It is entirely possible that such ancient ideals were translated by the evacuated children into a dedication to excel, coupled with a refreshing lack of complaint in periods of adversity—a kind of perseverance and sense of personal worth that rarely faltered. The writer found, on numerous occasions during the interviews, when attempting to draw out painful memories of events, that the person being interviewed would simply comment to the effect that one is expected to bear such things in life. Those who chose to detail the personal tragedies of their evacuation were few in number. More usual was to observe a person become highly emotional during the interview, but continue to answer the questions, with only tears, hastily wiped away, or a tremor in the voice, or nervous gestures of the hands or feet to belie the calm recital. It seems possible, then, that the accepted Basque cultural practices noted above may have prepared the children well to surmount the problems engendered by their evacuation at an early age.

Participant Observation

Besides the generalizations gained from answers to the questions asked by the writer, certain insights emerged from the writer's sustained participant observation done in Euzkadi, France, England, Belgium, and Mexico. As one example, the extent to which there appears to be a network of continuing relations among those who spent time in each host country was quite surprising. The periodic formal reunions enjoyed by those sent into France, England, and to a lesser extent Belgium and the Soviet Union, seem to serve a function beyond any possible catharsis of sad memories. It was not anticipated that there would be a web of middle-aged adults in several countries who feel a bond made manifest in their exchange of educational opportunities for children, in business, in *compadrazgo* relations, and in marriage arrangements. This network includes, naturally, the citizens from each host country who assisted the refugee children at some point. So as not to trivialize the emotive function of the periodic meetings of large or small groups of former refugee children, the writer notes that the recapturing of the past, a feature of each such gathering, permits the discharge of emotions of anger and grief among friends who shared in that past. In contrast, however, one ardent reunionist told the writer, "The best proof that our exile was good is the camaraderie at our reunions."

Through participant observation it also became apparent that the network has operated in such a way that each of the evacuated children, as an adult, is fully aware that the education and professional status of the Sovieticos is superior to that of those who were sent to other host countries; that those sent to Mexico had a hard time there; and that the children in adoptive homes in Belgium were unusually well-treated (both materially and emotionally), while the people in France were generally cold. They are also aware that France withdrew its subsidy for refugees, while Belgium was unique in offering a family allowance. The contrast between the help from both the governments of Russia and Mexico and the lack of it in England is also common knowledge.

On an emotional level, it was clear to the writer that the hardest blow to cope with was the loss by death of a parent while a child was in exile. The children who spent several years in exile and were reunited to find as many as three new siblings in the family frequently had difficulty in redefining their role, now different from the one that they had enjoyed prior to evacuation. Conversely, those who were not repatriated and did not share the persecution under Franco, as did their friends or relatives, feel a certain guilt about not having returned.

One curious fact emerged out of the interview context itself. Several of the persons interviewed insisted that their children be present in order that they might hear everything. It became clear that many of those evacuated had spoken very little about the experience to members of their own family. Even clearer was the momentousness of this period of exile in the life of the respondent. For the majority, it represented the biggest trip they had ever taken, and certainly the first outside the confines of Euzkadi. But this dramatic sojourn had been unreported, swallowed up in the subsequent mass evacuations of World War II. Time and again, whether male or female, respondents wept as particularly poignant memories became overwhelming.

Without exception, all of those questioned commented that no one had ever interviewed them before about their exile. Many felt somewhat resentful that their sacrifice during the

Spanish Civil War had been so totally ignored for more than forty years. What had been crucial to them had evoked no apparent interest in anyone in Euzkadi. Many shared their writings, their few letters, photographs, and other memorabilia with the writer with enthusiasm, in the hope that, finally, this pitiful evacuation might receive some attention. They felt that history had forgotten them; that their forfeiture of home and country was unrecorded, except in their own memories and by the small plaques and young oaks they had placed in gratitude in the countries that hosted them. As a group, the Basque refugee children as adults persevered in their conviction that their trauma and exile had been in a good cause. Over and over again, especially among the men, comments such as "Our cause was just" or "We had to fight the Fascists however we could" were common. Perhaps their evacuation and exile are best summed up in the words of a man from San Sebastián, whose odyssey as a child began a month after Franco rebelled:

> Our war, our battles, were the first rehearsal of the coming worldwide conflagration, approved by the League of Nations and the Vatican. Why, even the arms, blessed by them for the invasion of Abyssinia, were used in Euzkadi. We only provided a bit of time for the great Allies before the struggle against fascism enveloped even them.

APPENDIX I

Summary of Basques Interviewed

		FRANCE	ENGLAND	BELGIUM	USSR	MEXICO
Number Interviewed		30	26	21	21	11
Sex:	Male	17	16	13	10	8
	Female	13	10	8	11	3
Urban		23	22	17	21	9
Middle Class Background		18	21	14	2	8
Evacuated with Siblings		15	19	7	7	11
Scale of Living:	Private Home	6		15		
	Small Colony	8	21	6		
	Large Instit.	15	5	0	21	11
Education in Host Country		23	18 irreg. 8 none	21	21	2 to 8 years

Educational Level Completed:	Primary	12	13	7		7
	Secondary	14	10	10		3
	Technical				8	
	University	4	3	4	13	1
Occupation:	Housewife	5	7	6	6	3
	MD				3F	
	Teacher	3	4	2F	2F	
	Professional	4	2	5	9M, 1F	2
	Proprietor			5		4
	Manager	8	2			
	Worker	9	4	3		2
	Unemployed		1			
Middle Class Status		21	20	14	20	11
No. Married		20	24	16	21	11
No. Who Married Basques		20	22	15	15	3
No. of Children		60	80	31	59	34
Range (Children/Family)		0–11	0–10	0–6	1–5	2–6
Positive Effects from Exile		26	25	17	21	3
Satisfied with Life		21	22	20	21	6

APPENDIX II

Cuestionario [as used in interviews]

1. Nombre y Apellido———. Fecha de nacimiento———. Provincia———. Población———.

2. Dígame, por favor, lo que usted recuerda de la guerra Civil . . . por ejemplo, los bombardeos, el hambre, los aviones, la fuga de su hogar . . .

3. Recuerda algo de su salida de España? De qué puerto salió? El barco, sus compañeros, las condiciones de la travesía, su llegada———.

4. De esos años que permaneció en———, qué es lo que recuerda con más lucidez?
   a. de sus compañeros, en particular, los de su pueblo o parientes, hermanos, amigos—permanecieron unidos, o fueron separados?
   b. de los que iban al cargo de su grupo—de los profesores, curas, enfermeras, cocineros—eran Vascos? Quedaron con usted en———?
   c. de las personas que le acogieron en la ciudad extranjera—le hicieron contenta/o y feliz?

5. Dígame, por favor, cómo se educó? Cuanto tiempo asistió al colegio? Dónde? Fué su educación principalmente académica o práctica? En general, que opina de su educación: sus profesores, fueron comprensivos y atentos? Le gustó el colegio? Pudo mantener el Vascuence durante su experiencia de enseñanza? Pudo compartir su cultura—fiestas, bailes, canciones, cuentos —algo típico de su población?

6. Cómo pasó usted esos años desde que salió su país? Después de terminar sus estudios, qué tipo de empleo consiguió? Y ahora?

7. Dígame, por favor, si casado algo de su matrimonio? Fué con Vasco/a? Sus hijos . . . nombres, edades, residencias, empleos, etc. Dígame lo que le gustó en experimentar ser padre/madre? Dígame lo que le gustó menos en experimentar ser padre/madre?

8. Dígame, por favor, puede mantener los lazos con el país Vasco? Habla Vascuence, escribe cartas a parientes, ha regresado a su patria, le han visitado parientes del país Vasco, es socio de algún

club Vasco, come usted la comida típica de su país, asiste en presentaciones Vascas, como deportes, bailes, conciertos, ceremonios, fúnebres, etc? Tienen sus hijos lazos al país Vasco? Entre sus amistades, hay personas Vascas? Es usted proprietario? Dueño de carro?

9. Dígame, por favor, está usted satisfecho con su vida tal como lleva?

10. Qué opina usted de esta esperiencia de ser refugiado—fueron mayores los efectos negativos o positivos? Cree usted que llegaría a ser el mismo hoy día si no hubiese salido del país Vasco?

11. Si usted se viera obligado a enviar a sus hijos a otro país por causa de seguridad, qué condiciones impondría usted para aminorar la experiencia de ser un niño refugiado?

Muchas Gracias

APPENDIX III

Embarkations from Bilbao, Santander, and Asturias from May 5 to August 25, 1937.

SHIP	DATE, PLACE OF DEPARTURE			DESTINATION	NUMBER EVACUATED
Goizeko Izarra	May	5	Bilbao	Pauillac	319
Habana	"	7	"	La Pallice	2,326
Marvia	"	9	"	Pauillac	1,000
Habana	"	13	"	"	3,796
Galea	"	21	"	Verdun	900
Zurriola	"	21	"	"	900
Goizeko Izarra	"	22	"	"	350
Kenfig Pool	"	27	"	"	750
Cabo Corona	"	27	"	Pauillac	1,283
Habana	"	31	"	La Pallice	3,738
Habana	June	5	"	"	4,500
Torpehall	"	13	"	Pauillac	750
Alice Marie	"	14	"	"	790
Habana	"	15	"	"	4,600
Marraquesh	"	20	Santander	La Pallice	1,500
Kenfig Pool	"	30	"	"	1,500
Candlestones Castle	July	1	"	La Pallice	1,600
Kelwyn	"	1	"	Saint Nazaire	1,250
Stancroft	"	2	"	Pauillac	2,000
Molton	"	3	"	Saint Nazaire	2,000
Perros Goirce	"	3	"	Saint Nazaire	1,100
Sarastone	"	6	"	"	2,500
Marvia	"	10	"	Pauillac	2,600
Pilton	"	15	"	Saint Nazaire	2,120
Stamwool	"	17	Rivadesella	Pauillac	870
Kelwyn	"	18	"	"	1,000
Alice Marie	"	20	Santander	"	1,460
MacGregor	"	21	"	"	1,420
Bramden	"	23	Gijón	Nantes	1,000
Sarastone	"	27	Santander	Pauillac	2,000
Thorpebay	"	28	Rivadesella	Nantes	1,740
Stangrove	"	30	"	"	590
Jacobus	"	31	Gijón	Saint Nazaire	1,200

Marvia	Aug. 1	Santander	"	2,750
Pilton	" 6	Avilés	Pauillac	2,500
Bramden	" 7	"	"	1,250
Stamwool	" 11	Rivadesella	"	1,350
Kenfig Pool	" 11	Santander	Saint Nazaire	2,000
Marvia	" 11	Rivadesella	Pauillac	2,400
Stangrove	" 14	"	Nantes	750
Branhill	" 14	Gijón	Pauillac	1,500
Nailsea Vale	" 14	Avilés	"	3,000
Thorpebay	" 17	Santander	"	2,100
Seven Seas Spray	" 20	Avilés	"	2,000
Remolcador *San Martín*	" 23	Santander	"	185
Ganguil *Raos*	" 23	"	"	814
Pesquero *Joaquin Asta*	" 23	"	"	19
Pesquero *Rosario*	" 23	"	"	15
Pesquero *Gure Ametza*	" 23	"	"	230
Pesquero *Pantzeska*	" 23	"	"	63
Pesquero *Noble Cabildo de S. Andrés*	" 23	"	"	40
Pesquero *Noble Cabildo S. Andrés M*	" 23	"	"	63
Pesquero *Itxaro Izarra*	" 23	"	"	27
Pesquero *Noble Cabildo S. Andrés N*	" 23	"	"	46
Pesquero *Piedi*	" 23	"	"	25
Pesquero *Lina*	" 23	"	"	46
Pesquero *Nuevo S. José de la Montaña*	" 23	"	"	58
Pesquero *La Polar*	" 23	"	"	18
Pesquero *Santo Cristo del Amparo*	" 23	"	"	58
Pesquero *Doris*	" 23	"	"	13
Pesquero *Gain Gaiñekoa*	" 23	"	"	180
Pesquero *Constante Juan*	" 23	"	"	488
Pesquero *Cántabro número dos*	" 23	"	"	110
Pesquero *Deseado número dos*	" 23	"	"	167

Pesquero *F. Jaureguizar*	" 23	"	"	70
Pesquero *Pasaya*	" 23	"	"	217
Pesquero *San Antonio*	" 23	"	"	110
Pesquero *Enrique Diego Magraza*	" 23	"	"	12
Marvia	" 24	Rivadesella	"	3,000
		Total:		83,126

Embarkations from Asturias Arriving in French Ports from August 26 to October 25, 1937.

SHIP	ARRIVAL	PORT	NUMBER OF PEOPLE
Stanwool	Aug. 31	Pauillac	1,441
Bramden	Sept. 1	"	915
Pesquero *Olivita*	" 1	"	31
Stangrove	" 2	La Pallice	1,928
Stamnore	" 6	"	3,143
Mieres	" 6	Pauillac	2,000
Lancha *Amparin*	" 7	"	8
Stangrove	" 10	"	850
Celta	" 11	"	846
Santiago Lopez	" 11	"	2,782
Stambrige	" 18	La Pallice	601
Bramden	" 21	Pauillac	1,577
Margaret Rose	" 24	"	477
Migdol	" 24	"	3,354
Hilfern	" 27	"	2,200
Stanray	" 28	"	1,740
Stanray	Oct. 9	"	1,700
Stangrove	" 9	"	700
Kelwyn	" 11	"	4,000
Musel	" 23	"	40
María Santiuste	" 23	"	659
Pesquero *Alfredo*	" 23	"	215
Alfonso	" 23	"	255
Cervantes	" 23	"	291
María Elena	" 23	"	1,800
Chalupa *L. no. 1*	" 24	"	5
Pesquero *Justiniano*	" 24	"	36
Pesquero *Adelina*	" 24	"	15
Manuel	" 24	"	254
Velero *Rubio*	" 24	"	130
Remolcador *Plutón*	" 24	"	184
Stangrove	" 24	"	706
Bramden	" 24	"	251

Bramhill	" 24	"	598
Hilfern	" 24	"	300
Stanlhei	" 25	"	17
		Total:	36,049

Summary No. 1

People evacuated from Bilbao, Santander, and Asturias from May 5 to August 25, 1937:

Evacuated from:		
Bilbao	26,002	
Santander	30,974	
Asturias		
Rivadesella	11,700	
Musel	5,700	
Aviles	8,750	83,126

Approximate distribution of these evacuees:	
Women	46,126
Children	20,000
Adults	5,000
Men over 45	6,000
Men under 45	6,000

Persons evacuated from Asturias between August 26 and October 25, 1937:		36,049
	Total:	119,175

In completion of the charge given me by the head of the [Basque] government, I hereby present you with this information for the government of Euzkadi.

/signed/ Fidel Rotaeche

Source: Fidel Rotaeche, *Informe, Evacuación*. Bayonne, February, 1938.

Summary No. 2

Basque refugees entering France

Up to October 7, 1936, by the frontier at Irún		12,500	
by sea		27,500	
From October 7, 1936, to May 7, 1937, by sea		2,000	
From May 7, 1937, to October 24, 1937, by controlled evacuation		103,115	
From the ports of Santander and Asturias, by various ships and by plane		5,000	
	Total:		150,115

Basque refugees removed to Catalonia		
Arriving mainly from Guipúzcoa before October 7, and transferred to Catalonia	32,000	
Repatriated through Hendaye, because of the "repatriation" ordered by the French authorities	36,000	
Transferred to Catalonia for the same reason	63,000	
Total:		131,000
Number of Basque refugees remaining in France		19,115

Refugees entering France since the fall of Catalonia		
Basque citizens (civilians and Gudaris) in concentration camps	5,000	
Civil population, the majority being women and children, in refugee homes	35,000	
Total:		40,000

Basque refugees in France in 1939		
Already there prior to the fall of Catalonia	19,115	
Entries from France since that time	40,000	
Total number of Basque refugees in France:		59,115

SOURCE: *Basque Refugees: A Preliminary Survey*. Bayonne, [1939].

APPENDIX IV

Basque Children Cared for in France in Colonies (as of February 14, 1938)

TOWN	NUMBER OF CHILDREN	GROUP PROVIDING FUNDS
Agen	33	Comité d'Accueil / CGT
Amalie-Soulac	30	Dutch Committee
Angers	90	Comité d'Accueil / CGT
Arraute	36	Comité d'Accueil / CGT
Asnières	28	Swedish Committee
Aulmay-sous-Bois	25	Comité d'Accueil / CGT
Avernes	24	Comité d'Accueil
Avignon	10	Municipal
Bayonne	280	Spanish Republican Government and Swedish Committee
Bievres	53	French Cooperatives
Bois Colombes	25	Swedish Committee
Bois Guillaume	25	Socorro Rojo Internacional
Cadajuac	110	Comité d'Accueil / CGT
Cevere	95	Comité d'Accueil / CGT
Champigny	68	Comité d'Accueil
Chanay	11	Comité d'Accueil / CGT
Chantilly	110	French Cooperatives
Chapelat-Limoges	91	Comité d'Accueil / CGT
Chateau de Quincy	15	Comité d'Accueil / CGT
Chateau les Halles	53	Swedish Committee
Chateau St. Hilarie	39	Comité d'Accueil / CGT
Chenay	36	Swedish Committee
Chinon	10	Secours Rouge International
Colombes	57	Swedish Committee
Compiègne	60	Comité d'Accueil
Dijon	66	Comité d'Accueil / CGT
Firminy	24	Municipal
Fontenay les Bains	10	Municipal
Garennes	48	Swedish Committee
Gueret	16	French State
Guethery	29	Basque Government
Ivry	25	Swedish Committee

Jatxu	34	Sr. Inchausti
L'Howre-Orphelinat	25	Comité d'Accueil / CGT
Mas Éloi	100	Comité d'Accueil / CGT
Mignes	48	Comité d'Accueil / CGT
Millan	24	French State
Monts Place	29	Comité d'Accueil/ CGT
Orly	90	French Socialist Party
Orthez	83	Basque Government
Pavie	83	Socorro Rojo Internacional
Poitiers	16	CGT
Rex-Orphelinat	22	Municipal
Saint Christian	70	Basque Government
St. Etienne	30	Municipal
St. Etienne	15	Municipal
St.-Jean-Pied-de-Port	419	Basque Government
Sirgues	8	Municipal
Valence	26	Comité d'Accueil / CGT

SOURCE: *Colonias de Niños Expatriados*, Bayonne, February 14, 1938, BGEA.

APPENDIX V

Basque Children Cared for in Belgium

GROUP PROVIDING FUNDS	NUMBER AND LOCATION OF CHILDREN	
Baskische Kinderwerk	1,304 children with families in Anvers, Liège, Namur, Brussels, Gan, Malines, Bruges, Mons, Tamines.	
Spanish Group in Defense of the Republic	312 children in adoptive homes	
Socialist Party of Belgium	1,000 children:	Marchin, 112
		Anvers, 57
		Rexousart, 57
		Luxembourg, 23, etc.
Socorro Rojo Internacional	320 children	
Belgian Red Cross	192 children	

SOURCE: *Colonias de Niños Expatriados*, Bayonne, February 14, 1938, BGEA.

APPENDIX VI

Basque Children in the Soviet Union

TOWN	COLONY		NUMBER OF CHILDREN
Odessa	Sanitorium:	October Revolution	200
Moscow	Sanitorium:	Obincue	346
Crimea	Sanitorium:	Proletarian	162
Crimea	Sanitorium:	Persian, Bepheck	229
Crimea	Sanitorium:	No. 4, Simeis	148
Crimea	Sanitorium:	Varanoff	98
Crimea	Sanitorium:	Red Flag	99
Crimea	Sanitorium:	Ai-Pandam Simeiz	117

SOURCE: *Colonias de Niños Expatriados*, Bayonne, February 14, 1938, BGEA.

APPENDIX VII

Basque Children in Colonies in England, Scotland and Wales. 1937–40

LOCATION	COLONY	NUMBER OF CHILDREN
Almondsbury, Huddersfield	Basque Children's Home Old Clergy House	20
Arkley (Barnet)	Rowley House	40
Aston, near Oxford	St. Joseph's House	10
Barnes	Old College	20
Berkhamstead	The Culvers	60
Birkenhead	Greenbank, Upton	—
Birmingham	Fr. Hudson's Homes	100
Blackboys (Sussex)		19
Bolton (Lancaster-shire)	Watermillock House	—
Brechfa (Wales)		—
Bristol	Basque Children's Home	50
Brixton	Salvation Army Home	40
Brooke (Bucks)	Basque Children's Home	—
Bromley		55
Bury	Southall	21
Camberley	Fern Hill, Hawley	80
Cambridge	Basque Hostel, Pampisford Vicarage	29
Cardiff		50
Carleon	Cambria House	20
Carlyle (Scotland)	Nazareth House	26
Carmathanshire (Wales)		—
Carshalton		20
Colchester		51
Colwin Bay (Wales)	Basque Children's Home	20
Darlington	St. Joseph's Home	25
Derby		50

Ditton	Nazareth House	20
Dorking	Basque Children's Home, Park Farm	20
Durham		61
Dymchurch		150
Elford (Staffordshire)	Elford Hall	—
Escambray		11
Evington	Evington Hall	—
Epping	Forest College	—
Fulwood (Rochdale)	St. Vincent's School	10
Freshwater (Isle of Wight)	Weston Manor	114
Frogatt	Guest House	—
Gainford	St. Peter's House	—
Great Yarmouth		50
Guildford	Ardmore House	40
Guisborough (Yorkshire)	Hutton Hall	—
Hadleigh	Salvation Army	100
Hertford	St. Vincent's Orphanage	13
Helston		30
Hexham-on-Tyne	The Larches	—
High Wycombe		46
Honiton		46
Huddersfield		20
Hull (Tarran Industries)	Basque Children's Home	60
Ipswich	Whereshead Park	102
Keighley	Riddlesdown Sanitarium	120
Kent	St. Mary's	80
Kingsey	Tythrop House	—
Lancaster	Nazareth House	10
Lancing	Beach House	—
Langham	Adelphi Centre	—
Leeds	Hill End Cottage	20
Leicester	Evington	70
Littlehampton	St. Joseph's Convent	25
Liverpool	Catholic Girl's Orphanage	150
Liverpool	Nazareth House	21
London SE	Convent of the Sacred Heart, Honor Oak	61
London W (Hammersmith)	Nazareth House	29
London EC	Clapton: Salvation Army	100

London W	Kingston	35
London	Theydon Bois, Leah Manning Home	20
Maidenhead	Bray Court	50
Manchester	St. Dominic's House	15
Manchester	St. Joseph's Home	50
Manchester	Nazareth House	20
Manchester	Our Lady of Lourdes Home	30
Margate		75
Middlesborough		20
Montrose (Scotland)	Dundee Breakfast Union	20
Newbury	Baydon Hole Farm	100
Newcastle-on-Tyne	St. Vincent's Home	50
Norfolk	Diss Basque Home	50
Northshields		20
Norwich		120
Preston	Moorfield Convent	50
Ramsgate	Salvation Army	100
Salford		25
Scarborough	Basque Children's Centre	85
Shormes		18
Southampton	Nazareth House	85
Southampton	Moor Hill House	—
Southampton	Training College	—
Southampton	Rownham's Mount	—
Street (Somerset)	The Grange	40
Surrey	Red Hill	50
Swansea (Wales)	Shetley Park House	80
Thame (Oxon)	Basque Children's House	50
Tynemouth		—
Tunbridge Wells	Rest Hall	63
Tottingham	Holly Mount	50
Tudhoe	St. Mary's Home	120
Wakefield	Old Hospital Park Lodge	65
Walsall	Aldridge Lodge	50
Westcott Park Farm	Basque Children's Home, Park Farm	—
Wigton		35
Wolsingham		18
Worthing		39

SOURCES: *Colonias de Niños Expatriados* (Bayonne, February 14, 1938), BGEA; "*Los Niños Vascos en Inglaterra*, mimeo, BGEA; Interviews, Press Reports.

NOTES

Preface

1. According to John Hope Simpson, *The Refugee Problem* (Oxford, 1937), pp. 30–38, some 132,000 Armenian children were rescued during the years 1915–30, including some 63,000 who went into France with their families. Other destitute Armenian children were gathered into orphanages: 30,000 in Russian Armenia, 10,000 in Greece. Of the Russian children orphaned by the Revolution, hundreds were cared for in Belgium and France.

Introduction

1. A discussion of the inheritance customs of rural Basques may be found in William Douglass, "Rural Exodus in Two Spanish-Basque Villages: A Cultural Explanation," *American Anthropologist*, vol. 73, no. 5 (1971), pp. 1110–17.

2. These specific blood factors include the highest rate in Europe of the blood type "O," and the lowest rate of type "B," plus the highest incidence in the world of the RH negative blood factor. See Morton Levine, "The Basques," *Natural History*, vol. 76, no. 4 (April 1967), pp. 44–51, for a review. These factors are made manifest in the Basques through their propensity for marriage within the kinship network, thus avoiding medical problems arising from the RH incompatibility common to exogamous marriages.

3. For a brief discussion of the *fueros*, see Stanley Payne, *Basque Nationalism* (Reno, 1975), pp. 15–28.

4. The history of Basque political institutions has been interpreted in various ways. These range from writers dismissing Basque claims to the early development of democratic forms as a "historic mythology" to the view perhaps best expressed in the *Times* of London (May 4, 1937, p. 17), which traced the Magna Carta and the British parliament to the system observed among the Basques at Guyenne in the eleventh century by Simon de Montfort, and brought by him to the British Isles.

5. The Carlists were committed to the restoration of traditional Catholic and Spanish institutions through accession of the Pre-

tender, Don Carlos, rather than a secularized, constitutional monarchy of moderate liberalism espoused by the supporters of the Queen Regent, Maria Cristina. See Payne, pp. 43–49, for a discussion.

6. The growth of Basque nationalism and the Partido Nacionalista Vasco is described in Robert Clark, *The Basques: The Franco Years and Beyond* (Reno, 1979), pp. 40–49.

7. According to Payne, pp. 117–48.

Chapter One

1. See "International Strategic Considerations and the Evolution of the Republican Government" in the collection of essays edited by Gabriel Jackson, *The Spanish Civil War: Domestic Crisis or International Conspiracy?* (Boston, 1967), pp. 53–54.

2. The number of histories of the Spanish Civil War continues to grow, unabated by time. Gabriel Jackson, *The Spanish Republic and the Civil War* (Princeton, 1965), pp. 231–46, provides a careful account of the war, its antecedents, and its course.

3. Stanley Payne, *Basque Nationalism* (Reno, 1975), pp. 163–66.

4. This information comes from interviews and correspondence with Jaime Marcellan Arrospide and José Antonio Ibarburu Garcia in San Sebastián in 1979–81.

5. Payne, p. 163.

6. Gabriel Jackson, *The Spanish Republic and the Civil War* (Princeton, 1965), p. 228.

7. George Steer, *The Tree of Gernika* (London, 1938) provides a vivid, eyewitness account of the Civil War in Euzkadi. For the Guipúzcoa battles in 1936, see pp. 21–44. The Spanish edition of this book was a prized, clandestine possession of several Basques interviewed.

8. Claude Bowers, *My Mission to Spain* (New York, 1954), pp. 281–83, also discusses the diplomatic maneuvers underlying the Non-Intervention plan.

9. Steer, pp. 32, 76.

10. Jackson, pp. 274–75.

11. Ibid., pp. 266–68.

12. See the monumental, three-volume work on the emigration occasioned by the Spanish Civil War, by Javier Rubio, *La Emigración de la Guerra Civil de 1936–1939* (Madrid, 1977). He describes the exodus from Guipúzcoa in some detail on pp. 37–40.

13. Steer, pp. 41–44.

14. According to a pamphlet, *Emigración Vasca* (March 18, 1938), pp. 5–6. Archives of the Basque Government-in-Exile (hereafter BGEA), Paris.

15. Martin Ugalde, in an interview published in Luis y Juan Jime-

nez Aberasturi, *La Guerra en Euzkadi* (Barcelona, 1978), pp. 287–317, describes the flight of his family from Hernani, Guipúzcoa, p. 302.

16. Correspondence with Jaime Marcellan Arrospide in 1980 is the source of this figure.

17. Ugalde, p. 302.

18. Payne, pp. 169–71.

19. This material is found in a pamphlet *Why the Basques Fight Franco* (n.d.), BGEA, Paris. This also appeared in the Catholic journal, *The Tablet* (London), February 27, 1937, p. 422.

20. Payne, p. 171.

21. Ibid., p. 178.

22. Ibid., p. 188.

23. According to the magazine *Gudari* (Bilbao), April 24, 1937, p. 1.

24. Ugalde, p. 304.

25. Payne, p. 188; Jackson, pp. 302–3, 377.

26. This letter, signed by Bronwen Lloyd-Williams and Lydia Mary Gee, of the Save the Children League, appeared in the *Manchester Guardian*, April 9, 1937, p. 6.

27. Payne, p. 179.

28. Rubio, p. 160.

29. The two major newspapers consulted in Euzkadi for material on the Civil War in the north were the Communist paper, *Euzkadi Roja*, which had the largest circulation in Euzkadi in the spring of 1937, and the afternoon daily *La Tarde*, a more moderate Left paper. The PNV newspaper *Euzkadi* was also consulted. The ration figures quoted appeared in *Euzkadi Roja* December 10, 1936, p. 4.

30. Steer, pp. 127–29, and material from interviews.

31. Steer, pp. 127–29.

32. Ibid., p. 90.

33. This discussion of the blockade of Bilbao is based on James Cable, *The Royal Navy and the Siege of Bilbao* (Cambridge, 1979), pp. 44–54.

34. Ibid., p. 76.

35. This letter appeared in the *Manchester Guardian*, April 19, 1937, p. 6.

36. Michael Alpert, "Great Britain and the Blockade of Bilbao," *Anglo-American Contributions to Basque Studies* (Reno: Desert Research Institute, 1977), p. 130.

37. Steer, pp. 196–209.

38. *Euzkadi Roja*, April 21, 1937, p. 1.

39. Steer, p. 128.

40. *Euzkadi Roja*, April 21, 1937, p. 3.

41. Payne, pp. 183–84.

42. According to a testimonial published in *Garaia* (San Sebastián), October 14, 1976, pp. 36–37.

43. Steer, pp. 152–59.
44. Ibid.
45. Steer, p. 167.
46. The bombings of Durango and Guernica are well described and meticulously documented in Herbert Southworth, *Guernica, Guernica* (Berkeley, 1977). The fatalities for Durango are given on page 358.
47. *Euzkadi Roja*, April 8, 1937, p. 1.
48. Alberto de Onaindia, *Experiencias del Exilio: Hombre de Paz en la Guerra* Buenos Aires, 1974), p. 282.
49. *Euzkadi Roja*, June 1, 1937, p. 3.
50. Steer, p. 180.
51. *La Tarde* (Bilbao), April 19, 1937, p. 1.
52. Southworth, pp. 12–16. The low figure is taken from Castor Uriarte Aguirremalloa, *Bombas y Mentiras Sobre Guernica* (Bilbao, 1976), p. 138.
53. Southworth, p. 12.
54. Steer, pp. 184–86.
55. Ibid.
56. John Hope Simpson, *The Refugee Problem* (Oxford, 1937), p. 330, gives a concise description of the organization of the CGT colonies in France.
57. Ibid., p. 331.
58. This column appeared on page 4 of *Frente Popular*, a Communist daily in Santiago, Chile.
59. Published material on the role of the French Left in provisioning Spanish civilians was provided by M. Valmont in an interview in Paris in 1980. The source of the statistics quoted is *Editions de Secours Populaire* (Paris, June 1938), pp. 14–15. Another source in the Archives of the Communist Party in Paris was *Union des Coeurs* (Paris, June 1938), pp. 24–25.
60. *La Croix Rouge de la Démocratie Espagnole* (Paris, June 1938), pp. 36–37, also from the Archives of the Communist Party, listed these colonies as being situated at Puigcerda, Landes, the Gironde, Hérault, the Rhône, Haute-Loire, on the island of Oléron, in Limoges, in Haute-Garonne, Seine Inférieure, two sites in the Loire, and at St. Étienne.
61. Ibid.
62. This letter of 1937 from the private papers of the late Mrs. Lydia Mary Gee, a prominent member of both the "Save the Children Fund" and the Society of Friends, was generously made available to me in 1980 by Miss Ruth Marsden of Northampton, Great Britain.
63. Bowers, pp. 282–83.
64. The publication of the International Brigade, *Volunteers for Liberty* (Barcelona), December 27, 1937, vol. 28, p. 8, describes these projects.
65. Simpson, p. 167.

66. *Euzkadi Roja*, January 9, 1937, p. 1.

67. Onaindia, p. 282; *La Tarde*, January 10, 1937, p. 2.

68. According to Payne, p. 153, quoting Javier Tusell, et al., "Las Elecciones del Frente Popular" (Madrid, 1971), vol. 2, pp. 307–40.

69. *La Tarde*, January 18, 1937, p. 1.

70. Ibid., March 3, 1937, p. 1.

71. Ibid., March 5, 1937, p. 2.

72. Ibid., March 3, 1937, p. 1.

73. This notice appeared in the semi-official organ of the Basque Delegation in Paris, *Euzko Deya, la Voix des Basques* (Paris), April 1, 1937, p. 1.

74. *La Tarde*, March 30, 1937, p. 1.

75. Simpson, p. 166.

76. This is discussed in Juan Iturralde, *El Catolicismo y la Cruzada de Franco* (Toulouse, 1955–56), pp. 268–76.

77. Cable, p. 112.

78. Ibid.

79. *Euzkadi Roja*, May 9, 1937, p. 1.

80. The evacuation of Basque noncombatants is detailed in a report written by F. Rotaeche, *Evacuación* (Barcelona: February 5, 1938), pp. 1–10. BGEA.

81. Ibid., pp. 1–2.

82. Leah Manning, in her autobiography, *A Life for Education* (London, 1970), presents a detailed eye witness account of the evacuation of Basque children to Great Britain.

83. Cable, p. 118.

84. These letters may be found in Yvonne Cloud, *The Basque Children in England* (London, 1937), pp. 1–8.

85. Teresa Pamies, *Los Niños en la Guerra* (Barcelona, 1977), pp. 109–11.

86. But the cruel war goes on
And these dramas mean nothing to it.
Thus, each family kissed its children,
And, with all haste,
Seizing their precious cargo,
The buses departed.
Some children were weeping and others
Were waving goodbye with their little hands.
Their white handkerchiefs seemed like white doves
That in tragic flight fled from the shell of the hunter.
And still the planes and the bombs
Seed terror and death.
The night of that day I went
To my humble attic window,
To my nest, bereft and disordered,
And wrote some words of counsel to my sons.

87. Rotaeche, pp. 7–10.
88. Steer, pp. 328–31.
89. Rotaeche, pp. 3–6.
90. Ibid., p. 3.
91. Cable, p. 150.
92. *Le Peuple*, June 18, 1937, p. 1.
93. Rotaeche, pp. 4–5; Rubio, pp. 56–57.
94. Payne, p. 220.

Chapter Two

1. According to Robert Whealey, "Foreign Intervention in the Spanish Civil War," *The Republic and the Civil War in Spain*, Raymond Carr (London, 1971), p. 214.

2. Luis de Castresana published a moving account of his experiences as a refugee child in France and Belgium, *El Otro Arbol de Guernica* (Madrid, 1967). Following a film version of this book, he wrote a second book on this theme, *La Verdad Sobre 'El Otro Arbol de Guernica'* (Bilbao, 1972), which contains the passenger list of the March expedition, pp. 246–47.

3. "Euzkadi Liberated"; "Proletarian Brothers, United"; "We must Fortify."

4. *La Tarde* (Bilbao), March 19, 1937, p. 3.

5. The leave-taking is described in Castresana, *El Otro Arbol de Guernica* (London, 1972), pp. 58–60, in the words of a boy of eleven.

6. *La Tarde* (Bilbao), March 21, 1937, p. 1.

7. Ibid.

8. A detailed document, *Informe* (Bayonne, October 19, 1937), pp. 1–12, from the Housing Minister, Sr. Zarrabeitia, to Minister of Justice and Culture, Sr. Jesús Leizaola, from the Basque Government-in-Exile Archives (BGEA) is the source of these statistics.

9. Charles Mowat, *New Cambridge Modern History* (Cambridge, 1962), pp. 541–44.

10. These events were well documented in the Leftist press, with the Communist daily, *L'Humanité*, Paris, May 9, 1937, p. 1, and May 28, 1937, p. 1, as well as the Socialist daily, *Le Peuple*, Paris, June 18, 1937, p. 1, being the sources for this section. Srta. Panchica Berraza of Irún kindly shared her collection of the French press for 1936–39 with me.

11. *L'Humanité*, May 30, 1937, p. 1.

12. Ibid., May 5, 1937, p. 2, and May 15, 1937, p. 1.

13. According to *Editions du Secours Populaire* (Paris, June 1938), pp. 21–22.

14. These totals are found from an analysis of two documents from the BGEA: *Emigración Vasca* (Paris, March 18, 1938), pp. 5–6, and the more extensive *Colonias de Niños Expatriados* (Bayonne, February 14, 1938), pp. 1–56.

15. John Hope Simpson, *The Refugee Problem* (Oxford, 1937), p. 331.
16. *L'Humanité*, April 2, 1937, p. 1, and passim.
17. *L'Humanité, Le Peuple*, May 5, 1937, p. 1, and passim.
18. Castresana, pp. 84–86.
19. *Le Peuple*, April 27, 1937, p. 1.
20. A detailed account of the colony is entitled *Memoria de la Colonia Infantil de Mas Éloi* (Limoges, 1937). This was made available by Piru Ajuria of the PNV in Bilbao in 1980. Reference here is to pp. 1–19.
21. Ibid.
22. This letter from Comrade Ranz to the Director of Social Assistance Gracia, now in Paris, dated November 24, 1937, is from the BGEA.
23. This final letter from Comrade Ranz to Director of Social Assistance Landaburu, dated November 24, 1939, is in the BGEA.
24. *Euzkadi Roja*, May 6, 1937, p. 1.
25. *Le Peuple*, May 5, 1937, p. 1.
26. Ibid., May 5, 1937, p. 1.
27. *L'Oeuvre*, May 13, 1937; May 9, 1937, p. 1.
28. *Çe Soir*, June 15, 1937, p. 1.
29. *L'Humanité*, June 15, 1937, p. 1.
30. Simpson, pp. 331–32.
31. Ibid., p. 333.
32. *Colonias de Niños Expatriados*, pp. 30–32.
33. Catholic and PNV assistance to Basque children in France was reported in *Le Petit Jour*, April 30, 1937, p. 1, passim, usually by correspondent Pierre Dumas. The story of this help is also detailed in Don Alberto de Onaindia, *Experiencias del Exilio: Hombre de Paz en la Guerra* (Buenos Aires, 1974) pp. 287–90.
34. Stanley Payne, *Basque Nationalism* (Reno, 1975), pp. 187–88.
35. *Euzko Deya*, (Paris), March 11, 1937, p. 2.
36. Ibid.
37. *Euzko Deya*, May 10, 1937, p. 1.
38. Material for this section comes from an interview with the widow of Vicente Amezaga, published in the periodical *Garaia* (San Sebastián), October 14, 1976, pp. 42–43.
39. Ibid.
40. These circumstances are described in Herbert Southworth, *Guernica, Guernica* (Berkeley, 1977), pp. 152–55.
41. Ibid.
42. This eyewitness material was provided by Madame Renée de Monbrison in personal correspondence of May 4, 1980. Mme. de Monbrison was a founder of SIFERE, an aid organization which merged with the Comité de Coordination d'Aide à l'Espagne. Dur-

ing the Spanish Civil War, Mme. de Monbrison worked closely with the British Quakers through Miss Edith Pye.

43. F. Rotaeche, *Informe* (Bayonne, February 3, 1938), pp. 1–2.

44. This material appears in a pamphlet of the Ligue Internationale des Amies des Basques (hereafter LIAB), (Paris, 1938), pp. 1–4, and from an interview with Claude Bourdet in Paris in 1980. Bourdet was treasurer of the Committee for Civil and Religious Peace in Spain, and was himself a prominent journalist. An example of the work of the Committee appears in *L'Aube*, May 8, 1937, p. 1, entitled, "Pour le Peuple Basque." An account of the atrocities of Durango and Guernica followed, signed by François Mauriac, Georges Bidault, Jacques Maritain, Emmanuel Mounier, Paul Vignaux, Claude Bourdet, and others.

45. According to a pamphlet published by the Comité National Catholique de Secours à Réfugiés d'Espagne, entitled *Report no. 1* (Bordeaux, June 1939), pp. 1–8, in the BGEA.

46. Ibid.

47. *Le Petit Jour*, April 30, 1937, p. 2.

48. *Le Jour*, July 25, 1937, p. 1.

49. Onaindia, p. 201; two interviews with Don Alberto de Onaindia in St.-Jean-de-Luz, 1979–80.

50. Señora Jesusa Castillo, infirmary cook at La Citadelle, supplied this information in an interview in Bermeo, Vizcaya, in 1979.

51. *Garaia*, October 14, 1976, p. 42.

52. *Le Petit Gironde*, June 22, 1938, p. 1.

53. The preceding material comes from interviews with people who lived at La Citadelle as children, and from a very detailed *Rapport Général sur le Colonie St.-Jean-Pied-de-Port* (1939), pp. 1–9. BGEA.

54. Castillo, 1979.

55. *Garaia*, October 14, 1976, p. 43.

56. From an anonymous handwritten letter, 1938. BGEA.

57. *Euzko Deya*, October 23, 1938, p. 1.

58. Pedro de Basaldua, *En España Sale el Sol* (Buenos Aires, 1946), pp. 261–64; *Garaia*, October 14, 1976, p. 43; and an interview with Jesús Pascual Eraso, son of the art professor at the colony, in Bilbao, 1979.

59. Basaldua, pp. 298–99.

60. This material comes from an interview with the president of the Basque Government-in-Exile, Jesús Leizaola, in San Sebastián, in 1979.

61. *Rapport Générale sur le Colonie St.-Jean-Pied-de-Port*, pp. 1–9.

62. *Colonias de Niños Expatriados*, pp. 23–24.

63. Simpson, pp. 332–33.

64. *Informe*, Sr. Zarrabeitia, p. 10.

65. Pamphlet, LIAB, p. 2.

66. Sra. Irene Arrien of Guernica, formerly a member of *Elai Alai*, provided this information in an interview in Guernica in 1979.

67. Elena Castendyk, "Refugee Children in Europe" *Social Service Review* (Chicago, 1939), no. 4, pp. 588–91.

68. *Euzko Deya*, October 12, 1938, p. 1.

69. A report entitled *Decreto*, prepared by Asistencia Social (Paris, July 22, 1938) BGEA.

70. A letter from Senor Gracia, Director of Asistencia Social, to President Aguirre, dated February 1, 1938. BGEA.

71. A letter from Ambassador Azcarate to Sr. Gracia, dated February 10, 1938. BGEA.

72. From the response of Sr. Gracia to Sr. Azcarate, February 21, 1938. BGEA.

73. These anecdotes are found in the *Reportage de Colonias Vascas*, undated. BGEA.

74. Cable, p. 155.

75. Mowat, *New Cambridge Modern History*, pp. 543–45.

76. Rubio, pp. 51–54.

77. Ibid.

78. Simpson, p. 328.

79. *Euzko Deya*, July 2, 1938, p. 1.

80. *Informe*, October 19, 1937, pp. 1–12.

81. According to the document, *Censo, Vascos Refugiados en Francia*, December 1937. BGEA. These figures are given:

In fifteen colonies sponsored by the Basque government	3,940
Maintained as families by Basque government	1,800
Basque children's colonies	816
Children in adoptive homes	7,000
Artist colonies (Eresoinka, Elai Alai)	1,000
Basques in three residences of PNV	440
Maintained as families by PNV	1,500
In Spanish refugee colonies	400
In French refugee colonies	1,500
Living on their own	6,000
	24,000

82. *Colonias de Niños Expatriados.*

83. *Censo General de Acogidos en las Residencias Vascas* (Paris, April 1939). BGEA.

84. Ibid.

85. *Presupuesto del Gobierno de Euzkadi*, January 1940. BGEA.

86. *Basque Refugees, A Preliminary Survey* (Bayonne, not dated, though probably mid-1939).

87. *Relación de Refugiados Vascos Procedentes de Cataluña* (November 1937). BGEA. In this report, a file with the names of 4,687 persons

from Guipúzcoa, including 1,920 from San Sebastián and 1,653 from Irún, compiled by the Inter-Municipal Commission, was described.

88. *Informe*, October 19, 1937.

89. According to the *Nota Obtenida del Informe del Departamento de Asistencia Social en Cataluña Correspondiente a Agosto de 1938*. BGEA.

90. Howard Kerschner, *Quaker Service in Modern War* (New York, 1950), p. 29, is the source of this eyewitness account.

91. *Colonias de Niños Expatriados*, p. 40.

92. The work of the International Red Cross is summarized in the *Rapport Complementaire sur l'Activité du Comité International de la Croix-Rouge Rélative à la Guerre Civil en Espagne* (Geneva, April 1938), pp. 29–33.

93. Kerschner, pp. 56–64.

94. Ibid., p. 176.

95. Ibid., p. 156.

96. From an interview with Claude Bourdet, Paris, 1980.

97. According to the *LIAB Memorandum*, 1938. BGEA.

98. LIAB *Report: 1939*, pp. 1–4. BGEA.

99. Ibid.

100. M. Bourdet.

101. The brochure for the Foster Parent Plan was kindly made available by Sr. Javier Rubio.

102. M. Bourdet.

103. Ibid.

104. Monbrison (see note 42 in this chapter).

105. Simpson, p. 167.

106. Ibid., p. 331.

Chapter Three

1. Herbert Matthew, *Half of Spain Died* (New York, 1973), p. 149; Robert Whealey, "Foreign Intervention in the Spanish Civil War," in Raymond Carr *The Republic and the Civil War in Spain* (London, 1971), p. 214.

2. "Why the Basques Fight Franco", *The Tablet*, February 27, 1937, p. 442.

3. Michael Alpert, "Los Niños Vascos en Inglaterra," *Sábado Grafico* (Madrid, June 1975), p. 18, discusses this relationship. He also expands this subject in "Great Britain and the Blockade of Bilbao, April 1937," *Anglo-American Contributions to Basque Studies: Essays in Honor of Jon Bilbao* (Reno: Desert Research Institute, 1977), pp. 127–33.

4. Richard Ellis, "Four Thousand Basque Children," *The Lancet* (London), May 29, 1937, pp. 1303–7.

5. Alpert, "Great Britain and the Blockade of Bilbao, April 1937," p. 128.

6. A full set of the minutes taken at the meetings from 1937 until 1942 of the Basque Children's Committee of the National Joint Com-

mittee for Spanish Relief was made available by Ms. Yolanda Genge of the Hague, Netherlands. Those quoted are from the meeting on February 25, 1937, p. 1.

7. Ibid.

8. Minutes, NJCSR, March 22, 1937, p. l.

9. This interesting diplomatic initiative is described in James Cable, *The Royal Navy and the Siege of Bilbao* (Cambridge, 1979), p. 78.

10. London *Times*, April 28, 1937, p. 1; April 29, 1937, p. 1.

11. According to the British Cabinet meeting of April 28, 1937, as quoted in Cable, pp. 102–4.

12. *Minutes*, National Joint Committee, May 15, 1937, p. 1.

13. In her autobiography, *A Life for Education* (London, 1970), Dame Leah Manning details her work in Bilbao in arranging for the evacuation of 4,000 Basque children to Britain. The difficulties placed by the Home Office and by Mr. Stevenson on this undertaking are noted on pages 125–27.

14. *Euzkadi Roja* (Bilbao), April 30, 1937, p. 1.

15. *Times*, April 30, 1937, p. 8.

16. *La Tarde*, May 10, 1937, p. 1.

17. *Euzkadi Roja*, May 7, 1937, p. 4.

18. Richard Ellis, "Basque Children in England," *Guy's Hospital Gazette* (London, June 1937), p. 6.

19. Ibid.

20. Ricardo González Etxegaray, *La Marina Mercante y el Tráfico Maritimo en la Guerra Civil* (Madrid, 1977), pp. 121–22.

21. This letter appeared in the *Manchester Guardian*, May 19, 1937, p. 12.

22. According to a telegram from Leah Manning to Dr. Richard Ellis, contained in the personal album of Dr. Ellis, kindly made available in 1980 by his son Stephen Ellis of Hertfordshire.

23. Bishop Mateo Múgica's letter was published in *The Tablet*, April 28, 1937, p. 682.

24. Manning, pp. 125–26.

25. *Euzkadi Roja*, May 21, 1937, p. 4.

26. Ellis, "Basque Children in England," p. 25.

27. *The British Medical Journal* (London), April 29, 1937, p. 985.

28. According to H. C. Maurice Williams, Medical Officer of Health and Port to the County Borough of Southampton, in his report, "The Arrival of the Basque Children at the Port of Southampton," in *British Medical Journal* (London), June 12, 1937, pp. 1207–10.

29. This is detailed in an unpublished manuscript by a young Basque who wrote a retrospective history of his experiences. Amador Diaz-Campillo, "When 4,000 Basques Landed in Southampton"

(not dated), pp. 1–3, describes the rigorous measures to control vermin on the children, and their aftermath.

30. Alpert, "Los Niños Vascos," p. 19.

31. *The Daily Telegraph* (Southampton), May 24, 1937, pp. 13–14.

32. *Times* (London), May 24, 1937, p. 11.

33. Ibid.; *The Daily Telegraph*, pp. 13–14; and Alpert, "Los Niños Vascos," p. 19.

34. Yvonne Cloud, in *Basque Children in England* (London, 1937), pp. 33–55, gives an eyewitness account of the organization of the Stoneham Camp during its first few weeks. This slim green volume, complete with clear photographs, was a prized possession of several of the Basques interviewed who had stayed on in Britain.

35. Ibid., pp. 38–40.

36. Ibid., pp. 42–45.

37. Ibid., p. 37.

38. This material comes from interviews with nine Basques whose parents were Socialists.

39. Ibid.

40. According to Eric Pittman, treasurer at Stoneham Camp, and later to be treasurer of the West London Basque Children's Committee.

41. Diaz-Campillo, p. 4.

42. Ellis in *The Lancet*, May 29, 1937, p. 1303.

43. These anecdotes were supplied by Professor Helen Grant, of Cambridge. Mrs. Grant visited the children in Southampton, and was associated with the Basque Children's Hostel in Birmingham, 1937–40.

44. This was supplied by the late Manuel Irujo, of the Basque Autonomous Government, in an interview in Pamplona in 1980.

45. Ibid.

46. This section is based on interviews with Basques who had been teen-aged boys upon evacuation.

47. Diaz-Campillo, p. 3.

48. Pittman; Cloud, pp. 41–49.

49. *Colonias de Niños Expatriados* (Bayonne, February 14, 1938), pp. 47–50. BGEA.

50. According to the Minutes of the Basque Children's Committee, July 5, 1938, pp. 4–5.

51. Minutes, July 30, 1939.

52. *Memoria, Junta Provisional por Repatriación de los Menores Expatriados*, 1932–39 (Diputación de Vizcaya, Publicaciones de la Excelentisima Diputación Provincial de Vizcaya, Bilbao), pp. 23–24.

53. Grant interview.

54. Minutes, BCC, June 7, 1937, pp. 2–5; and according to the *Basque Camp Report* no. 1, June 11, 1937, p. 1. This series of reports from the site director at Stoneham Camp are from the Genge Collection.

55. Minutes, BCC, June 5, 1937, p. 2.
56. *Basque Camp Report* no. 5, June 27, 1937, p. 1.
57. *Basque Camp Report* no. 11, August 17, 1937, p. 1.
58. Minutes, BCC, July 20, 1937, p. 2.
59. Ibid., July 29, 1937, p. 4; February 8, 1938, pp. 6–7.
60. *The Tablet*, April 28, 1937, p. 682.
61. Ibid., June 19, 1937, p. 894.
62. Interviews with children (now adults) from the Socialist group, in 1980.
63. Pedro Basaldua, *En España Sale el Sol* (Buenos Aires, 1946), p. 290.
64. *The Tablet*, May 22, 1937, p. 728.
65. According to Don Benito Larragoetxea, in an interview in Oñate, Guipúzcoa in 1980. Don Benito was assigned to Weston Manor, Isle of Wight.
66. Basaldua, pp. 292–93.
67. This section is based on interviews with several Basque women who lived at Weston Manor in 1937–38, with Don Benito, and with Laura Markham, who was cook's helper at the colony.
68. *Basque Camp Report*, no. 11, August 17, 1937, p. 1.
69. Minutes, BCC, July 5, August 21, 1937, p. 5.
70. *New Statesman and Nation* (London), August 21, 1937, vol. 14, pp. 277–78.
71. Minutes, BCC, July 20, 1937, p. 2.
72. According to Eric Pittman, treasurer of the West London BCC.
73. *Program*, Wyndham Theatre, London, April 22, 1938.
74. Minutes, BCC, May 3, 1938, p. 3.
75. Ibid., July 5, 1937, p. 1.
76. Ibid., July 20, 1937, p. 2.
77. Ibid., October 13, 1938, p. 2.
78. Ibid., February 5, 1938, p. 1.
79. Ibid., p. 2.
80. Ibid.
81. Ibid.
82. Ibid., p. 3.
83. According to the *Bulletin no. 11*, entitled, "They've Not All Gone Home," National Joint Committee for Spanish Relief (London, March 1938), p. 2.
84. Minutes, BCC, October 22, 1938, p. 2.
85. Ibid., July 25, 1938, p. 2.
86. Ibid., February 8, 1938, p. 4.
87. Ibid., July 5, 1937, p. 1.
88. This request appears in the BCC Minutes for December 9, 1938, p. 2.
89. Material for this section comes from interviews with the co-director of this colony, Mrs. Emma Plank, its treasurer, Eric Pittman, and one Basque who lived in this colony as a child.

90. This anecdote was related by Mrs. Plank in an interview in Oakland in 1979.
91. Emma Plank, "We Bargained for Futures," *Progressive Education* (October, 1944), pp. 17–19.
92. Ibid.
93. According to a letter of appeal written by Eric Pittman, London, October 20, 1939.
94. According to the Treasurer's Report, April 1939, prepared by Eric Pittman.
95. According to the Financial Statement of the BCC, July 25, 1939, from the Genge Collection.
96. This material is found in a *List of Basque Children*, published by the BCC, December 1945, from the Basque Children's Committee Papers in the Genge Collection.

Chapter Four

1. Emile Cammaerts, *The Keystone of Europe* (London, 1939), pp. 192–97.
2. *Le Peuple* (Brussels), April 27, 1937, p. 1.
3. Ibid., May 14, 1937, p. 1.
4. Ibid., May 20, 1937.
5. Luis de Castresana, *El Otro Arbol de Guernica* (Madrid, 1967; London, 1972), p. 83.
6. F. Rotaeche, *Evacuación* (Barcelona, February 5, 1938), p. 6. BGEA.
7. *Le Peuple*, May 20, 1937, p. 1.
8. This is the total reported in the document *Colonias de Niños Expatriados* (Bayonne, February 14, 1938),p. 46. BGEA.
9. *La Voix du Peuple* (Brussels), July 7, 1937, p. 1.
10. Ibid., July 1, 1937, p. 1.
11. Ibid.
12. Ibid., July 8, 1937, p. 1.
13. Ibid., July 1, 1937, p. 1.
14. Ibid., July 29, 1937, p. 1.
15. *La Voix du Peuple*, July 8, 1937, p. 1.
16. *Le Peuple*, May 22, 1937, p. 1.
17. Ibid.
18. *Le Peuple*, July 2, 1937, p. 1.
19. Ibid.
20. *Colonias de Niños Expatriados*, p. 46.
21. Correspondence from Msgr. Múgica to Ernest Cardinal Van Roey was made available by Martin Aguirre. These letters also appeared in the *Gazete von Antwerpen* (Antwerp), May 27, 1937, p. 1, a Flemish newspaper.
22. This document from the Archives of the Archbishop of Malines was made available by Martin Aguirre of Mortsel. It is undated.

23. This document, entitled "List I: Enfants Basques Placés par le Comité de son Eminence" (n.d.), is from the Archives of the Archbishop of Malines.
24. Also from the Archives of the Archbishop of Malines.
25. Alberto de Onaindia, *Experiencias del Exilio: Hombre de Paz en la Guerra* (Buenos Aires, 1974), p. 287.
26. *Gazete von Antwerpen*, May 31, 1937, p. 1.
27. Ibid.
28. According to a letter from Msgr. LeClef to Izaurrieta, May 13, 1937. Archives of the Archbishop of Malines.
29. Letter from Izaurrieta to LeClef, May 24, 1937.
30. Letter from Izaurrieta to LeClef, June 7, 1937.
31. Letter from Izaurrieta to LeClef, June 17, 1937.
32. *Gazete von Antwerpen*, June 30, 1937, p. 1.
33. These figures are extracted from List I of note 23.
34. Ibid.
35. This material is based on interviews with two of the Basque priests sent into exile in Belgium with the Basque children, Don Jesús Orbe, and Don Dionisio Oartete, and the periodical of the Basque clergy, *Anayak* (St.-Jean-de-Luz), April 1–15, 1939, p. 24.
36. Don Jesús Orbe, interview, Bilbao, 1979.
37. Pedro de Basaldua, *En España Sale el Sol* (Buenos Aires, 1946), p. 287.
38. Castresana, pp. 171–75.
39. This material comes from interviews with two teachers sent to Belgium (Srta. Carmela LeClerq, and Sra. Begoña Olabeaga), interviewed in San Sebastián in 1980.
40. Quoted in a letter writen by Cardinal Van Roey on November 11, 1938. Archives of the Archbishop of Malines.
41. This is found in a document *Politica No. 51*, March 20, 1938. Archives of the Archbishop of Malines.
42. According to a letter from Ambassador Ruiz to Minister Leizaola dated January 18, 1938. BGEA.
43. Castresana, p. 94.
44. See note 8 in this chapter.
45. According to the writer's work on second-language acquisition in *Schooling and Language Minority Children* (Los Angeles, 1981), pp. 83–116.

Chapter Five

1. David Cattell, "Soviet Military Aid to the Republic," in *The Spanish Civil War*, ed. Gabriel Jackson (Boston, 1967), pp. 70–76.
2. Ibid.
3. George Steer, *The Tree of Gernika* (London, 1938), pp. 35–38, describes the extent and utility of Soviet war materials sent to Euzkadi.

4. The first full reports of the proposed expedition to the Soviet Union were printed in the Communist *Euzkadi Roja* of May 23, 1937, in a long article, pp. 4–5, although *La Tarde* (May 8) published a short piece two weeks earlier, on p. 5.

5. Martin Ugalde is the source of this anecdote, from an interview in Fuenterrabia in 1980.

6. This material comes from interviews in Mexico City in 1979 with five Basques who were sent from Spain to the Soviet Union in March 1937.

7. The evacuation of Basque children to the Soviet Union was fully reported in the Soviet press in 1937–38. This account appeared in *Pravda* (Moscow), June 23, 1937, p. 6.

8. Stanley Payne, *Basque Nationalism* (Reno, 1975), p. 185.

9. Payne, pp. 189, 194.

10. Ibid., p. 199.

11. *Euzkadi Roja*, April 2, 1937, p. 3.

12. Ibid., May 8, 1937, p. 5.

13. Alberto de Onaindia, *Experiencias del Exilio: Hombre de Paz en la Guerra* (Buenos Aires, 1974), p. 294.

14. *Euzkadi Roja*, May 25, 1937, p. 5.

15. Ibid., May 30, 1937, p. 3.

16. Ibid., June 11, 1937, p. 5.

17. Letter from Jesús Leizaola to the Spanish ambassador in Paris, October 30, 1937. BGEA.

18. *Pravda*, June 23, 1937, p. 6.

19. Ibid., June 25, 1937, p. 6.

20. Ibid., June 28, 1937, p. 6.

21. Ibid., July 6, 1937, p. 6.

22. Ibid., July 17, 1937, p. 6.

23. Ibid., August 14, 1937, p. 6.

24. Jaime Camino, *Intimas Conversaciones con la Pasionaria* (Barcelona, 1977), 172–174; translated by the writer.

25. *Pravda*, September 29, 1937, p. 6.

26. Ibid., March 31, 1938, p. 6.

27. Jesús Hernández, *La Grande Trahison* (Paris, 1953), p. 183.

28. Rafael Miralles, *Españoles en Rusia* (Madrid, 1947), pp. 206–13.

29. Javier Rubio, *La Emigración de la Guerra Civil de 1936–1939* (Madrid, 1977) pp. 107–108.

30. The figure quoted in Valentín González, *La Vie el la Mort en URSS, 1939–1949* (Paris, 1950), p. 184, appears high.

31. This section is based upon the booklet, *Colonias de Niños Expatriados* (Bayonne, February 14, 1938), and on interviews with nineteen Basques in San Sebastián, Bilbao, and Eibar who had been evacuated to the Soviet Union in 1937–38, and had lived there

twenty years. These interviews were conducted in 1979–80. A final interview was conducted with a Sovietico in Madrid in 1982.

32. *Euzko Deya* (Paris), July 9, 1939, p. 1.

33. These appeared in the *Literaturnaya Gazeta*, March 10, 1937, p. 9; and June 30, 1937, pp. 3, 5.

34. This material was drawn from interviews with a ballet teacher from Eibar, who had spent twenty years in the Soviet Union, part of which as a member of the Moscow Ballet.

35. González, p. 190.

36. Hernández, pp. 222–23.

37. Aleksandr Solzhenitsyn, *Gulag Archipelago*, vol. III, p. 51; vol. I, p. 86.

38. Colin Colomer, *Historia Secreta del la Segunda Republica* (Barcelona, 1959), pp. 219–25. Colomer paints a dismal picture of the life of the Spanish children evacuated to the Soviet Union.

39. Teresa Pamies, *Los Niños en la Guerra* (Barcelona, 1977), p. 119.

Chapter Six

1. *Euzkadi Roja*, May 16, 1937, p. 1.

2. *Colonias de Niños Expatriados* (Bayonne, February 14, 1938), pp. 51–52.

3. This colony is reported on in the *Rapport Complèmentaire de la XVII Conférence Internationale* (Stockholm, August 1948), p. 31, published by the Comité Internationale de la Croix Rouge.

4. *Colonias de Niños Expatriados*, pp. 51–52.

5. According to the *Memoria, Junta Provisional de Protección de Menores*, 1932–39 (Diputación de Vizcaya, 1940), p. 24.

6. Information on the Basque children's colonies in Denmark was found in the Archives of the Ministerio de Asuntos Extranjero in Madrid. Javier Rubio, in the Ministerio de Cultura, assisted me in locating certain documents, and shared useful documents in his personal collection with me in 1980–81. This information is contained in Letter no. 135 from the Spanish Republican delegate in Copenhagen, Sr. Salvador, to the minister of state in Barcelona. This three-page letter summarized the history of the refugee children in Denmark. The Matteoti Fund referred to monies from Social Democrats and the Amsterdam International, gathered to assist emigration for non-Communist Leftist trade unionists and political prisoners, according to John Hope Simpson, *The Refugee Problem* (Oxford, 1937), p. 189.

7. According to a letter from the ambassador from Germany to Denmark, Alfred Tveede, to the minister of foreign affairs for Nationalist Spain, in Burgos, April 9, 1938, pp. 1–3.

8. See note 6 above, Letter no. 135.

9. This data comes from a list provided by Javier Rubio in 1981, entitled *Relación de Niños Que Se Encuentran en la Colonia de Copenhagen* (Odense, June 31, 1938), pp. 1–3.

10. According to a letter from the Spanish Red Cross, Burgos, to the minister of state of Nationalist Spain, Sr. Sagroniz (Burgos, August 2, 1937).

11. Ibid.

12. Letter from Ambassador Tveede to the Spanish Nationalist foreign minister, April 9, 1938, pp. 1–3.

13. Ibid.

14. Ibid.

15. Ibid.

16. See note 6, above, Letter no. 135.

17. According to the newspaper *B.T.* (Copenhagen), May 24, 1938, p. 1.

18. Letter from Tveede to the Spanish minister of Foreign Affairs, August 10, 1938, p. 1.

19. See note 6, above, Letter no. 135.

20. According to *Dispatch no. 274* from the Spanish Republican Delegation in Copenhagen to the Spanish minister of state, Barcelona, September 27, 1938.

21. *Literary Digest* (New York), June 17, 1937, p. 4. See also F. Jay Taylor, "American Catholic and Protestant Attitudes toward the Civil War," *The Spanish Civil War*, ed. Gabriel Jackson (Boston, 1967), pp. 99–100.

22. Taylor, p. 99.

23. *Euzkadi Roja*, May 23, 1937, p. 1.

24. Taylor, pp. 90–91.

25. *America*, June 5, 1937, p. 198.

26. Ibid., June 19, 1937, p. 242.

27. Ibid., April 9, 1938, pp. 4–5.

28. *Literary Digest*, June 17, 1937, p. 4.

29. Ibid.

30. According to a letter from José Eiguren dated August 11, 1979.

31. William A. Douglass and Jon Bilbao, *Amerikanuak* (Reno, 1975), p. 361.

32. This material was made available by Javier Rubio, and appears in a Conference by Julieta Cabeza, entitled *México y los Niños Españoles*, in Ediciones Amigos de México (Valencia, December 26, 1937), p. 5.

33. *Boletín del Comité de Ayuda a los Niños del Pueblo Español* (Mexico, D.F., September 1937), no. 3, pp. 25–27. This was kindly made available by Emeterio Paya-Valera of Morelia.

34. Cabeza, 3.

35. According to Emeterio Paya-Valera, in "La Historia de los Niños Españoles de Morelia, *Elite* (Morelia), October 22, 1978, p. 7.

36. Ibid.
37. Cabeza, pp. 5–7.
38. Ibid., pp. 7–8.
39. Paya-Valera,"La Historia" (November 19, 1978), p. 7.
40. Cabeza, pp. 28–30.
41. *Boletín del Comité*, p. 24.
42. Vera Foulkes, *Los Niños de Morelia y la Escuela España-México* (México, D.F., 1953); Dolores Pla, *Los Niños de Morelia* (México, 1983).
43. The memoirs of Roberto Reyes-Perez, *La Vida de los Niños Iberos en la Patria de Lázaro Cárdenas* (México, D.F., 1940), describes in detail the school's vicissitudes during and after the term of Cárdenas.
44. Paya-Valera, "La Historia."
45. Reyes-Perez, p. 23.
46. Foulkes, p. 27.
47. Paya-Valera, "La Historia." February 25, 1979, p. 9.
48. Perhaps the strongest statement of this prejudice is found in Ricardo Alcazar, *El Gachupín, Problema Maximo de México* (México, D.F., 1934), pp. 40–48.
49. Paya-Valera, "La Historia," February 25, 1979, p. 5.
50. Rubio, p. 252.
51. For example, the editorial in *Excelsior* (México, D.F.), June 7, 1937, p. 5, written by Liciencado Querido.
52. This discussion is based on several sources, including Michael Kenny, "Twentieth Century Spanish Expatriates in Mexico; An Urban Sub-Culture," *Anthropological Quarterly* (1962), pp. 170–75; Patricia (Weiss) Fagan, *Exiles and Citizens*, Latin American Monographs (Austin, 1973), pp. 40–48; and Carmen Icazurriaga, "Españoles de Veracruz y Vascos del Distrito Federal," *Inmigrantes y Refugiados Españoles en México (Siglo XX)* (Tlalpan, 1979), pp. 167–223.
53. Kenny, pp. 170–75.
54. Reyes-Perez, p. 24.
55. *Excelsior*, June 6, 1937, p. 1; June 7, 1937, p. 5.
56. Lázaro Cárdenas, *Apuntes: 1937*(Mexico, D.F., 1972), pp. 369, 384, 393.
57. *Rapport Complémentaire* (See note 3).
58. Paya-Valera, "La Historia," March 18, 1979, p. 5.
59. Ibid.
60. *Rapport Complémentaire*.
61. Paya-Valera, "La Historia," January 21, 1979, p. 5.
62. Ibid., January 14, 1979, p. 5.
63. Reyes-Perez, pp. 79–85.
64. Ibid., p. 54.
65. Ibid., p. 131.
66. Ibid., p. 52.
67. Paya-Valera, "La Historia," February 11, 1979, p. 9.
68. Ibid., December 31, 1978, p. 9.

69. Reyes-Perez, p. 88.
70. Foulkes, pp. 30–31.
71. Paya-Valera, "La Historia," March 11, 1979, p. 13.
72. Ibid., February 4, 1979, p. 14.
73. This section is based on interviews with eleven of the Basques who lived in the Escuela España-México in Morelia as children. All were interviewed in 1979 in Mexico City.
74. (Weiss) Fagan, p. 55.

Chapter Seven

1. *Gaceta del Norte* (Bilbao), July 11, 1937, p. 1.
2. Ibid., passim.
3. Ibid., July 23, 1937, p. 2.
4. Ibid., July 27, 1937, p. 2.
5. Ibid., August 4 and 5, 1937, p. 2.
6. Ibid., August 5, 1937, p. 2.
7. Ibid.
8. Quoted in Pedro Basaldua, *En España Sale el Sol* (Buenos Aires, 1946), pp. 265–313.
9. *Gaceta del Norte*, October 19, 1937, p. 1.
10. Robert P. Clark, *The Basques: The Franco Years and Beyond* (Reno, 1979), pp. 80–84.
11. *Gaceta del Norte*, October 11, 1937, pp. 3, 11.
12. Ibid., October 14, 1937, p. 3.
13. Ibid., October 19, 1937, p. 5.
14. Ibid., October 23, 1937, p. 6; also noted is that the USSR had spent two million rubles on the child refugees.
15. Ibid., October 28, 1937, pp. 2, 4.
16. Ibid., p. 4.
17. *Sobre Niños, Mujeres y Ancianos*, author unknown, Archives of the Ministry of Interior (Madrid, n.d.), pp. 1–4.
18. *Gaceta del Norte*, September 7, 1937, p. 1.
19. Ibid., September 10, 1937, p. 1.
20. Ibid., September 4, 1937, p. 3.
21. Minutes of the Junta Provisional de Protección de Menores (Bilbao, September 25, 1937), pp. 118–122. Archives of the Diputación de Vizcaya.
22. *Gaceta del Norte*, October 1937, passim.
23. Ibid., November 29, 1937, p. 1.
24. *Euzko Deya*, February 20, 1938, p. 1.
25. Information volunteered by Don Alberto de Onaindia in an interview in St.-Jean-de-Luz in 1980.
26. This discussion is based on an article by Isidro Griful, "La Tragedia de los Niños Vascos en el Extranjero," *Razón y Fe*, a Catholic publication (San Sebastián), April 1938, no. 483, p. 402.

27. José Antonio Aguirre to Angel Ossorio, Paris, September 3, 1937. BGEA.

28. *Euzko Deya*, August 20, 1937, p. 1.

29. Census Form, 1937. BGEA.

30. This document of eighteen pages, *Censo y Estadistica de Expatriados*, written by Pablo de Azkue to Elias Etxeberria (Bayonne, September 27, 1937) details the position of the Basque government on repatriation. BGEA.

31. Diplomatic note to the information office of the Secretaria General de Su Excelencia el Jefe del Estado (SIFNE 18335), October 28, 1937.

32. This was noted in a letter from Sr. Uranga to José Antonio Aguirre, August 14, 1937, pp. 1–2. BGEA.

33. *Rapport Complémentaire Relative à la Guerre Civile en Espagne*, Comité International de la Croix Rouge (Geneva, May 1948), p. 31.

34. *Memoria, Junta Provisional de Protección de Menores de Vizcaya, 1932–39* (Diputación de Vizcaya, 1940), p. 22.

35. *Gaceta del Norte*, November 6, 1937, p. 4.

36. The headline in full read: "Today, Our Children are Arriving, Rescued from the Anarchist-Separatist Kidnapping," in *Gaceta del Norte*, November 13, 1937, p. 1.

37. *The Tablet*, May 22, 1937, p. 728.

38. *New Statesman and Review*, May 24, 1937, p. 1.

39. Minutes of the Basque Children's Committee (BCC), July 5, 1937, p. 3.

40. Sir Nairne Stewart-Sandeman, quoted in the *Bulletin of the National Joint Committee*, no. 11, March 1938, p. 2.

41. According to the Foreign Office Report 371 21372, noted in James Cable, *The Royal Navy and the Siege of Bilbao* (Cambridge, 1979), p. 155. Later BCC reports in the *Times* (London) noted only thirty-nine requests had been received in two months (September 6, 1937).

42. Cable, p. 106.

43. Minutes, BCC, July 28, 1937, pp. 1–2.

44. *Times* (London), August 20, 1937, p. 6.

45. BCC Minutes, July 28, 1937, p. 2.

46. Ibid., September 20, 1937, pp. 1–2.

47. Ibid., October 1, 1937, pp. 1–8.

48. Letter from Sr. Uranga to Juan Gracia, August 14, 1937, pp. 1–2. BGEA.

49. Ibid.

50. *Gaceta del Norte*, August 14, 16, 17, 1937, p. 3.

51. See note 30.

52. This section is based on BCC Minutes, October 21, 1937, pp. 2–4, and *The Tablet*, October 30, 1937, p. 606.

53. *News-Chronicle*, October 24, 1937, p. 3.

54. *Times* (London), November 13, 1937, p. 3.
55. Ibid.
56. Ibid., November 14, 1937, p. 3.
57. Personal journal of Mrs. Lydia Mary Gee, made available by Miss Ruth Marsden.
58. *Gaceta del Norte*, December 14, 1937, p. 1.
59. *Times* (London), December 14, 1937, p. 1.
60. This supper was catered by Eusebio Legarreta, founder of the chain of coffee bars in Bilbao, "Cafes Legarreta" (see note 58).
61. Minutes, BCC, November 23, 1937, pp. 2–6.
62. *Memoria, Junta Provisional*, p. 21.
63. Minutes, BCC, February 8, 1938, p. 4.
64. *The Tablet*, September 24, 1938, p. 390.
65. Pogroms began in Germany in November 1938, and Jewish refugee childen arrived in Britain on December 2, 1938, according to John Hope Simpson, *Refugees* (Oxford, 1939), p. 60.
66. Genge Collection.
67. Minutes, BCC, June 24, 1939, p. 2.
68. Betty Morgan to adoptive parent Mrs. Baish, dated October 4, 1939, made available by Joaquín Sánchez Velado in London, 1980.
69. This letter, from the Genge Collection of the BCC was written by Dr. Byloff to Betty Morgan, June 19, 1939.
70. This letter, written in English, was made available by Joaquín Sánchez Velado in London, 1980.
71. Cable, pp. 164–65.
72. *Memoria, Junta Provisional*, p. 23.
73. *Gaceta del Norte*, September 1, 1937, p. 1.
74. *La Métropole* (Brussels), August 25, 1937, p. 1.
75. *Gaceta del Norte*, September 11, 1937, p. 4.
76. Ibid., September 11, 1937, passim.
77. Ibid., September 21, 1937, p. 4.
78. *Memoria, Junta Provisional*, p. 23.
79. *Gaceta del Norte*, October 15, 1937, p. 4.
80. *Memoria, Junta Provisional*, p. 24.
81. Letter of January 18, 1938, from Ambassador Mariano Ruiz Funes, Barcelona, to Jesús Leizaola, Paris. BGEA.
82. *Euzko Deya*, October 31, 1937, p. 1.
83. Ibid.
84. *Memoria, Junta Provisional*, p. 24.
85. According to a letter from the Belgian foreign minister to José Antonio Aguirre, March 23, 1939. BGEA.
86. *Rapport*, pp. 32–33; see note 33.
87. This material comes from an interview with Martin Aguirre in Antwerp in 1980, and from President Aguirre's autobiography, *De Guernica a Nuevo York, Pasando por Berlin* (Buenos Aires, 1943).

88. Javier Rubio, *La Emigración de la Guerra Civil de 1936–1939* (Madrid, 1977), p. 168.

89. Vera Foulkes, *Los Niños de Morelia y la Escuela España-México* (México, D.F., 1952), p. 52.

90. Ibid., p. 54.

91. This is clearly set forth in letter no. 3088 from the Spanish Republican embassy in Paris to Pedro Basaldua of the Basque Delegation in Paris, dated September 31, 1938. BGEA.

92. Alberto de Onaindia, *Experiencias del Exilio: Hombre de Paz en la Guerra* (Buenos Aires, 1974), p. 295.

93. This material is based on an interview with Jesús Leizaola in San Sebastián in December 1979; on Onaindia, p. 295; and as reported in *Euzko Deya*, August 13, 1938, p. 3; and in a letter from Leizaola in the BGEA dated June 21, 1939.

94. *Rapport*, pp. 31–32, and see note 33.

95. Onaindia, pp. 295–296.

96. *Euzko Deya*, August 13, 1939, p. 3.

97. As found in a letter from President Aguirre to Juan Gortazar, Bayonne, April 25, 1939. BGEA.

98. This is contained in a letter from the LIAB to Enrique Dueñas, Paris, February 10, 1940. BGEA.

99. As noted in interview with Jesús Leizaola in 1979.

100. Letter from the Partido Communista de España to Jesús Leizaola, Paris, June 10, 1945. BGEA.

101. Letter from LIAB with attached Lista (children and visas), October 9, 1946. BGEA.

102. *Euzko Deya*, February 3, 1946, p. 1.

103. As reported in the major Mexico City daily, *Excelsior*, January 24, 1946, and February 6, 1945.

104. Letter from the Partido Communista de Euzkadi to the Basque government, March 2, 1946. BGEA.

105. Letter from the Comité Internacional de la Cruz Roja to the Basque government, April 5, 1946. BGEA.

106. As noted in a letter from LIAB to M. Charles, French minister of foreign affairs, on October 9, 1946. BGEA.

107. This is discussed in a letter from Sr. Durañona to Ambassador Bogomolov, December 4, 1947. BGEA.

108. Letter to M. Vasse from the Basque government, Paris, February 25, 1947. BGEA.

109. According to the document *Relación de Niños Vascos en la URSS* (Paris, June 1, 1947). BGEA.

110. Rafael Miralles, *Españoles en Rusia* (Madrid, 1947), p. 208.

111. Rubio, p. 797.

112. Santiago Carrillo, "Los Niños Españoles en la URSS," Supplement no. 89, *Mundo Obrero* (Paris, August 1947), pp. 1–31.

113. This information was provided by Irena Falcon, long-time secretary to Dolores Ibarruri, in an interview in Madrid in 1980.

114. *Pravda*, November 16, 1956, p. 3.

115. *Gaceta del Norte*, June 28, 1956, p. 1.

116. Ibid., August 22, 1956, p. 1.

117. Ibid., September 27, 1956, p. 1; September 29, 1956, p. 1; September 30, 1956, p. 13; October 10, 1956, p. 1; October 23, 1956, p. 3; November 24, 1956, p. 1; December 19, 1956, p. 1.

118. This material is based on interviews with nineteen Basques in Bilbao, Eibar, and San Sebastián who were evacuated to the USSR in 1937 and chose repatriation in 1956.

119. This incident was described spontaneously by several of the Sovieticos interviewed in Euzkadi.

120. As reported in *Interviu* (Madrid), March 1980, pp. 74–77.

Chapter Eight

1. See *Censo y Estadistico* (Paris, 1939), prepared by the Basque Government-in-Exile. BGEA.

2. Javier Rubio, *La Emigración de la Guerra Civil de 1936–1939* (Madrid, 1977), pp. 301–20.

3. *Censo y Estadistico*.

4. Rubio, pp. 115–24.

5. Ibid., pp. 128, 170.

6. Ibid., pp. 389–91, 852–55, 865–67.

7. Ibid., pp. 330–31, 857–63.

8. Ibid., p. 412.

9. Ibid., pp. 842–43; see also Patricia Weiss Fagan, *Exiles and Citizens* (Austin, 1973) 47, quoting *Excelsior* (Mexico City), March 31, 1939, p. 1; April 2, 1939, pp. 1, 11.

10. Rubio, pp. 875–77.

11. Ibid., p. 182.

12. Ibid., p. 196.

13. Ibid., pp. 170–99.

14. Ibid., p. 130.

15. Ibid., pp. 135–39; see also Fagan, pp. 47–59.

16. Rubio, pp. 139–50.

17. Ibid., p. 141.

18. According to a letter of instructions, written in 1939. BGEA.

19. *Basque Refugees; A Preliminary Report* (in English) (Bayonne, n.d.), p. 5.

20. This is reported in German Arcineaga, "Los Vascos en Venezuela," *Memoria del Centro Vasco* (Caracas, 1957) and in Diego Ibarbia, "Homenaje al Comité Pro-Inmigración Vasca," *Memoria del Centro Vasco*, Buenos Aires, 1968).

21. Ibid.

22. Rubio, p. 397.

23. *Memoria, Junta Provisional de la Protección de Menores1932–1939* (Diputación de Vizcaya, 1940), p. 22.

24. According to a *Presupuesto* (Paris, January 1940). BGEA.

25. Rubio, pp. 401–10.

26. Address at the airport at Montalivet, November 5, 1946, reported in *Bidasoa en Gurraztiak* (Ustaritz, 1975), no. 1, p. 26.

27. This material is taken from the Archives of the Toulouse Project of the Unitarian Service Committee, Harvard Divinity School. They are uncatalogued.

28. Ibid.; brochure of the Simón Bolívar Colony.

29. Rubio, pp. 788–89.

30. An interview with Pedro Beitia in San Sebastián in 1980.

31. Minutes of the Basque Children's Committee, March 21, 1939, pp. 1–3.

32. This is taken from a Report of the BCC dated June 1939.

33. This material is found in a pamphlet by Jessie Stewart, *Recuerdos, the Basque Hostel at Cambridge* (n.d.), pp. 10–11, made available by Professor Helen Grant of Cambridge.

34. Susan Isaacs, *The Cambridge Evacuation Survey* (London, 1941), p. 196; James Cable, *The Royal Navy and the Siege of Bilbao* (Cambridge, 1979), p. 198.

35. *New York Times*, July 11, 1940, p. 1.

36. *Mundo Obrero* (Toulouse), October 11, 1946, pp. 1–2.

37. Amador Diaz-Campillo, "When 4,000 Basques Landed at Southampton," (n.d.), p. 2.

38. BCC Minutes, May 3, 1939, p. 1.

39. *Action* (London), April 8, 1939, p. 16.

40. Diaz-Campillo, personal communication, 1981, p. 2.

41. Several copies of *Amistad* were kindly made available by Joaquín Sánchez-Velado and José María Villegas in London in 1980. Amador Diaz-Campillo also discussed this magazine from his vantage as the publication's illustrator and sometime editor. This material is taken from *Amistad*, May 1940, no. 1, pp. 9–10.

42. According to Manuel Irujo, in an interview in Pamplona in 1980.

43. Diaz-Campillo, 1981, p. 2.

44. *Amistad*, May 1943, no. 25, pp. 1–18.

45. Cable, pp. 168–69.

46. This material is based on interviews during April and May 1980 with ten Basques who were not repatriated from Britain.

47. Diaz-Campillo, personal communication, 1981, p. 2.

48. Ibid., p. 6.

49. According to the preliminary data Ms. Yolanda Genge has located. Another source noted that, even today, the expatriate

Basques and their children are not accepted into Basque political circles, and that considerable friction remains between those who returned after 1975 (Franco's death) and those who never left, and thus had to endure the persecution and shortages in Euzkadi under Franco.

50. According to a series of letters in the BGEA from Pedro Beitia in London to Javier Landaburu in Paris in 1946. Correspondence from a group of Basques residing in France attest to the reunion of nearly two dozen children from Britain with their parents or other relatives in France after World War II.

51. *Memoria, Junta Provisional*, p. 22.

52. According to an interview with the directress of this hostel, Sra. Paulina Urteaga, in Fuenterrabía in 1980.

53. This material comes from extended interviews in 1980 and correspondence in 1981 with Martin Aguirre, of Mortsel, near Antwerp.

54. Ms. Ariadne Pascual-Rosendorf has shared her diaries of her years in the Soviet Union with me, and has offered other material in interviews and correspondence from 1979–82, p. 2.

55. Ibid., p. 3.

56. Irena Falcon, secretary to Dolores Ibarruri, is the source of this material, from an interview in Madrid in 1980.

57. Pascual-Rosendorf, p. 5.

58. Ibid., p. 4.

59. Ibid., p. 5.

60. Ibid., p. 4.

61. Ibid., p. 6.

62. Rafael Miralles, *Españoles en Rusia* (Madrid, 1947) pp. 201–07.

63. Jesús Hernández, *La Grande Trahison* (Paris, 1953), pp. 223–24.

64. Ibid., p. 224.

65. Valentín González, *La Vie et le Mort en USSR* (Paris, 1950), pp. 183–94.

66. *Alkartu* (Toulouse), December 7, 1945.

67. Ibid., November 7, 1945, p. 3; January 22, 1946, p. 3.

68. Santiago Carrillo, "Los Niños Españoles en la URSS", Supplement 89, *Mundo Obrero* (Paris), September 1947, pp. 14–20.

69. Ibid., p. 22.

70. Ibid., p. 5.

71. Ibid., p. 31.

72. Vera Foulkes, *Los Niños de Morelia y la Escuela España-México* México, D.F., 1953), pp. 43–45.

73. Ibid., pp. 54–59.

74. Ibid., pp. 52–53.

75. Ibid., pp. 54–55.

76. Emeterio Paya-Valera, "La Historia de los Niños Españoles," *Elite* (Morelia), February 11, 1979, p. 6.

77. Ibid., March 4, 1979, p. 3.
78. Rubio, pp. 169, 786–87.
79. Carlos Blanco Aguinaga, personal communication, 1980.
80. Dolores Pla, *Los Niños de Morelia*, (Mexico, D. F., 1983), p. 172. The figures are: 2 suicides among 456 adults, compared to 18 per 100,000 expected according to suicide statistics for Mexico.
81. William A. Douglass and Jon Bilbao, *Amerikanuak*, (Reno, 1975), p. 264.
82. This material came from interviews with several score Basques who had been evacuated abroad, later repatriated, and are now living in Euzkadi.
83. Robert P. Clark, *The Basques: The Franco Years and Beyond* (Reno, 1979), p. 82.
84. *Euzko Deya*, October 16, 1939, p. 1.
85. Teresa Pamies, *Los Niños en la Guerra* (Barcelona, 1977), pp. 127–35.
86. Diaz-Campillo, p. 6.

Chapter Nine

1. *The Bulletin of the National Joint Committee for Spanish Relief* (no. 5, December 1937), p. 2, noted: "The presence of 4,000 of these [Basque] children is a small attempt to deal with the vast new modern problem of the evacuation of civilians from war areas."
2. This term, of uncertain coinage, appears, for example, in the *San Francisco Chronicle* of August 20, 1979, p. 3, in an article which estimates the total present refugee population worldwide as eleven million, of which two-thirds are children.
3. See, for example, Charles Zwingmann and Maria Pfister-Ammende, *Uprooting and After* (New York, 1973), p. 1, which begins, "During the first half of the 20th century, more than 100 million people in the Northern Hemisphere left their homeland or were forcefully separated from it." Eugene Brody, *Behavior in New Environments* (Beverly Hills, 1975) includes an article by Henry David, entitled, "Involuntary International Migration," p. 73, which gives the figure of fifteen million refugees in 1968.
4. Javier Rubio, *La Emigración de la Guerra Civil de 1936–1939* (Madrid, 1977), pp. 140–41, 199–201.
5. J. Donald Cohon, "The Refugee Experience and its Relation to Psychological Adaptation and Dysfunction," mimeo (1980), and "A Preliminary Analysis of Indochinese Refugee Mental Health Clients," mimeo (1980), both available at the International Institute, San Francisco.
6. A. M. Dalianis, "Children in Turmoil During the Civil War in Greece, 1946–1950; A Thirty Year Follow-up Study," mimeo (Stockholm, 1982), Karolinska Institute.

7. John Bowlby, *Maternal Care and Child Health* (Geneva, 1952), pp. 1–29.

8. Anna Freud and Dorothy Burlington, "Reactions to Evacuation," in *Uprooting and After*, ed. Charles Zwingmann and Maria Pfister-Ammende (New York, 1973), p. 107.

9. Anna Freud and Dorothy Burlington, *Infants Without Families* (London, 1943), p. 107.

10. Ibid., pp. 30–35.

11. Anna Freud and Dorothy Burlington, *Young Children in Wartime* (London, 1942), p. 80.

12. Anna Freud, quoted in Bowlby, p. 132.

13. Bowlby, p. 15.

14. Susan Isaacs, *The Cambridge Evacuation Survey* (London, 1941), pp. 53–55.

15. Ibid., p. 196.

16. Freud, *Young Children in Wartime*, pp. 71–72.

17. This is the conclusion reported from long-term health studies, as O. Odegard, "Emigration and Mental Health," *Mental Hygiene* (1936), vol. 20: pp. 546–63, for Norwegian populations; and B. Malsberg," Migration and Mental Disease among the White Population of New York State," *Human Biology* (1962), vol. 34: pp. 89–98, for the United States.

18. H. David, "Involuntary International Migration," quoting Maria Pfister-Ammende, in Brody, p. 80.

19. A. A. Weinberg, "Mental Health Aspects of Voluntary Migration," in *Uprooting and After*, p. 113.

20. Anna Freud, "Six Children of Terezin, An Experiment in Group Upbringing," *Psychoanalytic Study of the Child* (1951), no. 6, pp. 127–68.

21. Sarah Moskovitz, in her book, *Love Despite Hate: Child Survivors of the Holocaust in their Adult Life* (New York, 1983), discusses this issue in depth.

22. This moving book, *War Through Children's Eyes*, in the unedited words of the children involved, was prepared by Irena Grudzinska-Gross and Jan Tomasz Gross (Stanford: Hoover Press, 1981), p. xxxviii.

23. H. B. M. Murphy, "The Low Rate of Hospitalization Shown by Immigrants to Canada," in *Uprooting and After*, pp. 221–34.

24. David, p. 87.

25. David, p. 80.

26. Margaret Hicklin, "War-Damaged Children," *Bulletin of the Association of Psychiatric Social Workers* (London, n.d.), p. 6.

27. Bowlby, p. 26–29.

28. Ibid., p. 137–38.

29. In interviews with Leftist Basques, this point was repeatedly made.

30. Bowlby, p. 127.
31. H. B. M. Murphy, *Flight and Resettlement* (Paris, 1955), p. 97.
32. Ibid., Pfister-Ammende, quoted in Murphy, p. 161.
33. William Douglass and Jon Bilbao, *Amerikanuak* (Reno, 1975), p. 364.
34. Michael Kenny, "Twentieth Century Spanish Expatriates in Mexico: An Urban Sub-Culture," *Anthropological Quarterly* (Oct. 1962), p. 175.
35. Hicklin, p. 12.
36. Howard Kerschner, *Quaker Service in Modern War* (New York, 1950), p. 62.
37. Jessie Stewart, *Recuerdos* (Cambridge, n.d.), p. 7.
38. Teresa Pamies, *Los Niños en la Guerra* (Barcelona, 1977), p. 105.
39. Pfister-Ammende, quoted in Murphy, pp. 150–71.
40. Douglass and Bilbao, pp. 407–12.

BIBLIOGRAPHY

I. Official Publications and Archival Collections

Archives of the Archbishop of Malines. Malines, Belgium.

Archives of the Basque Government-in-Exile (BGEA). Paris.

Archives of the Communist Party. Paris and Madrid.

Archives of Eugenio Goyenetxe. Ustaritz, France.

Archivos del Ministerio de Asuntos Extranjeros. Madrid.

Harvard Divinity School Archives: Toulouse Project of the Unitarian Service Committee.

II. Unpublished Reports and Memoirs

Genge Collection. The Hague, Netherlands. Includes:

a) Basque Camp Reports, Numbers 1–21, from June 11, 1937 to October 18, 1937.

b) Basque Children's Committee:

Minutes of Meetings from May 31, 1937 until August 1, 1939.

Financial Statements.

Lists of Basque Children, 1937–45.

Diaz-Campillo, Amador. "When 4,000 Basques Landed in Southampton." Southampton, n.d.

Ellis, Richard, M.D. Album and Papers, n.d.

Gee, Mrs. Lydia Mary. Private Papers, Correspondence. Northampton, n.d.

Pascual-Rosendorf, Ariadne. "Russia and My Wartime Family." Austin, Texas, n.d.

Pittman, Eric. Reports, Treasurer's Reports, Correspondence. London, 1937–39.

III. Unpublished Studies

Cohon, J. Donald. "The Refugee Experience and its Relation to Psychological Adaptation and Dysfunction." International Institute, San Francisco, 1980.

———. "A Preliminary Analysis of Indo-Chinese Mental Health Clients." International Institute, San Francisco, 1980.

Dalianis, Mando. "Children in Turmoil During the Civil War in Greece, 1946–50: A Thirty Year Follow-up Study." Karolinska Institute, Stockholm, 1982.

Ressler, Everett. "Unaccompanied Children in Emergencies." Geneva, 1983.

IV. Books

Aberasturi, Luis y Juan Jimenez. *La Guerra en Euzkadi*. Barcelona, 1978.

Aguire y Lecube, José Antonio. *De Guernica a Nuevo York, Pasando por Berlin*. Buenos Aires, 1943.

Alcazar, Ricardo. *El Gachupín, Problema Maximo de México*. México, D.F., 1934.

Azpiazu, Inaki. *El Caso del Clero Vasco*. Buenos Aires, 1957.

Basaldua, Pedro de. *En España Sale el Sol*. Buenos Aires, 1946.

"Beltza." *El Nacionalismo Vasco en el Exilio: 1937–1960*. San Sebastián, 1977.

Bowers, Claude. *My Mission to Spain*. New York, 1954.

Bowlby, John. *Maternal Care and Mental Health*. Geneva, 1952.

Brody, Eugene, ed. *Behavior in New Environments*. Beverly Hills, 1975.

Cable, Sir James. *The Royal Navy and the Siege of Bilbao*. Cambridge, 1979.

Camino, Jaime. *Intimas Conversaciones con la Pasionaria*. Barcelona, 1977.

Cammaerts, Emile. *The Keystone of Europe*. London, 1939.

Carr, Raymond, ed. *The Republic and The Civil War in Spain*. London, 1971.

Cárdenas, Lázaro. *Apuntes: 1937*. Mexico, D.F.: Universidad Nacional Autonomo de México [UNAM], 1972.

Castresana, Luis de. *El Otro Arbol de Guernica*. Madrid, 1967.

———. *La Verdad sobre 'El Otro Arbol de Guernica.'* Bilbao, 1972.

Cierva, Ricardo de la. *Historia de la Guerra Civil Española* (2 vols.). Barcelona, 1971.

Clark, Robert. *The Basques: The Franco Years and Beyond*. Reno, 1979.

Cloud, Yvonne. *The Basque Children in England*. London, 1937.

Colomer, Colin. *Historia Secreta de la Segunda Republica*. Barcelona, 1959.

Coverdale, John. *Mussolini and Franco*. Princeton, 1975.

Douglass, William. *Death in Murélaga*. Seattle, 1969.

Douglass, William A., and Jon Bilbao. *Amerikanuak*. Reno, 1975.

Eiguren, Jose. *The Basque History*. Boise, 1970.

El Clero Vasco Frente a la Cruzada Franquista. Toulouse, 1966.

Fagan, Patricia Weiss. *Exiles and Citizens*. Latin American Monographs. Austin, 1973.

Freud, Anna and Burlington, Dorothy. *Young Children in Wartime*. London, 1942.

———. *Infants Without Families*. London, 1943.

Foulkes, Vera. *Los Niños de Morelia y la Escuela España-México*. México, D.F.: 1953.

González, Ricardo Etxegaray. *La Marina Mercante y el Tráfico Maritimo en la Guerra Civil*. Madrid, 1977.

González, Valentín. *La Vie et la Mort en la URSS*. Paris, 1950.

Gross, Jan Albert, ed. *United Nations Series: Belgium*. Berkeley, 1945.

Grudzinska-Gross, Irene, and Jan Tomasz Gross. *War Through Children's Eyes*. Stanford, 1981.

Hermet, Guy. *The Communists in Spain*. London, 1974.

Hernández, Jesús. *La Grande Trahison*. Paris, 1953.

Irrizar, Fabian. *Txingo Gertaldi; Ibilikariak*. Bilbao, 1973.

Isaacs, Susan. *The Cambridge Evacuation Survey*. London, 1941.

———. *Children in Institutions*. London, 1948.

Iturralde, Juan. *El Catolicismo y la Cruzada de Franco*. Toulouse, 1955–56.

Jackson, Gabriel. *The Spanish Republic and the Civil War*. Princeton, 1965.

———, ed. *The Spanish Civil War: Domestic Crisis or International Conspiracy?* Boston, 1967.

Kerschner, Howard. *Quaker Service in Modern War*. New York, 1950.

MacArdle, Dorothy. *Children of Europe*. London, 1949.

Manning, Dame Leah. *A Life for Education*. London, 1970.

Martinez Bande, J. M. *El Final del Frente Norte*. Madrid, 1972.

Mowat, Charles, ed. *New Cambridge Modern History*. Cambridge, 1962.

Miralles, Rafael. *Españoles en Rusia*. Madrid, 1947.

Moskowitz, Sara. *Love Despite Hate: Child Survivors of the Holocaust in Adult Life*. New York, 1983.

Murphy, H. B. M. *Flight and Resettlement*. Paris, 1955.

Onaindia, Alberto de. *Experiencias del Exilio: Hombre de Paz en la Guerra*. Buenos Aires, 1974.

Pamies, Teresa. *Los Niños de la Guerra*. Barcelona, 1977.

Payne, Stanley. *Basque Nationalism*. Reno, 1975.

Pla, Dolores. *Los Niños de Morelia*. México, D. F., 1983.

Reyes-Perez, Roberto. *La Vida de los Niños Iberos en la Patria de Lázaro Cárdenas*. México, D.F., 1940.

Matthews, Herbert. *Half of Spain Died*. New York, 1973.

Rubio, Javier. *La Emigración de la Guerra Civil de 1936–1939*. 3 vols. Madrid, 1977.

Simpson, John Hope. *The Refugee Problem*. Oxford, 1937.

———. *Refugees*. Oxford, 1939.

Solzhenitsyn, Aleksandr. *Gulag Archipelago*. New York, 1973.

Southworth, Herbert. *Guernica, Guernica*. Berkeley, 1977.

Steer, George. *The Tree of Gernika*. London, 1938.

Talon, Vicente. *Arde Guernica*. Madrid, 1972.

Thomas, Hugh. *The Spanish Civil War*. New York, 1961.

Wilson, Francesca. *In the Margins of Chaos*. London, 1961.

Zwingmann, Charles, and Maria Pfister-Ammende, Comps. *Uprooting and After*. New York, 1973.

V. Pamphlets

Arcineaga, German. "Los Vascos en Venezuela." *Memoria del Centro Vasco*. Caracas, 1957.

Basque Refugees, A Preliminary Report. Bayonne, n.d. (probably mid-1939).

Bidasoa en Gurraztiak. Ustaritz, 1975.

Boletín del Comité de Ayuda a los Niños del Pueblo Español, no. 3. México, D.F., September 1937.

Bulletin of the National Joint Committee for Spanish Relief, no. 5. London, December 1937.

Bulletin of the National Joint Committee for Spanish Relief, no. 11. "They've Not All Gone Home." London, March 1938.

Cabeza, Julieta. "México y los Niños Españoles. "Ediciones Amigos de México. Valencia, December 26, 1937.

Carrillo, Santiago. "Los Niños Españoles en la URSS." *Mundo Obrero*, supplément no. 89. Paris, September, 1947.

Censo: Colonias de Niños Vascos en Francia. Paris, February 3, 1939.

Censo y Estadístico. Paris, 1939.

Censo y Estadística de Expatriados. Bayonne, September 27, 1937.

Censo General de Acogidos en las Residencias Vascas. Paris, April 1939.

Censo: Vascos Refugiados en Francia. Bayonne, December 1937.

Colonias de Niños Expatriados. Bayonne, February 14, 1938.

Emigración Vasca. Archives of the Basque Government-in-Exile. Paris, March 18, 1938.

Evacuación y Repatriación del Sanitoria de Gorliz. Bilbao, 1937.

Foster Parent Plan, n.p., n.d.

Ibarbia, Diego. "Homenaje al Comité Pro-Inmigración Vasca." *Memoria del Centro Vasco*. Buenos Aires, 1968.

"La Croix Rouge de la Démocratie Espagnole." *Edition Universelle*. Paris, 1938.

Ligue International des Amies des Basques. Paris, 1938.

Memoria, Junta Provisional por Repatriación de los Menores Expatriados de Vizcaya, 1932–1939. Bilbao, 1940.

Nota Obtenida del Informe del Departamento de Asistencia Social de Cataluña Correspondiente a Agosto de 1938. Barcelona, August 1938.

Presupuesto de Gobierno de Euzkadi. Paris, January 1940.

Ranz, J. *Memoria de la Colonia Infantil de Mas Éloi*. Limoges, 1937.

Rapport Complémentaire sur l'activité du Comité International de la Croix Rouge Rélative à la Guerre Civil en Espagne. Geneva, April 1958.

Rapport Complémentaire de la XVII Conférence Internationale. Stockholm, August 1948.

Rapport Général sur le Colonie St.-Jean-Pied-de-Port. 1939.

Rapport No. 1, Comité National Catholique de Secours a Réfugiés d'Espagne. Bordeaux, June 1939.

Relación de Refugiados Procedente de Cataluña. Barcelona, November 1937.

Réportage de Colonias Vascas. Bayonne, n.d.

Rotaeche, F. *Emigración Vasca*. Bayonne, February 5, 1938.

———. *Emigración Vasca*. Paris, March 8, 1938.

Stewart, Jessie. *Recuerdos, the Basque Hostel at Cambridge*. Cambridge, n.d.

Uriarte Aguirremalloa, Castor. *Bombas y Mentiras sobre Guernica*. Bilbao, 1976.

Why the Basques Fight Franco. BGEA. Paris, n.d.

VI. Articles in Books and Periodicals

Alpert, Michael. "Great Britain and the Blockade of Bilbao." In *Anglo-American Contributions to Basque Studies*, ed. W. Douglass, R. Etulain, and W. Jacobsen. Reno, 1977.

———. "Los Niños Vascos en Inglaterra." *Sábado Gráfico*. Madrid, June 1975.

Cattell, David. "Soviet Military Aid to the Republic." In *The Spanish Civil War*, ed. Gabriel Jackson. Boston, 1967.

David, Henry. "Involuntary International Migration." In *Behavior in New Environments*, ed. Eugene Brody. Beverly Hills, 1975.

Douglass, William. "Rural Exodus in Two Spanish-Basque Villages: A Cultural Explanation." *American Anthropologist*, vol. 73, no. 5, 1971.

Ellis, Richard. "Four Thousand Basque Children." *The Lancet*. London, May 29, 1937.

———. "Basque Children in England." *Guy's Hospital Gazette*. London, June 1937.

Freud, Anna. "Six Children of Terezin: An Experiment in Group Upbringing." *Psychoanalytic Study of the Child*, no. 6, 1951.

Freud, Anna, and Dorothy Burlington. "Reaction to Evacuation." In *Uprooting and After*, comp. Zwingmann and Pfister-Ammende. New York, 1973.

Griful, Isidro, "La Tragedia de los Niños Vascos en el Extranjero." *Razón y Fe*, no. 483. San Sebastián, April 1938.

Hicklin, Margaret. "War-Damaged Children." *Bulletin of the Association of Psychiatric Social Workers*. London, n.d.

Icazurriaga, Carmen. "Españoles de Veracruz y Vascos del Distrito Federal." *Inmigrantes y Refugiados Españoles en México, Siglo XX*. Tlalpan, 1979.

Kenny, Michael. "Twentieth Century Spanish Expatriates in Mexico: An Urban Sub-Culture." *Anthropological Quarterly*, vol. 35, no. 4. Washington, October 1962.

Legarreta-Marcaida, Dorothy. "Effective Use of the Primary Language in the Classroom." In *Schooling and Language Minority Students: A Theoretical Framework*. Los Angeles, 1981.

Levine, Morris. "The Basques." *Natural History*, vol. 76, no. 4, April 1967.

Malsberg, B. "Migration and Mental Disease among the White Population of New York State." *Human Biology*, vol. 34, 1962.

Murphy, H.B.M. "The Low Rate of Hospitalization Shown by Immigrants to Canada." in Zwingmann and Pfister-Ammende, *Uprooting and After*. New York, 1973.

Odegard, O. "Emigration and Mental Health." *Mental Hygiene*, vol. 20, 1936.

Paya-Valera, Emeterio. "La Historia de los Niños Españoles de Morelia." *Elite*. Morelia, 1978–79.

Plank, Emma. "We Bargained for Futures." *Progressive Education*. October 1944.

Taylor, F. J. "American Catholic and Protestant Attitudes Toward the Civil War." In *The Spanish Civil War*, ed. Gabriel Jackson. Boston, 1967.

Weinberg, A. A. "Mental Health Aspects of Voluntary Migration." In *Uprooting and After*, comp. Zwingmann and Pfister-Ammende. New York, 1973.

Whealey, Robert. "Foreign Intervention in the Spanish Civil War." In *The Republic and the Civil War in Spain*, ed. Raymond Carr. London, 1971.

Williams, Maurice. "The Arrival of Basque Children in the Port of Southampton." *The British Medical Journal*. London, June 12, 1937.

VII. Newspapers and Periodicals

Action. London. 1939.
Alkartu. Toulouse. 1945–46.
America. New York. 1937.
Amistad. London. 1940–43.
Anayak. St.-Jean-de-Luz. 1938–39.
British Medical Journal. London. 1937.
B.T. Copenhagen. 1937–38.
Çe Soir. Paris. 1936–38.
The Daily Telegraph. London. 1937–39.
Elite. Morelia. 1978–79.
Euzkadi. Bilbao. 1937.
Euzkadi Roja. Bilbao. 1937.
Euzko Deya. Paris. 1937–40.
Excelsior. Mexico City. 1937, 1946.
Frente Popular. Santiago. 1936–37.
Gaceta del Norte. Bilbao. 1937–39, 1956.
Garaia. San Sebastián. 1976.
Gazeten von Antwerpen. Antwerp. 1937–39.
Gudari. Bilbao. 1937.
Informe. Bayonne. 1937.
Interviu. Madrid. 1980.
La Métropole. Brussels. 1938.
La Tarde. Bilbao. 1937.
L'Aube. 1937.
La Voix du Peuple. Brussels. 1937–39.
Le Petit Gironde. 1937–39.
Le Petit Jour. 1937–39.
Le Peuple. Brussels. 1937–39.
Le Peuple. Paris. 1937–39.
L'Humanité. Paris. 1936–39.
Literary Digest. New York. 1937.
Literaturnaya Gazeta. Moscow. 1937.
L'Oeuvre. Paris. 1937.
Manchester Guardian. Manchester. 1937–39.
Mundo Obrero. Toulouse. 1946.
News-Chronicle. London. 1937.

New Statesman and Nation. London. 1937–39.

New York Times. New York. 1937, 1940.

Pravda. Moscow. 1937–39, 1956.

San Francisco Chronicle. San Francisco. 1979.

The Tablet. London. 1937–38.

The Times. London. 1936–45.

Volunteers for Liberty. Barcelona. 1937–38.

INDEX

Adoptive Homes: France, 35, 55, 58–59, 61–62; Britain, 120; Belgium, 140–41, 148–49
Aguirre, José Antonio de: leads All-Basque Junta, 17–18; organizes defense, 26; plea for Basque children, 40; meets with Leah Manning, 57, 71, 102, 136, 138, 174–75; hides in Belgium, 228, 230, 243, 251, 320
Alava, 2–3, 5, 9; refugees from, 18; base for Northern Campaign, 18, 158
Alcalá-Zamora, Niceto de, 6
Aldasoro, Ramón (Minister of Commerce and Supply), 20–21; in evacuation, 42
Alkartu (Solidarity), 274
Alphonse XII and XIII of Spain, 3
Amezaga, Vicente de: promotes Basque language schools, 65–66; at La Citadelle, 73, 77–78; leaves for Catalonia, 78
Amistad, 258–61
Anarchists, and Confederación Nacional de Trabajo (CNT), 4, 5; not represented in Aguirre's cabinet, 18, 38, 61, 115, 158, 184
Antoniutti, Msgr. Hildebrando, 79–80, 87, 178; sent to repatriate children, 202; activities in repatriation from England, 206, 208, 210, 211, 217; in Belgium, 225–26, 228
Arana, Sabino de: organizes Basque Nationalist party, 3–4; Gudari battalion in his name, 26, 93
Argentia, offers refugees help, 246, 286
Ariztimuño, José de (Aitzol), 26
Armenian child refugees, x, xi, 100, 142
Asturias, 6; Basques evacuated to, 33, 46–50, 141, 157; children evacuated to USSR, 165, 176, 244, 261, 268, 276, 277
Atholl, Duchess of, 127, 130, 289
Atleti (Atletico) de Bilbao, 151, 155, 262
Autonomy, Statute of: drafting, 5; ratification, 16–17
Auxilio Social (Franco), 203; assists Basque repatriates, 219–20, 226, 284–85
Azaña, Manuel de, 5; Gudari battalion, 27

Barcelona, 46–47, 79; Basques in, 83–84, 104, 172, 219, 244. *See also* Catalonia
Basque Boys Training Committee, 257–59
Basque Children's Committee (BCC), 11, 45; formation of, 100–103; sets up colonies, 115–16, 119, 123; problems of, 120–30, 130–34; during repatriation, 211–25; after World War II, 252–64. *See also Amistad*; Concerts
Basque Delegation: in Bayonne, 58, 77, 83, 86, 231; arranges emigration, 244; in Paris, 83–84; arranges censuses, 89–91;

Basque Delegation (*continued*) deters repatriation, 208–10; in London, 116, 118
Basque people, 1, 29–30
Basque Republic: autonomy, 5; evacuation of 1936, 14; military defense, 18; composition of, 28; plans evacuation, 37–42; moves to Santander, 48; problems with Spanish Catholic church, 64; mounts cultural events, 84–86; problems in France, 81, 86–90; work in Catalonia, 90–91; in exile (after fall of Republic) in France, 90–91; conforms to British model, 99–100; evacuation to Britain, 106; combats repatriation, 209, 214; tries to reclaim USSR children, 229, 333–34; presses emigration, 245–46; evacuates Paris office, 247; after World War II, 250–51, 320–21
Basque priests: executed by Franco, 19; as mentors, 75–76, 79, 81, 121–23, 147–52, 292, 315–17
Basque culture: ethnic identity, 66; maintained in exile, 78–86, 112–14, 121–23, 125–26, 149–52, 318–19. *See also Amistad*; Concerts
Battalion, Gernika, 247–48
Batzoki, 66, 292
Begoña: Our Lady of, 17, 45, 75; Treasure of, 79–80, 149, 293
Beitia, Pedro, 251, 376
Belgian Family Allowance, 135, 152–53, 264, 305
Belgium, xi; politics in 1936, 135; helps Basque refugee children, 137–46; repatriation, 225–58; after World War II, 264–66
Beorlegui, Colonel, 11–12
Berck-Plage, colony of, 86
Bilbao, 3, 4; exodus to in 1936, 15; during Northern Campaign, 18, 25, 30–32; evacuation of, 38–39, 41, 46, 53; fall of, 60, 62, 68, 70, 73, 79, 83, 106, 114–16, 122, 127, 139, 143, 147, 201, 211, 215
Blockade: begins, 20; becomes total, 23; broken, 24–25; menaces evacuation, 46
Blum, Léon, 11, 36, 51, 88, 305
Bourdet, Paul, 71, 96–97
Bowlby, John, 298–99, 309–10
Britain, xi; reacts to blockade, 23–25; offers help to refugees, 40; ships in evacuation, 54; Home Office and BCC negotiate, 101–107; recognizes Franco, 127; repatriation, 213; allows Basque employment, 256; evacuates British children to USA, 256; during World War II, 255–56; Basque boys in army, 261–62
Byloff, Dr. Helen, 223–24

Caballero, Largo, 16
Cagnotte (colony), 81–82, 93–94
Cambo (colony), 86, 249
Cambridge (colony), 233–34, 310, 323–24
Canada, 41, 239
Cárdenas, Lázaro, 184; assists child refugees, 186–89, 191–93, 229; helps Spanish Republican refugees, 243, 278, 282, 294, 305
Caritas, 174–75, 250
Carlist Wars, 2, 6, 9, 11; *requete* of, 16
Carrillo, Santiago, 234–35, 275–76
Catalonia, 6, 88, 90; refugees in, 36–37, 41–43, 69, 90–91, 124, 128, 183, 241, 324
Catholic church (Spain), 1, 3, 5, 6, 28, 62, 120
Catholic press, 67–68, 97, 121, 180
Census work of Basque Government, 89–91
Centres de triage (transition centers), 35, 53, 147, 301
Centros Vascos, 200, 246, 315
Chamberlain, Sir Neville, 127, 305
Chile, offers refuge, 243–44, 246

Chilton, Sir Henry, pro-Franco sentiments, 29, 41
Ciboure (colony), 81
Civil War (in Spain), x, xiii, 4, 8, 9; Basques in, 10; 1936 evacuation, 12; later evacuations, 99, 134. *See also* Insurgents; Bilbao; Northern Campaign
Clapton colony, 117–19, 310
Cohon, J. Donald, 298
Comité d'Accueil aux Enfants d'Espagne (CAEE): organized, 34–35; aids Basque children, 55–64, 93, 137. *See also* Confédération Générale du Travail
Comité National Catholique de Secours aux Réfugiés d'Espagne (CNC): formed, 71; helps refugees, 72–73, 82, 93, 95–96, 208; in Belgium, 72
Commerce and Supply, Minister of. *See* Aldasoro, Ramón
Committee for Civil and Religious Peace in Spain, 71, 95
Communists: in Spain, 4, 5, 6, 18; role in refugee evacuation, 38, 61; in France, 62, 84; growth in Basque country, 159; help in Belgium, 135, 137, 140; in USSR, 157–58, 183; in Denmark, 177; role in JARE, 244; in World War II, 273
Concentration camps in France, Basques in, 47, 92, 96, 241, 244, 247, 249
Concerts (Basque children's): in France, 76, 84–85; in Britain, 123, 125–26, 129, 133–34; in Belgium, 149–50; in the USSR, 169–70; after World War II, 257, 260; importance of, 318–19
Confédération Générale du Travail (CGT): begins help, 35–36, 39, 55–57, 82, 97; in Belgium, 58
Cooperatives, in France, 35, 64; in Britain, 131–32
Cuba, help to refugees, 243–44, 273
Czechoslovakia, offers help, 126, 246
Daladier, Édouard, 88
Dalianis, Mando, 298
Decree of Responsibility: promulgated by Franco, 87–89; repealed, 235; menaces repatriated children, 247, 265, 286, 288, 323, 325
Delegation for Evacuated Children (Spanish Republic), 82; in Belgium (Casa España), 154
Del Rio, Felipe, 33–34
Denmark, xi, 40; Basque children in, 175–79
Dispersion: to colonies in France, 57–62; to adoptive homes, 62–64; in Britain, 116–17; in Britain, to Leftist colonies, 130–34; Catholic colonies, 119–23; in Belgium, to colonies, 136–41, Catholic placements, 141–46; in USSR, to sanitoriums, 163–64, to Children's Houses, 167–71
Durango, bombing of, 28–29, 32, 44, 58

Eden, Sir Anthony, 100–101, 127
Education, 250, 252, 255, 277, 289; in France, 35, 37, 63, 65–66, 73–81, 85–86, 91; Britain, 118–19, 121, 132; Belgium, 146–53; USSR, 161–71. *See also* Escuela España-México
Egypt, sponsors colonies in France, 41
Eiguren, Jose, 182–83
Ellis, Doctor Richard, 100; in evacuation, 104–107; in Britain, 112–13, 261, 323
Elai-Alai, 84–85
Emigration: LIAB assists, 95; policy of Basque Government, 243–46, 264–65
Escuela España-México, 188–89, 193–99, 279–80, 294, 310, 314, 321
Euzkadi, 2, 3, 4, 5, 6, 8; blockade in, 23–25; war in, 27–34; evacuation of, 34–50, 70, 83, 85, 89, 101, 103, 136, 147, 157–58, 183,

Euzkadi (*continued*)
197, 209, 276; repatriation to, 282–90
Euskera (Basque language), 3, 16, 75, 91, 111, 112, 144, 145, 155, 197, 289, 318
Euzkadi Roja, 160, 174, 179, 201
Euzko-Deya, 85, 231–32
Evacuation: after 1936 battles, 14–15; prelude to 1937 evacuation, 34–37; begins, 39; Basque Government role, 41–43; vessels used, 42, 104; first contingent, 56–58; later expeditions, 60–62; PNV-sponsored, 64–70; to Britain, 103–107; to Belgium, 137–40; to USSR, 157–58, 193–96, 197–99

Falange (Youth groups), 15, 205–207, 213, 217–18, 223, 283, 286, 289–90
Fascism: in Spain, 9, 11–12, 34, 88; in Britain, 127–28, 139–40, 157, 169, 203, 217, 223, 230, 243, 272. *See also* Franco, Francisco
Food: wartime shortages, 21–22, 73–74, 77–78, 87; in France, 55, 59, 82; in Britain, 107, 109–10, 117, 131–32; in Belgium, 137, 140, 144; in USSR, 162–63; in Mexico, 185–86, 192, 196–97; in Euzkadi, 284–85; overall importance, 321–22
Foreign Legion (Spanish Morocco), helps Insurgents, 12–13, 15, 30, 105–106, 120
Fortunato (Unzueta), 75, 79, 80–81
Foster Parent Plan, 96
France, xi; importance of border, 10; offers help to Spanish Republic, 40, 51–52; closes ports to refugees, 49; prohibits landing, 68; offers subsidy to refugees, 77, 80; requisitions La Citadelle, 81; moves to Right, 88; withdraws support, 88; copes with 1939 refugees, 91–97, 240–51; refuses permission to dock, 106; recognizes Franco, 208; defeated by Hitler, 247, 265; helps in repatriation, 208–11
Franco, Francisco: leads coup in Spanish Morocco, 9, 12; takes few prisoners, 13; begins blockade, 23; offers refugees neutral zone, 41, 67, 126, 176, 181; objects to Basque evacuation, 99, 101, 182, 201, 211; repatriates British children, 215–18; joins United Nations, 235; repatriates Sovieticos, 235–38; Allies accommodate after World War II, 251; repression of Basques, 281–90, 298. *See also* Decree of Responsibility
Freud, Anna, work with Jewish refugees, 299–300, 302, 309
Fueros (foral rights), 2, 3

Gabana, Father Roca: during repatriation, 202, 207; in Britain, 213–16, 219, 283; in Belgium, 226–27
Gracia, Juan: assumes leadership of Social Assistance, 18; organizes evacuation, 38, 42, 56, 60–61, 86; repatriation, 160, 206, 214–15
Gee, Lydia Mary: in Euzkadi, 32, 37; role in repatriation from Britain, 216–18
Germany: provides military help to Insurgents, 10, 23, 25–28, 30, 34, 105, 135, 164; Non-Intervention Plan, 10–12; Condor Legion, 32, 101, 145
Gomá, Cardinal Isidro, 64–65, 205
González, Valentín (El Campesino), 166, 168, 171, 272
Gudari (Basque militia), 16; commissary begun, 20, 22; organization, 26; in Northern Campaign, 27, 47–48, 53, 88; abandon villages, 41, 47; in

France, 61, 77–78, 83, 241
Guernica (Gernika), x, 2; Basque election in, 18; bombed by Condor Legion, 32, 55, 65–67, 73, 84, 85, 103, 126, 136, 140, 145, 149, 164, 261, 297
Guipúzcoa, 2, 3, 4, 5; Civil War in, 9–12, 15; refugees from, 18–19, 46, 66, 90–91, 183, 197, 204

Habana (in evacuation), 42, 49, 69, 74, 105–106
HAVAS (news service), 67
Health of Basque child refugees: in France, 61, 77–78; in Britain, 112–13, 130, 133; USSR, 163–64; Mexico, 193–95
Hernández, Jesús, 161, 166, 171; helps emigration, 232, 272
Hicklin, Margaret, on refugees, 311, 322–23
Hitler, Adolf, 8, 68, 127, 128, 192

Ikastolas (Basque language schools), 20; in exile, 66–67; refugees as teachers in, 318
Ikurriña (Basque flag), 3; with children in exile, 77, 122, 125, 126, 147, 150–51; under Franco, 253; as symbol, 290
Indarra (fortitude), 330
Insurgents, 3; coup by, 9; navy, 12–13, 15–16; executions, 19, 286; propaganda, 81, 120; blockade by, 20–25; air raids, 30–33, 98, 135, 165, 208; strafes refugees, 46–47, 49, 52; repatriation, 130, 176, 180; as occupation army, 207, 210
International Brigade: helps refugee children, 37; organized in France, 156–57
International Commission for the Assistance of Spanish Child Refugees (ICASCR). *See* Kerschner, Harold
International Committee for Spanish Child Relief (Britain), 259–61
International Red Cross: help to child refugees, 93, 137, 191–93; repatriation, 205, 210, 227, 229–30, 233; sponsors hostal, 264–65
Iron Ring (Bilbao's defense), 26, 30, 41, 83
Irujo, Manuel de: in Popular Front, 17–18, 113–14, 180; in Britain, 260, 320
Italy: military help to Insurgents, 10, 12, 13, 28, 30, 164; Non-Intervention Plan, 10, 11, 135
Izarriueta, Jose de, 72, 142–44

Jauregui, Julio, 244
Jewish child refugees, 94, 130, 220–21
Juan Carlos (King of Spain), grants autonomy to Basques, 251
Junta de Auxilio a los Republicanos Españoles (JARE), 198, 244, 278

Kerschner, Harold, 92, 94, 95, 323
Kingston (colony), 131–34, 317

La Citadelle: formation, life in, 73–81, 208–10, 247; reunions of, 290–91, 310
Landaburu, Javier de, 96, 320, 376
La Pasionaria (Dolores Ibarruri), 157, 158, 159, 163, 165, 168, 169, 172, 175, 232
Lauzirica, Archbishop, 65, 202–203
League of Nations, 8
LeClef, Monsignor, 142–43, 153
Leizaola, Jesús de, 65, 81, 153, 161, 230, 232, 320
Lendekari. *See* Aguirre, José Antonio de
Ligue des Amis Basques (LIAB), 95, 96, 97, 231–33

Lice, 69, 74, 79, 108, 197
Limoges. *See* Mas Éloi
Listowel, Lord, 102, 126

Maquis, Basques in, 247–48, 251, 262
Manning, Dame Leah, 42; with Basque children in Britain, 102–106, 124, 213, 216; colony at Theydon Bois, 255
Maritain, Jacques, 71
Mas Éloi (colony), 57–60, 136
Mathieu, Bishop of Dax, assists Basque children, 71–73
Mauriac, François, 71
McNamara, Captain James, 100, 127, 211
Mexico: sends garbanzos, 21; military help to Republic, 12, 192; assists refugees, 41, 183, 244, 273. *See also* Cárdenas, Lázaro; Escuela España-México
Mola, General Emilio, 3; in Navarra, 9; in Madrid, 10; fall of San Sebastián and Irún, 11, 14, 17; launches Northern Campaign, 27; predicts victory, 28; closes in on Bilbao, 30–31; takes southern Vizcaya, 32; reaches Iron Ring, 34; takes Bilbao, 40
Moragrega, Narciso, 44–46
Moskowitz, Sara, 302
Mounier, Emmanuel, 71
Múgica, Bishop Mateo, 64–65, 70, 106, 119, 141
Mussolini, Benito, 8

National Joint Committee for Spanish Relief (NJCSR): letter published, 31; formed and works in Britain, 97, 100–103, 105–107, 116, 119, 128–29, 134, 156, 183, 211, 224; in World War II, 254
Navarra, 2, 3, 5, 9; Insurgent troops in, 18, 158
Nazi extermination camps, Basques in, 247, 310
Niños de Morelia, 186–200, 277–78, 289–92; reunions of, 310, 314–15. *See also* Escuela España-México
Non-Intervention Policy, genesis, 11, 12, 41, 156, 242, 252
Northern Campaign: blockade as prelude, 23; launched, 27; Basque defense inadequate, 40, 48, 50; fall of Bilbao, 53, 60, 62, 68, 73, 83, 160, 162, 165, 244

Older boys: food riots in France, 87; problems in Britain, 117–19, 123–25; shipped to France, 213; problems defused in Belgium, 152; Mexico, 185, 191
Oléron (centre de triage): first contingent arrives, 39; life there, 52–59, 69, 136
Onaindia, Alberto de, 33, 67, 207

Pamies, Teresa, 45, 172
Partido Nacionalista Vasco (PNV), xiv; growth of, 3–5, 6; members flee coup, 9; joins Popular Front, 10; in Basque Government, 18; role in evacu ation, 38; refugee assistance, 62–82; in Britain, 110–11, 254, 320
Partido Obrero Unificación Marxista (POUM), 6, 171
Payá-Valera, Emeterio, 280, 295
Pelayo, Don (Pello), as mentor, 75–76
Pope Pius XI (Papal State), 8, 180; recognizes Franco, 202; sends funds for repatriation, 202; names Msgr. Antoniutti to repatriate, 87, 204; blesses Italian troops in Abyssinia, 284
Popular Front: Spain, 6; municipal governments in, 10; unity effort, 16; lack of help to

Basques, 60, 138, 160; French, refugee assistance, 35–36, 41, 51, 55–56, 62, 97, 174–75, 208; Chile, 35; Belgian, 137–40; British, visits Durango, 29, 87, 99; Mexico, 186, 191; Denmark, 174
Poyanne (Landes) colony, 72, 81, 96
Press: on Guernica, 32, 46–47; Catholic, 41, 67–68, 72, 79, 97; British, 103, 115, 117–18, 121, 124–25; British Catholic, 91, 211, 213, 216, 219; Fascist, 258; Belgian, 136–37, 146, 225; Soviet, 162–64, 166, 169, 235; Franco press, 191, 201; Mexico, 191; USA, Catholic, 180–82; Basque, 85, 102, 231–32. *See also Euzko-Deya*; *Euzkadi Roja*, HAVAS, *Pravda*, etc.
Purges (Stalinist), 171–73

Quakers, 37, 41, 94, 97, 199, 223, 250

Ranz, Comrade, 58–60
Repatriation, 87; preparation for, 201–207; from France, 208–11; Britain, 211–14; Belgium, 225–28; USSR, 229; Mexico, 229
Reception (of refugee children): Russian, Armenian, x, xi; Basques in France, 67–69; in Britain, 107–108; in Belgium, 137; in the USSR, 162–64; in Mexico, 186; importance of, 308
Reyes-Perez, Roberto, 188, 193–97, 279
Rivera, Primo de, 3, 4
Roosevelt, Eleanor, 179, 262
Rosarie (hospital), 86
Rotaeche, Fidel de, 42, 48
Royal Navy, 24, 101
Rubio, Javier, 189, 280

Salvation Army (colonies), 117–19, 127, 129, 207, 308
Santander: food ships to, 32; Basque evacuation to, 46–50, 67, 73–74, 91–92, 138–39, 141, 143, 165, 175, 176, 203, 206, 244
Santo Domingo, accepts Spanish refugees, 243–44, 273
Scabies, 77–78, 108, 124
Separation trauma, xiii; 133, 145–47, 152, 192, 298–301, 311–13
Sendotasuna (strength of character), 331
SIFERE, 97
Situational factors, 303–304, 307, 315–21
Social Assistance (Asistencia Social): organized, 18, 19; in evacuation, 38–40, 44, 87, 90, 91, 104, 160, 206, 253
Socialists: Spanish, 4, 5, 6, 38, 61, 89, 184; French, 51, 55–57; Belgian, 136–37, 139, 152–54; British (Labour), 103–106; Swiss, 175; Danish, 175–78; Basque Socialist children in Britain, 253–55, 257
Socorro Rojo (Secours Rouge), 36, 91, 93, 137
Sovieticos, 158, 161, 168, 172, 238–39, 270, 272, 276–77, 294
Spain: monarchy, 3; dictatorship, 4; Second Republic, 5, 91, 99, 261; Spanish Government in Basque evacuation, 41, 50; refugee help, 82–83; in Belgium, 138, 140, 154; affirms Basque right to educate children, 209; in emigration, 305
Spanish Club of Moscow, 234, 277, 294
Stalin, Josef, 157, 164, 171, 235, 305
Steer, George, 101, 290
Stevenson, Consul, 101, 212
Stoneham Camp, life in, 108–16, 123–24, 127, 212
Structural factors, 303–304, 308–313
St. Vincent de Paul, 71, 208, 209
Switzerland, xi, 40, 275–76

Swedish Committee for Republican Spain, 40, 93, 104

Unión General de Trabajo (UGT), 4, 38, 89, 184
Union of Soviet Socialist Republics (USSR), xi, xii; military help to Spanish Republic, 12, 57, 157; hosts Basque children, 156–74; education, 166–71; during World War II, 266, 268; repatriation, 229
United States of America (USA): group formed to bring in Basques, 179–83; none allowed in, 184; takes in British children, 256
Unitarian Service Committee, 248–50
Uruguay, 41, 246

Van Roey, Cardinal (Archbishop of Malines), 137; Baskische Kinderwerk, 141–46, 153–54, 225–27; repatriation from USSR, 230, 264
Venezuela: offers refuge, 233–34, 243; Centro Vasco, 246
Vichy Government, 247, 305
Vitoria: Insurgent base, 28; seat of Basque Government, 251
Vizcaya, x, xiv, 2, 3, 4, 5, 9; 1936 exodus towards, 14; aid set up for refugees, 16; hiatus in war, 18; refugee services, 20; war in, 25–33, 41; evacuation, 51–52, 73, 79, 88, 101, 102, 202; autonomy, 251

Weinberg, A. A., 302–303
Weston Manor, 121–23, 220, 292
Wilson Repatriation Committee, 212